Cities of Jiangnan
in
Late Imperial China

SUNY Series in Chinese Local Studies

Harry J. Lamley, Editor

Cities of Jiangnan
in
Late Imperial China

Edited by
LINDA COOKE JOHNSON

State University of New York Press

Published by
State University of New York Press, Albany

© 1993 State University of New York

For information, address the State University of New York Press,
State University Plaza, Albany, NY 12246

Production by Christine Lynch
Marketing by Theresa A. Swierzowski

Library of Congress Cataloging-in-Publication Data

Cities of Jiangnan in late imperial China / edited by Linda Cooke
Johnson.
      p.   cm.—(SUNY series in Chinese local studies)
    Includes bibliographical references (p.) and index.
    ISBN 0-7914-1423-X (CH : acid-free).—ISBN 0-7914-1424-8 (PB :
acid-free)
    1. Cities and towns—China, Southeast—History. 2. Urbanization—
China, Southeast—History. 3. Land use, Urban—China, Southeast—
History. I. Johnson, Linda Cooke. II. Series.
HT147.C48C58 1993
307.76'0951'2—dc20   92-14140
                                                                  CIP

10 9 8 7 6 5 4 3 2 1

CONTENTS

ILLUSTRATIONS

PREFACE

This volume represents an effort on the part of six scholars of four different nationalities to gather materials on the urban history of several cities in a single core region of China: the region traditionally known as "Jiangnan"—literally: "South of the River," more recently identified as a major component of the Lower Yangzi macroregion.[1] In its original Tang designation "Jiangnan" covered a large area encompassing most of the modern provinces of Jiangsu, Jiangxi, Anhui, and Zhejiang on the south side of the Yangzi River.

The term underwent several stages of modification in the period between Tang and Qing; in the first part of the Qing it was briefly revived as the name of Jiangnan province, but in province form Jiangnan lasted only a short while, for in the Kangxi reign it was divided again into the two modern entities of Anhui and Jiangsu. All that remained was the familiar colloquial term "Jiangnan," designating that region "south of the river."[2] In this volume, the city of Yangzhou, in Jiangsu province, although on the north bank of the Yangzi and therefore technically part of what is sometimes called "Jiangbei" (north of the river) or "Subei" (northern Jiangsu), is considered together with Suzhou, Hangzhou, Nanjing, and Shanghai as socially and culturally part of Jiangnan.

Slightly smaller in size than modern France, Jiangnan by all accounts was the most prosperous and most highly urbanized region of the empire in the late imperial period. Two imperial capitals—Hangzhou in the Southern Song and Nanjing in the Ming—were located here, as was Suzhou, capital at varying times of independent kingdoms. By the late imperial period Suzhou was a major urban entity with a population of over a million persons. Yangzhou, the famous salt-city on the north bank of the river, which had been celebrated as the epitomy of southern culture in the Sui and Tang periods, assumed renewed prominence in the later Ming and Qing periods. Lastly, Shanghai, in the heart of China's cotton producing region, a city that had been a prominent port and county seat since the Song, developed an important role as a coastal and ocean port in the Qing. The five papers in this volume examine four Jiangnan cities: Suzhou, Hangzhou, Yangzhou, and Shanghai, from the Southern Song through mid-Qing (1150–1840) across a time span of seven hundred years. Of the principal cities of Jiangnan during the period covered by this volume, only a study on Nanjing is regrettably lacking.

These five papers on four cities examine different aspects of urban history in China through their respective individual case studies. Three of the papers, the first Suzhou paper and those on Yangzhou and Shanghai take a predominantly economic view, while two, the second Suzhou paper and the paper on Hangzhou, concentrate on urban conflict and class differentiation, aspects of social history.

By limiting the scope of this study to a single geophysical and economic region, we have attempted to provide a measure of synchronic spatial depth; no city in this collection is more than 100 kilometers from its neighbors. At the same time, we have tried to address a somewhat broader time span, in order to provide a wide diachronic scope. Implicit in the selection of the papers and the cities to be included is our contention that the Jiangnan region, unquestionably the most heavily urbanized region in the Chinese Empire in the late imperial period, was also in some ways distinguished from other regions of China. As G. William Skinner has argued—an argument that the papers in this collection support—Jiangnan enjoyed a full hierarchy of urban development, ranging from small lower-level market towns with less than one hundred families to major cities with over a million inhabitants.[3] But as these papers demonstrate, the hierarchy shifted over time. Hangzhou and Nanjing were both prime cities during the era when each was an imperial capital, but Hangzhou in the Ming suffered a marked decline from its Song prominence and Nanjing diminished in the latter Ming after the capital was moved to Beijing. As a result the apex of the urban pyramid remained at Suzhou throughout most of this period. Yangzhou obtained importance in the Ming and Qing periods, and Shanghai rose only fairly late, becoming a major port city during the Qing period.

As befits its prominence, this volume has two papers on the city of Suzhou. Suzhou was the most populous, elegant, and prosperous city in Jiangnan—some might say in the Empire—in the late imperial period. During the Southern Song, Hangzhou, the de facto capital of the empire, was larger, but it declined rapidly both in size and influence after the Mongol conquest. Suzhou, by contrast, not only benefited from Hangzhou's proximity in the Song, but went on to become even larger and more important in the Ming and Qing eras. So similar were these two Jiangnan cities, that a popular saying, quoted by Professor Marmé, equated both with the halls of Heaven. Suzhou retained both its size and prominence even during the early Ming when nearby Nanjing, also a city of the Jiangnan region, was named as the capital of the Empire; when the Ming capital was again shifted to the north and Nanjing declined, Suzhou was the beneficiary of renewed centrality. Thus, as the papers of Professors Marmé and Santangelo demonstrate, Suzhou retained its prominence throughout this period, but often at the cost of individual impoverishment and suffering. Professor Marmé's paper traces economic development and its costs in this city across a three hundred year span of time. Professor Santangelo's paper on the late Ming and early Qing period examines the development and differentiation of elite and working classes in the city in the next several hundred years.

Meanwhile, the ratio of secondary urbanization varied over the course of time, with—at various periods—Hangzhou, Nanjing, Yangzhou, and finally Shanghai assuming important positions in the Jiangnan region. Hangzhou, now the capital of Zhejiang province and seat of its governor, was an important city in its own right even after the transfer of the imperial capital. The internal politics and social movements in the city become the focus of the paper by Professor Fuma, who demonstrates that social protests in the Ming period were generated by specific local grievances and did not come about as generalized protests against dynastic corruption or eunuch control.

Yangzhou, a city that owed much of its economic prosperity to the salt monopoly, is not literally "south of the river," but has always been considered culturally to be a part of Jiangnan ever since Sui Yangdi enjoyed the comforts of the south in its environs. In the Ming and for most of the Qing period, as Professor Finnane shows us, the city shared the social and cultural characteristics of Jiangnan and enjoyed its own economic prosperity which placed it among the top urban entities of the late imperial period.

Shanghai was the most recent Jiangnan city to assume a degree of economic prominence, but, as the paper by Professor Johnson demonstrates, it had been a significant seaport since the Song dynasty and its economy was greatly reinforced during the Ming with the development of the cotton industry in that area. Its significance as a port increased after the Kangxi emperor's lifting of sea prohibitions in the mid-seventeenth century, but the city's greatest expansion came about in the late eighteenth and early nineteenth centuries as merchants from south China congregated there to participate in China's renewed maritime trade opportunities.

A second aspect of the present volume is that it brings together scholarship on the subject of urban history of the Jiangnan region from four continents: three of the participants in this effort, Linda Cooke Johnson, Michael Marmé and William T. Rowe, are from the United States; Paolo Santangelo is from Italy; Antonia Finnane is from Australia; and Susumu Fuma represents Japanese scholarship. This selection reflects a cross section of international scholarly inquiry, gathered here in concentration on a single subject, urban history, with a regional focus on the cities of Jiangnan. Regrettably the volume lacks a participant from China to make it fully representative, but as every paper in this selection demonstrates, we are all indebted to our Chinese colleagues for much of the material we have studied.

That these papers differ in scope, focus, and level of detail provided by the authors is a reflection of the diverse modes of scholarship brought together in this volume. The English language writers are sensitive to contemporary methodological discourses, and discuss issues dealing with paradigms of geographical organization, economic interpretations, and incipient imperialism. They tend to be more analytical but, within the space available here, offer less descriptive detail than do the two papers from different scholarly traditions. The Japanese and Italian papers, by contrast, concentrate on social issues and are distinguished by the remarkable depth of their scholarship in Chinese primary sources and by the meticulous detail they provide to the reader.

Finally—although in point of fact it comes *before* the other papers—Professor Rowe's introduction places these papers into the context of urban studies in Chinese history. Rowe not only covers the state-of-the-field scholarship, but he also articulates several of the critical questions raised by these studies, questions regarding space, economic development or stagnation, continuity, technology, government intervention, and social conflict. He addresses the issue of regional analysis in Chinese studies, and discusses the complex relationship between a city and its hinterland: How embedded were these cities in their respective hinterlands and to what degree did differing urban and rural interests contribute to social conflicts described in the papers by Santangelo and Fuma? This is a question that underlies and informs the discussions in all five papers.

The genesis of this book was a panel on urban history of Jiangnan which Professor Michael Marmé organized for the 1989 meeting of the Association for Asian Studies, held in Washington D.C. To Professor Marmé go our thanks for conceiving the project and organizing the panel which got it started. Professors William T. Rowe and Evelyn S. Rawski were the discussants for this panel, and gave us much helpful guidance and commentary. Professor Rowe's introduction is evidence of his continued assistance; Professor Rawski's assistance and encouragement have been much appreciated. I would also like to thank Professor Roland Higgins who has been informative on the topic of Nanjing and who recruited Professor Fuma's paper for this volume. Our thanks also to Professor Rowe for persuading Professor Santangelo to join the project. Thanks also to William C. Johnson for his help in designing and executing the computer graphics in this volume and to the cartography lab at Michigan State University for the maps.

—Linda Cooke Johnson

INTRODUCTION
City and Region in the Lower Yangzi

William T. Rowe

Since the publication in the mid-1970s of the pioneering conference volumes edited by G. William Skinner and Mark Elvin, our knowledge of and appreciation for the Chinese urban experience of the past millennium has grown enormously.[1] Simple, undifferentiated models of "the Chinese city" have become increasingly untenable; the perceived disjunction between Western inspired treaty ports and indigenous urban centers has narrowed (or at least blurred); once popular views of urban and rural in Chinese society as either unmediated opposites or, conversely, as mutually indistinguishable, have gradually given way to more contextually sensitive portrayals of urban metropolis and regional hinterland. Most importantly, we have become much more aware of a pattern, or patterns, of Chinese urban change over time.

Unquestionably the most productive instrument in advancing our knowledge of Chinese cities in the post-Skinner years has been case studies, either monographic "urban biographies" or more specialized studies of politics, women, labor, businessmen, and so on, in the context of individual cities.[2] There have, however, been at least two biases apparent in the work that has appeared so far in English, both of them resulting from the reasonable desire of working historians to concentrate on the highly visible, the seemingly important for the understanding of our own day, and, not least, the well-documented. One is that we now know far more about *big* cities than we do about the second, third, and even lower-rank central places where probably the bulk of late imperial urbanites spent their lives. Rectification of this scholarly imbalance may not lie too far in the future, but for the moment we must live with it. Second, the work of the past decade has concentrated heavily on cities of China's industrial era (the twentieth century) or, at most, the last century of imperial rule. It is this deficiency which the present volume attempts to redress, by maintaining an awareness of the common concerns pointed up by writers on later era cities, yet moving the inquiry back in time another seven hundred years.

Each of our contributors devotes significant attention to the question of the use of space in their particular cities—Suzhou, Hangzhou, Yangzhou, and Shanghai—and the way land use patterns changed over time. In doing so they draw upon the stimulating theses advanced some years ago by F. W. Mote in a series of articles on Suzhou and Nanjing, in which he identified as a distinguishing feature of Chinese urbanism a truly remarkable long-term stability of city form.[3] In his own study of Suzhou in this volume, Michael Marmé invokes Mote's ingenious overlay of outline maps of that city dating from 1229 and 1945, explicitly endorsing Mote's conclusion that little had changed, and Antonia Finnane argues that this same observation "could just as well be applied to Yangzhou."

Yet in the descriptions they offer of the pattern of growth of these cities, our authors are remarkably consistent, and the common processes they depict seem in tension with the morphological stagnation posited by Mote. In all these cities, periods of economic prosperity led to great spatial expansion, an expansion clearly seen by our authors as driven by the market. This meant a movement beyond the city walls (though in at least some cases walls were *re*-created to reflect the new realities of urban growth), the development of extramural commercial suburbs at the termini of major trade routes, and the incorporation of outlying market towns into a greatly enlarged metropolitan area (what Marmé terms "the urban penumbra"). Accompanying this was a long-term decline of the planned aspects of the Tang-style city: a collapse of the system of formally segregated official markets, an increasingly "haphazard" street plan, greater multicenteredness, increasingly complex residence patterns, and a tendency toward more functionally integrated land use. At the same time, all of our cities to some extent witnessed a continuing or even heightened spatial separation of the official and the commercial sectors, corresponding in general to the intramural-extramural division, though by no means very neatly so.

What then are we left with: a morphological stagnation imposed by political authority, or a dynamic fluidity driven by private enterprise and market determined land values? Is Marmé simply incorrect in emphasizing the strength of "the state's impact on the organization of

urban space," and Finnane in arguing that "the basic spatial organization of the city had been set by . . . precedent . . . and by a political
and cultural tradition which supported the gentry-official stratum"?
Mote's celebrated maps suggest that they are not. And yet the evidence presented in this volume, as well as other recent work, cautions
against the acceptance of easy or one-sided conclusions on this issue.

This same tension or ambiguity underlies a second critical question
addressed in these studies, that is, why do cities (in this instance
Chinese cities) rise and decline? Not surprisingly, the answer our authors offer begins with the balance struck, successfully or unsuccessfully, between ecology and technology. Under a given level of technology, topographic or other ecological features favor the centrality and
prosperity of some cities over others; with a shift either in ecology or
technological level, relative advantages also change, promoting new
central places and sending others into decline. Countless examples of
this might be cited from China itself (the promotion of Changsha over
Xiangtan due to the introduction of the steamship) or from elsewhere
in the world (the promotion of Baltimore over Charleston, or Chicago
over St. Louis, due to the introduction of railroads).

In the Lower Yangzi, the construction of the Yangzi-Huai section
of the Grand Canal in Han times offered stimulus to the rise of Yangzhou, whereas the subsequent shift of the Yellow River to a southern
route diminished that city's potential centrality. Suzhou, for its part,
was favored over Hangzhou by the *re*-construction of the Canal in the
Ming Yongle reign. Shanghai owed its earliest ascendence to a shift in
the course of the Wusong river in the eleventh and twelfth centuries, a
shift that sent the once prosperous Qinglong into permanent obscurity.
Its growth was further stimulated by the *collapse* of the Grand Canal
route in the early nineteenth century, which prompted the shift to the
coastal route for shipments of northbound tribute grain.

In each of these instances, it was the technology of transport that
was decisive, but other technological innovations could play major
roles as well. For example, Suzhou could not become an important city
based on its extraction and redistribution function within its hinterland
until the problem of waterlogging in that fertile but low-lying territory
was solved by massive construction of waterworks, first in the Song
and again in the early Ming. Shanghai's rise was likewise aided by successive waves of innovation, beginning in the thirteenth century, in the
technology of cotton cultivation, the staple of its own delta hinterland.
Yangzhou's prosperity, needless to say, was conditioned by technological developments in salt production, which offered the Liang Huai

product competitive advantages or disadvantages over salt produced in other regions (despite its state monopolistic aspects, the actual command of markets by various salt production areas was often in large part a function of consumer choice).

Beyond the factors of ecology and technology, however, our authors present strikingly insistent evidence to argue for the pivotal role of administrative decisions in the relative rise and fall of cities. This is not wholly unexpected. The model of "the Chinese city" bequeathed by Max Weber would of course predict as much, and even the *doyen* of the historical study of Chinese urbanism in this country, G. William Skinner, in his model of regional cycles driven first and foremost by market factors, was careful to point out the potential of political acts such as relocation of an imperial capital or the institution or abolition of bans and monopolies on foreign trade on the relative fortunes of metropolises and their regions.[4] The evidence is so strong in the studies included here, however, to lead one to suspect whether, Skinner's marketing model notwithstanding, the political factor might indeed have been *unusually* important in a centralized bureaucratic state of vast territorial scale such as China, in determining relative status within the hierarchy of central places.

Among lower Yangzi cities, Nanjing, with its history of dramatic shifts in administrative rank, would of course be expected to have its fortunes profoundly affected by such decisions (much like the Kaifeng of Hartwell's classic study).[5] But Marmé argues that Suzhou, too, found its prosperity affected rather directly by political decisions, in the area of Grain Tribute policy. Most surprising is the case of Shanghai, the economic city *par excellence*. Linda Cooke Johnson's chapter here repeatedly points out the impact of administrative actions on the city's fortunes, even in the pre-treaty port era. Shanghai's initial rise was precipitated by the establishment of an Office of Overseas Trade in 1277; the Ming relocation of the capital to Beijing and institution of the sea ban drove it into temporary decline; and the early Qing reopening of foreign trade and establishment of the Jianghai Customs in 1730 made it once again a major conduit for interregional and international commerce. Indeed, when Johnson argues that "nearly all of the growth of Shanghai, both inside and outside the walls of the city, can be attributed to mercantile and commercial interests," it would be well to remember that it was in large part political decisions which put the merchants there in the first place.

The case of Yangzhou, as presented here by Finnane, demonstrates the critical role of the political factor in the most striking terms. Though Yangzhou is usually conceived of as a center of "commercial capitalism,"[6] a characterization Finnane would perhaps not refute, she argues that the true basis of its regional primacy was always political: Yangzhou usually enjoyed high rank in the administrative hierarchy of central places, and its rising or falling commercial fortunes followed directly upon its administrative status. Presumably, Finnane's argument implies, another central place in the Jiangbei area might equally well, or even better, have served the regional city function which Yangzhou enjoyed by virtue of bureaucratic favor.

Assuming, then, that the prominence of these great cities was determined by some complex interplay of ecological, technological, and political factors, the question posed by the contributors to this volume might be stated in terms of whether or not the political decisions involved were made out of economic rationality, so as deliberately to capitalize on the advantages of centrality offered by the other factors. In general, Marmé and Johnson argue that they *were*—Marmé speaks of a pattern of "ad hoc decisions taken to exploit existing opportunities for imperial advantage." Finnane's work suggests, on the contrary, that in her case they were *not*, that administrative decisions were made à priori of any serious consideration of economic geography (or of the interests of the area's population), and that Yangzhou was "imposed on the landscape, rather than growing out of it," with all of Jiangbei suffering as a result.

To get at this question more effectively, we need for a moment to shift our scale of analysis up a bit from the city to the region. What, first of all, is a "region"? As I use the term here, and as I see it used most often in the field of China studies since the work of Skinner, a "region" is not a *zone* within which some key factor—say, language or religion or staple economic product—is held constant and uniform, but rather it is a *system* of localities of varying degrees of centrality, held together by a relatively strong pattern of interdependent exchange relationships. A region, then, is characterized not so much by internal homogeneity (though sharing of certain secondary factors such as dialect is likely to occur) as it is by a functional heterogeneity.[7]

A region so defined in not a finite or closed system, but rather fits into nested hierarchies of various magnitudes and scales. Thus, the region which this volume announces as its subject, Jiangnan, was also a component of a larger system, the Lower Yangzi "macroregion," which itself fit into the still larger system which was the Chinese Empire. (This is so notwithstanding Skinner's persuasive argument that, *in general*, it was the intermediary "macroregional" units which in China's late imperial era had greater functional integrity than either the empire as a whole or "sub-regions" such as Jiangnan.) Nor do individual central places necessarily participate in but a single regional system. Certainly they belong simultaneously to systems of differing magnitudes; Suzhou and Shanghai, for example, were important components of both the Jiangnan subregion and the Lower Yangzi macroregion. In certain cases, however, a given central place may also fit into two adjacent regional systems of comparable scale. This seems to have been the case with Yangzhou, a fact which has complicated life for most analysts of its economy and society. Looked at from one perspective, Yangzhou is clearly the regional city for the Jiangbei subregion; looked at from others, it is just as clearly a component of the adjacent subregion of Jiangnan. The boundaries of regional systems, in other words, are soft, and vary not only over time but also with differing functional perspectives.

The period under consideration in this volume, that from the early twelfth to the early nineteenth centuries, was one in which the Lower Yangzi macroregion became ever more prosperous and ever more clearly the metropolitan region within China as a whole. This fact, perhaps first formally articulated by Chi Ch'ao-ting in 1936 and demonstrated in detail in the work of Shiba Yoshinobu, Fu Yiling, and many others, is further reinforced in the research presented here.[8] Each of the cities studied in this volume participated in and benefited from this process. There were short-term reverses and epicycles, to be sure, but the long-term trend was very positive. Of course, not all subregions or localities shared equally in this increasing prosperity and influence. We have already seen how urban decline for certain cities like Qinglong was an inherent byproduct of the streamlining of the macroregional system as a whole. More interestingly, Yangzhou's Jiangbei hinterland did consistently (and notoriously) less well than did the southern portion of the lower Yangzi macroregion. Clearly a basic cause of this was the relative poverty of its resource endowments, but, as Professor Finnane argues, there were other, human factors at work as well.

What factors determine the fortunes of a region's or subregion's economic development? The trigger, according to American economic historian Douglass North,[9] is most often provided by the discovery of an export staple which is able to find a steady, cost-effective, and lucrative extraregional market (North offers the example of timber in the American Pacific northwest). In Jiangnan such a role seems to have been assumed in turn by rice, silk, and cotton. Almost invariably this export staple forms one half of a reciprocal two-way interregional trade, and frequently the cost effectiveness of this staple's export will be enhanced by a prior demand for a regional *import* (or imports); merchants, bringing a needed item into the region, will seek return freights (if only as ballast) at often very depressed rates. In Johnson's Shanghai, for example, high value-per-bulk cotton textile exports found markets in North China as return cargo on vessels bringing in the needed soy-cake fertilizer, along the southeast coast as return freights for imports of lumber and sugar, and in the Middle Yangzi in exchange for imports of grain. In Marmé's Suzhou, imports of coarse grain facilitated exports of the higher value rice, and, somewhat ironically, the seemingly onerous political requirement to ship tribute grain north after the Ming Yongle reign facilitated imports from North China of raw cotton (despite legal prohibitions), hence further stimulating the region's export cotton textile trade.

Obviously, however, the successful development of an export staple does not in itself guarantee rising regional prosperity, in either absolute or relative terms. If it did, Jiangbei's fortunes would have been much different, for its most distinctive product, salt, had extraordinary advantages as an export staple: guaranteed and steady extraregional demand, weak outside competition, high value-per-bulk, fairly low production costs, and inexhaustible supply. Yet Jiangbei apparently failed to capitalize upon this and follow the further pattern of successful regional development. This pattern would call for development of a regional market structure which conformed to a balanced and symmetrical central-place model, favoring redistributive as much as extractive commodity flows, rather than a dendritic layout oriented exclusively towards exports. Its regional product structure would gradually diversify, rather than remaining concentrated on a monoculture dictated by external, metropolitan demand. Its internal consumer market would develop accordingly. Regional industry, too, would develop and diversify, rather than remaining at a low level and highly specialized, serving merely the instrumental needs of the metropolitan market.

Late imperial Jiangnan is clearly the very model of a successfully developing regional economy. Its metropolis during most of this era, Suzhou, initially developed its silk textile industry under imperial monopoly control. Yet, as Paolo Santangelo shows us, this industry was gradually taken over by the private sector (seemingly unlike the salt industry in Yangzhou), and technologies developed for silk production were eventually adapted to the even greater scale cotton trade. In the wider region, Marmé and Johnson demonstrate the development of a balanced marketing hierarchy. Jiangnan progressively diversified its export base to include tea, paper, and other commodities beyond the proliferating variety of cotton and silk textiles. It saw a gradual diffusion of handicraft technology and production throughout the region (into less as well as more urbanized localities), accompanied by an increasingly sophisticated functional specialization of handicraft labor: spinners, weavers, dyers, calendarers, and tailors, as well as transport and commercial workers. All of this contributed to the rise of popular buying power and a broadly based indigenous market not only for extraregional imports (obtained at favorable terms of trade in exchange for more highly processed exports) but for local products as well. The results were very positive. As Marmé argues, with perhaps but slight exaggeration, "The system centered on Suzhou probably did provide better for more people than any previous [regional] system in world history."

In each of these regards Jiangbei did notably less well. If Yangzhou was not, as Finnane argues, a "colonial city," it was almost certainly a company town. Its region saw nearly no diversification of export base beyond salt (except, significantly, increasing exports of manual labor unable to find work at home). Despite the fact that much of the region was potentially suited to cotton cultivation, it remained essentially a monocultural rice producer (Finnane's suggestion that political authorities may have had some role in preventing product diversification, so as better to concentrate Jiangbei's energies on rice and salt, is most telling). Some minor residentiary industry did develop, notably rush mat weaving, but its level remained low and its profits lower still. Jiangbei did so poorly, in fact, that at least by the mid-nineteenth century its natives had developed a reputation outside the region for cultural inferiority (a stigma which clearly in some fashion further contributed to subregional immiseration).[10] A major cause of Jiangbei's woes, again, was the area's ecological fragility. However, as Professor Finnane contends, a large portion of the blame may in fact have lain with Yangzhou itself, and with its peculiarly adversarial relationship with its hinterland.

I have suggested that a "region," as used these days in Western studies of China, refers not to a zone of continuity but to a system of interdependent exchange relationships, and is therefore characterized more by internal heterogeneity than homogeneity. This implies internal *inequality* as well. Within a regional system of central places, the regional metropolis will almost always do better than any other participant in the system. At the very least, it will enjoy the considerable advantages of centrality: greater multifunctionality, greater economic diversification, greater leverage in exchange relations, and so on. Therefore, that the regional metropolis is by far the most prosperous locality within a region is not in itself a necessary indication either of an unusual degree of exploitation, or of systemic dysfunction.

Still, under differing conditions the prosperity of a regional metropolis may be good for that of the region as a whole, or else a negative factor, being achieved at the region's general expense. The literature on early modern European urban development provides neatly contrasting models of these "generative" and "parasitic" cities, in the work of E. A. Wrigley on London and David Ringrose on Madrid.[11] The key questions posed in these models are: (1) Is consumption in the regional metropolis primarily of goods produced within the region (as in the case of London), or does it constitute an expenditure of regional capital on luxury goods from without (Madrid)? (2) Is extraction from the countryside primarily through processes of reciprocal market exchange, or is it commandeered in the form of rents, tithes, and taxes? (3) If via exchange, how fair—free from political or other extraeconomic manipulation—are the terms of trade? The answers to these questions in turn hinge on the function of the city within the region, and the character of the city's elite.

We see in this volume several examples of the potentially generative role of regional metropolises. The original rise both of Suzhou *and* its hinterland in the Southern Song is attributed by Marmé, at least in part, to the consumer demand of the region's major city of that era, Hangzhou. (One is reminded again of the corresponding role of Kaifeng during the Northern Song, as presented by Hartwell.) The increasing regional importance of sericulture and, later, cotton culture in the Ming and Qing seems to have enhanced the generative aspects of both Suzhou's and Shanghai's relations with their hinterlands. Both activities were mediated by a complex web of reciprocal market relationships, and a proliferation of small-scale shippers, brokers, processors, and handlers which served to disperse the profits of the trade from metropolis to surrounding region. The salt enterprise, with its ambiguous status somewhere between the state and private market sectors, seems not to have provided Yangzhou with the same generative possibilities relative to Jiangbei.

But there are more troubling questions here as well, which at least in part confound the attempt to interpret our case studies according to clear and simple models. Suzhou and other areas around Zhu Yuanzhang's capital at Nanjing, for example, were subjected to effectively confiscatory tax rates for centuries after the Ming founding, and yet

Marmé argues that these had no clear negative effect on balanced regional development. Suzhou was also notorious for the number and wealth of its absentee landlords, yet this, too, we are told, did not impede regional progress (at least not until the cataclysmic class warfare of the late Ming). Yangzhou, which from an outsider's perspective would seem to have been dominated by an elite, not of tax-farmers and rentier landlords like Suzhou or Hangzhou, but of merchants and entrepreneurs, apparently proved more "parasitic" than either of those two cities.

One way in which our contributors seek to address questions of the quality of city-hinterland relations is through focus on the level of "embeddedness" in the regional society. One way to assess this issue might be to ask to what degree the city's elite was comprised of natives to the region, and to what extent of (presumably rapacious) extra-regional sojourners. I am less than satisfied with this methodology. Indeed, I would propose as very general rules that, in *any* city of late imperial China, (a) a direct correlation would pertain between the socioeconomic status of any individual and the distance from that city of the individual's native place; and (2) socioeconomic dominance by nonlocals would be greater the higher one rose in the hierarchy of central places, because of a greater orientation of the city to trade (or administration) of broader geographic scale. We also see in this volume a number of other hints that the percentage of extra-regional sojourners cannot be used as an index of a given city's "parasitism." Yangzhou, portrayed here as a drain on its hinterland, was certainly dominated by outsiders; but no less so was Shanghai, depicted by Johnson as a force for regional growth, dominated by Ningboese, Fujianese, and Cantonese. Suzhou, too, as Santangelo reminds us, numbered Huizhou and Ningbo merchants among its commercial elite. Moreover, the available evidence by no means supports a simple conclusion of extraction of capital by sojourning merchants as a crippling blow to regional fortunes. We know that Huizhou salt merchants active at Yangzhou did put a large percentage of their profits into landholding in their home prefecture (arguably, this hurt Huizhou more than it did Jiangbei),[12] but Finnane's evidence on the luxurious gardens they constructed, as well as the celebrated aesthetic pleasures of Yangzhou generally, suggest a pattern of significant investment in their host locality as well. Nor is there any reason to believe that sojourning merchants at Shanghai or Suzhou were any less eager to withdraw resources from the host community and its regional system. The fact was that local identities in late imperial China were complex and multistranded, and under these circumstances ethnic analysis of urban elites as a means of assessing the quality of city-hinterland relations is problematic at best.

Another way to approach the question of embeddedness would be via analysis of a city's trading partners. In my own work on Hankou I argued, perhaps too offhandedly, that the greater importance within the city's economy of *entrepôt*, or interregional transshipment functions, relative to direct extraction, supply, or redistribution functions for its own regional hinterland, suggested a fairly low degree of embeddedness. In this volume, Professor Finnane notes something similar for Yangzhou, invoking the work of Paul Hohenberg and Lynn Lees on European cities to argue that a "network" model describes cities oriented primarily to interregional trade more closely than does the familiar central place model, which situates the city more firmly within a regional urban hierarchy. The same point has been made by the geographer James Vance, who in his analysis of "gateway" cities such as Chicago points out that the central place model itself was derived essentially to describe the territorial implications of *retail* trade, and that accounting for wholesale trade may necessitate a basically different type of analytical conceit.[13] My own view is that the two models are by no means mutually invalidating, and that higher magnitude central places, including all the cities studied in this volume, are part both of interregional networks and regional systems. But evidence presented here may cast in doubt the wisdom of drawing hasty conclusions about a given city's embeddedness based on analysis of trade flows, since the interregional *entrepôt* function seems to have been relatively *less* central in Yangzhou than in either Suzhou or Shanghai, and yet Finnane argues, plausibly, that Yangzhou's level of embeddedness was lower than that of the other two.

How then is "embeddedness" to be measured? The best way might be through detailed analysis of lower-level marketing hierarchies and of functional relationships of central places within their regions. Our contributors offer us some information on this score, though none treat the issue systematically. Abundant research, however, has been done on precisely this topic in China during the past decade, and to lesser extent in Taiwan and Japan as well.[14] The conclusions of this new corpus of scholarship basically accord with those of our contributors here. Jiangnan, the regional hinterland of first Suzhou, then Shanghai, was endowed from Ming times on with a balanced hierarchy of small cities and towns, which steadily increased in number and density of deployment over the landscape. As most of these markets continued to grow in size, some, those at the lower end of the scale, graduating from periodicity to permanency, became more functionally complex while others tended to specialize in a given commodity or process. Ever greater numbers of them were no longer merely collection and distribution centers but hubs of organization for handicraft activity. Thus, they assumed a greater variety of roles with respect to their surrounding rural-dwellers: they were no longer simply receptacles for marketing occasional surplus grain and sources of a few necessary consumer goods, but sources of employment, capital, marketing services, technological diffusion, and the raw materials of rural handicrafts. In this fashion, Suzhou and Shanghai, at least through the end of the preindustrial era, became increasingly embedded in their regional hinterland, with whose fortunes their own prosperity tended to move in tandem. By mid-Qing times, indeed, it might be better to conceive of Jiangnan not as two or three major cities in a surrounding rural hinterland, but rather as an "urban region," an area of widely diffused urbanness not unlike northern Italy or the Low Countries in Europe of the same period.[15]

Jiangbei was a different story. As Finnane's chapter reminds us, Yangzhou's hinterland was far from desolate of markets, but it does appear that these were largely of a different order from those of Jiangnan. Although he was only able to trace comparatively recent historical developments, the great sociologist Fei Xiaotong in a 1984 field survey may have captured this essential difference when he noted that, whereas the Jiangnan countryside was profusely covered with fairly populous market towns (*zhen*), in Jiangbei the comparable central place was no more than a "fair" (*ji*), with but a marginal claim to permanent settlement. He added:

> I am convinced that a real town could only come into existence when rural commodity production has attained quite a high level of development, which cannot easily be achieved by expanding agricultural production alone. Industry must be established on the village-township level. The fact that there are towns but no fairs in southern Jiangsu is probably due to the fact that commodities were produced there by rural handicraft industries in very early times. . . . In northern Jiangsu, where traditional rural industries are backward, fairs alone can handle commodity circulation in localities that produce only farm produce. As a result, towns cannot be established there easily.[16]

The picture presented by Fei is of a classic dual economy, with the metropolis of Yangzhou, relating perhaps more closely to Jiangnan than Jiangbei, of marginal significance for good *or* ill in the fortunes of its subsistence-oriented agricultural hinterland. This may be accurate as far as it goes, but of course there was more to the story than this. Through its direction of the regional salt industry, its administrative and fiscal role, its demand for labor and food supply, and perhaps above all its financing and direction of regional water conservancy works,[17] Yangzhou was in fact of critical significance to the prosperity of Jiangbei, just as Suzhou and Shanghai were to Jiangnan. In late imperial China, *all* major cities were embedded in their hinterland to a very considerable degree.

This by no means denies the possibility of conflicts between urban and rural interests. Both Paolo Santangelo's study of Suzhou and Susumu Fuma's of Hangzhou show how these two cities had come to experience tensions between urban insiders (in Fuma's term, "citizens") and an ever-growing number of newly arriving outsiders. In Fuma's study, we see as well how systematic had become the pattern of urban-rural contention over distribution of tax assessments by the late Ming period. Keep in mind that these tensions arose, not in "colonial" cities like Yangzhou nor in allegedly "foreign implants" like Shanghai, but rather in provincial capitals, to all appearances fully integrated into their local and regional hinterlands.

All five of our studies, it seems to me, demonstrate the evolution by the late imperial period of an autonomous urban culture, one characterized (in Santangelo's words) "by frenetic activity, daily habits and customs, impulses and conflicting emotions." This runs counter to the argument of Max Weber, updated by Mote, that Chinese cities were relatively less distinctive from the countryside, in cultural terms, than were their Western counterparts. Most striking in the studies of Fuma and Santangelo is the specific preoccupation of both urban elites and urban administrators with *urban* problems, both groups being completely accustomed to assuming the discreteness of the municipal unit as a locus of managerial responsibility. A remarkable demonstration of this came in the 1720 Suzhou public security reform, described by Professor Santangelo. The result of this reform was a style of urban societal self-policing, fully "recognized" by the imperial state but managed by urban economic elites, that was highly systematic and hierarchical, and completely discrete to the municipality.

In Professor Fuma's paper on Hangzhou we see an even more striking early attempt at creation of an urban public security force.

Though this grew out of a hoary tradition of *corvée* assessment for street patrolling duty, what emerged in the 1560s and 1570s was in fact a remarkably bold experiment in a rather fully bureaucratized municipal police force, built upon a fiscal base of specifically urban property tax assessments. Fuma's study essentially analyzes why this precocious system, proposed by popular initiative "for the sake of the city," could not take hold. The chief impediment, it appears, was the internal conflict it generated within an increasingly stratified urban society. The major struggle was not that between capital and labor, but rather between an upper elite and an emerging urban middle class, capable of being rallied to self-awareness by a quasi-professional political activist, Ding Shiqing.

Based on Fuma's study one is led to reconsider the broader processes of urban socioeconomic change of the mid and late Ming. Specifically, one wonders whether the "sprouts of capitalism" debate, with its Marxist presumptions of the primacy of the mode of production in generating structures of conflict, has led us to miss the point of what was really going on in late imperial Jiangnan cities.[18] It seems from the evidence presented here that the "sprouts of capitalism" were probably very real, in Hangzhou and elsewhere, but that they were only ancillary to many of the major social conflicts of the era. We see in sixteenth-century Hangzhou a process of embourgeoisement, which was fairly independent of any early capitalist transition. There is little in the lines of cleavage presented here that necessarily presupposes major changes in work organization of the sort associated with the rise of capitalism. Rather, although the social configurations, which Fuma describes, appear to be new to his era, and rooted in the rapid mid-Ming urbanization of Jiangnan, the key factors in structuring conflict seem to be the emergence of an intense urban consciousness, based on residence rather than occupation or production relations, and catalyzed by issues of rents and taxes on urban residential property.

One of the most satisfying contributions of the case studies which follow, at least to this reader, is their collective effect of discrediting the "anomalous case" approach to Chinese urban history. It was all too easy in the past to discuss Shanghai as an implanted cancerous growth (or outpost of progress, depending on your perspective), extraneous to the "normal" path of Chinese urban development, just as it was convenient to treat Yangzhou as an isolated, state-sponsored "special economic zone" of commercial capitalism, and Hankou as an inexplicably overgrown commercial suburb, and Jingdezhen as an oddly-misplaced Chinese Birmingham (or, more accurately, Stoke-on-Trent), all of them too widely deviant from the norm to require more than a passing aside in general treatments of "the Chinese city."

What emerges from these studies, more clearly than from other recent work, which has edged in this direction, is a view of even the most distinctive of late imperial cities not as anomalies, but rather as points within a wide spectrum of possible Chinese urban types. This is most striking in Professor Johnson's contribution, where, building on the work of Mark Elvin, she effectively demolishes the "sleepy fishing town" notion of pre-treaty port Shanghai. Obviously, the city that the foreigners built at Shanghai was something quite new to China, as were many of the techniques of trade, transport, and manufacture they introduced along the way. But Shanghai had been an important and growing commercial center for centuries before 1842, and indeed had come to assume paramouncy in precisely the role for which it has been celebrated in its later history, as interlocutor between the trade of its own and adjacent regions, on the one hand, and the emerging international market on the other. Treaty-port Shanghai thus fitted into an endogenous trend of rather long duration, however much the foreigner might have provided in the way of new direction.

Michael Marmé takes this refreshing approach still further, when he asks whether we might trace to Suzhou and other cities of the early Ming, or even the Southern Song, Marie-Claire Bergère's "attempt to find indigenous roots for twentieth-century Shanghai," a cosmopolitan urban tradition which she has dubbed "the other China." Marmé, probably wisely, refrains from answering decisively in the affirmative the question he has posed, but the weight of his evidence suggests that not only the late nineteenth-century treaty-port phenomenon but also the late Ming "sprouts of capitalism," built upon, rather than creating ex nihilo, an ongoing and flexible Chinese urban tradition. This tradition may, in fact, have represented less an "other" China than an integral part of a highly complex, almost infinitely malleable, and yet cohesive and distinctive, experience of Chinese urbanism. It was an experience which offered, as Antonia Finnane points out, "a diversity of models."

Ctr for Cartographic Research and Spatial Analysis, Michigan State University

Fig. 1 The Jiangnan area in the Yuan dynasty

Chapter 1
Heaven on Earth: The Rise of Suzhou, 1127–1550

Michael Marmé

Shang you Tian tang, xia you Su Hang.

The city of Suzhou first entered the historical record around 500 B.C., when the prince of Wu made it his capital. Thus, when the phrase, "Above there is Heaven; on earth, Suzhou and Hangzhou" was first used, Suzhou was already a millennium-and-a-half old.[1] The phrase is a reflection of China's march to the tropics, that southward shift in China's center of economic, cultural and political gravity with which we have long been familiar. Its currency should not obscure the fact that, for Suzhou, this formula marked the beginning of a new stage in the city's development, *not* its culmination.

SONG SUZHOU: FROM THE "LAND OF RICE AND FISH" TO "HEAVEN ON EARTH"

During the half century which separated the fall of the Tang dynasty (618–906) and the consolidation of the Song (960–1276), Suzhou was the seat of the northernmost prefecture of the kingdom of Wu-Yue, whose capital was at Hangzhou. Although it consisted of little more than the modern province of Zhejiang and the southeastern corner of Jiangsu throughout most of its existence, the kingdom was among the most prosperous and stable regions of China during the interregnum.[2] Its ruler voluntarily submitted to the Song in 978. The new government was based, as those who ruled the Middle Kingdom had always been, in North China. It reorganized the area south of the Yangzi and north

of Fujian as the Liang Zhe circuit. The circuit was an administrative
level below the central government controlling a group of neighboring
prefectures. The officials in charge at this level—typically, of military,
fiscal, judicial, and supply commissions—had "different functional responsibilities and powers [in] the same area, sometimes with disparate
but overlapping geographical jurisdictions."[3] These divide and rule tac-
tics were intended to prevent the accumulation of power at the regional level which had undermined the Tang. Boundaries not only varied
with function, they also shifted over time. Liang Zhe itself was periodically divided into two circuits—a distinction which persisted even when
not officially in use. In this scheme, Suzhou was assigned to Zhexi
("Western Zhe").[4]

Among the thirteen prefectures of the Liang Zhe circuit, Lin'an
(Hangzhou) remained the most important. In 1010, its eight counties
had a registered population of 163,700 households. Suzhou's five
counties—Wu, Changzhou, Wujiang, Kunshan, and Changshu[5]—had
only 66,139. The 1077 commercial tax quotas tell a similar story.
Although their assessments ranked both Hangzhou and Suzhou among
the empire's most important trading centers, Hangzhou's quota was
fixed at 170,813 strings of cash, Suzhou's at a mere 77,076 strings.[6]
Suzhou was designated Pingjiang *fu*, one of Liang Zhe's five "superior" prefectures (*fu*), in 1115. But it could not rival Hangzhou—much
less the Song capital at Kaifeng.[7] No discernible social or economic
trends promised to alter this situation.

In the 1120s, the Jurchen, a Tungusic tribe from Manchuria,
broke through the Song's northern defenses. In 1126, they sacked
Kaifeng, capturing the emperor and three thousand members of his
court. In disarray, what remained of the Song government fled south,
with Jurchen armies in hot pursuit.[8] In 1129 the newly proclaimed
emperor Gaozong halted in Pingjiang, but only for a few days. Subsequent developments proved that, in this case, discretion was the better
part of valor. On the twenty-fifth day of the second month, 1130, Jurchen units appeared at Pingjiang's southern gate. Breaking into the
city, the invaders "plundered government offices and private residences, [helping themselves to] sons and daughters, gold and silk, the
accumulation of granaries and storehouses. They committed arson and
fire spread. Smoke could be seen for 200 *li*. In all, the fires burned for
five days and nights."[9] When open hostilities settled into a military
stalemate and an uneasy truce after 1141, the emperor chose Hangzhou as *Xingzai* or "temporary imperial residence." Not only was it a
far more important place than Pingjiang but it was also more centrally

located within the truncated realm and must have seemed marginally more secure than places to its north.

Such political choices had social and economic consequences. With Lin'an as the "temporary" capital of the Southern Song (1127–1276), all of the Liang Zhe circuit benefited. When Marco Polo visited the area—after Mongol conquest had reunified the country and returned the capital to the north—he found Suzhou, "a large and magnificent city. . . the number of [whose] inhabitants is so great as to be a subject of astonishment," a city as noted for its role in trade and manufacture as it was as a center of learning. Yet, four days' journey to the south lay the "noble and magnificent city of [Xingzai], a name that signifies 'the celestial city,' which it merits from its preeminence to all others in the world, in point of grandeur and beauty, as well as from its abundant delights, which might lead an inhabitant to imagine himself in paradise."[10]

One must conclude that the gap separating Hangzhou from Suzhou widened rather than narrowed over the twelfth and thirteenth centuries. The years which followed brought Suzhou repeated, often bloody conquest, higher taxes, and the exile or execution of its social, economic, and cultural elites. These scarcely seem ideal conditions for overtaking the more affluent, populous, and developed center to its south. Nonetheless, scholars East and West agree that by the sixteenth century Suzhou had emerged as the economic and cultural center of the Middle Kingdom's richest, most urbanized and most advanced region. It remained the central metropolis integrating (and dominating) that region well into the nineteenth century.[11]

Military defeat, confiscatory taxation, and decimation of local elites are not usually regarded as keys to local prosperity and increased influence. Analysis of so unlikely an ascent should help us better understand the processes of development in late imperial society. It should also allow us to address a number of other issues. If contemporaries regarded Suzhou as "All under Heaven's Heaven on Earth," did this suggest incorporation in, or transcendence of, the imperial order? Ming Suzhou was famous for its riots and its eremitism;[12] it was an urban corner of a huge agrarian empire. Was it already home to that "other China" which Bergère invokes in her attempt to find indigenous roots for twentieth century Shanghai—a China urban rather than rural, commercial and capitalist rather than "feudal," a secular society rather than a bureaucratic state, cosmopolitan rather than closed, open-ended rather than orthodox?[13]

Recent work demonstrates that we can certainly trace much of this "other China" back to the early nineteenth century. At least at the great central Yangzi port city of Hankou, many characteristics conventionally attributed to Western impact have been shown to have roots in an indigenous tradition which long predated the treaty ports. Not only was Hankou sharply distinguishable from the countryside which surrounded it, it was also run for (and, de facto if not de jure, largely by) its merchant community, a community with its own commercial capitalist interests and values.[14] If "truly urban" cities can be found in the Middle Kingdom prior to 1842, it becomes necessary to ask how far back this indigenous urban tradition—a tradition hardy enough to survive, even flourish, without charters or an autonomous military arm—can be traced. How widely distributed was it spatially? In particular, can we trace the origins of an autonomous, commercial capitalist tradition fundamentally at odds with the orthodox, agrarian, bureaucratic state as far back as Ming Suzhou—as much of the work on the sprouts of capitalism seems to imply? Or is this "other China" a separate, and much more recent, development?

Analysis of these issues must begin in the Song. Suzhou/Pingjiang prefecture occupied the lowest lying portions of Jiangnan: much of it was, and still is, below the water level of Lake Tai and the Yangzi River.[15] Thus, the fact that this region was developed after other parts of Jiangnan is not surprising. Without immense investment in water control, the area would remain, quite literally, a backwater. If sodden marshes were to become productive fields, dikes had to be built, and the waters behind them drained. The network of polders and canals which resulted was extremely delicate. A blocked channel miles away might result in flood waters breaching an ill-maintained dike, returning paddy field to lake. Too many polders would leave high water nowhere to go, increasing the pressure on dikes throughout the system. Dredging the delta's principal river channels was too large an undertaking to be left to individuals or localities: local officials, using *corvée* labor, periodically addressed this task.[16] The work of reclaiming fields from the waters was however usually left to private individuals. Both public and private efforts were extremely labor intensive. That the number of households registered in Pingjiang prefecture almost doubled between 1184 and 1275 (rising from 173,042 to 329,603)—precisely the period in which construction of polders was transforming the entire Yangzi delta—thus comes as no surprise.[17] Since creation of polders on this scale required both coordination and the ability to subsidize many hands while dikes were built, fields drained and a first harvest ripened, leaving the task to improving landlords insured that high tenancy rates would result as certainly as expansion of the area under cultivation.[18]

It is hardly surprising that the landlords who organized and guided this process did not go to the trouble merely to expand the area for subsistence agriculture. Pingjiang's population doubled as early-ripening rice and multiple cropping techniques were becoming widely known in this part of China, but these new technologies were not employed in Pingjiang *fu* [prefecture]. No ecological conditions barred their use and yet Suzhou peasants continued to specialize in lower yield, but more commercially valuable, strains of rice.[19] This choice clearly reflected the interests of market-oriented landlords, their eyes on the inexhaustible market of *Xingzai*, rather than those of self-sufficient peasants. As the Suzhou poet Fan Chengda (1126–1193) wrote, "Never once in their lives have they [the peasants] tasted/Rice clean and bright as the cloudstone."[20] Water control after all not only raised fields above the waters, the carefully dredged rivers and intricate system of canals provided a superb network for transporting bulky commodities cheaply and efficiently. This elaborate web of streams and channels facilitated export of high-value grains *and* made possible the import of coarse grains for consumption. Without imports, the peasants could not have sacrificed quantity for quality.

Change marked the city as well as its hinterland. Yet a sturdy framework to which all but the most powerful forces would have to adapt was already in place. Suzhou's moat provides the most obvious example: a section of the Grand Canal, which linked Jiangnan with North China's Central Plain, formed part of the river system ringing the city. The area within these waters was crisscrossed by canals and surrounded by a wall. Local legend credited Huang Xie, a Chu official enfeoffed at Suzhou in 263 B.C., for both walls and the grid-like pattern of canals within them. From Tang times on, local tradition held that the Jade Emperor had appointed Huang "god of the walls and moats"—as city gods are styled in Chinese—of his old fief. The choice may have owed as much to his work as canal-builder as to his role as wall-builder. City walls not only protected the inhabitants and their property from hostile forces, they also reorganized space, creating a "pivot of the four quarters," which endowed mundane arrangements with cosmic significance.[21] Yet, at Suzhou, the canal system was equally important: not only had it improved transport and communication within the city but it also protected the area within the walls from flood.[22] Over the centuries, residents and officials had elaborated on

Table 1: Temple Building in the City of Suzhou

Period	Length in years	No. Temples	Rate (per year)
Pre-Tang		12	
Tang (618–906)	289	8	0.028
Five Dynasties	55	2	0.036
N. Song (960–1127)	168	13	0.077
S. Song (1127–1276)	150	39	0.260
Yuan (1176–1368)	93	40	0.430
Ming (1368–1506)	139	4	0.029
Source: *Gu Su zhi* (1506): juan 29.			

Huang Xie's initial design: dozens of bridges were thrown across the canals, and, in 922, the city wall had been rebuilt in brick.[23]

A rough indicator of the rhythms of development within this frame is available: the record of temple building within the city. (Table 1) These figures are obviously incomplete.[24] But, flawed as they are, the general thrust—particularly the dramatic increase in activity during the Southern Song and Yuan—seems too marked and too markedly at odds with the Chinese tendency to prefer early origins to more recent ones, to be attributed to inadequate data. Although the scenic northwestern quarter continued to have the greatest concentration, by the end of the Yuan, Buddhist temples and Daoist monasteries could be found in every quarter of the city.

Even more dramatic changes can be traced in the commercial sphere. Although a few specialized markets had already been established in other parts of the city, as late as 1008–1016, the principal business district was still the east and west markets at either side of the Yue Bridge. These central markets were a continuation of the Tang system of organizing urban space by wards rather than streets, a system which facilitated careful control and official regulation of the market.[25] By the end of the Song, the commercial district had expanded in every direction, usurping broad stretches of the urban landscape (see map 1). In the same period, secondary market districts had developed; the most notable were north of the Changzhou county yamen and beside the Xihe.[26]

With trade came industry: in addition to textiles, Suzhou was a center for agricultural processing of rice and vegetable oils, the production of wine and vinegar, the manufacture of articles for daily use (ropes, bottles, stoves, shoes), boat building, rush-sail making, and the armaments industry. It was also a center for building trades, for copper work, and for financial transactions. Much of this activity was carried on within the boundaries of the (much expanded) market. Yet, by the end of Song, such limits had become too constricting. The area within the northeastern gates was given over to stables and pasture for travelers' mounts; boat-building yards had taken over the area north of the Wu county yamen as well as several neighborhoods in the southern half of the city; the southeast corner had become a center for grain processing; and textiles were being produced north of the Changzhou county yamen as well as in the area south of the prefect's offices.[27]

There are clear signs of guild organization, at least in some trades: as early as the Northern Song, there was a Jisheng *miao* (temple to the Loom Spirit) northeast of Yue Bridge. Although this structure had disappeared by Yuan times, a *Wujun jiye gongsuo* (Guild of the Wu Commandary Loom Industry) was then headquartered in the Yuanmiao Daoist Temple, itself northeast of Yue Bridge.[28] As the location of these organizations suggests, the link between temple building and economic activity was intimate and complex: not only did economic growth generate funds which might be put to pious use but also temples, once built, might be used to organize economic activity.[29]

Even if we no longer think of the imperial Chinese city as "the yamen writ large,"[30] the state remained a prominent feature of the cityscape. Suzhou, a prefectural capital and the seat of two counties, was no exception. Indeed, the prefect's compound, situated in the eastern half of the city, was literally a city within the city. Its walled *Zicheng* occupied almost 5 percent of Suzhou's total area. Separate compounds housed the local county magistrate of Wu (governing the western half of the city and the areas south and west of the wall) and of Changzhou (in charge of the eastern half, plus the hinterland north and east). In addition, schools, examination halls, tax offices, granaries, arsenals, and temples of the state cult were scattered throughout the city. There were even twenty-eight separate barracks in which units of the military were housed. Little wonder that the official complex remained one of the most striking features of the *Pingjiang tu* of 1229.[31] (See Fig. 2.)

The state's impact on the organization of urban space was even greater than this catalog suggests for, in addition to preempting broad portions of the landscape, the state's activities also shaped the uses made by others of what remained. Most obviously perhaps, so large an official establishment required an even larger complement of sub-officials, of clerks and runners, were it to rule as well as reign. A sub-

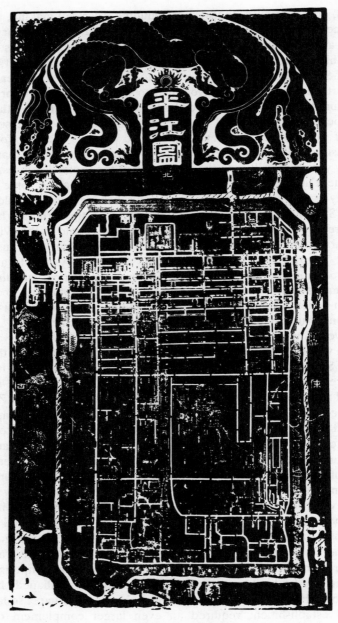

Fig. 2 Engraved Song Map of "Pingjiang" dated 1229
Source: Suzhou Bowuguan

stantial portion of the urban population must have been employed, directly or indirectly, by the public sector. More subtle were the ways in which official power shaped the residential patterns of the local elite. In Song times, Wu was far and away the most successful of Suzhou's counties in achieving membership in the scholar-official elite. Yet these successful families elected to establish urban residence in the *eastern* (Changzhou) side of the city—farther from home perhaps—but closer to the prefectural yamen.[32]

Clearly Southern Song Suzhou was impressive; few thirteenth-century cities anywhere in the world could compare in size, in beauty or in wealth. Yet as long as Hangzhou remained the capital, Suzhou would remain a prosperous satellite in a Hangzhou-centered universe.

YUAN AND EARLY MING SUZHOU: "A LARGE AND MAGNIFICENT CITY"

Mongol conquest reduced Hangzhou from a blazing sun to the status of another planet. It still exerted a considerable gravitational pull in its own neighborhood, but it was no longer the body around which all others revolved.

In 1234, the Song conspired with the Mongols, an Inner Asian group which had recently emerged from the steppe, to destroy the Jurchen Jin dynasty in North China. This military triumph led not to Song recovery of the north, but to the substitution of a new and far more formidable barbarian menace for the old. Effective defense required mobilization of all the Southern Song's resources. Yet attempts to do this, ranging from Jia Sidao's public field laws to requisitioning of merchant vessels, undercut elite support for the dynasty.[33] The Mongols routinely asked those under attack to surrender voluntarily; if they refused and were defeated, the Mongols would show the vanquished no mercy. Chinese officials at Changzhou, the prefecture north of Suzhou, had chosen resistance; defeat and massacre had followed. The benefits of Song rule clearly were outweighed by the risks of defeat and the costs (expropriation, higher taxes) of loyalty. In early 1276, Pingjiang surrendered to the Mongols without a fight.[34]

Under the Mongols the center of political power (and with it, the chief beneficiaries of tax revenue) returned to the Central Plain. As a result, the Hangzhou region stagnated.[35] Pingjiang *lu* (as Suzhou was officially designated from 1277 to 1356 and from 1357 to 1368) on the other hand, experienced dramatic growth; in the fifteen year period from 1275 to 1290 the prefecture's registered population rose from 329,603 households to 466,158.[36] The government's decision to send southern grain north by sea was a primary cause of this expansion.

Taicang, in the northeast corner of Pingjiang *lu*, became a key center of this grain traffic. By one estimate, its port city, Liujiagang, had a population of half a million people in the early fourteenth century.[37] Suzhou, the prefectural capital, prospered as well: if we are to judge by the rate of temple building, growth rates in the Yuan surpassed those of the Southern Song. Officially sponsored factories were established east of the prefect's yamen; the area outside the southeast gate specialized in the building and repair of ocean-going ships; the northwest (Chang) gate had become a major commercial center complete with shops, warehouses, and a grain processing industry.[38] Indeed, so many merchants collected in the northwest suburbs that, when the city wall was rebuilt in late Yuan, a moon wall was added to protect them. This moon wall gave Suzhou its distinctive bulge.[39]

Suzhou's prosperity did not necessarily imply stagnation elsewhere. Did other centers within Jiangnan thrive in equal or greater measure? In particular, was this the case at Nanjing which, from 1356, had been the capital of Zhu Yuanzhang, the rebel who would succeed in founding the Ming dynasty? An extremely influential sketch of Jiangnan's urban history posits a Nanjing cycle between the Hangzhou cycle of Song times and the Suzhou cycle of late Ming and high Qing.[40] If this sketch is accurate, Suzhou's development in Southern Song and Yuan times must be regarded as a mammoth false start, checked if not reversed by the triumph of political forces hostile to it. Did the pathological hostility of the victor bring social and economic developments to a grinding halt, as the received version of events would suggest? Or was Nanjing's ascent simply more rapid than Suzhou's?

Let us first review the received version. Shortly after rebellion broke out in 1351, it was clear that the Mongols would not regain power. Although by convention the Mongol period extends to 1368, the 1350s and 1360s were in fact a period in which rival warlords fought among themselves for the succession. From 1356, Suzhou was the capital of one Zhang Shicheng, erstwhile salt-smuggler and self-styled King of Wu. Down to 1367, he was Zhu Yuanzhang's main rival for the imperial post. Only after a ten-month siege, involving some of the most bitter fighting of a bitter civil war, did Zhu's armies prevail.[41]

According to Zhu Yunming (1461–1527)—a Suzhou native famous as a calligrapher and writer—the victor, proclaimed first emperor of the Ming the following year, was:

> . . . exasperated with the city [of Suzhou]. For a long time
> it did not submit. He hated the people's adherence to the ban-

dit [Zhang Shicheng]; moreover, he suffered difficulties from the mansions of the wealthy [for] they were defended to the end. For these reasons, he ordered his men to seize all the rent registers of the powerful families and to calculate what was handed over to them [in rents]. The civil officials obeyed, making the fixed tax equal to this amount. Taxes were therefore plentiful and the levy especially heavy in order to punish the evil practices of one time.[42]

The prefecture's tax quota was tripled. The land of absentee owners and of prominent supporters of the Zhang Shicheng regime became "official land." Tens of thousands of families, especially families of the wealthy and skilled, were forced to move to distant parts of the empire. Many were executed for crimes real or imagined. The exceptionally heavy tax quotas persisted down to the late nineteenth century.[43]

Thanks in no small measure to the wealth, culture, and examination success of Suzhou men in the Ming and Qing, this series of measures is one of the most famous examples of imperial autocracy in all Chinese history. The individual elements are well-documented. And at least some shreds of the evidence we have already examined—the dramatic decline in temple founding during the early Ming shown in table 1—suggest that these blows were real and that their impact was lasting. Yet scrutiny of the evidence for the rise of Nanjing and analysis of the real impact of Zhu Yuanzhang's punitive measures leads us to a different conclusion.

Since Nanjing started from a more modest base, it would have to have prospered even more dramatically in the thirteenth and fourteenth centuries to have overtaken, then surpassed, Suzhou. It is a proposition worth testing—and testable. Under premodern conditions, population is a reasonable proxy for the size of an economy. Thus, we can use the figures for 1290 and 1393 in the three regions—centered on Hangzhou, Suzhou, and Nanjing—which made up the Lower Yangzi macroregion to compare developments during the fourteenth century. (See Graph, Fig. 3.) The Nanjing region, smallest of the three in 1290, was still the smallest in 1393.[44] Although all three regions lost population, the Nanjing region lost it at twice the rate of the other two. Suzhou was the only core prefecture which maintained or increased its size.

Thus, *even after* a generation of forced deportations from Suzhou and a generation of concerted efforts to make Nanjing a city worthy of

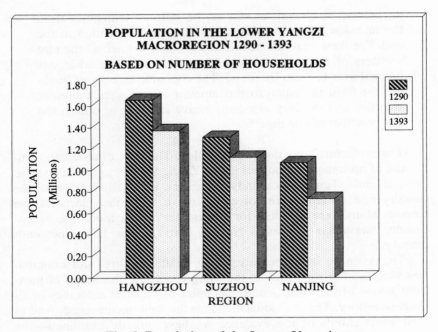

Fig. 3 Population of the Lower Yangzi
Macroregion 1290–1393[45]

a Son of Heaven, the Nanjing region had fallen farther behind the rest of Jiangnan than it had been in late Song and early Yuan. After twenty-five years of effort (1368–1393), the Nanjing cycle remained a gleam in the first emperor's eye. He had failed to re-channel developments which, since the thirteenth century, had contributed to the rise of Suzhou.

What then of the infamous land tax? Ming Hongwu (reign 1368–1398) had tripled Suzhou's tax quota, extracting more grain from this single prefecture than from whole provinces, producing a tax rate that averaged ten times that elsewhere in the empire. Although real, this allocation of the tax burden was much less capricious than the sources imply.[46] The highest taxes were rent on "official fields" (*guantian*) some of the most valuable arable in the empire. "People's fields" (*mintian*) were taxed at rates similar to those imposed in other parts of the realm. All governments need money; those attempting to establish military control over a subcontinent arguably need it more than most. And as the Ministry of Revenue reported to the throne in 1370:

Taking the land tax and comparing it, only in Zhexi are there many wealthy households. In the single prefecture of Suzhou, commoners annually submit grain. Four hundred ninety households submit one hundred to four hundred *shi*; fifty-six households submit five hundred to one thousand *shi*; six households, one thousand *shi* each; and two households submit an amount between two thousand and three thousand eight hundred *shi*. In all these five hundred fifty-four households annually submit more than one hundred fifty thousand *shi*.[47]

Analyzing the figures presented by the Ministry of Revenue, and applying the average official rate of 0.54 *shi* per *mu*, these households controlled an average of 500 *mu*.[48] Even assuming that the wealthiest households paid at the highest rate on the official land, those two households controlled ten times that much. It is not necessarily unfair or unreasonable to make the wealthiest 0.1 percent of households, households possessing 3.5 percent of the registered land, bear 7 percent of the tax burden. When we turn to the way this system was actually administered, it is even more difficult to regard this system as the spiteful act of an arbitrary despot. Taxes were routinely remitted, in whole or in part, in time of natural disaster and, once military control was essentially complete, the dynasty modestly reduced the quota demanded.[49] As long as the complex of land taxes and labor services was administered as originally intended, the strain on local resources would seem to have been sustainable.

If we examine the relationship of tax quota, agricultural production and population district by district, however, this argument demands qualification. Consider Wu and Changzhou, the counties whose capitals were located within the walls of Suzhou city. [See Appendix Two, Table 1.] Changzhou retained a minimum 20.47 *shi* of husked rice per household in the late fourteenth century. (If we assume that all the arable land Qing officials could locate three hundred fifty years later was already under cultivation, this figure rises to 27.46 *shi* per household.) Yet Wu was left with a mere 11.77 *shi* per household (14.98 *shi* if 1725 acreage figures are used). This was far less than the 20 *shi* per annum conventionally regarded as necessary to support a family. Such tax rates would certainly seem to justify contemporary complaints. Indeed, if Suzhou were merely "the land of rice and fish," depopulation would have been the inevitable result. The figures for early Ming trade imply that commerce in nonagricultural commodities

was equal to 30.78 percent of the maximum agricultural production for
Wu and Changzhou, however.[50] Foodstuffs were tax exempt but, in
light of Suzhou's leading position in the wholesale grain trade from the
Southern Song to High Qing,[51] commerce in agricultural commodities
must have accounted for at least as much activity. Suzhou's ability to
prosper while paying these taxes depended from the outset on the
thoroughly commercialized character of the local economy. The prefecture was as much the victim of its economic maturity as of its political indiscretions.

Late fourteenth-century Suzhou was no longer the half-submerged,
underpopulated and semi-developed area that it had been at the beginning of the Southern Song period in the early twelfth century. Yet, had
his successors continued the Hongwu emperor's policies, building up
Nanjing at the expense of Suzhou, Suzhou would have been no more
able in the Ming than it had been in the Song to avoid subordination to
the capital. Political changes delegitimated and destabilized this design
before the Ming founder's plans could reach fruition.

MID-MING SUZHOU: "DAZZLED BY ITS BRILLIANCE"

In 1399 the Jianwen emperor (1399–1403), grandson and successor of
the Ming founder, announced that differential tax rates were inherently
unfair and ought to be abolished.[52] This policy did not survive its imperial sponsor. It may well never have been implemented, for the emperor was preoccupied throughout his brief reign with the problem of
bringing his uncles (Zhu Yuanzhang's sons) under control. The most
able of these drove his nephew from the Dragon Throne in 1403. This
usurper, who reigned as the Yongle emperor (1403–1424), could ill-
afford a tax reduction. He was determined to move the capital from
Nanjing to his base in the north, a decision which required both the
costly and extensive rebuilding of Beijing and the restoration of the
Grand Canal. The canal was to funnel tax grain north to supply the
bureaucracy and Ming armies which defended the Middle Kingdom
against a Mongol resurgence. The emperor repeatedly launched major
military operations in Inner Asia in hope of keeping the Mongols
at bay. Simultaneously, Ming forces sought to quell resistance to
the annexation of northern Vietnam. And, he dispatched his eunuch
Zheng He on a series of voyages to the South Seas. Such activism required additional surcharges on the land tax and dramatic increases in
the labor service burden.

The period was one of increasing activism at the local level as well:
in Suzhou the Yongle reign saw the second most intensive concentra-

tion of activity with respect to water control in the entire Ming period. Although maintenance of purely local irrigation systems was left to private initiative,[53] an area as low-lying and as dependent on trade as Suzhou relied on official coordination of regional efforts physically and economically. Much of the work had to be done far from the places most immediately threatened by failure to keep channels open; the peasants' desire for more land clashed with the system's need for clear channels and ample reservoirs.[54] Problems were acute enough by 1399 to trigger official concern, but continued flooding made clear the ineffectiveness of measures adopted in response. In 1403, the emperor ordered the Minister of Revenue, Xia Yuanji, to take charge of the water control efforts in the Suzhou area personally. Using *corvée* labor, he opened the Wu Song River and its attached streams and ponds; the effort extended over Kunshan, Jiading, Changshu, and Shanghai counties. In 1407, the dikes and banks of the Lou River were repaired; the work was done in Wujiang, Changzhou, and Kunshan counties. In 1411, more than seventy *li* of stone and earth ponds, bridges, and roads between Suzhou city and Jiaxing were repaired, affecting one hundred and thirty-one places. And, in 1415, on the initiative of the vice magistrate of Wujiang, the areas around Lake Tai were dredged. This time portions of Changshu, Kunshan, Changzhou, Wu, and Wuxi counties were involved.[55] As necessary as such efforts were for the viability of Suzhou's urban and rural economy, they placed additional strains on a population already heavily burdened by state demands.

If more were being demanded, less care was taken to allocate burdens equitably. As surcharges increased, the wealthy refused to pay them. The additional burdens thus fell on their less fortunate and well-connected neighbors. Eventually many small-holders were forced to choose between taking flight and commending themselves to the protection of those better connected.[56] Either strategy decreased the number of taxpayers, thus augmenting the burden for those who remained. Massive tax remissions may well have benefited those whose wealth and connections made it easy to evade payment rather than the general run of taxpayers.[57] Natives of Wu and Changzhou passed the provincial examinations in record numbers during the Yongle period.[58] Although in theory a career open to talent, success in the examinations required years of strenuous preparation—one had first to memorize the classics, then to master the commentaries as well as the specialized forms of essay writing. It was a game at which only the wealthy and well-born could usually compete—as accounts of the rare exceptions

prove. Thus, Chen Yuanmo, journeying every third year to the capital
in tattered clothes and ruined shoes to try (always without success) to
pass the metropolitan examination, stood out.[59] The Yongle emperor's
anxiety to co-opt elites here seems to have combined with the auto-
crat's indifference to mundane details of local administration. If one
were well placed and unscrupulous, this combination of apathy and
appeasement provided numerous, readily exploited opportunities to
advance personal and family interests. If the number of years that
"illustrious officials" occupied key local posts is any guide, Suzhou was
worse governed during the Yongle era than at any other time in the
history of the Ming.[60]

The results of early Ming policies were not necessarily detrimental
to the interests of Suzhou as a collectivity. However unwelcome to the
individuals involved, the exile of elite and artisan families—a practice
which affected natives of Suzhou more often than it had those of most
other places—had the unintended effect of creating an unusually dense
and well-developed network of particularistic contacts in every corner
of the empire. Such networks played a critical role, particularly in
trade, throughout the late imperial period.[61] The decision to shift the
capital from Nanjing to Beijing, although not implemented until 1421,
was made in 1403—just ten years after the census indicating Nanjing's
emergence as a rival for regional primacy was still incomplete. Reconstruction of the Grand Canal insured that Suzhou would play a key
role in the integration of the Middle Kingdom's now separate economic and political centers. Even the need to ship grain to the new
capital had its advantages: each year the armada of grain barges
carried some ten thousand tons (ten million kilograms) in authorized
private cargo. It was an open secret that these quantities were regularly exceeded and the prohibition on using the empty barges to ship
northern goods south ignored.[62]

If Suzhou and its elites could tolerate the emerging reality, neither
the imperial treasury (faced with a rise in the number of tax evaders
and an increase in uncollected taxes) nor the area's poor (increasingly
forced to shoulder alone a tax burden assessed with less and less attention to ability to pay) were able to do so. In the 1430s and 1440s a
complex series of reforms that were designed to reduce both the
sphere for evasion and the costs of compliance were introduced. The
prefecture's tax quotas were slashed by seven hundred and twenty
thousand *shi* per year; approximately a third of the burden was then
converted from grain to silver at half the current market rate.[63] Responsibility for administration was shifted from local notables, the "tax

captains," to the county yamen. Since the most heavily burdened tax-payers were permitted to use the most favorable method to settle their accounts, the erosion of the local elite's role in tax collection merely reinforced a growing distaste for service in the sub-bureaucracy. Conversion of so substantial a portion of the land tax to specie presupposed an economy which was already highly monetized. Insofar as tax assessments in the 1440s still reflected ability to pay, the introduction of Gold Floral Silver should have (1) encouraged the wealthy to orient themselves even more intensively toward production for the market. If the wealthy had long since concluded that land on the tax rolls was an investment for fools, this stimulus would have (2) been felt by the peasantry. In either case, a growing proportion of the population became involved in commercial transactions a growing percentage of the time. The velocity of circulation, hence the level of economic activity, should have increased as a result—even if the population and silver supply remained constant.[64]

Thus, in and of themselves, the measures introduced in the early fifteenth century should have been a catalyst of further commercialization. Suzhou was, and remained, a major center of the wholesale grain trade. But growing commercialization and monetization were made possible, and in turn encouraged, by the spread of textile production. The prefecture had produced linens, ramie, hemp cloth, and silk for centuries. Nonetheless down to the twelfth century, its products were deemed inferior to those of North China.[65]

However, from the Southern Song on, Suzhou was famous for its silk. The warmth and humidity of its mild climate and watery ecology proved an ideal environment for transforming tiny silkworm eggs into fabric. The population explosion of the twelfth and thirteenth centuries provided the huge labor force needed to take advantage of this potential economic opportunity. Not only did raising worms require 'round-the-clock attention, but obtaining the maximum quantity of the highest quality silk also demanded a delicate touch and exquisite judgment. The rituals of sericulture—cultivating mulberry, raising silkworms, feeding them on mulberry leaves, tending the cocoons, reeling the raw silk, winding it, warping it, sizing it, weaving it—were henceforth part of the annual local routine. "The third and fourth months of the lunar calendar were called "silkworm months"; every family shut its doors and stayed at home."[66]

Cotton had only come to be widely cultivated in Jiangnan during the Yuan. Yet it was the production of cotton which expanded most quickly in Ming times. By the beginning of the sixteenth century, every

county in Suzhou prefecture was producing cotton cloth.[67] Even earlier, in 1466, cotton cloth merchants from Jiading, Kunshan, and
Suzhou (i.e. Wu and Changzhou) jointly established a guild at Linqing, a key trading center in Shandong.[68] Since cotton was not grown
in the water-saturated soils of Wu and Changzhou, commercially significant production from these counties implied organized importation
of the raw fiber from areas bordering the Yangzi, where sandy soils
were favorable to cotton.

Given the ready availability of raw silk, the reputation that Suzhou
silk enjoyed and the higher prices silk commanded in the market, commercial production of cotton cloth in the areas bordering Lake Tai may
seem puzzling. Yet, in the early Ming, silk weaving remained a highly
specialized skill, the monopoly of male artisans in the prefectural capital. The expense of the looms and the need for specialized training
restricted entry into silk cloth production. Only in the Xuande reign
period (1425–1436) did silk production spread to the capitals of Suzhou's subordinate counties, a process which demanded importation
of skilled labor from the prefectural seat. The looms needed to weave
cotton cloth were cheap, the skills peasants honed in centuries of producing linen and hemp cloth readily transferable.[69] Not until demand
for silk "sky-rocketed" in the 1470s and 1480s did silk weaving finally
cease to be an urban monopoly, tapping the labor power available in
the countryside.[70]

The expanded production of silk cloth in the countryside may well
originally have been sponsored, and controlled, by members of the
local elite anxious to seize new economic opportunities.[71] Suzhou's
hinterland was, however, densely populated, and its canals provided
such excellent transport and communications that peasant households
were tied directly to higher level markets. A twentieth-century survey
measured 27.8 miles of navigable canals and rivers in one square mile
of Suzhou's immediate hinterland.[72] Boat ownership seems to have
been widespread, and an agency system may already have been in
place in the fifteenth century. In the early twentieth century, agents
made their money marketing peasant output for fixed commissions.
They provided free transportation to and from town, even making
purchases for their clients, purchases they delivered free of charge.[73]
As a result, standard markets—periodic markets dealing in a limited
range of daily necessities, which organized village economic and social
life in most of rural China—did not exist here.[74]

Shi and *zhen* near the prefectural capital were open daily; even
the smallest market towns seem to have housed several hundred

families.[75] Many of these central places had recognized specialities: vegetable oils were produced at Hengtang and Xinguo, rice wine (and butchered pigs) were specialities of Hengtang, Xinguo, and Hengjin. Mudu was famed for metal work, Lumu *zhen* for pottery and fan "bones."[76] As descriptions of the Hushu/Yuecheng complex make clear (see below), some of these market towns were so thoroughly integrated with Suzhou city that attempts to classify them as separate economic entities would be pointless and artificial. Given their operation all day every day, the number of resident households, the population of their catchment areas, and the range of goods and services they offered, most of the other towns rank as central markets.[77] Through them, merchants like Qin Yunyan (1467–1506), a fifth generation descendant of a holder of the highest degree, "superintended the capital of resident and traveling merchants, dispersing it to "shuttle and loom" households and gathering the [finished] bolts of cloth in order to return them to the merchants."[78] Local merchants were essential for the smooth operation of the putting-out system, for only those who had well-developed networks of particularistic ties possessed the detailed knowledge of skill and trustworthiness it required. As prosperity and a taste for ostentation spread from the court to the elite in the late fifteenth century, demand for Suzhou's premium products expanded. The stimulus was rapidly felt throughout the system, creating a boom economy which awed visitors and was recognized even by natives as unprecedented.[79]

Nonetheless, as a now-standard pairing of the Pingjiang *tu* of 1229 [See Fig. 2, p. 24] and a U.S. Air Force reconnaissance photo of 1945 suggests,[80] the effect on the cityscape was less dramatic than one might expect. Indeed, in the course of seven centuries, almost nothing seems to have changed. The most obvious innovation within the walls was officially inspired. Since Zhang Shicheng used the Zicheng as his palace, Ming Hongwu regarded attempts to refurbish it as evidence of subversive intent.[81] The area was abandoned in favor of a new, more modest prefectural compound on the west side of the city. This change had its impact on the residence patterns of others: clerks and runners congregated in the southwest corner of the city, while members of the local elite—in Ming times drawn almost equally from Wu and Changzhou—concentrated inside the Chang Gate, in the northwest quadrant of the city.[82] The last remnants of the official market system disappeared. By the middle of the sixteenth century, commerce had been diffused throughout the city, shops lining every street.[83]

Within individual trades, institutional as well as physical constraints appear to have fallen away. The guild system, which had persisted from early Song to Yuan times in the textile industry, seems to have disappeared. As the 1466 founding at Linqing suggests, the guild concept had not been forgotten by Suzhou natives. In Song and Yuan, guild organizations were often located in temples dedicated to the god of the trade (as was the Jisheng *miao*) or attached themselves to preexisting temples (as the Guild of the Wu Commandery Loom Industry, headquartered in the Yuanmiao Daoist Temple, did). Yet examination of the sources on temples and monasteries in the *Gu Su zhi* (1506) failed to provide evidence of guilds with headquarters in religious institutions. The earliest records of independent guilds date to the Wanli era (1572–1620).[84] Specialized markets for those with particular skills continued to exist: satin workers at Flower Bridge, those who specialized in thin silks at the Guanghua Monastery Bridge, spinners of silk at Lianxi *fang*. At each, professional intermediaries (*hangtou*) matched prospective employer and employee.[85] Careful mapping has shown that these were precisely the areas in which guilds devoted to these specialities were subsequently established.[86] Some sort of organization clearly persisted, but lack of physical headquarters suggests that such organization was weaker and less formal than it had been in Song and Yuan or would be in late Ming and Qing.

If the city's activities had outgrown inherited institutional forms, they had also outgrown the physical constraints imposed by encircling walls. The most striking embodiment of early Ming prosperity was found outside the city gates—particularly the northwestern Chang Gate. The 1379 edition of the prefectural gazetteer listed no lanes (*xiang*) outside the ramparts, a result of the incorporation of pre-Ming suburbs in the city proper when the wall was rebuilt in late Yuan.[87] By 1506, there were ten new lanes outside the Chang Gate; one of these, the Yizhe Lane, "although narrow, was nonetheless the spot at which merchants collect."[88] Yuecheng was "the place where merchants from the two capitals and various provinces assemble. Nan and Bei *hao* as well as Shang and Xia *tang* [nearby] had also become markets. [The area] was especially prosperous."[89] By the middle of the sixteenth century, in the area between Chang and Xu Gates and "extending to the west, cottages sit close together like teeth of a comb. It is almost the same as the area within the city wall. Sojourners dwell here in large numbers."[90] Zheng Ruoceng, (fl. 1505–1580), a Kunshan native, who compiled an atlas to aid in the defense of China's coastal areas, noted that nine-tenths of the pirates' interest in Suzhou during the mid-sixteenth century *wokou* crisis had centered on the area outside the wall. He wrote that:

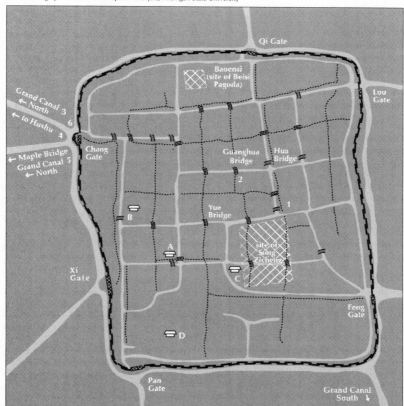

based on maps from Ming and early Qing gazetteers of Suzhou prefecture.

A Suzhou Prefectural yamen	1 Lianxi fang
B Wu County yamen	2 Yuanmiao (Daoist) Temple
C Changzhou County yamen	3 Bei hao
D Prefectural School	4 Shang tang
	5 Nan hao
	6 Xia tang

Fig. 4 Ming dynasty Suzhou

. . . from the Chang Gate to Maple Bridge is a distance of ten *li*. On both the north and south shore [of the Grand Canal] the residents are as close together as the teeth of a comb, especially on the south shore. In general, as for goods which are difficult to obtain in the four quarters [of the world], there are none which are not found here. Those who pass through are dazzled by its brilliance. Maple Bridge in particular is the spot where the seaworthy vessels of the merchants converge to go up river. North of the river is the center of a great trade in beans and grain and in cotton. Guest [merchants] from north and south come and go, holding the oar and weighing the anchor. All are here.[91]

The key point outside Chang Gate was, however, Hushu, a market town twenty-five *li* (eight miles) northwest on the Grand Canal. A police station and a relay post from the beginning of the Ming, it was designated one of the seven Inland Customs stations created in the mid-fifteenth century. The choice no doubt reflected the fact that it was already "the place where the goods of the fourteen provinces converge, and that merchant boats come and go, each day in their thousands."[92] Here, around 1506, "the common people dwell by the side of the water, peasants and traders living side by side. It is a great market."[93] By the end of the Ming, it had become the empire's major wholesale grain market, commodities trading overshadowing its traditional role as a center of handicraft production.[94]

The city's other suburbs developed more slowly and on a less imposing scale. By 1506, the Feng Gate was the only other area in which settlements outside the city walls had been formally organized into lanes.[95] A century later all save the southern gate had officially designated lanes, yet their combined number was less than that of the lanes outside the "Golden" Chang Gate.[96] The Xu Gate, south of the Chang Gate in the west wall and linked most directly to Lake Tai, was usually referred to as an extension of the complex to its north. Thus, its three lanes can be viewed as a southern continuation of the Chang Gate's twenty-two. In spite of its recognized specialty (frames for raising silkworms),[97] the environs of Pan Gate, located in the southwest corner of the wall, seem to have been relatively deserted.[98] The Qi Gate, in the northern wall, was known as a center for kiln workers and makers of rattan pillows by the early sixteenth century.[99] A hundred years later, "brokers" or middlemen (*yakuai*) were said to converge "like spokes at the hub of a wheel" in these "humbler suburbs."[100]

Significant in themselves, the rise of these suburbs tied the villages more closely to the city, a development reflected by the growing concentration of village population in the urban penumbra.[101] As Table 2 in Appendix Two demonstrates,[102] such integration was vital if Suzhou's population were to support itself. Commerce and manufacture permitted this area to evade Malthusian constraints, which would otherwise have forced residents to choose between migration and starvation. *All* the post-1368 increase in the population of Wu—in city, suburb *or* village—and virtually all the more modest increase in Changzhou is attributable to the expansion of trade and handicrafts, not to agriculture.

By the beginning of the sixteenth century, Suzhou's economic primacy was recognized by all; the important Fujian port of Zhangzhou boasted that it was a "little Su Hang."[103] As was true of political hegemons in antiquity East and West, as long as the constellation of forces, which brought it into being persisted, such universally recognized dominance was no less effective for the lack of institutional form. Such economic hegemony brought cultural hegemony in its train. Ming policies had pushed the trends which made this hegemony possible further and faster than would otherwise have been the case. Yet, we should not replace the time-honored image of a dynasty bent on impoverishing the base of its defeated rival, Zhang Shicheng, with an image of Ming policies as an elaborately disguised effort to promote the development of Suzhou. The Ming imposed taxes, moved the capital, refurbished the Grand Canal, and modified administrative structures for its own reasons. In doing so, the dynasty was making the most of existing possibilities. If Suzhou had not been as highly commercialized, as admirably equipped with cheap and efficient water transport, as open to new commercial and handicraft possibilities as it was, Ming policies would have proved unworkable as well as arbitrary.

Once in place, the brittleness of the Ming fiscal system made the dynasty hostage to the continued well being of so important a source of its revenues. Not only did Suzhou provide a tenth of the state's total annual revenue, but the Ming system of allocating particular taxes from particular areas to particular ends severely limited the government's ability to cope with fluctuations. Far better to intervene in time of need to support a Suzhou than to rejigger the entire fiscal system.[104] Tax remissions, water control, and the quality of local administrators all reflect this interest.[105] Yet, insofar as Suzhou's rise from prominence to eminence was the work of the state, it was the produce of ad hoc decisions taken to exploit existing opportunities for imperial advantage.

"A REPUTATION FOR RICHES AND ABUNDANCE," YET "ACTUALLY FULL OF WANT AND DISTRESS"?

Suzhou's development was no more the result of the machinations of canny local elites than it was of the polity. The material and human

surpluses Suzhou's success generated were substantial. Yet, during
Suzhou's rise there was neither evident need to advance a political and
economic program nor the social space to articulate one.

China's population in the early Ming was sixty million, approximately that of periods like the mid-Tang in which the state had successfully regimented society.[106] Ming Hongwu was determined, particularly in areas he deemed crucial, to organize the whole population
along lines imposed by the government.[107] Individual patrilines sought
to take advantage of the opportunities that the area's rise afforded. A
few individuals suggested ways in which local administration might be
improved.[108] A concerted attempt to advance the interests of Suzhou or
its elites as a whole was beyond their means, their imaginations, and
their needs. In early Ming, extended kinship organizations were weak,
guilds nonexistent.[109] Both appear in the late sixteenth century,[110]
attempts by those who had succeeded either in the market or the examination hall to consolidate their hold on wealth and status. The environment's overall stability afforded little solace to individual families,
each of which faced an extremely volatile situation. Fortunes might be
lost as well as made in the market and the competition in the examination halls grew more intense as population increased. Given the level
of the land tax and the practice of partible inheritance, land did not
provide a secure base for future generations either. Confronting such
uncertainties, families were understandably less concerned with improving a generally favorable context than in making the most of the possibilities that context afforded.

Consider the case of Tu Yunfeng. The Tu family was not
prosperous—or lucky: the father, a merchant who traveled to Shandong and areas north of the Yangzi, encountered brigands who not
only seized his goods but also beat him within an inch of his life. The
mother, Ms. Chen (1479–1521), was the issue of an uxorilocal marriage. When her husband was robbed and injured, she laid aside her
scarf and began to participate in business, "cutting back on consumption and regulating expenditure. The family daily flourished." When
her husband died, Ms. Chen was already ill. Although she sought to
comfort her orphaned children, her health deteriorated and she died
soon afterward. Her eldest son, then a youth, was already engaged in
trade. On her deathbed his mother,

> . . . weeping silent tears said, "Now you trade for profit in
> order to support your parents. Yet your father is dead and
> now I also am dying. In future, who will there be to support?

Yet, if you become a scholar, my death will not be a death."
[At this, her eldest son,] Yunfeng was moved. He roused himself to study Confucianism. In a short time he filled a vacancy in the prefectural school.[111]

Not until 1555, thirty-four years after his mother's death, did Yunfeng become a Tribute Student.[112] Given the events described in his mother's funerary inscription, he would thus have been about fifty by the time he finally reached this lowest rung of upper degree status. Achievement at so advanced an age could not influence his own marriage prospects or those of his children. No one else bearing the Tu surname from either Wu or Changzhou counties achieved upper-degree status in the two hundred and seventy-seven years of the Ming. Tu's success demonstrates that those who achieved even a modest competence could aspire to elite status. The absence of other men surnamed Tu also suggests that however dogged their pursuit of that goal, formidable barriers confronted those who hoped to translate individual achievement into family distinction.

Nonetheless, Tu's success placed him in the upper tier of a two-tiered society. For the fortunate few, Suzhou had indeed become "All Under Heaven's Heaven on Earth." Uneasy though they might be regarding their descendants' ability to enjoy the same levels of wealth and status, their lives combined opulence with cultivation. Almost all surviving evidence relates to the apex of local society. We must depend on statistics, stray (and usually very general) comments, and inferences from lists of local products, land-man ratios, and the like to reconstruct the lot of the majority. This evidence suggests that the overwhelming majority of Suzhou's population continued to work hard, to live in squalor and to die young.[113] As the Wu district magistrate from 1559 to 1563, Cao Zishou emphasized, Suzhou's affluent exterior could be deceiving:

Now the people are numerous and yet the sources of profit are few. Presently the common people of Wu do not purchase land; they live by [producing] goods and beckoning merchants. The area around the walled Chang market looks like an embroidered tapestry. [There] luxurious feasts and splendid clothes compete in extravagance. The people in consequence vie for trifling amounts of profit; this does not offset the cost [of such display]. When taxes are levied, all [their wealth] goes out; a single stint of *corvée* duty breaks up families. Those who

discuss the matter say that labor services weary the native people; the profits are the possession of the merchants. Will you
not find it really so? Hence externally Suzhou had a reputation
for riches and abundance, yet within it is actually full of want
and distress.[114]

Cao's description may well betray a physiocratic bias, yet it reson-
ates with demographic realities, as well as with Zhou Chen's paintings
depicting the people of the streets of Suzhou "Beggars and Street
Characters" (1516).[115] Suzhou's impressive population growth between the later fourteenth and the early nineteenth centuries is consistent with a life expectancy at birth of 22.55 years for females and 23.36
for males.[116] As officials emphasized in their accounts of the late Ming
riots, many in the city lived from day to day.[117] Shortly after arriving at
his post, Cao had seen just how desperate the situation could become:

1559 was a year of severe drought, and the harvest was
seriously influenced. In the city young hoodlums boasted of
their skill with their fists and their martial prowess. They
united to form gangs. In sport, they attacked and wounded
men; though they inflicted harm, none dared to protest. Even
though night had not fallen, they plundered and robbed without fear. If those affected offered resistance, the hoodlums
smashed their wares and violated their women. If they came
across a man in the street, they attacked him; seeing him take
to his heels in fear made them laugh. It reached the point that
the marketplaces were deserted, all [respectable people] shut-
ting their doors and going into hiding. Those who came from
afar were compelled to abandon what they had brought [with-
out compensation]; they did not pursue the matter. The leaders all were known by name and native place inside the city
and out. Yamen underlings and the apprentices of butchers
and shopkeepers were in league with them. Even the scions of
good families were involved.[118]

When the authorities rounded up the ringleaders, their followers
set fire to the yamens of Suzhou prefecture and Changzhou county.
The prefect and the newly installed Wu local magistrate, Cao, shut
the city gates and conducted a house-to-house search for the male-
factors. Arrest was followed swiftly by confessions of guilt and summary
execution.

Such incidents have attracted less attention than the clashes of textile workers and eunuch taxgatherers some decades later.[119] But this affair reveals much about the social tinder that underlies them all. Drawing on some of the evidence we have already cited—the fact that some textile workers depended on selling their labor power each day for their livelihood, the existence of specialized labor markets for craftsmen with particular skills—P.R.C. historians have sought to establish the existence of proletarians in late Ming Suzhou. There were of course both rich and poor in Ming Suzhou. Yet, if those who lacked the means of production and hence had to sell their labor to others in order to live existed,[120] a separate class, which monopolized control of the means of production, using that monopoly with an eye to exacting the maximum surplus value, did not. "[C]lass happens when some men, as a result of common experiences (inherited or shared), feel and articulate the identity of their interests as between themselves, and as against other men whose interests are different from (and usually opposed to) theirs."[121] To speak of a proletariat, one must have a bourgeoisie; the two are inseparable. Ming Suzhou, for all its cultivated gentlemen and wealthy merchants, learned scholars and prosperous shopkeepers, did not have a bourgeoisie.[122]

Proto-proletarians were an atypical minority, outnumbered by apprentices and yamen underlings, hooligans and beggars, boatmen and stevedores, shopkeepers and merchants. Not surprisingly, study of late Ming urban riots provides scant evidence of an emerging working-class consciousness or working-class solidarity. We can document popular participation in food riots, tax riots, and criminality—just as we can in urban centers throughout the preindustrial world. It is now clear that these are not, in and of themselves, symptoms of a new world aborning in the womb of the old. Given the small size of most establishments at Suzhou, the sophistication of the labor market, and the absence of a guild framework,[123] silence regarding struggles between masters and craftsmen is apt to reflect Ming realities as well as the ravages time may have exacted on our sources. Tensions between masters and men no doubt existed, but tension on so atomized a scale as to escape the notice of contemporaries and the efforts of the historian.

Life at the urbanized core was a bit easier than life on the periphery, and mid-Ming Suzhou was the core of the core of the empire's wealthiest region. By 1559, Suzhou had been systematically drawing food and raw material from other parts of the Lower Yangzi macroregion, from Jiangxi and from Huguang for centuries. Location, infrastructure and the skills and industry of its people gave the area real advantages. Once the imperial fisc saw, and exploited, those advantages, the polity had a vested interest in doing what it could to maintain the area's prosperity. There were, however, alternative centers, centers which combined similar advantages with lower tax rates: not only Hangzhou and Nanjing but also Changzhou and Jiaxing, the prefectures immediately north and south of Suzhou, come to mind. The Ming-Qing Empire was, after all, an extraordinarily open system; people moved from province to province. The best technology spread from more to less advanced areas, and investors—many of whom were outlanders sojourning at Suzhou[124]—were quite capable of shifting their resources if better returns were available elsewhere. Had living standards (labor costs) been substantially higher for the general populace here than elsewhere, resources would have shifted away from Suzhou. The affluence of the few should not lead us to exaggerate the modest (and hard-won) competence of most, or to forget the wretchedness of many. The system centered on Suzhou probably did provide better conditions for more people than any previous system in world history;[125] access to imported grain in time of crop failure and the availability of multiple ways of earning a living provided its residents cushions less fortunately situated areas lacked. Under premodern conditions, any substantial population reasonably confident of earning its bread (or rice) by the sweat of its brow was a fortunate one. In these more modest terms, Suzhou's reputation may have been justified for the many as well as for the few.

Intimately tied to the existing order and providing so well for its population in the terms recognized by that society, Suzhou's rise was a remarkable achievement. It was the result of individual actors making the most of the opportunities available to them at each stage. However distinctive the outcome, whatever its tensions with the imperial agrarian order in which it was embedded, Suzhou and the empire were products of a common history.

To be sure, Suzhou is virtually the only large premodern city which subsidized the state rather than being heavily subsidized by it.[126] Although its sons enjoyed great success in the examination halls, there is ample evidence that the relationship between Suzhou men and the state, which sponsored those examinations, was a strained one. Most of those who passed held low-rank office for short periods and close to home. Some of Suzhou's most famous figures evaded government service altogether, preferring self-cultivation and pursuit of an amateur ideal to official rank. Others led the opposition to imperial autocracy.

Yet the city—urban, commercialized, alienated from and critical of the polity though it was—could thrive only because a symbiotic relationship successfully embedded the urban aberration in a world of landlords and peasants, emperors and bureaucrats. Suzhou continues to be central to our understanding of China's social, economic, and cultural development in the Ming and Qing. Indigenous shoots of an "other China" must be sought in places less central to, and less happily integrated with the late imperial order than Suzhou.

Chapter 2

Late Ming Urban Reform and the Popular Uprising in Hangzhou

Susumu Fuma

Translated by Michael Lewis

Ming village society underwent a major transformation during the Xuande and Zhengtong periods (1426–1449). Excessive taxation and labor service demands, plus unfair distribution of these burdens, shook the *lijia* system of collective responsibility for tax and service obligations. The system by which rural communities were organized had been established by the dynasty's founders. But by late Ming farmers, who earlier had shouldered their tax and labor service responsibilities, began to flee in large numbers from villages. This flow from the countryside further weakened the village *lijia*, worsened the already unbalanced tax burden, and contributed to a widespread sense of injustice. To cope with such changes in rural society, the state enacted reforms including the equal-tax system, the Single Whip tax, and equal-field and equal-labor service systems.

Numerous studies have examined changes in rural society and the reforms in tax and labor duty systems[1]. The transformation of urban society in cities receiving massive numbers of absconding farmers and the reform of various urban systems after the influx are issues that have gone largely unstudied. Even in the investigation into the "sprouts of capitalism," a central theme in the study of Ming history, the concentration has been on the silk, cotton, ceramics, iron, and other handicraft industries. Questions have been limited to what types of "capitalistic" factors appeared within these handicraft industries. As a result, attention has not been directed toward the city itself. The types of problems that arose from the urban transformation and the development of ameliorative reform policies are still largely neglected issues.

The first issue addressed in this essay will concern aspects of urban labor service reform. Urban residents of Ming cities were required to serve as *zongjia* (unit headmen) and as *huofu* (watchmen) in the watch system as part of their labor service obligation. The first task of the *zongjia* was ". . . to prevent altercations. In cases of serious disputes, this officer was to report to officials and, after proper investigation, rely upon officialdom for punitive measures. Should thievery break out, he was obliged to lead people in taking preventive steps."[2] As for the *huofu*, ". . . he was charged with standing night-guard both within and without the city walls. Originally designated as a guard against fire, he also prevented theft and robbery."[3] In fulfilling labor service obligations, the *huofu* led by *zongjia*, patrolled the city and were responsible for preventing the outbreak of fire or theft. In Beijing, the system was organized so that the ranks of *zongjia* and *huofu* were determined by the rank of the individual's household. Upper households were designated *zongjia* (headmen); middle households, *xiaojia* (subordinates); and lower households, *huofu*.[4] Originally, *zongjia* and *huofu* duty had required that urban residents serve in person, but gradually the system was modified so that others could be hired for pay to fulfill these obligations.

This essay first addresses reforms in the *zongjia* and *huofu* systems in Jiangnan regional cities by focusing on urban problems; it will then go on to examine how the changing system of labor services in the city was related to reforms in rural villages. The second issue to be taken up will examine the type of riots that broke out when urban reforms were obstructed. In Hangzhou, as in other Jiangnan cities, urban reforms went forward but they did not always advance smoothly. On the contrary, when reforms were frustrated, massive rioting occurred on a scale that led one shocked contemporary observer of the 1582 uprising to comment: "Rioting of this magnitude in major cities is simply unprecedented."

Research on Ming urban unrest has heretofore concentrated on the series of city riots that broke out from 1599 to 1614.[5] Eunuchs were deeply implicated in all of these uprisings, which were sparked by cruelty and the imposition of taxes that ignored or violated customary practice. The popular uprising at Hangzhou differed in that it broke out in response to the local citizens' apparently well-intentioned and fair-minded attempts at urban reform. On this point, we will see in the

Hangzhou uprising aspects that present an image altogether different from that evident in previous studies of urban rioting. We must first clarify what was problematic in the development of the reforms at Hangzhou and then proceed to look at the concrete circumstances of the riots. In so doing, we can see not only class conflict but also an increasingly organized expression of political consciousness and the aspirations of lower-strata urban residents.

REORGANIZATION OF ZONGJIA AND HUOFU POSTS IN JIANGNAN CITIES

In Jiaxing county in Jiaxing prefecture, Zhejiang, the posts of *zongjia* and *huofu* were transformed into hired or paid positions during the Longqing period (1567–1572). Within the city wards, or *fang*, consisting of one hundred household administrative divisions, sundry labor service posts such as *zongjia* and *huofu* were assessed after the reform according to a formula based on the household tax. The assessment was made to correspond with the amount of rent paid.[6] (A discussion on the house tax problem by one Sun Zhi provides details on the changes in taxation practices.)[7] According to Sun, the excessively heavy labor service duties required of farmers in rural districts was removed after Pang Xiangpeng enacted an equalization law. But there was no corresponding reduction in the burdens placed on urban residents. Services required of city dwellers, posts such as *zongjia*, *huofu*, *yiguan* (guardian), and *fangmin* (ward-leader), were not subject to equalization under the law. In contrast to the wealthy and shrewd urban residents, who resorted to bribery to evade service, the poor and the honest had to shoulder the labor service burden unceasingly and with no opportunity to transfer the duty to others.

Shi Yuguo, a resident of the city's Fangsheng district, appealed; as a result, the house tax or *mentan* law was enacted. According to this law, the residences of members of the official class as well as prefectural nominees, tribute students, tribute students by purchase, and government students were not assessed this tax, but

> . . . an evaluation was to be reckoned upon the housing of all others. If this valuation came to ten silver *taels*, then rent usually came to one *tael*. If rent totaled one *tael*, then the annual tax assessed on the dwelling would not exceed 0.085 *taels*. The assessment would fluctuate according to the movement of the dwelling's estimated value above or below the one-hundred *tael* level. [If the dwelling was] located on an out-

of-the-way alley, corner, or if the residents were impoverished, then the evaluation would be reduced and not determined strictly according to the standard.[8]

Tax money collected in this manner would be used by officials to hire
substitutes for local residents to fulfill the *zongjia* and other city labor
duties.

The significance of this change was that, as a result of transforming
labor service posts into paid positions and paying for services at fixed
rates, taxes actually underwent an extraordinary reduction. Before the
revision, those people who wished to pay their labor service obligation by an additional tax payment were assessed a stiff levy. For example, an individual with residential property, carrying an assessed valua-
tion of one hundred *taels* or less, seldom saw an assessment for a
month of *zongjia* service dip below seven or eight *taels*. But after the
change a dwelling evaluated at even more than one hundred *taels* was
assessed less than a single *tael*. In his "Epitaph for County Magistrate
Cai," Feng Gaomo provides a source for understanding the reform of
house taxes and general changes in *huofu* labor service practices in
Haiyan county.[9]

According to Feng, two problems existed before tax reform. The
first involved the mobility of small scale merchants (*fanfu*) and the difficulties this posed for collecting the household tax. On this point he
notes of such persons, ". . . today one would think that their domicile
was here, but tomorrow they move it there, and the next day they quit
their business and leave altogether."[10] The second problem concerned
the *huofu* labor obligation. As was the case in Jiaxing in Haiyan county
too, officials, examination students and official functionaries were given
tax exempt status. Moreover, the shrewd and cunning could avoid
labor service, which consequently left the burden entirely to the poor
and powerless. The similarity of the problems in both places led to
similar attempts at reform. In Haiyan city, as was the case in Jiaxing,
"assessments would be levied on the basis of the householder's rents"
and the money collected would be used to hire individuals to perform
labor services.

As evident in Sun Zhi's discussion of the house tax, these urban
reforms were inspired by the revisions in rural tax policies undertaken
by Pang Xiangpeng. Reforms in both places arose from similar complaints about labor service exemptions and illegal evasions. Indeed, the
features common to urban and rural reforms enable us to see just how
difficult it is to separate city and countryside. Still, urban and rural

conditions were not identical. One obvious distinction, given the fluid nature of city life, was the difficulty in collecting tax money from renters for hiring substitutes for labor services.

Reforms also went forward in cities in Changzhou prefecture. According to the Wanli period (1573–1620) gazetteer for Changzhou, the post of *huofu* in the prefectural city of Wujin was established from 1537. Aside from certain exempted categories, the city's entire residential population was subject to the labor service, which was to be carried out under the direction of *zongjia*. Despite the measure's egalitarian basis, the wealthy sought to evade the law and shifted the burden to the poor. At this juncture, the county magistrate, Xu Tu, assessed a 10 percent tax on rents to generate revenue so that substitutes could be recruited for performing labor services.[11]

Even before the reform was enacted, it appears that renters as well as the owners of dwellings were subject to the unpaid *huofu* service. Yet, because most owners were well-to-do, they managed to evade the work so that those people who actually fulfilled unpaid labor service obligations were the renters. The compiler of the Changzhou prefectural gazetteer, Tang Hezheng of Wujin county, pointed out the following regarding the transformation of *huofu* to a paid position:

> In this region, at the beginning of the Wanli period a person named Zhou introduced a policy of money taxation. Every year ten percent of the amount received in rents would be assessed and be applied against the cost of hiring [for labor services]. Dwelling owners had benefited under the old unpaid labor system. But by assigning the owners a cash assessment and making them pay, renters, who in contrast to owners had to work for a living, came to enjoy an easing of their circumstances. In general, most dwelling owners were people of influence and renters were small-time merchants and women peddlers. [The change] was thus seen as excellent policy for inflicting losses upon the owners and profiting the tenants.[12]

According to the new system, renters, who had had to carry the burden of *huofu* service before the reform, were freed from duty after the reform; *huofu* service was transformed into a hired position paid for by collecting taxes from the owners of dwellings. It meant an extraordinary benefit for renters and, conversely, a severe loss for owners. Although they shared a common identity as city residents, renters and owners, who were involved in this single concrete urban reform, found that their interests differed. In Wuxi and Yixing counties in Changzhou prefecture, the *huofu* also changed into a hired position.[13]

In the case of Nanjing, labor service guard patrols within the city walls initially alternated among families which formed *huofu* groups composed of one *zongjia* and five *huofu*. The *zongjia* and *huofu* would assemble at watch-boxes (*gengpu*) and then patrol during the nighttime hours when passage on city streets was generally prohibited. This obligatory duty required that city residents work in a cooperative structure with soldiers.

Although the poor were supposed to do the work themselves, labor service regulations recognized the right of the wealthy to privately hire substitutes. Problems arose, however, when the *zongjia* hired by the richer city residents colluded with official functionaries in perpetrating widespread abuses within the system. Consequently, city residents mounted a movement that appealed for changes to replace the private hiring of substitutes to one in which labor service posts would be filled by official recruitment. The movement succeeded in causing the entire system to be reformed around 1609. Hereafter, cash assessments would be categorized and collected according to a division of "three ranks and nine categories" (*sandeng jiuze*) and officials took responsibility for recruiting for the labor service.[14]

In Jiading county in Suzhou prefecture labor service was also changed to one that could be fulfilled by cash payment. Peddlers and itinerant workers became overburdened because members of notable and wealthy families in most cases evaded labor service (*paimen fu*), an obligation demanded of every household within the city. As a result a property assessment system became widely used. According to this method of taxation in lieu of labor services, the entryway or other dimension of a house were used to determine dwelling size for assessment purposes.[15]

A similar movement was initiated in Suzhou city itself. Suzhou and Hangzhou, both centers of high quality silk production, shared many similarities including the manner in which labor service systems were reformed. In both cities, the transformation of the labor service guard patrols was accomplished within the *baojia* system. An examination of the Suzhou reform is instructive, and is possible because of the existence of the extremely important source, the *Zhen Wu Lu*, [A Record of the Pacification of Suzhou], which records in detail the efforts of Jiang Liangdong, a military commander charged with putting down unrest in Suzhou and revamping civilian labor service patrols.[16]

Suzhou had already experienced the well-known weavers (*zhi-*

yong) uprising in 1601. This riot became an occasion for strengthening the *baojia* system whereby city residents organized in *bao* and *jia* units kept guard, patrolled nightly, and manned street gate checkpoints throughout the city.[17] Such methods were found wanting when it came to controlling the violent political actions such as the popular uprising of 1601 and the student (*shengyuan*) riot mounted at the examination hall in 1603.[18] At this time, when changes were made in the *baojia* system and unrest ensued, Jiang Liangdong was moved to defend Suzhou.[19]

On the inconveniences created within the city by the *baojia* patrol system, the street gate checkpoints, and the prohibition of nighttime movement, he pointed out the following:

1. The street gate checkpoints create obstacles in coping with medical emergencies and in the delivery of babies. Doctors and midwives cannot be hurriedly summoned.
2. The poor city residents in the eastern half of the city of Suzhou specialize in weaving. Everyday they travel to the homes of the wealthy, work [at weaving] throughout the day, and return home at nightfall. If they inadvertently violate the curfew they are invariably subject to merciless squeezing by the constables.
3. Merchants selling from carrying poles hawking goods carried on their backs, commoners who sell vegetables and sweets—such people always leave the city around four A.M. to conclude transactions with brokers and restock their wares. If these [petty merchants], whose sales for an entire day amount to little in their struggle for a tiny profit, are caught up [in the restrictions on movement within the city] and are thereby rendered unable to do business, then their families must go hungry for a day.
4. Thieves and robbers are deft of hand and light of foot. Moreover, they are thoroughly familiar with the lay of city streets. Even with the street gate checkpoints, they can evade capture. But conversely, the patrols themselves are obstructed by the street gates and cannot capture [offenders].
5. The *baojia* is a good law, but in Suzhou scholars and officials are overwhelmingly numerous. Owing to their privileged exemptions, others have gathered around the influential so that they, too, may avoid labor service. As a result, only the poor and weak from the lower households are serving on patrol. The common targets of most thieves and robbers, however, are the grand houses [of the rich and powerful]. Consequently, when

only the poor are called upon for policing, they can work up
little enthusiasm for the job.
6. For the poor, the oil bill for keeping lanterns lit at each doorway produces an extraordinarily steep expense which they must
bear on their own.[20]

Of particular note here are his second and fifth observations. As
for the inconvenience to weavers, it is worthwhile to compare Jiang's
observations with those of Xu Yigui in the *Zhigong dui* [Weaver's Re-
sponse], a source which has become controversial in the "sprouts of
capitalism" debate.[21] In contrast to the weavers who appear in the *Zhigong dui* as resident laborers (*jugong*), the weavers who appear in the
account of the *Zhen Wu Lu* are commuting workers hired on a day-
labor basis. Furthermore, in contrast to the weavers described in the
Zhigong dui, who might continue to work as usual until around 9:00
P.M. (the hour of the second drum), the weavers in the *Zhen Wu Lu*,
despite the possible need to work late, were in principle supposed to
return home before the curfew began.[22] If on one hand we have the resident laborers and, on the other, the commuting laborers, it should
probably be expected that we could see a difference in working hours.
The problem is that, following the narrative in the *Zhen Wu Lu*, it
seems that commuting laborers, especially those engaged in weaving,
lived in the eastern part of Suzhou, and it appears that their way of life
represented a general pattern for city residents.

The prohibition on nighttime movement—the erection of street
gates, the demands of *baojia* patrol—these restrictions greatly fettered
the lives of city residents and came to constitute an additional urban
problem. The commuting workers, the petty merchants and vendors
mentioned in Jiang's third point, required both freedom of personal
movement and freedom from time restraints. Speaking of poorer city
residents, he observed that ". . . they worked their utmost throughout
the daytime hours shouldering heavy loads to make a living and they
coveted the nighttime with its promise of a leisurely rest."[23] For them
the work that awaited the next day was more important than anything
else. Thus, the various arrangements introduced to check urban unrest
became extraordinary restraints placed upon those common people
who formed the mainstay of the city's commerce and handicraft industries.

Jiang's observations on the problems posed by exemptions from
labor service, his fifth point, are also worth noting. True, exemptions

and evasion were issues that were not just limited to city labor services. But given the general tendency of this period of social transformation "from rural residential landlords to city residential landlords," it is clear that the problem was one that became increasingly an urban issue.[24] Of Suzhou, it was even said that ". . .those holding exemptions in Suzhou, including gentry, second-degree graduates, national university students, first-degree licentiates, unranked subofficial functionaries, clerks, and scribes, now total between seventy and eighty percent of the city's population."[25] These widespread exemptions meant that *baojia* labor service groups came to be exclusively comprised of ten-family groups of weavers and petty merchants. Furthermore, they were forced to guard the mansions of the gentry, homes which were the favorite targets of robbers and thieves. Here, in the context of the *baojia* system and night patrolling, can be seen the latent conflict between two urban strata.

In the abstract, this conflict was between the "rich" and the "poor." But in more concrete terms, it was nothing other than a conflict between specially privileged city residents of the gentry-official strata, individuals empowered to grant exemption from labor service, and those people without such privileges, such as the weavers and petty merchants. On a deeper level, as was evident in the case of Changzhou, the conflict was also one that pitted the powers of the owners of dwellings against renters. There is no doubt that renters who flowed into many cities became weavers and petty merchants. Their strata was that which most demanded freedom of activity and which was the most earnestly desirous of reform of the urban labor service.

In Suzhou, the *huofu* labor service obligation had already been transformed into a hired position before the question of freedom of movement within the city became an issue.[26] Despite this change, the tendency toward equalization of duty was reversed when *baojia* units, which were comprised largely of the poor, were repeatedly pressed to take responsibility for *huofu* and similar labor service burdens. The soldier, Jiang Liangdong, who witnessed the inconvenience caused by the middle and lower strata of city residents, advocated ending *baojia* patrolling, removing street gate checkpoints, and reforming the city's policing structure by leaving it exclusively to soldiers. The issue of the difficulties created by assessing the *baojia* for *huofu* and other labor services, the relationship of soldiers and city people, and the various matters concerned with the abolition of labor services by urban residents will be taken up next in our discussion of events in Hangzhou.

THE HANGZHOU CITY REFORM MOVEMENT

Problems confronted in Hangzhou were the same as those faced in other Jiangnan cities, so it is not surprizing that similar reform movements appeared in different places. In Hangzhou attempts at reform concentrated on two issues: reduction of the *jianjia shui*, or house tax, and abolition of compulsory labor service for city policing that had traditionally been carried out in connection with *baojia* membership by neighborhood groupings. Ding Shiqing, a school teacher, played a pivotal role in both reforms and was central to the popular uprising that broke out later.

The *Jianjia* Tax Reform Movement

Ding Shiqing was involved in the movement to reform the formula of special tax assessments known as *jianjia* taxes, that were levied against Hangzhou residents. Originally from Shanyu county, Shaoxing prefecture some eighty kilometers from Hangzhou, Ding taught at a local community school in the Dongli district and was himself a renter in the Ping An neighborhood.[27] Through his leadership of the opposition to the *jianjia* tax, he effected a genuine reduction in taxes. The *jianjia shui* was a heavy tax assessed only against the residents of Hangzhou; it was not levied in other major cities in the region.[28] As historical sources note, ". . . the *jianjia shui* was not relied upon in other provinces, but was a problem of Hangzhou city only."[29] In the earlier cases of cities in the three counties of Jiaxing prefecture (Jiaxing, Xiushui, and Haiyan), residential tax laws generally specified that assessment would be based upon the size of the gate or entryway as determined by the number of bays or *jian*. This was true not only for various cities in Jiangnan but also in the North China region as well. As Lu Kun states in his *Shi Zheng Lu*, ". . . in general, in fixing the *jianjia*, the primary standard was the number of *jian* measures in the doorway."[30] In Hangzhou, however, things were different. The standard was not based on the bays in the entryway, but the size of the plot on which the dwelling rested, measurement known as the "plot-*jianjia*" (*jidi jianjia*).

During the early Ming period, the formula for the Hangzhou *jianjia* tax specified that land upon which city residents had their particular dwelling was to be differentially assessed on the basis of "official's land" (*guanjidi*) and "commoner's land" (*minjidi*).[31] The principal difference was that those designated as official landholders had only to pay regular taxes but were not obligated to perform labor services. Those designated as common (*min*) landholders, conversely, were only required to fulfill the labor service obligation and were free of other cash or in-kind tax payments. However, as shown in the table on the next page, the tax assessment of one *ding*, the standard unit of tax liability, for every ten *jian* measures—the rate that was established at the founding of the dynasty—had increased to a levy of one *ding* for every seven *jian* after the middle of the Jiajing reign (1522–1567). The increase did not pose a major problem as long as the assessment affected only nonofficial owners. But from 1568, the situation worsened because ". . . the heavy burden of field taxes in the rural area resulted in the inclusion of urban nonofficial taxpayers into the rolls of regular taxpayers. Heretofore, this group had been free of other cash or in-kind tax payments." Moreover, ". . . The heavy burden of rural labor service obligations resulted in the inclusion of urban official landholders into the rolls of those owing regular obligations. Heretofore this group had been exempt from the labor service."[32] In other words, with the unavoidable shifting of the rural tax burden to the city, the taxation formula that was applied to commoners and officials living in the city was made uniform. The taxation rate of one *ding* per seven *jian* came to be extended to owners of the official lands.

As for the popular response to the shift to heavy urban taxation, it was reported that ". . . although all Hangzhou city people complained bitterly of the exceedingly heavy levies, not a soul came forward to make overtures to the government."[33] When no one came forward, Ding Shiqing alone appeared to appeal the tax system's impracticality and to present a plan for tax reduction. Simply put, his reform plan called for reducing the tax on city land holdings from the then current level of one *ding* for every seven *jian* (equivalent to 0.35 *mu*) to a level equal with that assessed on rural land or at a rate of one *ding* for every two hundred *jian* (or ten *mu*). He advocated that on the basis of the high rural tax burden being combined with the light city tax burden, and because the assessment standards were being made uniform and equal, then his reforms should be adopted to enable reality "to match the name of equality (*paping*)."[34]

The provincial governor, Xu Shi, indicated that he thought that Ding Shiqing's suggestion was essentially correct. Yet, the magistrates of Renhe and Qiantang counties, even as they, too, tended to acknowledge that Ding's plan was reasonable, tempered this view by noting that "the righting of evils should be done a little bit at a time." They

Table 1: City Tax Reduction Proposals in Renhe and Qiantang
Counties, Hangzhou city

Early Ming period: nonofficial *jianjia*: 0.5 *mu* (10 *jian*) = 1 *ding*
Pre-reform rate: 0.35 *mu* (7 *jian*) = 1 *ding*
Ding Shiqing's proposal: 10.00 *mu* (200 *jian*) = 1 *ding*
County magistrate's proposal: 1.0 *mu* (20 *jian*) = 1 *ding*
Prefect's proposal: 2.5 *mu* (50 *jian*) = 1 *ding*
Provincial Administration Commissioner's proposal: 1.0 *mu*
    (20 *jian*) = 1 *ding*
Rural tax rate: 10 *mu* (200 *jian*) = 1 *ding*

---

viewed Ding's tax reduction plan as far too extreme, and accordingly
proposed to assess the *jianjia* tax at a rate of one *ding* for every twenty
jian.

The prefect, who received the two magistrates' proposal, thinking
that the people were greatly burdened, suggested a scale in which fifty
jian would equal one *ding*, but this proposal went nowhere. Gentry
members Chen Shan and Ma Sancai also submitted individual opinions
to the provincial governor. As a result, the Provincial Administrative
Commissioner, the Administrative Vice-Commissioner, and Assistant
for Police Affairs submitted a joint proposal recommending that twenty *jian* equal one *ding*. This plan was accepted and, for the time being,
the matter was considered resolved.[35] (See table above.)

A comparison of the contents of Ding Shiqing's tax reduction
proposal, which attempted to treat city and countryside alike, with that
of the Provincial Administrative Commissioner, the plan that was finally adopted, suggests why Ding's proposal might be called "revolutionary." True, the provincial governor thought Ding's ideas to be just;
even county magistrates to a certain extent recognized his proposal's
reasonableness in principle. But Ding's ideas ignored the practical
differences between the city and the farm village, and thus resulted in
nothing more than a formally logical tax equalization plan.

Fang Yang, who became prefect in Hangzhou in 1582, commented
on taxes and assessments based on land measurement by noting that
urban land values were worth twice as much as farm land; after all,
people concentrated in cities and were able to do business that yielded
great profits. According to Fang, "if tax assessments are determined
solely by the single uniform standard of land area, then a majority of
tax revenue would be lost."[36] Even though land areas might be the

same, based upon the great difference in profitability between city and farm land, it was only natural that a divergence in land values would also emerge. Ding's plan, which attempted to alleviate the heavy city tax burden and make urban assessment levels uniform with those of farm villages, at first glance appeared to be fair. But to follow Ding's proposals would in fact give special treatment to the city in comparison with that afforded rural villages. Not surprisingly, city-based merchants and craft industry workers gave Ding's reform ideas an exceptionally warm welcome.

Which strata of the city's residents actually benefited from the proposed policy of special treatment? On that question and on the relationship of city to farm village, the Provincial Commissioner's proposal provides valuable hints:

> Those people who owned numerous city dwellings without fail owned fields in rural villages. Lowering urban taxes and increasing rural taxes by the same measure did not significantly benefit them. However, for poor people, those who had a dwelling but did not possess fields, this measure was a great blessing.[37]

In other words, the *jianjia* tax reduction issue was of great concern to common urban residents who did not possess rural fields. City-based landlords simultaneously owned many urban residences and invariably also enjoyed extensive holdings of farm land. For such people, to reduce the *jianjia* assessment on their urban residences, simply to turn around and increase levies against rural fields did not translate into a tax reduction. In contrast, lowering the *jianjia* tax meant an immediate and real tax cut for the middle and lower strata of the urban residents. Ding Shiqing's proposal thus brought forth an extraordinary chorus of welcome from the general run of the urban population. It found wide support among people who did not own farm fields: that is, those of the middle to lower strata of the city's population who relied exclusively upon trade and the handicraft industry to maintain their livelihoods. From their perspective, Ding's plan was the superior *urban* plan, a reform proposal that could be undertaken *for the sake of the city*.

The Movement To Abolish Labor Service Policing

Another movement shouldered by Ding Shiqing was the abolition of civilian guard duty, a labor service undertaken by city residents in conjunction with their participation in the *baojia* system. Civil guard within Hangzhou was charged to *huojia*, groups made up of *zongjia* and *huofu*. Both posts had already been changed into paid positions prior to 1545 and expenses required for the change had been covered by the *jianjia* tax revenues. In Hangzhou, as in other cities, the major problem with the *zongjia* and *huofu* posts was that the rich used bribery to avoid service and the poor found themselves overburdened to the point of being unable to fulfill their obligations.

In 1545, a change in the system was carried out according to a petition submitted by Chen Yu, a city resident. The reform changed the system so that, with the exception of certain exempted categories of citizens, the *jianjia* tax would be assessed on taxable groups divided into high, middle, and low categories. *Zongjia* and *huofu* would thus be recruited from revenues generated by the fixed rate of equal taxation within each of the three broad divisions.[38]

Although the post of *huojia* had already become a hired position, it appears that around 1555 city patrolling came to be carried out as an additional policing duty assigned to members of unpaid units organized within the *baojia*. Around this time, *baojia* were organized in Hangzhou to prepare against and ferret out spies acting on behalf of bands of Japanese pirates and thieves. Hangzhou had been so pressed by these outlaw groups in 1555 that the duty of serving as residential watchmen on a rotating basis within the *baojia* jurisdiction had also become obligatory. The arrangement was one in which civilian watchmen came to cooperate with the *huojia* in carrying out night patrols, despite the fact that the *huojia* had already become the "professionals" hired expressly for this purpose. The measure was originally nothing more than a matter of temporary convenience, but with time it became customary practice. In short, city residents themselves were once again being forced to take part in policing. Worse yet, labor service obligations within the *baojia* expanded to require citizens to take additional responsibility for repair work at all Hangzhou government offices.[39]

Ding Shiqing opposed the inconvenience and unfairness of such practices and put forth plans for remedial measures. Upon observing the difficulties suffered by Hangzhou residents, he submitted the following appeal:

> It should be sufficient to make use of the one hundred seventy laborers assigned to repair work at government offices when dispatching [units] for night patrol service. To requisition *baojia* labor service—on top of assessing each house for payment of the *jianjia* tax so that *zongjia* and *huofu* can be hired—is to

go too far and to leave citizens totally exhausted, both financially and physically. Please act to end all labor service requirements demanded of city residents.[40]

This appeal, first raised in 1559, was also circulated in following
years to Pang Xiangpeng, who had implemented the Single Whip law
in Zhejiang province.[41] Despite the repeated petitioning, the system
was not easily changed. Indeed, for lower-level officials, who oversaw
the repair of government offices and who were responsible for policing
the city, it was an excellent arrangement, one that drove the citizenry
into labor service and thereby enabled minor functionaries to make
money through graft.

Just when it seemed that the reforms had gone forward, a setback
would occur that would play to the strengths of such clerks. To protect
their extra-legal income, they even accused Ding Shiqing of "upsetting
established laws." On as many as three occasions judges, who failed to
investigate the allegations fully, ordered Ding to be flogged, bound in
manacles, and returned to his home in Shanyu county.[42] But in 1572,
Ding's petition was finally accepted. Once more in 1574, he returned
to Hangzhou and petitioned on this issue and from this time forward
labor services were to be completely eliminated. Nevertheless, Ding
was justifiably concerned about the persistent anti-reform movement
and fearful of yet another reversal that would nullify his efforts. He
accordingly had a description of the process leading up to the reforms
carved on stone steles. In 1577 [Wanli 5] he had these erected at
Zhenhai tower and Wulin gate as a perpetual testament.

Whether the issue was the *jianjia* tax, abolition of night patrol
duty, or displeasure over other miscellaneous labor service requirements, the common people found it extremely difficult to have their
views reflected in regional administration. Although these issues were
of pressing importance and despite the fact that ". . .the entire citizenry of Hangzhou spoke among themselves of the heavy burdens,
there was not a single person who would appeal to officialdom." For
protest to begin they waited for someone like Ding, a low ranking intellectual and a man of indomitable spirit who would "three times suffer a brutal flogging and shackling, and be returned to Yue."[43] Chen
Shan, the compiler of the Wanli gazetteer for Hangzhou was an eyewitness to the reform movement and judged Ding Shiqing's actions as
an example of "righteous conduct." Despite Chen's position as a member of the gentry—rather, *because he was a member of the gentry* and
therefore unable to carry the burden of the reforms so obviously needed
—he felt remorseful. Chen left the following intriguing reflection:

The harm ensuing from labor service and night patrol extends
not to scholars and officials. Therefore it is rare that the gentry have anything to say on the matter. Furthermore, those who
are thoroughly familiar with this issue are, again, few. Upon
reading Ding Shiqing's "The Record of Fraudulent Labor Service in Hangzhou," I could not help but weep and feel deeply
awed. With nothing to gain and all to lose he fearlessly sets
out his case in twenty articles. And with what earnestness and
clarity these are presented! [I feel as if during my] thirty years
as an official I have stolen my salary. I have mistakenly trailed
behind high officials and have not been able to spare my home
region calamity. But Ding Shiqing, although a solitary wander-
er, felt indignation, pressed his petition from start to end for
eighteen years, and in the end accomplished his aim.[44]

Here, of course, we can make out the voice of the Confucian intellectual, a single member of the upper gentry and an individual susceptible
to the emotionalism of the Wang Yangming school.[45] Such considerations aside, what is of greater importance is Chen's admission that he
has "mistakenly trailed behind." This statement can be perceived as a
general image of high officials and the gentry elite. Members of these
groups "inevitably held much land in rural regions and the harm of
night patrol duty did not reach them." It was indeed likely that their
attitude toward the urban reform movement would hinder effective
measures of reform. At the same time that officials and gentry were
city residents and urban landlords, they also commonly enjoyed the
status of a specially privileged citizenry. The difference in attitudes toward a common city problem—on one side the city residents who enjoyed special privileges and on the other the commoners who were
without such privileges, those who "held no land in the countryside"
and therefore could not evade labor service—suggested the direction
that city administration would later take. The separate attitudes on the
part of the two broad urban groups, and the conflicting interests that
underlay their estrangement, frustrated reform attempts by Ding and
others and brought on the "anti-gentry" Hangzhou popular uprising.

THE 1582 HANGZHOU POPULAR UPRISING

The Military Uprising

The Hangzhou popular uprising of 1582 (Wanli 10) was sparked by a
military uprising raised by soldiers stationed in Hangzhou who made
demands related to their own livelihood. Before directly considering

the civilian uprising, it is essential to first look at the deeply rooted relations between soldiers and civilians, and the links between civilian
and military uprisings.[46]

Among the soldiers who raised the disturbance were those with
glowing military records. They had achieved success in the north
fighting against the Mongol tribes, and in the south, led by the famous
Hu Zongxian, had been instrumental in suppressing Japanese pirates.
Their glorious battle record had reverberated throughout the nation.
"Soldiers of Zhejiang" (*Zhebing, Zhebing*) were troops esteemed as
steadfast and reliable.

The issue of soldiers' rations and pay became a problem in the
autumn of 1581 when fiscal stringency resulted in demands for cuts in
various government expenses. Up to then, each soldier received one
tael (or 9.5 *qian*) every month, but reforms now called for this to be
cut by one-third. Furthermore, a debate arose about making one-
half (or perhaps one-third) of this payment in "new cash" (*xin qian*).
In Hangzhou, unlike in Beijing, the new cash had the same value as
the old or was considered slightly inferior in value to the old currency.
Since it appeared to be only plain copper, the new cash did not circulate as widely in Hangzhou.[47]

After five months, soldiers, who not only suffered a partial pay cut
but also were forced to accept payment in the new copper cash, found
the situation intolerable and turned to forceful protest. On the second
day of the third month of 1582, the soldiers, led by Ma Wenying and
Yang Tingyong, called upon Governor Wu Shanyan to press him to
restore the method of payment to precisely that which had existed before the introduction of changes. In defending their unilateral action
they argued that:

> Our present actions are taken because we are temporarily
> pressed by extremities of hunger and cold. We have not
> attempted to raise a rebellion or commit criminal acts which
> cannot be forgiven. Who can call our action open public
> disobedience?[48]

The soldiers' protest was indeed organized, orderly, and disci-
plined. The two ringleaders, Ma and Yang, and other soldiers gave
assurances that "we do not kill people; do not steal property" and it
appears that not a single incident of arson or violence aimed at the
citizenry was seen during the protest.[49]

On the connections between the military and civilian uprisings one

point that cannot be overlooked is that at the very time the soldiers
raised demands in support of their livelihood, they also complained on
behalf of civilians. In particular, they pointed out to officials that
". . . various burdens can be counted among those endured by civilians, *but first and foremost is the labor service.*"[50] Regarding the labor
service issue, soldiers, who had a rather good understanding of and
sympathy for the living conditions faced by the citizenry, presented the
demands of city residents before their own.

The day after they had submitted their demands, the soldiers' two
ringleaders, who had had their hands bound by their own men, turned
themselves over to the governor to await punishment. As an ameliorative measure, officials acknowledged the position advocated by the soldiers and, for the time being, the two leaders were pardoned. The
troops they represented were granted not only a five-month food
ration allotment, but were also advanced an additional three-month
supply. At this juncture, the military uprising ended.

The announcement "outbreak of military insurrection in Hangzhou" astonished the Beijing government. Central government officials, having experienced previous and repeated incidents of military
uprisings, fully realized the dangerous nature of soldiers and the difficulty of controlling unrest in the ranks. They appeared to believe that
the Hangzhou uprising might spark rebellion by soldiers garrisoned
elsewhere who harbored the same kind of dissatisfactions. If that happened, then the situation would become irrevocable. Zhang Juzheng,
the Grand Secretary at the time, selected Zhang Jiayin, who had suppressed the Nanjing military uprising, to put down the Hangzhou unrest. Upon receiving this order, Zhang Jiayin hurried to Hangzhou and
learned at Chongde county in Jiaxing that "the civilian uprising continues." Zhang's very first question after hearing the report was,
"Have the portion of garrison troops assigned to sea duty left yet?" His
second was, "Have the troops that remain joined forces with the
civilians?"[51] Nothing was to be feared more than the conjunction of
military and civilian uprisings.

The Civilian Uprising

Ding Shiqing, the hero of the tax reforms, now became the leader of
the civilian uprising.[52] Ding had studied for the examinations during
his youth in his home region of Shanyu county, where it was said that
"he studied composition . . . from childhood and often argued the provincial examiner into silence."[53] Accounts of his life also note that

"when there was civil litigation, people would always come to discuss the matter with Ding Shiqing."[54] There is no doubt that he was an intelligent individual, one not easily intimidated by officials. Once settled in Hangzhou he was again sought after to help with lawsuits, which he repeatedly managed to win. Thus, he developed a reputation as a mediator in resolving local disputes.[55] That he had earned the confidence of Hangzhou's citizens is suggested by the comment that "many in Hangzhou sent their children to study with him."[56] For an apparently insignificant school teacher to raise a movement to reform the *jianjia* tax administration and to abolish civilian labor services was indeed an accomplishment. For such an individual to successfully put forth such "revolutionary" proposals and succeed in swaying the administration of a major provincial capital symbolically marked the opening of a new era.

Despite these successes, anti-reform machinations persisted. We have already seen how minor officials, who superintended labor services or were responsible for night patrols, opposed the reforms. Such local conservatives were joined by far larger numbers of gentry and Beijing bureaucrats of Hangzhou origins who possessed even greater power to oppose the abolition of civilian labor services. The father and son Shen Jin and Shen Pian were representative of the opposition group.

The Shen family seems to have become one of Hangzhou's foremost families about the time that Shen Jin's father, Shen Jian, became sexton of the Hong Lu temple, a post that he probably acquired as a purchased title.[57] Shen Jin took the *shengyuan* degree at the county level and thereafter obtained the post of deputy director of the same temple. His son, Shen Pian, took the *jinshi* degree in 1554 and thereafter served successively as Investigating Censor on the Guangdong (or Huguang) circuits.[58] In 1579, he quit official life to return to his home district in Hangzhou, two years after Ding Shiqing had erected a stele to convey forever the abolition of civilian labor service and to prevent the reversal of the reforms.

Shen Pian's rise to the position of Censor enabled his father, Shen Jin, to receive honorary titles.[59] As their titles and careers attest, both father and son were "gentry" in every sense of the word. Indeed, they were commonly called "local dignitaries" (*xiangdafu*) or "gentry-censor," and their words and deeds exerted powerful influence on regional administration.

Although night patrol labor service had finally been abolished, a change instituted in 1580 resulted in the reinstatement of mandatory civilian labor service. The shift prompted Ding Shiqing to immediately petition the provincial intendant as well as the prefectural and county magistrates. The matter was then handed over to the sub-prefect of Hangzhou, Wu Riqiang, who was to conduct hearings and to decide whether to continue the civilian labor service or change to a hired service. This development led Shen Pian, the "local censor," to counter that the transformation from civilian duty to professional or hired service was not permissible, while the "local dignitary," Shen Jin, averred that "*huojia* service [in this case, night patrol by *baojia*] cannot be discontinued."[60] It can be said that the 1580 reversion to labor service from the hired service post generally conformed to the views of the resident gentry on this issue.

After gentry pressure caused the failure of Ding's appeals at the regional government offices, he next dashed off to Beijing to argue his case. But here again he was duped by an "illustrious official" and his efforts came to nothing.[61]

Who was the "illustrious official" who deceived him in Beijing? Although the sources are not absolutely clear on this point, Chen Sanmo is a likely candidate. At the time of the popular disturbance instigated by Ding, Chen's home was marched upon and burned down. Chen had risen to *jinshi* status in 1565 and it appeared likely that Shen Pian, a man from the same region and successful contemporary of Chen, worked through him in exerting influence in the capital.[62] It was in 1580, just at the time that Chen Sanmo had been promoted from a high post in the Censorate to vice-minister in the Court of Imperial Sacrifices and was coming into the peak of his influence as an "illustrious official," that Ding Shiqing arrived in Beijing.[63] It is probable that Chen Sanmo was central to the process whereby officials originally from Hangzhou but now serving in Beijing maintained contacts with resident Hangzhou gentry to block Ding's reforms.

At a time when each new day brought disappointment as central and regional bureaucrats and gentry blocked reform, the Hangzhou soldiers mounted their uprising. Ding witnessed the insurrection and observed that:

> Perhaps officials think we are easily tamed. . . . If the soldiers' monthly rations are cut slightly, the garrison troops immediately tie back their sleeves, mount an uprising, and no one dares to say even a single word. But even if [we civilians] suffer day after day, not a single measure is given. We always get blamed even when dogs and chickens are noisy.[64]

Stirred by what he witnessed of the military insurrection and incensed over the better treatment afforded soldiers who joined it, Ding was thoroughly dissatisfied with the lack of consideration given to the civilians. Thus, he began to whip up the citizenry and make plans to burn down the homes of his most hated antagonists, the father and son, Shen Jin and Shen Pian.[65] But someone informed the Shen Pian household of his plans against the gentry. A secret report was made to the appropriate legal officials, whereupon Ding was arrested. In addition to being flogged with a bamboo rod, manacles were placed on his hands, feet, and neck after which he was pilloried for display in the city.[66]

At the time this punishment was being inflicted, he is reported to have cried out to city residents: "From the very beginning my appeal over night patrol duty was made for you. Now I alone must suffer. Why don't you do something to help me?"[67] And, "It was for you that I appealed over night patrol duty, but I alone am bound in shackles and have been whipped. Can you bear this?"[68] In response, the citizenry called back, "Ding Shiqing has been punished for us. We must save him," whereupon several hundred people took up this call, rushed to the Provincial Court of Justice and released him.[69] This dramatic sequence of events culminated in the outbreak of the popular uprising.

It is at this point in the narrative of the Hangzhou incident that Ding, formerly the man of "virtuous conduct," suddenly yields center stage to Ding the "cunning hooligan," "rebel," and "cruel and crafty character."[70]

The rioters who rescued Ding not only formed groups to tear down every nightwatch tower but also attempted to burn Shen Pian's home to the ground.[71] By now approximately one thousand people had joined the insurrection. Chen Liangdong, magistrate of Renhe county, along with the magistrate of Qiantang county, rushed to the scene in an attempt to somehow save the situation. But instead they found themselves surrounded by angry citizens. Order had deteriorated to the point where the two only managed to slip away during the night by disguising themselves.

With nightfall, the pitch of the insurrection reached its zenith. Rioters occupied every lane and alley. From the homes of gentry, they took red undergarments to hang from poles as banners. They also placed lanterns at each house and at every tenth house ordered that a banner be raised. The night glowed as bright as daylight.[72] The city had fallen to rioters' control and crowds attacked and burned the homes of Chen Sanmo and those of other gentry. People who tried to protect the mansions of the rich could do nothing other than take an attitude of warm welcome toward Ding Shiqing. It was reported that at the homes of Chen Sanmo and Ma Sancai cooks were ordered to prepare fresh dishes of meat and to await Ding's appearance. Upon arriving he was warmly welcomed with music and by the wives of gentry who greeted him on their knees while expressing their deepest regrets for the treatment that he had endured.[73]

The next day, a crowd of rioters pushed into the provincial judicial office where they took custody of Hao, the Surveillance Commissioner. They then called upon Zhang Wenxi, the Regional Inspector, in an attempt to have an audience with him. The door to the Inspectorate was locked so the crowd smashed through it. But because the inspector had fled through a break in the outer wall, the crowd deposited Hao at the office gate and all turned their attention to looting.[74]

On the first day of the fifth month, the rioters, whose number now reached two thousand, had virtually destroyed bazaars and had torn down almost all of the street gates and nightwatch towers.[75] On this day, Zhang Jiayin, who had been named provincial governor and had been ordered to suppress the military uprising, arrived at the governor's yamen in Hangzhou city. At nightfall, more than two thousand city residents converged on the office where they raised a tremendous clamor outside its gate. Zhang Jiayin ordered the outer gate opened and riding in a sedan chair accompanied by only a few soldiers went out to face the citizenry at Wangxian bridge.[76] While surrounded, Zhang is reported to have negotiated with individuals in the crowd in the following way:

> Zhang: You have undoubtedly suffered and have important reasons for complaint. Tell me of these.[77]

The city people responded saying:

> We are suffering because of night guard duty. The influential families, the noble and powerful houses, they can evade their obligations. We have appealed to the provincial intendants and to the county magistrates, but it is as if they have no ears. This is why we complain.[78]

And

It is wrong for clerks to falsify and take bribes. It's criminal that they turn the nightwatch into their private business venture. But complaints to higher officials are suppressed. This is why we complain.[79]

Zhang Jiayin is said to have listened to the crowd's lament and to have answered by advising those gathered to disperse:

This is a simple matter. Why do you allow momentary anger to risk the death of your entire family? I fully understand your difficulties and will speedily remedy them. I came to this place to spare your lives, to save you. . . . Listen to my words and disperse. Aside from ringleaders no one will be charged with any offense. But if you won't do this, go ahead and kill me. I am not a person who fears death.[80]

Zhang Jiayin's promises to meet the residents' demands caused the crowd to begin to scatter. But once a citizenry has risen up, it does not always know when to stop. Thus, Ding Shiqing and others, who did not believe Zhang Jiayin's replies, seem to have continued their agitation.[81]

Taking advantage of the night, rioting citizens again made a round of the many mansions of the rich where they joined in looting. Throughout the city, flames reflected in the night sky and the noise of wailing and shouting continued to fill the streets until dawn. Zhang Jiayin hurriedly put together an official proclamation advising the populace to accept his promises of improvements that would come once the uprising ended and threatening dire consequences if it continued. By morning the notice had been posted on the city's major thoroughfares. Nevertheless, the citizenry seemed unimpressed; copies of the proclamation were ripped up and looting grew even more fierce.[82]

Zhang Jiayin now thought that the only remaining alternative was to resort to force. He summoned the two leaders of the military insurrection that had broken out before the civilian uprising. Up to this point soldiers had watched the rioting without taking any action. Zhang requested that the two soldiers "lead your followers on our behalf and capture the rioters. If you are successful not only will your crimes be pardoned, but you will be granted an imperial reward."[83] The offer was a startling change of fortune for Ma Wenying and Yang

Tingyong. After the military protest, they had had themselves bound
and turned over to the provincial governor, and had resigned themselves to suffer death for their role in the protest. Their resignation was
such that they had already told their soldiers to "furnish us with coffins
and burial robes and provide for our wives and children."[84] They
strongly sympathized with Hangzhou's citizenry. Recall that they had
expressed this sentiment in stating that "many are the burdens endured
by civilians." But such sentiment was no match for Zhang Jiayin's
enticement. He succeeded in preventing the coalition of civilians and
soldiers, the outcome most feared by officialdom, and at the same time
brought the military into direct combat against the citizenry.

On the second day of the fifth month, street fighting spread to the
Caishi bridge, the Zhangjia bridge, the Guanxiang portal, the Chujia
embankment, and to virtually every avenue leading into Hangzhou
city. After this the civilian uprising was crushed. (See map Fig. 5.)
More than one hundred and fifty people, including Ding Shiqing, were
rounded up and of these, more than fifty were immediately beheaded
and their heads put on public display.[85] This incident, which "was virtually unprecedented as a civilian uprising in a major city," had lasted
four days from start to finish and ended with the executions.[86]

Were the promises given to the citizens at Wangxian bridge actually kept after the popular uprising was suppressed? This indeed seems
to have been the case. In implementing a sweeping reform, Zhang
Jiayin immediately had the night patrol labor service changed and
abandoned the *jianjia* tax.[87]

A FEW OBSERVATIONS

Two central points help explain why city residents had no other recourse than rebellion. The first is that popular resistance to the gentry
and officials who obstructed reforms and persecuted common citizens
served as motivation for attacks on the homes of specific persons and
wealthy merchants. The second reason, a demand that the state allow
personal freedom of movement, resulted in the tearing down of watchtowers and street gates which to Hangzhou's citizenry were the physical embodiments that symbolized their persecution.

The consciousness and actions of the general citizenry, during the
uprising, clearly expressed opposition to both the state's control and
"gentry rule." The gentry's attempt to control the night patrol labor
service, as seen in the words and deeds of the father and son Shen Jin
and Shen Pian, interfered with regional administration. Citizens in

Ctr for Cartographic Research and Spatial Analysis, Michigan State University

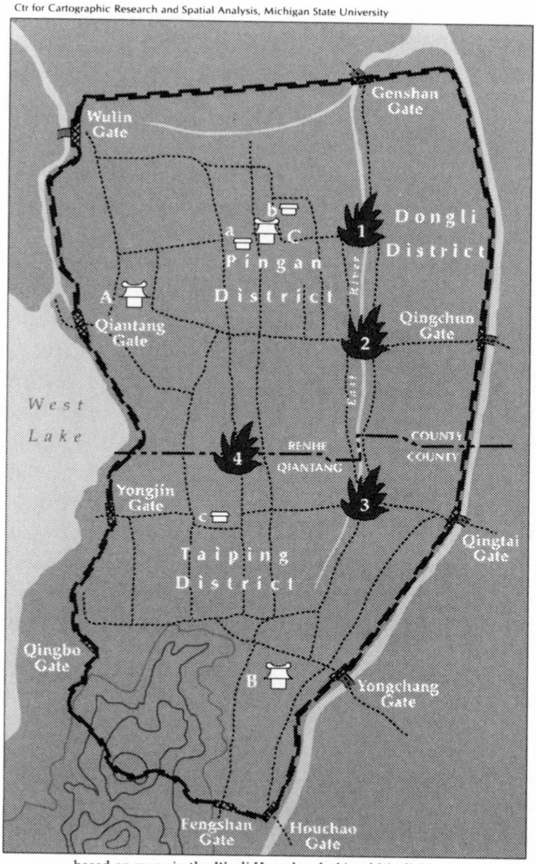

based on maps in the *Wanli Hangzhou fuzhi and Wanli Qiantang xianzhi.*

A Provincial Court
B Provincial Governor's Palace and Offices
C Examination Hall
a House of Ma Sancai
b House of Shen Pian
c House of Mo Rui

Sites of disturbances

1 Chujia Embankment
2 Caishi Bridge
3 Zhangjia Bridge
4 Guanxiangkou Street

Fig. 5. Ming dynasty Hangzhou

general responded to such actions by demonstrating their lucid awareness that "the assignment of city residents to labor service depends on
the intervention of the individual officials Chen, Chai, and Shen."[88]
"Chen" stood for Chen Sanmo, "Shen" for father and son Shen Jin,
and Shen Pian, and "Chai" was Chai Xiang, a *jinshi* who had taken his
degree in 1556 and had served successive terms in the Nanjing
Inspectorate.[89]

Mo Rui and Ma Sancai have also been identified as individuals
whose property was targeted for attack.[90] Mo Rui had already become
a *juren* holder by taking a first in the provincial examinations in 1573
and had passed the examinations leading to the *jinshi* degree in 1583.[91]
His role as a "scholar" enabled him to reach a position by 1582 from
which he could intervene in regional administration. Ma Sancai, a *jinshi* of 1546, had returned to his home after serving in various high-
ranking posts.[92] Once installed in his home district, he also participated in regional administration as a member of the local gentry. We
have already seen in discussion of the *jianjia* tax problem that he and
Chen Shan provided the government all manner of opinions on this
issue in 1578. Ma was also linked by marriage relations to Gao Gong,
who became a prime minister. The relationship was one in which his
son, Ma Yinghua, married Gao's daughter, and, to return the favor,
Gao's son took Ma Sancai's daughter. From this nexus of connections
the Ma family became one of Hangzhou city's famous lineages.
Although the patriarch, Ma Sancai, was dead by 1580, it is likely that
his son, Ma Yinghua, already a student-scholar at the capital (*tai
xuesheng*) and Gao Gong's son-in-law, continued to exert sufficient
power to influence local administration.

In other words, the five families identified: Shen, Chen, Chai, Mo,
and Ma comprised Hangzhou's local patrician elite, who occupied positions from which they could influence regional administration. It was
reported that during the Hangzhou uprising more than forty homes of
gentry families, who were materially or symbolically associated with
these five families, were attacked and set afire.[93] Another source goes
so far as to report that, ". . . of the gentry or great houses, not one
escaped destruction."[94]

The rioting city residents clearly understood whom they opposed.
Based on this understanding, they roamed the city targeting the homes
of individual elite families. The map of the Hangzhou popular uprising
shows us that the homes of Mo Rui, Shen Pian, Shen Jin, Ma Sancai,
and Ma Yinghua were among those which suffered attack.[95] Mo Rui's
home was in the vicinity of Guanxiangkou, but Ma Sancai's residence

was located to the west of the examination hall, some two kilometers to the northwest. Ma Sancai's home and that of Shen Pian were separated by the huge provincial examination hall building. The three homes of elite families were therefore each separated from one another by considerable distances. (See map of Hangzhou.) The map of the protest suggests that the fire attacks on gentry homes were not random, but were instead carried out against carefully selected targets.

In contrast to the damage done to the homes of unpopular gentry, the case of Chen Shan, whose home went through the uprising undamaged, is quite significant. Chen, who is credited with compiling the Wanli edition of the Hangzhou gazetteer, maintained a residence near that of Mo Rui. But Chen's property was not destroyed when Mo's home was attacked and burned. City residents who joined in the riot are said to have been particularly solicitous of Chen Shan's property, even "mutually warning one another, 'Be careful not to harm that place.'"[96] This example strongly suggests that what occurred was not simply a case of attacking whatever was at hand, but that the citizenry's action was controlled in an exceedingly orderly manner.

Hangzhou rioters attacked the homes of wealthy merchants as well as gentry property. But such actions were not just because the merchants were rich. In his speeches intended to instigate the crowds, Ding Shiqing detailed some of the reasons why merchant property was targeted for arson and destruction:

> The rich merchants dress in fine clothing and dine on delicious food. Embracing beautiful concubines they live in gorgeous mansions. With money they evade the labor service. [But] you people live in rented dwellings and even if you pay the *jianjia* tax there is no way to become exempt from [labor service]. [You] suffer cold through the long night, hold your empty stomach, and roam through the darkness. Not even the male slaves owned by rich merchants do [the kind of work forced upon you].[97]

It appears that wealthy merchants were also involved in the institutions of local administration and that they attempted to manipulate these organizations to their own advantage. For example, large numbers of Xin'an merchants had moved their residences to Hangzhou city. In cases in which the prefectural magistrate was of the same native place as a Xin'an merchant, it appears that extraordinary arrangements developed.[98]

If the merchant's aim was to ingratiate himself with local officials, then the most effective strategy was to curry favor with none other than the gentry. Why? Because the compass needle of regional administration spun according to their power. Wu Ding, a Hangzhou resident of the Jiajing period, provides the following commentary on gentry influence:

> The gentry in the countryside now receive noble ranks and high salaries and are regarded as among the ranks of high officials. They associate with local officials as if associating with equals. Just a casual word [from them] and anything is possible. Even though they attempt to monopolize for themselves all that is beneficial, no one dares dispute this. If they are warm to one, one can survive. But if they blow cold then one simply shrivels up and dies. If one works through officials to quash a suit brought by the [gentry], then a thousand *tael* bribe is paid and although clerks may be set bustling about, [nothing comes of the matter].
> . . . Those holding positions of local officials are captured by their own selfish concerns and try to gain favor [among the gentry].[99]

In Wu's words, the clerks who opposed Ding Shiqing's reforms were the very ones who, in accordance with earlier changes, were now paid in cash for night patrol service; they found that they could no longer collect bribes and thus were no more than "small fry." But the gentry, who monopolized regional administration and drew in enormous bribes, could be described as no less than "great whales." While the gentry, the equivalent of a group of specially privileged city residents, attempted to control city administration by intervention, they also tried to place other non-privileged city residents under their control. "Gentry rule" thus appears to have become an established feature of city life.[100]

What kind of awareness did Ding Shiqing and others like him have of "gentry rule?" He provided the following view when Shen Jin and Shen Pian obstructed the making of night patrol labor service into hired work:

> This is not the will of the officials. From the very beginning the obstructionist actions of various wealthy and powerful families have vexed the officials. If I thrash [the likes of the Shens] and

burn their homes, then even officials would probably feel good
to hear of this. Heed my words.[101]

According to his lights, regional officials and gentry were not identical. On the contrary, local officials suffered because of gentry monop-
olization of regional administration; for Ding and his supporters to ex-
tirpate the gentry represented a development that officialdom would
welcome.

The Confucian administrative principles of Chinese government
had always insisted on the "rule of avoidance," whereby an official was
never assigned to his home district in order to avoid precisely the kind
of influence at question in this case. Nevertheless, he could exert his
influence in his home district either through powerful friends and family members or after his retirement and through such privileges as exemption from service. Indeed, Ding appeared to believe such interfer-
ence, commonly called "gentry rule," which came between the state
and the people, created a barrier that divided like-minded people inside and outside the government. He thus argued that the barrier presented by gentry should be removed. The state should maintain direct
relations with its subjects. In short, his criticism of "gentry rule" was
consistent with the principle of unity of the sovereign and the people in
national administration. This view was not unique to Ding. Indeed, the
Hangzhou popular uprising is categorized in the *Ming Shi Lu*, the
annals of the Ming administration, under discussion of resentment
against the gentry.[102]

The nature of the Hangzhou uprising was entirely different from
the "popular rebellion against eunuchs" theme of research which has
formed the conventional image of the common people and their protests. Scholar officials frequently joined in the many anti-eunuch popular uprisings. They were accompanied by numerous leading merchants
and large numbers of the gentry who sympathized with and demonstrated their approval of the anti-eunuch popular uprisings. But in anti-
gentry uprisings the large merchants and the gentry were the targets of
attack. Thus, it is not surprising that, with regard to the Hangzhou
popular rebellion, contemporary intellectuals failed to show the degree
of sympathy or approval which they had demonstrated in support of
other popular protests. On the contrary, they lavishly praised Zhang
Jiayin for his splendid crushing of the unrest. Almost all of the many
contemporary sources for the Hangzhou uprising share this perspective. Similar sentiments toward the rebellion can be seen in the attitude of gentry scholars from the region around Hangzhou. In compil-

ing the *Dufu Liangzhe dingbian yusong lu*, a panegyric preface to the
record of General Zhang's success, the authors demonstrated their
utmost joy on the suppression of this popular uprising.[103] It is also reported that all classes of Hangzhou people resident in Beijing showed
exceptional happiness upon learning of Zhang Jiayin's pacification
of the Hangzhou uprising.[104] What these references make clear is that
the Hangzhou popular uprising, with its clear "anti-gentry" aim, was a
political action.[105]

For those who joined the Hangzhou uprising to remove "gentry
rule" and restore direct relations between state and people, direct ties
definitely did not mean that the state could impose restrictions that
would limit the freedom of personal movement. Indeed, the series of
urban reforms aimed at eliminating obligatory city labor service was
nothing more than demands for personal freedom. The relaxation of
the nighttime curfew was among the items on Ding Shiqing's list of reform demands.[106] This was because freedom of movement was essential for small-scale merchants and handicraft workers; their demands
for reform constituted an attempt to gradually slip from the state's
restrictions.

City residents who joined in the uprising have usually been presented in various historical sources as "idlers" or "vagabonds." Actually, there are no materials that clearly define their occupations. Nevertheless, it is most accurate to think of the protesters as weavers, dyers,
small-scale merchants, and petty traders. Supporting this postulation is
the fact that the Ping'an district in which Ding Shiqing had rented
lodgings was at that time known as "the street of the weavers."[107] If
weaving work was conducted here, it appears that dyeing workshops
were located along the East River which flowed nearby.[108] Furthermore, the Chujia embankment, along which street fighting spread
during the uprising, was also in the Ping'an district. Other sites of
street battles were all within local markets. For example, fighting took
place in the Caishi and Zhangjia bridge areas, which were both vegetable markets, and in the Guanxiangkou, a lane in which the cloth market had become established.[109] This general area was the center of
activity of petty merchants within Hangzhou city and of those traveling
back and forth from nearby farm villages in pursuit of profits. Many
people from these areas undoubtedly joined in the uprising.

It is also likely that the protest participants were those people who
lived in rented quarters. This is evident in Ding's call to arms, "You
are renters but are not in the least spared the *jianjia* tax."[110] Undoubtedly, one section of the rioters were commuting laborers of a

type similar to those seen in Suzhou. In short, the participants in the uprising were those who rented their homes; those weavers, dyers, small merchants, and petty traders, and others who earned just enough day by day to sustain themselves. This type of middle-to-lower strata required a great deal of freedom to maintain their occupational activities.

Restrictions such as night patrol duty or serving at watchtowers after a full day's work posed extraordinary obstacles to the conduct of the daily lives of weavers, dyers, small merchants, petty traders, and others in the middle-lower level of city residents. It is reported that individuals absent from labor duty were subject to heavy fines. For example, "Those who did not arrive in time for the third watch (from shortly before eleven P.M. to one A.M.) had to pay a penalty of one *tael*; those absent from the second (from around 8:40 P.M. to just before eleven P.M.) and fourth (from around one A.M. to a little after three A.M.) were fined five *qian*, half as much."[111] It was further said, "Those who served on night patrol were required to keep watch the entire night and at dawn they were obliged to make their report. [Until this was completed] they were not able to return to making a living even if it were high noon."[112] That neighborhood watchtowers and street gates were the first things destroyed by the citizens during the rebellion indicates just how serious and negative an influence the night patrols exerted on the livelihood of the local residents.

The forms employed in organizing the citizens should not be overlooked. On the night of the uprising, immediately upon its outbreak, the city fell to the control of the rioting citizenry. Thereafter, the firing of the homes of the gentry proceeded in an orderly controlled manner, the speed and accuracy of which is only slightly less than amazing. How was this accomplished?

The answer is that rioters relied on the existing and unchanged traditional *baojia* system of neighborhood organization. The orders that went out to make banners from clothes taken from the homes of gentry, to hang a lantern at each house, and to raise a banner at every tenth house demonstrate the household organization system in which ten families constituted a *jia*. In other words, elements of precisely what Jiang Liangdong pointed out as inconveniences of the Suzhou *baojia* system, such as lighting a lantern at every doorway as obligatory *baojia* practice, reappeared in the Hangzhou events.

The *baojia* system, a traditional organization, which the state had originally imposed from above, was officially justified as an organization concerned with the public welfare. But it had become a system that impeded the daily lives of city residents. Moreover, it was one in which the gentry and the rich did not participate while only renters and other common citizens filled out the *baojia* ranks. To add insult to injury, it also required the mobilization of common citizens for the protection of the homes and property of the gentry and the rich. In short, the *baojia* had been transformed to the point where it had become an implement of "gentry rule."

Rioting city residents in Hangzhou reversed the use of the *baojia*; they transformed it from a system that restricted their personal activities and turned it to their own ends. They used it to organize action against the rich and powerful instead of protecting the gentry— attacking and burning their homes and destroying the watchtowers that symbolized the commoners' subjugation.

CONCLUSION

The population increase, resulting from the massive migration from countryside to city, gave rise to new urban problems. In major cities like Hangzhou the old residential population had declined to less than half of the total living in the city.[113] It can be said that almost all of the new arrivals lived in rented dwellings, kept no reserves of food or cash in their homes, and only by working day and night somehow managed to make a living. For weavers, other commuting laborers, and petty merchants—people who had to work every day—freedom of activity was essential. These people sustained the development of trade and handicraft industry within the city and it was they who felt that the imposition of obligatory labor service, the street gates, and a curfew on travel on city streets after dark were unbearable fetters. The unpopularity of such restrictions propelled urban reforms in Jiangnan cities during the late Ming period. City residents forced the abolition of labor service obligations, caused street gates to be torn down, and compelled the relaxation of nighttime curfews. Of course, there were occasional instances in which the shift from civilian labor service to hired services resulted in a worsening of public security and the move from civilian labor service to hired service was reversed. Nevertheless, the trend at the end of the Ming period was toward the abolition of labor service.

The period when large numbers of middle-lower strata city residents began living in rented dwellings corresponded to the period when large numbers of specially privileged city residents, landlords, gentry, and others, also began to live within the city's boundaries. Although all were equally "city residents," their opposing interests soon became apparent. The clash of the groups that enjoyed special privileges and those that did not caused society to change in differing directions.

One direction was toward the elimination of "gentry rule" and more direct ties with the state. Middle and lower income city residents bore the burden of this movement. That a school teacher and like-minded supporters could sway the administration of a great city, that they could even temporarily enact reforms beneficial to the middle and lower strata or urban residents, such events heralded the opening of a new age and testified to the expanding political awareness of the middle and lower level strata of city residents.

The massive dimensions of "gentry rule" smothered the movement and frustrated reforms. At that time, the logic used to criticize "gentry rule" was the logic of state control inherent in principles concerning the unity of sovereign and people. Compared to the exceedingly clear criticism of the gentry, criticism of the state is not to be found.

That middle and lower strata city residents, who were also residential tenants, singled out the urban gentry as their antagonists in the struggle to overturn "gentry rule," suggests that the position of the urban residential tenant relative to his putative social superiors was comparable to the relationship of the rural peasant-tenant to the village landowner. In cities, the practice of renters refusing to pay housing rents spread; in the village, harvest rent resistance by peasants also arose.[114] It was said that "those people who own many dwellings in the city invariably hold much land in the countryside." On the issue of opposition to the gentry, it can be said that poorer city residents and peasant-tenants historically stood on the same ground.

Chapter 3
Urban Society in Late Imperial Suzhou

Paolo Santangelo

Translated by Adam Victor

Suzhou is located in the heart of the vast Yangzi flood plain, northeast of Lake Taihu, where the Jiangnan section of the Grand Canal meets the Wusong River. With a low altitude, mild climate, more than adequate rainfall, fertile soil, and waterways and lakes full of fish, the region attracted a growing population from the fourth century onwards.[1] By the Song period it was the most prosperous area in the empire.

The city itself is one of the oldest settlements in the Yangzi basin, dating back to the Kingdom of Wu the sixth century B.C.[2] It was said that even then the town had eight gates, four on land and four on water.[3] During the Qin dynasty the city was included in Guiji prefecture (*jun*), and after a succession of administrative changes, became the seat of a sub-prefecture (*zhou*) in the Sui. Promoted to a prefecture (*fu*) by the Song, then called "Pingjiang-fu," the town regained the name of Suzhou under the Ming. The number of counties (*xian*) in Suzhou prefecture was increased from seven to nine in the Qing dynasty, when the city became the capital for Jiangsu province.[4] The administrative centers for Wu, Changzhou, and Yuanhe counties and many offices, schools, and temples lay within the city walls.

After the splendors of the Song, when Suzhou was China's center of weaving, the city felt the effects of Mongol policies and suffered first from the civil war that brought the Ming to power, and later from heavy taxation by the Hongwu emperor. The first decades of Ming rule

were a time of economic and intellectual oppression, when Suzhou's
wealthiest and most influential families were deported to Nanjing, then
to Beijing, and the so-called four talents of Wu suffered greatly.[5] But
from the fifteenth century on, the city's economy improved, providing
former peasants with opportunities for employment. Zhou Chen
(1381–1453), governor of Jiangnan, noted that only in Suzhou were
immigrants so happy with their new lives that they did not miss their
home villages.[6]

The city's recovery was described by eyewitness Wang Yi, who had
remarked on the destruction of the early Ming period, when,
"Although there were no massacres, many people fled. . . . Villages
were deserted, there was little to eat; passing travelers were horrified
by what they saw." Wang had visited the city at regular intervals between 1436 and 1464, but, ". . . though people claimed that the city
had regained its former splendor, to me the place seemed anything but
thriving." Only during the reign of Zhenghua (1465–1487) did he find
Suzhou "once again its flourishing self." He described the reinvigo-
rated city:

> In quarters where houses are packed as tightly as tiles on a
> roof, all the way up to the city walls and canals, here and there
> rise pavilions and palaces. The streets are all a-bustle with
> carts and crossroads are clogged with traffic, while a multi-
> colored throng of citizens enliven the old alleys and taverns
> are full to the bursting point. Ships gliding between the hills
> and boats blossoming with beautiful singers seem like fish dart-
> ing through the green waves and red pavilions. The melody
> of musical instruments, of songs and of dances, interweaves
> with the hustle and bustle of the market.

Wang remarked on the economic health of the city, with its "production of silks for the Court, of stationery, of flowers and fruit, of
articles both precious and rare" which were now "constantly rising."
While, "[t]he arts of engraving, weaving and painting learned from
Zhejiang in the Song era, so long forgotten" were now revived. "And
as for scholars," he said, "those of Suzhou fear no rival. The city's
scribes are specialists in traditional styles . . . their expertise on the
Han, Tang and Song is without equal."[7]

In 1488, the Korean official, Ch'oe Pu, praised Suzhou's splendor
and renown, recognizing it as the cultural center of the empire, home
to a large number of scholars; it was a place where every kind of

manufactured article, humble or valuable, could be found, [and] the destination of all the most skillful craftsmen and wealthiest merchants. "At the port of Changmen, merchant ships hailing from Hubei and Fujian gather like clouds."[8]

A few centuries later, Oliphant compared the bustle of boats on Suzhou's Grand Canal to that of the busy alleyways around London's Fleet Street in variety and color.[9] According to official documents, ships carrying as much as 4,000 *dan* of goods could dock at Xushu-guan, outside Suzhou's walls.[10] Washed on two sides by the Grand Canal, the city was one of the world's greatest ports. Suzhou at this period was a city of prime importance not only in the administrative hierarchy but also in the "natural" hierarchy of manufacture and distribution.[11] But, although Suzhou was the empire's granary and one of the most important centers of silk production, it was dependent on food imported from neighboring provinces such as Hunan and Guangxi.[12] Its silk industry made extensive use of raw silk from nearby Huzhou and Songjiang and other regions of China.[13]

During the late Ming Suzhou's preeminence extended from trade to manufacturing to financial services. Taxes levied here were paid in silver derived from China's export trade; part of the wealth flowed back to the city with merchants' purchase of "southern goods" (*nanhuo*). Surplus wealth not skimmed off by taxes became so-called usurer merchants' capital, spent on luxury items. Money was spent on art, on culture, and occasionally on public amenities and welfare. In the words of Ximen, protagonist of *Jin Ping Mei*, "money adores movement and abhors lying inert, Heaven created money not to be hoarded in dark corners, but to be used by men."[14]

The last years of the Ming coincided with the beginning of a period of stagnation; waterways were neglected, adversely affecting transport and agriculture.[15] Investments were transferred from the land to commerce; contraction of agriculture spurred the process of urbanization. As in nearby Nanjing, the value of the land declined as taxes on it increased; peasants had little choice but to sell and seek their fortunes in the city. No one bought land any more, the wealthy preferred to invest in trade, and soon it fell into abandon.[16] The effect on Suzhou's food supply was disastrous, contributing to outbreaks of revolts in the city. According to Gu Yanwu, agriculture around Suzhou became a marginal occupation because compared with handicrafts, trade or salt, it was hard work in exchange for low income.[17]

Suzhou surrendered without resistance to Qing troops, only to rebel against the imposition of a new code of hair styles. Repression

worsened the city's decline until recovery began during the last decades of the seventeenth century. Agriculture recovered due to a concerted program of waterway maintenance, and rising prices for produce encouraged investments in land again.[18] The end of the naval
blockade, resolution of the civil war and the arrival of English, Dutch,
and French instead of Spanish and Portuguese traders were all prime
factors in the Qing economic recovery. Exports of Chinese goods, including silks manufactured in Suzhou, cotton and tea, all increased,
and the city became known even to foreigners who had never visited it
as, ". . . the school of the greatest artists, the best known scholars, the
richest merchants, the best actors, most nimble acrobats, and also the
home of delicately made women with tiny feet. It rules Chinese tastes
in all matters of fashion and speech and is the meeting place of the
richest pleasure-seekers and gentlemen of leisure in China."[19]

Economic crisis of the late eighteenth century sent Suzhou back
into the downward spiral it had experienced in the last years of the
Ming; problems in state finances and competition from Shanghai and
Canton in manufacturing and commerce led to the neglect of water
control and financial decline.[20] To make matters worse, concentration
of land and water resources in the hands of big landowners began in
the mid-eighteenth century and gathered pace.[21]

Endemic nourishment problems suffered by poor urban residents
were recorded in the chronicles of the period. Hui Shiqu (1671–1741)
opposed a policy of reducing grain prices because such a measure
worsened the situation by keeping rice merchants away and ultimately
drove prices up.[22] Even so, Robert Fortune, who visited the city in the
1840s, recorded that "everything remarkable came from [Suzhou]; fine
pictures, fine carved-works, fine silks, and fine ladies."[23]

THE LIFE OF THE GENTRY

Our knowledge of the life of the gentry in the later imperial period is
mostly based on the achievements of the upper classes in Suzhou, a
city whose refined culture was admired by all. Gu Yanwu, a native of
the region, wrote in his *Historical compendium of geography*:

> The residents of Suzhou are intelligent and accomplished
> in traditional pursuits and skillful in imitating arts and crafts of
> days gone by. When they reproduce calligraphy or a picture,
> or fashion a sacrificial vase or tripod it is impossible to tell the
> copy from the original. In the realm of good taste, their au-

thority is absolute throughout the empire; what in Suzhou is considered elegant is considered elegant elsewhere, and everybody scorns what is scorned here as vulgar. Here, it is agreed by all, the true value of each object is appreciated. The furnishings, the decoration, . . . even stones and lengths of bamboo are fashioned into objects of great value, like Lu Zigang's jade, Ma Xiaoguan's fans [or] Zhao Liangbi's blades.[24]

Thanks in part to the prosperity of the area and to its economic and cultural development, Suzhou prefecture had one of the highest numbers of *jinshi* in the empire—a distinction it achieved despite the fact that a large proportion of its human resources were employed in trade and manufacturing. The prefecture gave birth to famous scholars and artists, including Zhu Yunming (1461–1527), Xu Zhenqing (1479–1511), Tang Yin (1470–1524), and Wen Zhenming (1470–1559), who by force of their heterodox ideas and original behavior left a lasting mark on fifteenth and sixteenth century cultural history.

The city's palaces and gardens served as premises for conversations among erudite men and high officials. Wealthy patrons, landowners, and rich merchants led a refined and luxurious existence, collecting rare books and works of art, immersing themselves in the company of writers and poets. One illustrious citizen was the expert administrator, Cao Yin (1658–1712), superintendent of the imperial textile factories, who debated with brilliant intellectuals of the caliber of You Tong, Han Tan, Peng Dingqiu, and Jiang Chenying. There were innumerable private libraries, including one called "The bell of the fragrant orchid" belonging to Zhu Huan, as well as libraries within the academies, temples, and monasteries. Suzhou's role in the annals of the well-known academies of Donglin and Fuzhe cannot be forgotten. Nor can that of circles of scholars, meeting formally or informally in the many villas surrounded by exquisite gardens, located in the countryside or on one of the Taihu islands, far from disturbances.

The home of Xu Qianxue (1631–1694), on Dongtingshan Island, often hosted Yan Roju, Gu Zuyu, Hu Wei, and Huang Yuji during their collaboration compiling the *Da Qing yitong zhi*. Hui Zhouti, on the other hand, built his "Library of the red soya" in the city's Yuanhe district, where he soon established a school of study famous for its interpretation of the Confucian classics. Hui Zhouti and his son Hui Shiqu (1671–1741) and grandson Hui Dong (1697–1758) looked after the School of Suzhou or Wu, carrying on the teachings of Gu Yanwu on textual and philological studies.[25] During the Kangxi reign a group of typographers founded a private academy for "the Veneration of Virtue."

The refinement of taste and the nonconformity of many circles of Suzhou was a source of alarm for orthodox groups, who recommended a return to Confucian studies and a strict code of morality. Tang Bin (1627–1687) warned that "although Suzhou enjoys high levels of culture and is more refined than many other parts of the empire, morals, in their original purity, are not wholly applied. Nothing is more important in a sound education than the Classic of Filial Piety. . . ."[26]

During the Ming and Qing eras many new gardens, built by rich local officials or by other court dignitaries were added to those opened under the Song and Yuan.[27] Designed by painters and architects, the fame of these gardens lay in the harmony of artificial hills and ornamental lakes, plants, small buildings, rocks, bridges, and paths, all of *chan* inspiration.

Social life was busy; visits paid and received were interspersed with poetry readings and gatherings of scholars.[28] There was no shortage of entertainments in Suzhou, a city renowned for its hedonism. Martino Martini, in his *Novus Atlas Sinensis* remarked that the pleasures of love and wine were expressed at the highest levels, in particular on the "Flower boats," which were more splendid than the most ornate palaces.[29]

The upper echelons of society did not, however, indulge exclusively in these pastimes. The gentry ran charitable organizations and looked after the maintenance of roads and bridges, the construction of schools, walls, and ditches.[30] They attended official and religious ceremonies, sometimes at the Confucian temple located in a park south of the city. Some chose to renounce a career in administration in favor of a freer, more independent life. These "urban hermits" (*shiyin*) represented scholars who preferred the well-being of their communities over political careers. Frequently, the gentry arbitrated in conflicts of interest between the state and the local population. It was not always possible to avoid tension and unrest.

Naturally, the greatest threats arose in periods of transition, when the scholars' position of political responsibility was called into question. The Ming-Qing transition was one such period. First the high-handedness of eunuchs and then the new Manchu leadership created chaos; in addition there were various local difficulties like the infamous "lament of the temple" incident of 1661.[31] Examples of the vicissitudes that befell the scholar-elite were the fates of Gu Yanwu and his relative Gu Bingqian in 1629.[32]

INDUSTRY AND TEXTILES

Textiles dominated Suzhou's economy. Lin Zexu (1785–1850) wrote: "Fifty to sixty percent of Suzhou's men and women earn their living by spinning or weaving."[33] A memorial from Lang Tinji, governor of Jiangxi, dated September 27, 1712, throws light on the subject. This note, drafted to champion the cause of Cao Yong as a future superintendent of the Nanjing Imperial Factories, mentions some important representatives of sections of the population involved in textile manufacture and distribution. The following categories, although referring to people from the Nanjing area, hold true for Suzhou. At the top of the list are middlemen, representatives of the manufacturer's guild, followed by owners of the spinning and weaving workshops, textile craftsmen, local raw silk guilds, and finally merchants who supplied raw silk from Zhejiang.[34]

Many local gentry families were directly or indirectly linked with these industrial activities; thus, members of the gentry were engaged as overseers and managers for the Imperial Textile Factories. It was common knowledge that the gentry enjoyed a series of political, financial, social, and penal privileges. At the beginning of the dynasty, Chen Youming, special superintendent of the Suzhou Imperial Factories, subsequent to its restoration, drew up a list of obligations concerning not only the richest textile owners but also members of the gentry.[35] As we will see, these obligations lay in the supply of raw silk destined for weavers and the delivery of the finished products to the factories. We may presume that these posts were filled by members of gentry families because weaving was the region's most profitable economic sector. One source reveals that spinning, the most widespread occupation, was even practiced in the homes of scholars and officials.[36]

Such was the renown of the quality of Suzhou's products that "its silk was worn throughout the empire."[37] From the end of the Ming dynasty onwards, the weaving and finishing of cotton was added to the processing of silk: "The fame of Suzhou cotton products spread throughout the empire from the area opposite Heaven's Gate (Changmen) where the goods were made."[38] At the conclusion of the Ming dynasty, no fewer than six different types of weaving machinery were on sale in the city.[39] Economic activity required a good deal of capital from merchants, entrepreneurs, independent artisans, and the state itself, yielding profits to fuel Suzhou's wealth, refined culture, and entertainments. The hundreds of thousands of people—from workers to businessmen—employed in the textile sector formed a hub around which the rest of society revolved: peasants, gentry, officials, and eunuchs alike.[40]

The textile industry conditioned local customs: on *Xiaoman* day, in May, the streets were thronged with peasants come from nearby towns and surrounding countryside to sell "new raw silk" (*mai xinsi*); friends and relatives from different villages gathered together, and cakes, fruit, fish, pigs feet, and flowers were sold in the streets. This particular festival came at the end of a period of intense work in the fields for peasants and farmers, and constituted a moment of close interaction between urban and rural areas.[41]

While silk production was concentrated in the eastern part of Suzhou, the western portions of Wu district provided a home for other crafts and trades in which inhabitants of Suzhou excelled. In the Qianlong period (1793) there were upwards of thirty paper mills, employing more than three hundred workers from all corners of the province.[42] There were at least a hundred candle factories and a multitude of metal and leather workshops employing craftsmen from Wuxi and Nanjing respectively.[43] Suzhou had important shipyards, and was famous for its jade and jewelry workshops.[44] In one of his accounts, Gu Yanwu notes that carpenters, brickmakers, builders, and stonecutters hired workers from other regions to cope with the burgeoning demand because immigrants accepted lower wages than local people.[45] And, according to Zhang Dai (1597–1684), even poor artisans could get great wealth and social advancement in various fields of production.[46]

THE IMPERIAL FACTORIES

The Imperial Textile Factories provided the backdrop for a large slice of the city's economic activity. In the Ming era, every artisan was in theory enrolled in a special register, and therefore had to do a certain quantity of work for the state, whether he lived permanently in the area of the factory or had to commute to the place of work.[47] Textile workers were organized according to a strict division of labor, based on each worker's level of skill and specialization. In addition to the superintendent's important role, members of rich local families involved in textiles, called "*tangzhang*," were assigned technical, financial, and managerial responsibilities on behalf of the manufacturers.[48]

From the second half of the fifteenth century onwards, the technical superiority of Suzhou's work force over smaller textile centers (in Jiangxi, Henan, Shandong, Hunan, and Hubei), accelerated the dominant position of Jiangsu production, regardless of the output of the Imperial Factories. The Imperial Factories, a collection of factories and

offices (located in the city center, east of the Tianxin Bridge in Changzhou district) administered by the ministries of finance and public
works, were refounded at the start of the Ming dynasty, continuing an
ancient tradition. Under the name of "Office of Weaving and Dyeing,"
the manufacturers supplied the court and government with the high
quality textiles required for international relations, national politics,
and the needs of the imperial family. The Imperial Factories, now
under the control of eunuchs, fell into decline as the Ming dynasty
weakened; more and more often, production quotas were met by
workers doing their share of hours for the state at home rather than in
the manufacturer's factories.[49] A system of contracting became popular, in which the wealthier textile owners, among those figuring on
local registers, assumed those responsibilities previously covered directly by the Imperial Factories; they assigned work quotas and often
had to pay out in advance.[50]

The new Qing dynasty restored and improved the Imperial Fac-
tories, in the process removing the eunuchs' centuries-old influence.
On the premises of the old "Office of Weaving and Dyeing" arose the
Northern Textile Factories, so-called to distinguish it from the new
Southern Factories, located in larger premises in southeast Suzhou (in
Yuanhe county, inside the palace formerly belonging to Zhao Gui,
Count of Jiading).[51] Under the guidance of the Office for the Imperial
Household, the excesses of the late Ming period were eradicated,
eunuchs gave way to *baoyi* in the management of the manufacturers,
and normal working conditions were reestablished in the factories.
Moreover, between 1485 and 1562 more and more artisans began to
follow a system whereby the *corvée* was replaced by direct payment;
the Qing abolished the whole system of hereditary professions and
registers.[52]

However, it would be a mistake to think that with these changes
the old "contracts" and extortions came to an end. Indeed, the protest
of the wealthy textile families prove the contrary.[53] In theory, the new
system was one in which the Imperial Factories purchased silk yarn
spun by peasants at the source of production, and then distributed it
among craftsmen employed in government mills.[54] In practice, however, finished products were often bought directly from silk merchants
or from artisans who worked at home, and not in Imperial Factories.[55]

The Superintendents of Imperial Factories effectively controlled all
activities relating to weaving, either by supervising guilds and regulating "private" businesses, or by issuing certificates granting manufacturing and trade licenses.[56] Although rarely entering into direct contact

with producers and craftsmen, the Superintendents kept up contacts with all sectors of economic and social life in the prefecture and throughout the province through professional guilds, wholesalers, and financial groups. All workers, from spinners to dyers (who often came from nearby Shanghai), were hired through their respective guilds or intermediaries (*hanghui, yahang*). The Imperial Factories generally purchased silk spun in Huzhou prefecture from wholesalers and brokers (*sihang*), and traded with big merchants (*dushang*) from Suzhou and Songjiang to secure important business.

If, on the one hand, the Imperial Factories stimulated production by placing large orders for high quality merchandise produced using advance techniques, on the other hand they were often agents of state exploitation and forced labor.[57] The private sector, producing for the marketplace, was a well-established alternative (if not antithesis) to the state sector, providing the main source of income for many local families. A memorial quoted in the *Veritable Annals* observed that "the poor dedicate themselves to weaving in order to make ends meet." Again, "poor workers depend on weaving for their livelihood,"[58] while local histories from nearby Songjiang prefecture state that, "weavers are wholly dependent on this activity for their nourishment."[59] This state of affairs was equally true for rich manufacturing businesses and for wholesale traders in silk, but it applied above all to cotton.[60]

State pressure on textiles probably accelerated the process of privatization, commercialization, and specialization among craftsmen.[61] The shift in control of the textile sector meant that taxes and obligations to the state fell squarely on small and medium-sized workshops, often ironically called, "rich families," while the more prosperous managed to avoid these burdens through a variety of means, sometimes by using people from orphanages or hospices to stand in their stead. If rich families were registered as textile workers, it was often a trick to avoid heavier taxation.[62]

MERCHANTS AND GUILDS

Merchants, particularly numerous in Suzhou, enjoyed the same privileges as their counterparts across Ming and Qing China—contrary to traditional Confucian attitudes. In Suzhou many of them succeeded in accumulating vast fortunes, either due to the many opportunities to be found in such an important trading center, or through borrowing and financial speculation.

Usury was so common that it was frequently practiced in the name of the Imperial Factories; according to Sun Pei, the manufacturers were forbidden in 1684 to issue loans in order to combat the well-rooted practice whereby certain powerful citizens of Suzhou, presenting themselves as agents of the Imperial Factories, took advantage of the poor by offering high interest loans, which often resulted in the ruin of the debtors.[63] An economic crisis afflicted many traders during the transitional period between the Ming and Qing dynasties, while others used the crisis to their own profit, as did Zhu Youming of Hangzhou. Son of a textile worker, Zhu began his career in his older brother's trading company. During the stagnation caused by the Manchu invasion, his speculations resulted in a hundredfold increase in his wealth.[64]

A great number of merchants came to Suzhou from all parts of the empire to buy textiles and, to a lesser extent, to sell goods produced in other regions. Qin Shan describes how big merchants from Hebei arrived in Suzhou with huge sums of capital after long journeys on mule or horseback, having either dragged their wagons over frozen rivers or transported them on the Yangzi ferries, heedless of the wind and rain.[65] Merchants from Shandong set up *Jidong* and *Jining* guilds in Shengzezhen, a nearby market town in Wujiang county. The majority of merchants who traveled to Suzhou during the Qing period hailed from Fujian, shuttling between the city and other provinces. Merchants from Huizhou, among the principal exporters of local silk and importers of foreign goods, played a crucial role in Suzhou's transformation into a flourishing marketplace from the middle of the Ming dynasty on.[66] In 1809 these merchants, together with counterparts from Ninguozhou, established the Huining guild in Shengzezhen, not to be confused with the Anhui guild founded in Suzhou in 1867. By the second half of the Qing dynasty, they, along with others from Hubei and Zhejiang, controlled the Suzhou grain markets.[67]

Equally well known were the Ningbo merchants, some of whom remained in Suzhou with their families, where they set up large trade emporiums. One of these, a certain Sun Chunyang, set himself up in business at the end of the sixteenth century after unsuccessfully sitting for the examinations. Beginning with a small workshop situated in Suzhou's trade quarters, his business soon expanded into a huge bonded warehouse situated in a building that would have done a government office proud. This warehouse developed into six stores, each one specialized in a particular type of merchandise, from continental products to overseas goods, salted meats to condiments and spices, sweets to candles. Such was this man's name that even the Qing Impe-

rial Household obtained its provisions from his warehouse. Earlier, at
the end of the Ming dynasty, a dandy such as Zhang Kui boasted of
using nothing but Sun Chunyang's lamps and candles.[68] Inside the
warehouse, clients would first pay the cashiers, from whom they
would obtain a receipt redeemable for the product of their choice.
Every day, warehouse administrators drew up accounts which at the
end of the year formed an annual total. This great warehouse retained the same ownership and prestige for most of the Qing dynasty.
Around 1840, Qian Yong exalted the establishment's efficiency and
prosperity.[69]

Merchants from farther afield, including Muslims (Uigers), almost
certainly based themselves in Suzhou. Their presence is referred to in a
treatise on customs and traditions in Suzhou, written by the poet and
painter Gu Lu at the beginning of the Ming period. On the subject of
the festival held on the fifteenth day of the third lunar month (honor-
ing of the god of money), the author noted that these merchants did
not eat pork; when sacrifices were made they were offered liquor and
beef.[70]

The fact that Suzhou was such a vast marketplace meant that
merchandise from all over China was readily available (goods from
Sichuan, Guangdong, Yunnan, Guizhou, Fujian, Jiangxi, Zhejiang
and Shandong). "West of the Feng Bridge cereals and pulses are on
sale."[71] Suzhou's streets were crowded with shops selling foreign
goods, leather articles, textiles, clothes, jewelry, medicine, and with
taverns, tea shops, and theaters. In 1688 there were at least one hundred and thirty-two wood merchants; in 1710 there were seventy-nine
goldsmiths and jewelers; soon after 1820 there were over a hundred
shops selling lamps and candles.[72] Gu Gongxie noted that such a concentration of rich merchants provided a boost for the local economy,
giving rise to a flourishing tertiary sector: restaurants, theaters, and
other entertainments which provided an honest living for hundreds of
thousands of people.[73] The most impressive shops in the city were
naturally those selling textiles, some of which took up two floors and
had a number of entrances.[74]

The biggest merchants possessed vast fortunes, and wherever
they traveled they did so with hundreds of thousands of silver *taels*.
They generally dealt through intermediaries for silk transactions and
through local guilds for other business. Guilds regulated bargaining
and opposed people who, though not guild members, acted as intermediaries.[75] Middlemen often depended on interprovincial merchants
for their income as if they were directly employed, so great was the

difference in wealth between themselves and their clients. But it was also true that merchants were forced to go through intermediaries, some of whom held a kind of local monopoly. As described in an inscription inveighing against abuses of the South Ditch, these intermediaries would "fall like flies" on ships arriving with goods from other provinces.[76] Since more often than not they had no direct contact with producers, interprovincial merchants, coming to purchase goods, had to conduct transactions through intermediaries.

Many craftsmen, workers, and merchants resident in Suzhou were immigrants from other parts of the empire. A portion of workers whose job it was to distribute silk were originally from Hangzhou; these merchants had their own guild, which distributed textiles all over China, and their own market near the city's northwestern gate.[77]

Guilds could either be predominantly trade or craft oriented, or both. Generally composed of craftsmen and merchants, they occasionally included civil servants too. The Jiangxi guild, founded in 1684 by merchants from Jiangxi who worked in Suzhou, is a good example of one such organization. In order to accommodate Jiangxi merchants, trading in items as varied as paper, pottery, textiles and foodstuffs, as well as to look after government officials from Jiangxi, the guild moved to larger and larger premises.[78] From the end of the Ming dynasty right through the Qing era, during a period of wide-ranging economic change, guilds sprang up to cater for every conceivable occupation, providing security and guarantees for their members—even for beggars and prostitutes.[79]

On the whole, the *huiguan* grouped together merchants or craftsmen who originated from a common native-place, such as the Jiangxi organization mentioned above. In contrast to Beijing, where most guilds were formed by candidates for examination, Suzhou *huiguan* were predominantly for commerce.[80] *Gongsuo* guilds, on the other hand, were generally organizations of a professional nature; examples were the *Zhifang gongsuo* guild for paper manufacture and the candlemakers guild, *Dong Yue*.

Over the Ming and Qing periods there were over forty *huiguan* and one-hundred-and-thirty *gongsuo* at Suzhou.[81] As well as promoting specific economic objectives, the guilds performed a statutory series of activities pertaining to religion, recreation, and welfare.[82] The Suzhou guild of silk merchants of Hangzhou origin, Qianjiang *huiguan*, which included both professional trade and geographic origin categories (*tongxiang tongye*), is a typical example of such a corporation. Founded in 1758 thanks to substantial contributions by wealthy merchants, the guild's objective was to promote the commercial activities of its members, offering warehouses for storing goods and temporary accommodations for merchants. The headquarters, as we see in an inscription from 1776, served as a site for ceremonies intended to strengthen the guild's unity and provide a place for members to socialize. Guandi, the god of war, was venerated there, as was Wenchang, the god of literature.[83] Each guild revered a divinity, patron either of a particular place or profession, to whom prayers and sacrifices were offered up. Town functionaries were often invited to participate in these ceremonies. The plasterers and carpenters guild worshipped Lu Ban, while the guild of doctors and apothecaries considered the "Three Sacred Emperors," renowned in the mythology of popular religion, to be their protectors.[84]

Within the larger context of guilds—that of regulating persons occupied in any given activity—disputes were resolved at meetings and ceremonies in order to avoid competition between men plying the same trade and coming from the same town. Guilds demanded absolute compliance with their internal rules and regulations. In 1872, a Suzhou goldsmith was bitten to death by a hundred fellow workers as a punishment for having broken the guild's rules regarding the hiring of apprentices.[85]

There were cases of conflict of interest between guilds and laws of the state, particularly with regard to rules prohibiting "market obstacles." On these occasions a guild would find its requests denied, as happened to the sandalwood guild when it denounced out-of-town merchants for selling wooden mirror frames in and around Suzhou in 1895. The guild's complaint was found to be without grounds in as much as the corporation was not, by law, allowed a monopoly in this specific sector.[86] Changes in government economic policy towards the end of the Qing period spelled an erosion of the guilds' influence along with a reduction of their privileges and powers.[87]

Almost all guilds carried out a series of charitable projects for the benefit of guild members who found themselves in dire straits. The corporation of traders in foodstuffs, the Liangxi *gongsuo*, founded in Suzhou at the beginning of the 1800s, supported members in financial difficulties, provided medical assistance for the infirm, and looked after burial of the dead. An 1878 inscription in Shengzezhen, belonging to the guild of rice merchants, shows that it, too, fulfilled a similar set of obligations towards its indigent members.[88] An 1895 inscription shows that the corporation of beauticians offered help to invalids, the aged, sick people without families, and provided funerals for deceased members who had no descendants.[89]

A further fundamental feature of the guilds was their cooperation with the state in a number of areas. Guilds collaborated with the authorities in fixing prices, taking responsibility for overseeing equity in conditions of sale and quality of merchandise. In addition they protected professional ethics, maintained standards of workmanship, collected taxes on trade, and registered itinerant merchants.[90] However, it must be noted that some guilds were simply exploitative organizations, using the veneration of a particular divinity or the provision of services for a given group of craftsmen as a cover to extort money from weaker groups.

THE JIHU

Information on the urban population is incomplete and partial, in as much as primary sources mainly refer to fiscal affairs or matters of public order. The term *jihu*, for example, which literally meant "textile families," was originally a fiscal term referring to families whose names featured in special registers instituted by Hongwu.[91] The so-called superior families or rich families (*shanghu*, *fuhu*), who were more prosperous, were the object of special attention on the part of fiscal authorities. Beyond having to produce a certain quantity of merchandise for the state, these families were given technical and managerial responsibilities, control over the award of contracts by tender, and roles such as that of foreman (*tangzhang*) in factories belonging to the Imperial Manufacturers, a position that entailed buying raw materials and managing labor. Until the beginning of the Qing dynasty the term *jihu* indicated rich families commissioned by the Imperial Factories to produce certain products.[92] From the beginning of the Qing on, the meaning of the term expanded to refer to craftsmen and workshops that either worked independently or for big companies.[93] The *jihu* were formally differentiated from ordinary employees of the Imperial Factories in that they were allowed a certain degree of independence.[94] But the term always indicated a craftsman in a private sector textile workshop as opposed to one who merely worked in exchange for a wage. All the same, at the start of the Qing dynasty the *jihu* were still listed in registers, which meant they depended in some way on government offices. As one source noted, "the population of eastern Suzhou to a large degree works in textiles, and the names of these textile firms are registered in government ledgers."[95]

At least until the eighteenth century the *jihu* were the production
units that made up family-run textile firms of varying size, owning one
or more domestic looms. These units accounted for the majority of
Suzhou's textile output. Richer *jihu* owned their own workshops
(*jifang*) and hired workers, and though some of the poorer craftsmen
worked for their richer neighbors, most worked for themselves.[96] Most
of these workshops were located in Suzhou's "industrial" zone, in the
east and especially northeast sectors of the city.[97] Here the streets were
lined with textile workshops whose enterprise was renowned throughout the empire.[98] According to one source in the Tongzhi period
(1862–1875), the *jihu* sold finished textiles.[99] Later they were said to
have been given raw materials from big merchant companies, for
whom they produced merchandise on their own premises, often hiring
workers to help complete their orders.[100]

According to Chen Zuolin, there were some very big trading companies, known as "accounting companies" (*zhangfang*) which, rather
than manufacturing themselves, regulated production, commissioning
work from the smaller workshops and independent craftsmen, providing raw materials and tools and paying by piecework according to the
putting-out system.[101] Finished products were often marked with the
brand of the accounting company that had commissioned the work.
These companies dealt principally with the business side of things,
while output was catered by a number of small workshops.[102] Despite
objectives and functions distinct from those of the Imperial Factories,
these companies often resorted to similar methods of organizing
production.[103] Thanks to a high degree of control over the textile market, they were able to buy up raw cotton from peasants or through intermediaries at very low prices.[104]

The big interprovincial traders and textile merchants always dealt
with guilds or intermediaries and never directly with the *jihu*, who
in turn never sold directly to wholesalers. The many intermediaries
charged a commission amounting to two or three *jiao* for every *pi* of
cloth sold.[105] Paradoxically, it was precisely the government policy of
limiting the number of looms per production unit to two, designed to
protect the interests of small factories, that helped the *zhangfang* to
control the market without ever having to become directly involved in
production. These big merchants were also aided by an increase in international trade which, in pushing up the price of raw silk, hastened
the process of concentration. The *jihu* of Suzhou subcontracted a
portion of their work to "delegated workshops." The stability of the
hierarchical relationships between the three levels of the production

MARKET ORGANIZATION FOR TEXTILE PRODUCTION

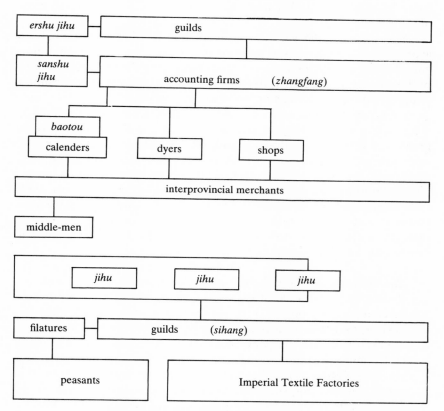

Fig. 6. Chart of Textile Production Organization

structure was reflected in local names for each tier; the advance company was known as "oldest uncle" (*dashu*), the workshop as "second
uncle" (*ershu*) and the delegated workshop as "third uncle" (*san-
shu*).[106] On occasion these relationships were formalized in written
contracts consonant with the regulations and practices of local
guilds.[107] The production and commerce of cotton required further
stages arranged between owners, dyers, and calenderers.

With the arrival of westerners in the second half of the nineteenth
and the first decades of the twentieth century, Shanghai and Canton
came to the fore as trading ports for foreigners, who did not deal

directly with accounting companies, from whom the orders filtered down to local traders, because negotiations took place through compradors.

The size of a *jihu* varied from workshop to workshop, though on average each one possessed three or four looms. Over time, the number of these workshops varied in accordance with the size and mobility of the market, particularly after cotton became a widespread consumer durable and cotton production overtook that of silk.[108]

Certainly, Suzhou and many smaller textile centers benefited as the result of development of and specialization in the manufacture of textiles. Suzhou, in addition to being the biggest producer of silk, became one of the major centers for merchants in textiles from Songjiang prefecture and from other provinces. It also became the most important location for the dyeing and calendering of cotton cloth, two typically urban industrial activities.[109] The trend towards urbanization based on textile production was a boon to smaller towns in the Suzhou prefecture. Thus, the story of Shengzezhen, in Wujiang county, is proverbial. Local histories relate:

> The weaving of damask and silk was, under the Song and Yuan, the prerogative of citizens of the administrative center, Suzhou. It was only during the Hongwu and Xuande eras (1425–1435) that local people began progressively to dedicate themselves to the weaving of silk, often making use of the craftsmen of Suzhou. By the end of the Chenghua and Hongzhi eras (1465–1505) the town achieved a mastery of the activity of weaving, such that all those living within a radius of forty or fifty miles around Shengze and Huangxi earned a living producing silks and damasks; the rich employed other craftsmen while the poor wove for themselves and put their children to work weaving. Those women who were not busy weaving spent all day and night spinning, and boys and girls from ten years of age on earned a living in this manner, working all day and all night.[110]

In one of his short stories, Feng Menglong described the prodigious growth of a *jihu* from this area. Over a period of ten years a husband and wife, poor farmers who raised silkworms, managed to create a large and prosperous textile factory.[111] The turnover from the sale of silk was so great that even after deducting the very high taxes levied, manufacturers always made a profit. Tang Zhen (1630–1704) described

Suzhou's importance as a silk production center, noting the huge profits.[112]

During the Qianlong era there were thirty thousand looms in Nanjing, which would seem to confirm the figures calculated by Shang Yue of around fifteen thousand looms and three or four hundred big dyeworks at Suzhou.[113] At the turn of the century, Suzhou had around fifty big accounting companies, each one running between one and two hundred looms.[114] In the same period, there were around a thousand small workshops in Suzhou, each one with an average of three or four employees.

In spite of contentions between *jihu* and their employees, some of which have been immortalized in inscriptions, relations between the two tended to be paternalistic. This can be judged from a number of expressions which exalt their mutual interests and propose the idea of common origins of all textile workers in Suzhou. It is to this purpose that an expression written at the end of the Ming dynasty extols the pride of belonging to the ancient lands of Wu, "We, citizens of Wu."[115]

Craftsmen employed in workshops were divided by specialization. They were generally paid by the day. Local histories and other sources confirm that although most production took place in the home, from the end of the sixteenth century on, it was common in Suzhou for a "semi-free" workforce to be hired; a large number of former peasants, having learned textile skills, were employed on a long-term basis.[116] Of those who could not afford to purchase the raw materials necessary for production, some worked at home on commission, while others went to work at the *jihu*. If a craftsman working at a *jihu* was dissatisfied with working conditions, it was not difficult for him to find work in another establishment. Likewise, workshop owners had little difficulty finding labor to fill gaps in the work force. In certain parts of the city— one for each specialization—large groups of unemployed workers gathered at dawn in the hope of finding a day's work. Some of these were seasonal workers, others were peasants who supplemented their incomes by working in the city from time to time. Some of these prospective workers had neither land nor means and maintained themselves on what work they could find in town.[117] People who were unable to find work over long periods sometimes joined gangs who roved the streets and lived by robbery, posing a threat to public order.[118]

The Imperial Factories frequently made use of the *jihu* either directly or indirectly, by ordering them to produce a certain quantity of textiles, or by taking on *jihu* craftsmen full or part-time. Each *jihu* was registered at the office of the Imperial Factories in categories based on their economic potential.[119] The wealthiest were placed in command of groups of workers fulfilling their work quota for the state. They managed the work, handed out contracts, and were responsible for both the quantity and quality of the final product. Frequently they had to provide yarn for weaving, pay out costs in advance, devise the work schedule, and send the finished products to the capital.[120] Such persons were known as *jiatou*, *tangzhang*, or *jigun*. As the duties imposed were extremely onerous, they tried as hard as possible to avoid being called up. Most state orders were placed at low prices, in line with the ancient fiscal tradition of so-called harmonious purchases (*hemai*), under which suppliers and workshops were required to sell specific goods at political prices.[121] Sometimes, however, the *jihu* succeeded in turning these duties to their own advantage, using the Imperial Factories funds for their own purposes, delaying payment and delivery, or substituting inferior yarn.

The practice of introducing private sector managers (*tangzhang*) into a state-run enterprise was peculiar to the Chinese socioeconomic situation. Along with the state monopolies, such a system was an example of the cooperation between private and public capital, which complemented the enforcement of the whole fiscal system. The relationship between an owner working on behalf of the Imperial Factories and the craftsman he hired to realize the commission at home was different from the usual relationship between a private contractor and his employee. In the first instance, the owner acted in force of his political obligation, in other words, he had the authority of his duties to the state behind him.

Sources show that most of the *jihu* were based on the family, though, depending on size, they relied on other subcontracting craftsmen and often hired other workers.[122] Only men were employed in the *jihu*, as women worked exclusively at home. When the *jihu* needed workers, they could go to the labor markets, one for each specialization, found in different parts of the city. But even in this case they had to do so through brokers, or intermediaries, from the various textile guilds.[123] Contracts with workers could be either long-term (the majority) or short-term, sometimes on a day-to-day basis. Wages were paid by the day, occasionally according to the quality and quantity of work, while payment in food was distributed each month.[124] Most of the goods produced were destined for the market rather than for local consumption.

CONFLICTS AND PUBLIC ORDER

It was not unusual for employers and craftsmen to argue over their respective obligations; the *jihu* often accused workers of improper use or unlawful appropriation of work tools and materials, or of illegally forcing pay raises. Demonstrations, strikes, occasionally even attacks on the dwellings of *jihu* leaders, seem to have been commonplace, as shown by two memorial tablets, one commissioned by the Changzhou county *jihu* at the beginning of 1735, the other placed opposite the headquarters of a textile guild in the Yuanhe county sector in the summer of 1822. Demonstrations and protests took various forms: either straightforward street protests, during which organizers stirred up the crowd against the *jihu* in support of wage raises, or union-like protests, coherent and well-ordered, which halted work in the textile workshops and sometimes even resulted in acts of violence, such as the destruction of employers' homes.[125] All of these forms of protest were considered illegal, in as much as they went against the prohibition of "market obstacles," as well as evidently violating laws against violence, theft, and so forth.[126]

Relations between owners and their workers or craftsmen has, over the years, been the subject of heated debate, particularly among Marxist historians in China and Japan. Some scholars interpret the few sources on the subject as proof of the existence of proto-capitalist relations rather than of relations based on a supposed feudal system.[127] Other more objective historians have found the relationship to be based on a framework of traditional, paternalistic links not dissimilar to those found within the familial clan. But, whenever there were conflicts between employers and craftsmen, the authorities invariably sided with the employers, condemning any and every form of protest. In 1734, for example, local authorities answered complaints by *jihu* from the Changzhou quarter by banning any form of demonstration under pain of arrest and pillory:

> The workshops [in] Suzhou city for the most part employ craftsmen to weave; workshop owners invest capital, while craftsmen receive wages for their work. Owners and craftsmen need one another, without recrimination from one side to the other. Yet there are some outlaws who, having lost their jobs through lack of skill and dedication to their work, nursed hatred and jealousy against their former employers. Under the

pretext of setting up a guild, these individuals have incited workers to strike and to demand higher wages, forcing the workshops to close and causing the craftsmen to lose their means of sustenance.[128]

Workers' grievances were often against the state because of excessive levies and taxes.[129] From the middle of the fifteenth century on, textile workers played a major role in the frequent revolts and popular uprisings against the rule of eunuchs such as Wei Yi during the Zhengtong period (1436–1439), Gong Hong during the Zhengde period (1506–1521), Diao Yong in 1523, Sun Shun, and Lu Bao at the beginning of the seventeenth century, and in 1628 against Li Shi.[130] Sources relate that during these uprisings weaving equipment was destroyed and workshops were closed down in the name of protests against excessive government taxation.[131] Often at the heart of these conflicts lay guilds that organized varied forms of protest, strikes, lock-outs, and demonstrations.

The 1601 protest, which broke out following the imposition of new taxes on production and commerce by the tax-inspector, Sun Long, is a classic example of conflict. A lock-out was declared by the *jihu*, effectively closing down weavers and dyers workshops. This act caused the widespread unemployment, which eventually prompted an assault on the houses of tax collectors.[132] Students from the Imperial University, *shengyuan*, and other members of the gentry took part in the protest. Ge Cheng, a craftsman who became famous for taking full responsibility for the incident, risked the death penalty, although, in the end, his sentence was commuted to a few years imprisonment.[133] The scholar Wen Bing (1609–1669) drew up a brief and clear account of the revolt:

At the time when Sun Long was the *Taijian* of the Imperial Factories of Suzhou and Hangzhou, and simultaneously holding the position of chief taxation officer, some evil men (*wulai*) infiltrated his administration, purporting to be regular tax inspectors. They set up customs checkpoints at each of Suzhou's six gates, and not a chicken nor a vegetable could pass into the city free of duty. The life of the people became more and more difficult, their thoughts became ever more turbulent. On the sixth day of the sixth lunar month, twenty-seven men, barefoot, and with unkempt hair, dressed in white, wearing short sleeves, each one holding a palm leaf fan, unexpectedly encircled the collectors' houses; after setting alight the houses and their furniture, they carried the tax collectors off to the main crossroads, where they killed them. The anger of twenty-seven men had broken with the force of a storm, and nobody dared stop them. All it took was a signal from their leader and they were prepared to do anything, even scale walls or climb to the top of the highest buildings.

When, on the next day, the men erroneously broke into a private house, the home of merchants who had done nothing wrong, their leader and his men apologized for the fright they had caused, before heading towards a nearby house where a tax clerk dwelt. Scared to death, the tax clerk threw himself into the river, but the men dived in after him, pulled him out and pounded him, gouging out his eyes and beating him to death. The account goes on to tell of several other incidents, including that of a rich man named Tong who was the Prefect's assistant in charge of the customs post of the River Liu. When the revolt broke out he tried to escape by swimming across the river, but died of cold. The rebels burned down his house, killing his family. His son survived, but only because he had been hidden at a neighbor's house. Sun Long also managed to survive by fleeing under cover of darkness to Hangzhou where he went into hiding. So, over three days, all those in charge of taxation were eliminated, one by one.

> On the fourth day a notice was hung on all the city gates, bearing the following message: "The tax officials' exploitation of levies was intolerable; we have taken it onto ourselves to rid the people of this evil. Now that our task is complete, the citizens are content; there is no longer cause for unrest.

The entire town was quiet that day and nobody went out into the streets. On the fifth day, the authorities began to order the arrest of the rebels. It was then that Ge Cheng decided to turn himself in at the Prefecture office, confessing his role as an instigator of the troubles:

> It was sufficient, he said, to punish him and him alone to reestablish the rule of law; otherwise, if common people were arrested, a full-scale revolt would follow. Thus it was that only Ge was arrested and sentenced to death. Later he was granted a pardon and released. Thirty years later, Ge, still alive, if questioned about the events of the revolt, refused to answer.

It is said that he was not the real leader, but that he turned
himself in to save the people.[134]

In this protest, the weavers demonstrated not only a high degree of
solidarity, unlike protesters in other rebellions against tax collectors
which broke out at the end of the dynasty, but also remarkable dis-
cipline and organizational ability.

The *Kaidu* uprising (1626) against the excesses of the eunuch Wei
Zhongxian is an example of collaboration between the gentry and the
urban population against an abuse of power. During this episode, the
gentry and intellectuals from the Donglin Academy found a natural
ally in the world of commerce and labor, at that time suffering under
the yoke of excessive taxes.[135] The gentry formed the vanguard of the
protest, attempting to moderate the behavior of the masses behind
them; they succeeded in occupying the government offices for a number of days.

Another common cause for protest was in times of famine or
natural disaster, when people turned out to demonstrate. An illus-
trative example is this lively report drafted in 1748 by Provincial Commissioner for the Guard, Weng Zao:

> In Jiangsu, during the second lunar month of this year, low-
> lying land flooded after torrential rain. On the fourth and fifth
> days of the fourth month hailstones fell in the prefecture of
> Suzhou and surrounding areas. . . . After the damage caused
> by flooding and hailstones, it is unrealistic to expect a decent
> harvest. The price of rice has risen; one *dan* of rice costs three
> or four *qian* more than the last month, and everywhere rice is
> being sold in order to fix the price.

In Suzhou, just as in other areas, this had been the policy since the
previous winter, but since Suzhou was a provincial capital, with a
dense population to feed, such regulations proved difficult to enforce,
and it seemed impossible to control market prices.

> On the twenty-fourth day of the fourth month, a trouble-
> maker, Gu Yaonian, appeared out of nowhere, carrying a sign
> on top of a bamboo pole which read "HOW CAN WE BUY RICE
> WITHOUT MONEY? LIFE IS TOUGH FOR THE POOR"—and then—
> "FOR THE COUNTRY AND THE PEOPLE, NOT FOR MYSELF!" This man
> went to the government offices, where he shouted his desire to

see the decree issued obliging rice shops to sell rice at lower prices. Then the Governor, An Ning, sent the magistrate of Changzhou, Zheng Shiqing, to investigate. But the followers [of the gang], fearing that their real motives would be discovered during interrogation, whipped up a mass demonstration to press for the release of those who had been arrested. . . . Gu Yaonian, who had been arrested, was freed by his companions Lu Gao and Wu Bao. The Prefect, Jiang Shunjiao, then ran as quickly as possible to the government offices, chased by demonstrators. The huge crowd which gathered around the offices broke down the palisade. The governor then called in the army, which arrested Ye Long and thirty-nine demonstrators; only then did the crowd disperse. Other men arrested included Gu Yaonian, the rebel Lu Gao and the well-known trouble-maker Cao Da, all of whom were tried without mercy in a bid to stamp out their bad example. On the twenty-fifth the governor reported the news to Court, replacing Prefect Jiang with Zheng Shiqing. On the twenty-seventh day of the fifth month Gu Yaonian, Lu Wenmo and Hua Long were sentenced to death by flogging; Cao Da, Lu Gao, Chen Liu, Ye Er, Chen San, Wu Hangong and the rest were sentenced to life imprisonment and corporal punishment.[136]

The authorities invariably attributed the responsibility for these rebellions to "evil men who took advantage of the situation to stir up the crowd," even though they were aware that uprisings were often provoked by bad administration, unfair assistance policies, and corruption among government officials.[137] During the Qing dynasty, famines causing rice prices to increase became more and more frequent in Suzhou, providing "urban trouble-makers" with increasing opportunities to spur on the population to attack government offices or raid warehouses and the homes of the rich. The authorities attempted to weed out the so-called "hoodlums" from the rest of the population. In 1686, the historian Wang Hongxu (1645–1723) suggested finding out the names of miscreants and arresting them at harvest time, when the people were in a peaceful mood. Similar ideas were repeatedly expressed on stone tablets erected by trading companies warning against action organized by "ruffian" elements among calenderers.[138] Another form of protest during the Ming dynasty was passive resistance and of evasion. One of the most serious problems facing the tax system was that craftsmen ran away, resulting in serious inaccuracies of tax records.[139]

It is worth noting the gangs of outlaws (*wulai*) that infested the outskirts of Suzhou. One type of illegal organization, gangs of outlaw calenderers, was probably the so-called "Cotton-beaters" noted in local records as causing a number of incidents.[140] The frequency of references to these phenomena in source material leads us to assume that in large towns juvenile delinquency and organized crime were as much of a problem as they are in modern societies today.[141] In those days, just as today, one of the biggest difficulties facing the authorities in their fight against crime lay in the invisible links between the criminal underworld and figures belonging to upper echelons of society, local notables, and members of the gentry. An eighteenth century source reported:

> The vice of gambling is extremely widespread in Suzhou, in spite of the very serious damage it causes. Whenever local officials look into the matter they just arrest small-time gamblers, because the heavyweight gamblers all belong to the gentry, to rich families. These people gamble away in well hidden corners of their houses and offices, protected by their attendants. The police are not able to arrest them, and nobody dares investigate too deeply. The stakes during these gambling sessions are enormous; entire fortunes are won and lost; land, houses, flourishing properties vanish, rich families find themselves suddenly paupers, and the sons of good families turn into rogues and bandits.[142]

Strictly speaking, the term *wulai* refers to a specific type of criminal organization, generally located in a town, closely linked to local administration through corrupt officials and servants, well connected with scribes, yamen guards, and under the protection of powerful families.[143] Leaders of these gangs governed both internal matters and links with the outside world, while members—for the most part of peasant origin, marginalized urban emigrants, or unemployed craftsmen—took up precise roles within the gang's structure. Such gangs offered a number of "services" to their clients, generally of an illegal nature, including violence, intimidation, and false testimony before judges. They raised money by robbing and extorting from markets or by setting up illegal middleman companies (*sihang*).[144] In and around Jiangnan during the Wanli reign (1573–1620) there were roughly three hundred groups of *wulai*, each one made up of dozens of men. As they were too many to arrest, the authorities tried to eradicate them by arresting gang leaders. But it was only with the strengthening of centralized power under the Qing, together with concurrent developments in the marketplace, that the traditional role of commercial brokerage filled by these gangs was undermined and they began to lose their importance.

A further type of criminal association was constituted by the so-called *jiaofu*, who dealt with the *corvée* of the conveyance of officials and their household goods to their new postings: arranged in guilds, both legal and illegal, they controlled all transport, from the goods that merchants wished to sell at town markets to funeral and marriage processions.[145] During the first period of the Qing dynasty, the power of the *jiaofu* reached huge proportions as increased agricultural and manufacturing production entailed a greater need for transport between town and country. Taking advantage of their position, the *jiaofu* extorted money from merchants and forced them to pay exorbitant prices, also going into the business of food supply and selling rice at high prices.[146] Following merchants' denunciation of the situation, the authorities attempted to clamp down, but the *jiaofu* often had links with the gentry and corrupt government officials. Towards the middle of the dynasty, however, the government succeeded in imposing control, thanks to a compromise reached between the authorities and the criminal associations.

Some examples of criminal associations in action are provided by Suzhou records:

> Violent men and vagabonds group together in gangs and secret societies. Some of them pretend to be bankrupt, others live by gambling and various expedients; they carry sticks and knives, commit crimes and attack the weak. If one of their number has a fight, all the others gather to get revenge. If one of them is sued, the others help him out. And when they come across orphans and widows from rich families, they really set to work: taking advantage of their weakness and inexperience, they send "con-men" to tempt the young men with gambling and loose women, or else they force them to lend money or push them to start legal proceedings. They convince soldiers and textile craftsmen to ally themselves with attendants from government offices, and together they cheat and steal their way to wealth. Always backing each other up, some of them intrigue to abet tax evasion or to block the course of justice.[147]

The existence of large numbers of craftsmen (many of whom were unemployed) concentrated in certain well-defined urban areas coupled with a continual passage of merchants, immigrants from the country looking for work, and individuals without their families or links with their homes—all these elements generated too many problems for local authorities to succeed in keeping public order. Therefore, following a well-trodden path, part of the responsibility for keeping public order was transferred to local districts such as the urban *fang* and suburban *xiang* and to trade corporations and wealthier business owners. Calenderers, too, were grouped together for collective responsibility, under the *baojia* model.[148] Many guilds in Suzhou were in practice delegated power over price controls, the registration of itinerant craftsmen and merchants and the collection of levies on trade in addition to their usual religious and benevolent activities. The leaders of a number of guilds oversaw de facto the hiring of craftsmen, while the heads of districts had to keep an eye on strangers, denounce lawbreakers, periodically report for duty, check that taxes were paid, carry out emarginated *corvées* and necessary tasks, and help out in emergencies.[149]

STRANGERS AND CALENDERERS

Strangers were generally regarded with suspicion, and they were often blamed as the source of disturbances and misdemeanors in town. Merchants and especially peddlers were included in this category. In the collection of Yongzheng "Vermilion Decrees" the superintendent for the Imperial Factories of Suzhou wrote:

> In the area of Suzhou bounded by Heaven's Gate (Changmen) and the South Ditch gather merchants from all over. In all they number around ten thousand, many of whom hail from Fujian. *Among these men are many good for nothing vagabonds, dissatisfied with their condition, ready to fight and commit crimes.* Craftsmen from dyeing and calendering workshops also congregate here; all 20,000 or so of these workers, originally from Nanjing, Taiping or Ningguo, now dwell homeless and without their families in Suzhou. *Each and every time that a crime is reported, there is always a calenderer implicated.*[150]

A memorial tablet commissioned in 1694 by the seventy-six businesses, which held the financial control of Suzhou's calendering workshops, referred to calenderers as "a gang of strong, violent men, all without their families, prepared to thieve and flee at a moment's notice; they come from all over, they all live together, they are all likely to commit crimes."[151]

Thus, calenderers (*chuaijiang* or *yajiang*) formed another restless, exclusively urban group of textile workers. The job of calenderers was to soften and polish cotton cloth after it had been pressed and rubbed in an operation not dissimilar to the fulling of wool. This process, developed during the Qing dynasty, came to be concentrated in the town of Suzhou for a number of reasons, even though the cotton cloth on which it was carried out was produced almost exclusively in other prefectures, especially, Songjiang. Calenderers occupied a rather low level of standing among urban fellow workers. They had to be strong men, considering the especially tiring nature of their job: using their arms as levers on wooden supports while balancing, they had to rock a huge forked stone with a ground base onto cotton cloth wrapped around a wooden roller which rotated in a groove in the base of the stone. The object of the process was to make cotton shiny and durable. The "grindstone," weighing several tons, could cost up to ten silver *taels* depending on its heat-conducting qualities, its workmanship, and the location of the pit from where it was quarried in the upper Yangzi.[152]

The calenderers, who typically came from rural areas of Jiangsu and Anhui, did not have sufficient resources to equip and open their own workshops; they were employed in the town's (*chuaifang*) factories where they were closely supervised. Most of the proprietors of these workshops were in fact managers or contractors, *baotou*, who maintained contact and drew up contracts with traders in exchange for money and cloth.[153] Workshops and equipment (the top and bottom grindstones, wooden rollers) were set up thanks to the money paid in advance to the *baotou* by big cotton merchants. This money also covered incidentals such as tools, food, furniture, and dormitories for the workers. Calenderers working for these contractors could expect to be paid a little over a cent for each *pi* of cloth they processed, although out of this they had to pay back thirty-six *qian* per month for the rent and upkeep of dormitories, equipment, and for living expenses. The contractors can be considered as agents for big merchants; they assumed responsibility for the money and goods received and naturally for the quality of the workmanship.[154] Their role as intermediaries and administrators can, to some degree, be compared to that of the *jihu* with respect to the Imperial Manufacturers or to the accounting firms. When, during the Qing dynasty, the Suzhou Manufacturers had to look after the dyeing of certain cloths, they most probably tried (and failed) to do so without the mediation of the *baotou*, who in practice appropriated most of the money earmarked for workers' wages.[155]

At the beginning of the eighteenth century, there were four hundred-and-fifty such factories in Suzhou. The fact that there were so many calenderers goes some way towards explaining their unpopularity with local authorities and townspeople who regarded them with a mixture of fear and contempt. A significant episode illustrating this uneasy situation occurred in the town of Changli, in the nearby Songjiang prefecture. There, at the beginning of the Kangxi reign, there were a large number of textile workshops employing many dyers and calenderers originally from Nanjing. New arrivals swelled the numbers of these workers until they were so numerous that the people of Changli considered them a threat. As time passed and the townspeople suffered more and more at the hands of these workers, their hatred of the immigrants grew, until one day they collected a huge sum of money, closed the city gates and threw themselves upon the immigrants, slaughtering many hundreds.[156]

Cut off from their families, isolated from the townspeople, and concentrated in one area of town, they created conditions which favored incidences of lawbreaking, or at the very least of behavior perceived as criminal. Moreover, these workers were financially unstable; their already low wages were reduced by the fees they paid the *baotou*, and their spending power diminished still further over time, as their wages failed to keep pace with price rises.[157] As the chart in Fig. 7 demonstrates, wages increased by just 3 percent in 1715 and a further 15 percent in 1772, for a total of 18 percent, while over the same period the price of rice almost quadrupled (price rises of 19 percent in 1715 and 336 percent in 1770).[158] The calenderers, paid in copper, were further penalized by a revaluation of silver against copper. As shown below, the ratio was eight hundred-and-fifty copper coins to one silver *tael* in 1730; it declined somewhat between 1730 and 1770, but began a steady rise after 1772, reaching 1300 by 1795.[159]

Besides the constraints of rising inflation, any type of welfare, such as the creation of a retirement fund or the setting up of an orphanage, hospice or hospital had to come out of the workers' own wages.[160] It is not surprising that after the price of rice rose in (a) 1670, then again in (b) 1693, (c) 1701, (d) 1715, (e) 1720, (f) 1739, and (g) 1795, the calenderers organized demonstrations and strikes to demand higher wages.[161]

Local administrators, aware that over 10,000 workers were kept in

	wages (taels)	cotton rate (per *pi* cloth)	rice (per *dan*)	ratio (1963)	silver/copper tael/cash
1693	0.011	100	0.98	100	
1698			1.00	102	
1701	0.011	100			
1707			1.25	128	
1708		168			
1709			1.35	138	
1712			0.80	82	
1715	0.0113*	103	1.17	119	
1718			0.96	98	
1723			1.10	112	
1727			1.19	121	
1729			0.94	96	
1730	0.0113*	103			1:850
1731			1.20	122	
1733			1.55	158	
1735			1.10	112	
1740					1:700
1748			2.00	204	
1759					1:750
1770			4.46	455	
1772	0.013	118			
1775					1:875
1786			4.30	439	
1795					1:1,300

Note: the standard ratio of silver to copper was 1:1,000; the lower ratios in the 18th century represent a favorable balance, while that after 1795 reflects a dramatic inflation in the price of silver.
*If rice prices exceeded 1.50 taels per *dan* workers were entitled to obtain a supplement of 2.4 *hao* (1/10 of a copper qian) per *pi*, an increase of 2.1%.
Source: MQBKJ, pp. 68–69.

Fig. 7. Prices, Wages, Cotton, and copper/silver ratios in the Ming period

check by just 300 *baotou*, did not underestimate the problems of maintaining public order.[162] They recognized the necessity of setting up a regulated, stable organizational structure, capable of ensuring a degree of social supervision. To this end, a stone tablet was erected in 1720 proclaiming a series of restrictions on these workers, circumscribing their freedom of movement and forbidding them to leave their quarters at night.[163] Associations formed by calenderers were dissolved as soon as they were discovered.[164] A 1723 communication from He Tianpei suggested more rigorous police control over the thousands of immigrant dyers and calenderers residing in Suzhou through traditional collective responsibility mechanisms. He wrote:

> As far as dyers and calenderers are concerned, they are all employed in their respective workshops where they are subject to supervision. Amongst these workers there are some good men, who respect their station, but there are also a good many drunkards and outlaws. In the fifth lunar month last year I uncovered a plot hatched by a gang of calenderers to rob wealthy citizens. Their plan failed because local officials arrested and tried the leader of the gang. The cotton cloth made in Suzhou, sold through merchants far and wide, needs to be treated by these dyers and calenderers. It is my humble opinion that each workshop that hires these workers should take full responsibility for their conduct, while local officials should keep their guard up. These actions would prevent ring leaders from finding hiding places in workshops; they would be forced to respect the law and behave themselves.[165]

In the same year, the Superintendent of the Imperial Factories exhorted the Emperor to increase checks: "It is my own modest conviction that all these people should be carefully watched; we must foresee, root out, purify and kill at birth any and every criminal act."[166]

As early as 1701 a tablet commissioned by cotton merchants already hinted at the desirability of organizing the *baotou* into a system based on collective responsibility similar to the traditional rural *baojia*. The *baotou* were organized in groups (*jia*) of ten, with one of their number acting as the overseer of the *jia*, collaborating closely with local police. The next step was to permit the temporary appointment of an experienced worker inside each factory to act as a "foreman" (*fangzhang*). There is also mention of the establishment of a register of calenderers, recording the name, place of birth, particulars of the guarantor, and the dates of employment, distinguishing between three categories of worker: (a) long-standing employee, (b) new employee, and (c) sacked employee.[167] The 300 *baotou* from Suzhou, who made up this complex organization, were split into groups of twelve, known as *jia*.[168] Members rotated at holding the position of "overseer" for one month each year. The overseer's job was to keep a register in his own name recording the names of all calenderers working for members of the *jia*; in addition, he kept a check on the other contractor-managers who were *baotou*.

But it is in the 1720 stele that plans for organization and control become more concrete, with the systemization of a "private" structure, recognized by the state, whose role was to forestall rather than repress crimes committed by immigrant workers and to stop them from organizing; here principles previously aired are repeated and refined, passing from the old system of supervision by the *baotou-jia*, to one in which each factory had a foreman, a direct employee who actually lived in the factory itself and answered to the "*baotou*," himself a manager of one or more factories. The tablet explains that as each *baotou* managed more than one business, employing on average around thirty workers, it was decided that there would be a single foreman for each workshop. Though they had less power than the *baotou*, nevertheless, they were important figures, particularly for the harmony of the manufacturing cycle.[169]

The foreman was in charge of hiring workers; consequently, he had to pay close attention to the calenderer's work history, making sure that behind each prospective employee stood a "guarantor." Between them, the *baotou* and foreman were held responsible for any illegal act perpetrated by an employee, including theft, gambling, disorderly conduct, association with prostitutes, criminal association, or incitement to riot.

The strongest, most respected *baotou* were selected to become "general supervisors" (*fangzong*), the top position in the control hierarchy. The "general supervisors" were a link between the private factories and local government; they informed local magistrates of suicides and breaches of the peace, and were empowered to investigate any misdemeanors committed within the work environment. These "general supervisors" were responsible for the *jia* overseers, issued identity documents and commanded guards and policemen. Should an illegal act occur, the foreman was obliged to report to the manager-*baotou*, who in turn met with the overseer of his *jia*, who sent a report to the "general supervisor," who began an investigation. As the "general supervisors" were twelve in number, we may infer that they, too, followed a system of rotation based on reciprocal responsibility.

When workers were first hired and their particulars entered into company registers, they were organized into their own system of collective responsibility based on groups of five. Workers' details were entered under four columns, following the procedure used in accounting ledgers (where the columns were divided into headings for residuals, expenditures, income, and balance). In the middle of each month, the *jia* overseers presented the registers to the "general supervisors" for checking.[170] The system of supervision and surveillance is analogous to the organization system found in the silk industry; both systems were cooperative structures grafted onto a merchant-entrepreneur base, whose goal of collective supervision and responsibility was intended to provide mutual benefits and limit competition.[171]

Several years later there were further cases of unrest, proving that the situation remained tense. The Governor of Zhejiang, Li Wei, in a communication to the Emperor, complained that: "Using sustenance as a pretext, a not inconsiderable number of them importune honest folk."[172] Li was referring to a news item dating back three months: a calenderer called "Luan Erji" had formed a gang numbering twenty-two people, all of whom had sworn their loyalty in a secret pact sealed with sacrifices to the gods. During the course of a nocturnal patrol in Suzhou, chief of police Xiao Chengxun arrested them, only to release them after being bribed. Luan Erji and his gang then went to the house of the *baotou* Qian Yuyuan, leaving a trail of death and destruction.

In a confession, it was revealed that the calenderers had in fact been in league with Yao Bingzhong, a student at the Imperial University who, having made money through "protecting" female and underage prostitution rackets, had taken on the gang, paying each member the sum of seven *taels*. The outlaws, who formed his private army, were paid handsomely for "exploiting the weak and furthering the criminal cause."[173] Another memorial, from early 1730, addressed to Yongzheng Emperor, reports the arrest of a secret society of twenty odd calenderers and implies that they had links with "bandits" operating on the coast.[174] Jingong, Luan's uncle on his father's side, had organized a sect of calenderers in 1723. His plan, scheduled for the fifth day of the fifth lunar month, was to sack and set fire to warehouses, killing any officials who tried to stop him and his gang and, if anything went wrong, to hijack a ship and escape to the open seas. His plan was foiled by the *baotou* Wu Jingfan, who discovered what was afoot and warned the authorities. Of the thirty-five gang members arrested, thirteen were sentenced to death. The leaders of the gang, however, managed to get away.[175]

Distrust and friction between local residents and immigrants are topics which reward careful analysis. There are some particularly curious cases to be found, in which strangers are accused of manifestly fantastic and irrational crimes. An example is the panic that broke out in Suzhou and surrounding areas in 1768, caused by so-called robbers of the soul. These sorcerers, generally chosen from the ranks of tramps and itinerant monks, were held responsible for this heinous behavior resulting in sickness and ultimately death.[176] These episodes always concerned strangers or immigrants, not part of local society, far from their homes and more often than not single.

During the Ming and Qing dynasties the inhabitants of Suzhou managed to exploit the town's strategic location and make use of equipment, techniques, and experience garnered from the silk industry to establish Suzhou as an important center for the commerce and processing of cotton, despite the fact that very little cotton was grown in the area. The situations and examples referred to in this paper do not claim to provide an exhaustive overview of the complexities of urban life, an existence characterized by frenetic activity, daily habits and customs, impulses and conflicting emotions. In concentrating on the textile sector, we have attempted to reflect the color and movement to be found in urban life without remaining exclusively within the bounds of a strictly socioeconomic framework. The same impulse towards development in manufacturing and trade that permitted the wealthy to cultivate refined tastes and indulge in luxurious life-styles had its darker side, expressed in severe imbalances on both social and psychological levels. Groups of immigrants and pockets of unemployed workers, all living on the fringes of society, made up a pool that criminal organizations regularly tapped. Frequently criminal elements were shielded by notables and members of the gentry in exchange for the occasional use of their services.

Economic development and its consequent social mobility and change unleashed on the urban population in the form of continuous waves of immigration and emigration could easily be interpreted by local inhabitants as dangerous for their identity and cultural heritage. The influx of many strangers could provoke irrational and ill-controlled reactions. The examples gathered here are emblematic of the social and economic development in Suzhou, a city whose impulses towards industrial manufacturing and trade had long ago altered its identity as a purely administrative center.

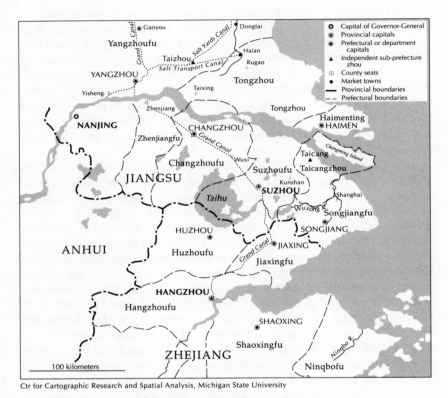

Ctr for Cartographic Research and Spatial Analysis, Michigan State University

Fig. 8. Jiangnan in the Qing dynasty

Chapter 4
Yangzhou: A Central Place in the Qing Empire

Antonia Finnane

The city of Yangzhou lies on the west bank of the Grand Canal, a few miles north of the Yangzi River. Now a modest provincial center, it was one of China's larger cities during the Qing dynasty and, at least until the end of the eighteenth century, also one of its most prosperous. In the mid-Qing period, when it was the administrative center of the Lianghuai salt monopoly, its population included some of the wealthiest merchants and best known scholars of the time. Its gardens, teahouses, and splendidly lit night markets brought it a renown which long outlasted its prosperity. While many of its features were typical of urban society in China, others were peculiar to the city itself, reflecting its particular past and its particular regional context as well as its unique supraregional role.

The present article is concerned with three aspects of the Qing city of Yangzhou: its spatial context, its internal spatial organization, and its social structure. An examination of these not only establishes much about Yangzhou that could have been predicted from the established body of scholarship on urbanization in China but also reveals the special features that were a function of its unique position within the spatial and economic organization of China in the late imperial period. More particularly, the case of Yangzhou draws attention to the role of the state in the delineation of the spaces, both literal and figurative, within which at least one section of Chinese society functioned.

THE CITY IN SPATIAL CONTEXT

Spatial organization in China was once understood largely in terms of the administrative boundaries which demarcated provinces, prefectures, departments, counties, and other jurisdictional areas. Viewed from this perspective, the city seemed primarily an administrative center and Chinese society was accordingly imagined as featuring a sharp urban-rural dichotomy.[1] G. William Skinner's identification of regional and macroregional distinctions, based on central place theory, has resulted in a rather different picture. Superimposed upon the administrative map we now see an economic one of eight macroregions, each boasting a distinctive hierarchy of local urban systems.[2] Within this framework the city in China is seen, in Skinner's words, as "at once embedded in society and essential to its overall structure."[3]

Central place theory seems to provide a ready explanation of Yangzhou's prominence during the Qing period. Situated close to the junction of two major waterways, this city was an obvious *entrepôt* for north-south trade. Near to it were located some substantial market towns, immediately suggestive of the characteristic hierarchy of trading places predicted by central place theory: on the Grand Canal to the north lay Shaobo; at the junction of the Grand Canal and the Yangzi to the south lay Guazhou; and on the Salt Transport Canal to the northeast lay Xiannuzhen. The traveler, journeying from Yangzhou along the Grand Canal or the Salt Transport Canal, would pass by lesser towns, too, before coming to one or another of the county-level capitals within the Yangzhou jurisdiction. Gaoyou was the closest capital to the north, Taizhou to the east, and Yizheng to the southwest. A map of the greater Yangzhou area, showing urban places and communication routes, clearly reveals Yangzhou's centrality. All roads, it would seem, led to Yangzhou.

An older spatial arrangement, however, underpinned the placement of all these towns relative both to each other and to the waterways by which they mostly stood. "Early markets," in the words of one scholar, "did not so much control space as they were controlled by spatial arrangements growing out of the organization of other kinds of social exchange."[4] In the strategically sensitive region between the Huai and the Yangzi Rivers this "social exchange" consisted essentially of an exchange of hostilities. Early spatial arrangements in this area were to an unusual degree influenced by military factors and such factors were obviously operative in the genesis both of Yangzhou and of the Grand Canal.

According to early historical sources, the city and the canal emerged simultaneously towards the end of the Spring and Autumn period (722–464 B.C.), when the southern state of Wu was threatening to "attack [the northern state of] Qi and usurp authority over China."[5] Wu's ambition was advanced by the excavation of a canal running northwards from the Yangzi to the Huai River and by the construction of a fort on Shugang, a small plateau immediately northwest of the present city of Yangzhou.[6] The canal was a forerunner of the Grand Canal while the fort, known as "Hancheng," is deemed the forbear of Yangzhou. In 319 B.C. the site was again walled by the ambitious ruler of a southern state, King Huai of Chu,[7] and in the uncertain years of the early Han the walls were reconstructed yet again by Liu Bi, nephew of the first Han emperor, Liu Bang (r.206–195 B.C.).[8] The story of concentrated human activity in this area up to this time basically concerns a struggle between rival aspirants to political power. The landscape through which the antagonists moved bore relatively few imprints of human activity and was peripheral to all the major centers of power. Its great importance was as a link, a means of communication, between north and south.

In this early period there was of course no real city or even, to our knowledge, permanent human settlement in the vicinity of Yangzhou. The paucity of pre-Han artifacts on Shugang shows that prior to the second century B.C. no more than a temporary garrison existed on this site.[9] During the Han, however, a city did develop on Shugang. Known as "Guangling," it was at first merely a military stronghold which served Liu Bi as a power base for the control of his fief, the kingdom of Wu.[10] From the security of this bastion, Liu Bi subsequently directed the development of salt production on the coast and the exploitation of local copper resources. These, it is said, enabled him to forgo levying a land tax and helped him build a base of popular support for the rebellion he raised in 154 B.C.[11] The first half-century of the Han dynasty seems, then, to have been crucial for the development of both the city of Guangling and the Huainan region. As the Han progressed, there was that movement in and out of the walls which Fernand Braudel regards as satisfying the notion of the town.[12] "Axles collided," runs the nostalgic *Wucheng fu* (Ballad of the Ruined City), "and people jostled; houses everywhere, and village gates; singing and piping filled the heavens."[13] The fifth century author of these lines may have been using the Han as a surrogate for his own dynasty, the early Song (A.D. 420–479), but the archaeological record, taken together with Guangling's administrative importance during the Han and strong evidence of regional development, suggests that the lines accurately convey the circumstances of Guangling in its Han dynasty heyday.

Guangling, in company with Gusu (later Suzhou), is in fact held to have been virtually preeminent among southern cities during the Han.[14]

The emergence of this flourishing town was clearly a function of the unification of North and South China, which was achieved first with the formation of the Qin empire then in more lasting form under the Han. The instability of political borders during the preceding Warring States period had fully exposed the military significance of the Huai River valley, which was such as to constitute, in the words of Chi Ch'ao-ting, "almost a 'permanent' check to the economic growth of the whole region between the Yangtze and the Hwai."[15] Only with the unification of north and south could a city of the size and substance of Guangling emerge in this region. When the Han dynasty collapsed, giving rise to the fabled "Three Kingdoms," the Huai-Yangzi area was again reduced to a war zone and the foundations of Guangling's prosperity were temporarily destroyed. According to the *Song shu*, vast tracts of land between the Yangzi and the Huai were uninhabited during the Three Kingdoms period and the counties of Hailing, Gaoyou, and Jiangdu, all part of the commandery of Guangling under the Later Han, ceased to exist.[16]

Not only was the unification of north and south a necessary condition for the prosperity of this city; the city itself was also intimately involved in the military and political processes which created and destroyed a succession of empires in China. In the sixth century A.D., Sui Yangdi purposely cultivated it as a southern seat of power for his northern dynasty.[17] During the Tang, it was the hub of a growing north-south trade and the base from which the rulers in the north developed the revenue potential of the south. For the Southern Song and later the Southern Ming, it served as the last bastion before the Yangzi, shielding these southern dynasties from northern invaders. During the Yuan, it was the forward position of defense for an alien northern dynasty, which was nervous of possible uprisings in the south.[18] Crowded sometimes with merchants, sometimes with soldiers, and sometimes with a mixture of the two, Yangzhou was a city which rose and fell in accordance with the political and military fortunes of the empire. The Qing scholar-official Yao Wentian (1758–1827) noted the unusual importance of the strategic factor in Yangzhou's position when he wrote:

[Yangzhou] is an important crossing between north and south. From the Qin and Han dynasties onwards it has acted as a thoroughfare for military forces. The rises and falls of its departments and counties, the changes in its boundaries, are many more than those of other jurisdictions.[19]

Its strategic significance made Yangzhou alternatively a military stronghold during times of political conflict and a thriving center of commerce and culture in times of unity. Commercial development in the Yangzhou area took place, however, within a spatial arrangement that had been developed primarily to satisfy the defense, communication, and economic needs of a succession of imperial dynasties. This is particularly evident from the crucial role played by the Grand Canal and the Salt Transport Canal in determining the pattern of urbanization in this area. Both of these canals were initially developed to help their respective creators increase their span of territorial control. Although they were subsequently to be used by private commercial traffic, it was official rather than private initiatives which ensured their extension, maintenance, and periodic restoration in later centuries. These official initiatives were designed to guarantee the tribute grain and salt transports, the former being a tax and the latter a government monopoly.[20] Private trade which developed in the wake of these official transports took place within an infrastructure designed primarily to benefit the imperial government. The key position held by Yangzhou within this infrastructure reflected the intimate connection between the development of this city and the creation and maintenance of the empire.

YANGZHOU: CITY, LOCALITY, REGION

Yangzhou had a local and a regional context as well as an imperial one. In its origins the product of exogeneous forces, it developed the roots in its locale which were essential to its long-term survival. During the Qing dynasty, a range of economic and administrative functions, intertwined in complex ways, connected it to the locality and the greater region which it helped define. An examination of these functions shows, however, that in some important respects this city stood apart from its hinterland under the Qing, at least during the eighteenth century.

Yangzhou's formal position within the Qing field administration was as prefectural and county capital. Early in the Qing dynasty it was recognized as one of the thirty "most important" (*zuiyao*) administrative centers in the empire, which signified that the posts of prefect and county magistrate in Yangzhou were "most important" posts.[21] As Skinner's analysis of post designations has shown, "most important" centers all possessed strategic significance but as well were typically large, busy, wealthy cities with jurisdictions which probably presented a range of administrative challenges and problems.[22]

The size of any jurisdiction was subject to change and during the late imperial period Yangzhou was affected by alterations of administrative boundaries at both county and prefectural level. According to the cryptic account provided in the prefectural gazetteer, Yangzhou prefecture retained its Ming form until the end of the Kangxi reign (1661–1722), and as such embraced the three departments of Taizhou, Tongzhou, and Gaoyou and the six counties of Jiangdu (Yangzhou's "home" county), Yizheng, Rugao, Taixing, Baoying, and Xinghua. A seventh county, too aptly named "Haimen" (sea gate), was in 1671 incorporated into Tongzhou after the county seat had been destroyed in coastal floods.[23] The prefecture was reduced in size in 1724, when Tongzhou became an independent department (*zhilizhou*) with jurisdiction over the counties of Rugao and Taixing. Two new counties, Ganquan and Dongtai, were subsequently created through the subdivision of, respectively, Jiangdu and Taizhou, giving the prefecture a total of two departments and six counties by the late eighteenth century.[24] Together these jurisdictions covered an area of around seventeen-and-a-half thousand square kilometres.[25]

Provincial boundaries were also susceptible to alteration. During the Ming dynasty, Yangzhou had been contained within the "southern metropolitan" province, Nan Zhili, which owed its particular status within the Ming empire to the importance of Nanjing, the "southern capital." Under the Qing this province was initially renamed Jiangnan but was divided early in the Kangxi reign to form the two provinces of Jiangsu, with its capital in Suzhou, and Anhui, with its capital in Anqing.[26] Yangzhou prefecture lay within Jiangsu.

Jiangnan did, however, survive as a sort of super-province. It was one of the two administrative divisions under the control of the Liangjiang governor-general, the other being the province of Jiangxi. A gazetteer of Jiangnan (*Jiangnan tongzhi*) was published in 1687, a second edition appearing in 1737. The literal meaning of "Jiangnan," "south of the Yangzi," did not of course, apply to the Qing province of Jiangnan, which stretched north of the Huai River as well as south of the Yangzi. The office of the Jiangnan director-general of river conservancy, created in 1728, had its seat in Qingjiangpu, near to the confluence of the Yellow and Huai Rivers, and had jurisdiction over the Grand Canal only down to the Yangzi.[27] Yet to some extent the literal meaning of Jiangnan seems to have informed the bureaucratic meaning. In terms of population, urbanization, wealth, culture, and political importance, the southern part of Jiangnan was clearly dominant over the area to the north. This dominance was given official recognition and expression in the location of provincial offices, which were all in southern cities. If there was a tendency for the term "Jiangnan" to be used mainly in reference to the south, this was but allowing the bureaucratic meaning to approach the literal meaning.

Qing Yangzhou is often thought of as being a Jiangnan city, quintessentially southern, belonging with Suzhou and Wuxi rather than with the definitively northern Huaian.[28] In the eighteenth century, however, even Huaian had something of a southern charm, evident particularly in its spread of southern-style gardens, which were collectively referred to as "little Yangzhou."[29] Indeed, before the breakdown of the inland waterway system and the boom in the coastal trade in the nineteenth century, links between the southern and central parts of Jiangsu were much closer than subsequently. In this period, Yangzhou's provincial context could clearly be referred to in some sense as "Jiangnan," a term which was rich with historical and cultural connotations and was at least as adequate as the term "Jiangsu" for conveying a general idea of the city's physical location. The inclusion of Yangzhou in the Lower Yangzi macroregion naturally adds strength to the association of Yangzhou with Jiangnan.

Properly speaking, however, Yangzhou belonged not to Jiangnan, in its literal sense, but to Jiangbei, that part of Jiangsu province lying "north of the Yangzi," and it is in this context that its particular characteristics are best understood.[30] The Jiangbei region was not defined by administrative boundaries but substantial waterways demarcated it from other parts of Jiangsu and Anhui. It was separated from the southern part of the province by the Yangzi; from the northern by the Yellow River, at this time occupying the bed of the Huai; and from neighbouring Anhui largely by the Grand Canal and the system of lakes which bordered it. Northeast lay the vast Hongze Lake, into which the waters of the Huai River were deposited. To the east lay the sea. In administrative terms, this region was largely divided between the Yangzhou, Huaian, and Tongzhou jurisdictions.

Internally Jiangbei was given cohesion by a network of waterways that supplied its major means of communication. The major transport routes were the Grand Canal, which connected Huaian in the north to the cities of Baoying, Gaoyou, Yangzhou, Yizheng, and various smaller market towns; the Salt Transport Canal (*Yunyan he*), which ran east from Yangzhou through Taizhou and connected these cities,

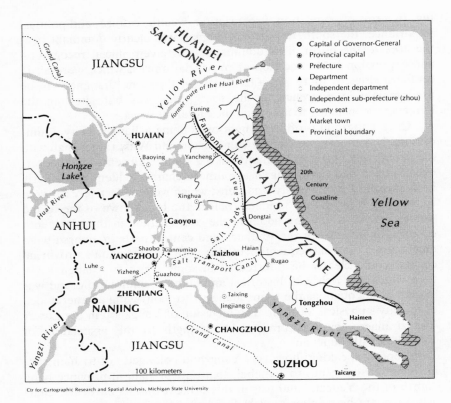

Fig. 9. Northern Jiangsu (Jiangbei) in the Qing
dynasty

via various tributaries, to the southeastern centers of Taixing, Rugao, and Tongzhou; and the Salt Yards Canal (*Chongchang he*), which extended north from the Salt Transport Canal and followed a route roughly parallel to the coastline, connecting the various salt yards and the cities of Dongtai, Yancheng, and Funing. The area defined by these perimeters was riddled with canals and lakes of greater or lesser dimensions, making transport notionally easy and efficient, but the area was also flood prone and the canals tended to silt up.[31] Carts and donkeys were in constant use around Yangzhou,[32] but overland transport for medium to long-distance trade can have been of significance only in the southeast of Jiangbei, where there were few canals, and in the hilly area west of Yangzhou.

In terms of its climate, land formation, and natural resources, the central part of Jiangsu province had more in common with the south than with the north. The Huai River was a natural climatic boundary, dividing the relatively dry North China plain from the wetter and warmer Yangzi valley.[33] Jiangbei formed the eastern part of Huainan, the region "south of the Huai," and not only enjoyed relatively high levels of precipitation but also served as the main drainage basin for Hongze Lake and the Grand Canal. It was for this reason that floods were a regular occurrence here.[34]

The generous water supply was an important influence on the regional economy. Paddy rice was the dominant agricultural product, fish were a valuable resource, and activities such as raising ducks and the cultivation of water lilies were important economic sidelines. Rushes growing in the marshes, by lakesides and along the coast supplied materials for the manufacture of articles such as mats, sandals, and hats.[35] This variety of natural resources helps explain the prosperity of Jiangbei relative to Huaibei, the region lying north of the Huai.

Relative to southern Jiangsu, however, Jiangbei was rather underdeveloped. The jurisdictions along the north bank of the Yangzi did present some of the economic characteristics of southern Jiangsu. In Tongzhou, for instance, cotton and indigo were being produced for export during the eighteenth century and corresponding amounts of grain were being imported, very much as was the case across the river.[36] From the Yangzi up to the Huai, however, there was a steady diminution in the intensity and diversity of economic activity. Due to the ever-present threat of floods and despite the introduction of fast-ripening strains of rice, harvests were uncertain. Landlessness and lawlessness were common problems. Throughout Jiangbei levels of urbanization were lower than in southern Jiangsu and marketing activity was more specialized and restricted.[37]

In its salt, however, Jiangbei had a resource of great value. According to a late Ming source:

> Of the six salt controllers in the country, only the Lianghuai salt controller [in Yangzhou] is powerful; of the three sub-controllers [in the Lianghuai region], the Taizhou sub-controller is foremost; and in Taizhou, Anfeng is the greatest salt yard. In this hideaway of merchants and salt masters, the profits from salt top the wealth of the south-east.[38]

Salt was Jiangbei's great export commodity. In fact, within Jiangbei only the Tongzhou-Haimen area had anything else to offer external markets and even here salt was the most important product in the eighteenth century. As is well known, however, the salt trade in China was a government monopoly and salt production was consequently tightly regulated and closely monitored. How the production and marketing of Huainan salt was organized helps to explain Yangzhou's dominance in Jiangbei.

The salt came of course from the coast. Indeed, the entire coastal area of the central and northern parts of the province was given over to salt production. Restrictions were imposed on types of land use permissible within this zone and although farming and fishing were common means of livelihood, the cultivation of land was often in breach of the law.[39] Salt making was in theory an hereditary occupation and salt makers were registered as such with the term "*zaoding*" (lit. salt men), which differentiated them from ordinary people, registered as "*min*" (lit. people). Like other *déclassé* groups, the salt makers were subject to different sets of regulations from those applying to the rest of the population. The mutual responsibility (*baojia*) system, for example, was introduced among the salt makers only in 1728, shortly before it was extended to other minority groups.[40] Like members of these other groups, the salt makers also found it difficult to shed their classification.[41]

The effective alienation of a large part of the land and population of Jiangbei created great social and economic problems, as shown by the problems of law and order encountered by officials stationed on the coast.[42] Some of the profits of the official salt trade were turned to uses notionally of benefit to the region, such as the stocking of famine relief granaries and the repair and maintenance of waterworks.[43] The nature of these undertakings will not be closely explored here but it should nonetheless be noted that the severity of Jiangbei's water control problems, which were responsible for periodic grain shortages in the region, were a direct consequence of state water control policies aimed at preserving the Grand Canal as a thoroughfare for the transport of tribute grain. In these circumstances, the attention paid to infrastructural maintenance in Jiangbei could only be equivocal in nature and effect, certainly as far as the agricultural sector in Jiangbei was concerned.

The structure of the salt monopoly did, by contrast, directly promote Yangzhou's development through the later seventeenth and eighteenth centuries, as it had done in the late Ming. Positions in the Lianghuai salt administration, centered in Yangzhou, were highly lucrative and the presence of salt officials alone would have ensured the city a measure of prosperity. To their numbers were added those of the salt merchants: the head merchants (*zongshang*), who had responsibility for returning the salt tax, were expected to reside in Yang-zhou,[44] and the many lesser merchants undoubtedly found it convenient to live there for business reasons. The result was that during the eighteenth century Yangzhou was the residence of some of the wealthiest men in China, let alone Jiangbei.[45]

Two other factors served to promote Yangzhou's dominance in Jiangbei. First, the city's administrative importance as prefectural capital was bolstered by its importance as center of the salt administration: the salt controller's authority extended beyond the prefecture into the Huaian and Tongzhou jurisdictions and also extended beyond salt into important regional matters such as water control.[46] Second, the fixed route for the salt transport, down the Salt Yards Canal and along the Salt Transport Canal to Yangzhou, greatly influenced the shape of the infrastructure in Jiangbei, helping determine the position of a number of important market towns and conferring centrality on Yangzhou itself. In these ways, it should also be noted, the salt trade contributed to the combination of administrative and economic features which gave Jiangbei some regional integrity.

Despite the state's appropriation of the salt trade, salt was a significant item in the regional economy. Most of the Jiangbei region was excluded from the official Lianghuai salt marketing area because it was too difficult to control smuggling in areas close to the salt production zone. This meant that salt was widely peddled in relatively small quantities throughout Jiangbei.[47] In addition, larger amounts of salt were smuggled out of the region for sale at competitive prices elsewhere.[48] The trade from which Yangzhou benefited must, however, be considered as fundamentally distinct from these dispersed activities rather than as an organic outgrowth of them.

If it is accepted that Yangzhou's size and wealth in the eighteenth century were primarily due to the functions devolving on the city from the official salt trade and were not a consequence of broad based economic development in Jiangbei, then central place theory by itself becomes inadequate as an explanation of the city's growth. Network system theory provides us with an alternative approach. This theory, proposed by Paul M. Hohenberg and Lynn Hollen Lees to account for long-distance trade in the context of medieval Europe, postulates that a given city may owe its existence or importance to its role as a gateway linking its hinterland to the network of long-distance trade beyond. In central place theory, distance and the difficulties of transport are regarded as disincentives which limit the economic importance of long-distance trade and consequently its significance as a stimulus for preindustrial urbanization. In network system theory, the profit motive is viewed as overcoming these disincentives. The existence of the network, in the words of Hohenberg and Lees, "testifies to the mercurial force of movable wealth and universal ideas. . . . At the heart of the system is an "internationale of cities," each determinedly autonomous and more concerned with the world at large than with its own backyard."[49]

When due allowance is made for the peculiarities of the Chinese case, where for many cities "the world" was, for all intents and purposes, the Chinese empire, this theory serves to make sense of the extensive system of trade across regions in a context where regional systems were still quite distinct. Eighteenth-century Yangzhou was unarguably the product of such a system. The Huainan salt distribution area, which yielded the bulk of Yangzhou's wealth, stretched from southwestern Jiangsu through Anhui, Henan, Hubei, Hunan, and Jiangxi to the periphery of Guizhou. In other words, Yangzhou's important economic relations were with places outside of the Lower Yangzi macroregion, contradicting the supposition that cities within a macroregion will all have stronger economic ties with each other than with cities in other macroregions.[50]

With respect to the supraregional role conferred on it by its position in the salt trade, Yangzhou showed one of the hallmarks of the network city: its potential for substitution by another town. Under the Qing it was largely by virtue of the Ming precedent that the salt administration was centered here. During the Northern Song, however, nearby Yizheng (then Zhenzhou) had been the more significant administrative center, had preempted Yangzhou's place in the tea and salt trades, and had flourished while Yangzhou stagnated.[51] Under the Qing, Yizheng continued to be the de facto export port for Huainan salt, but it was in Yangzhou, seat of the officials, that all important financial transactions took place.

In addition to its interregional trade Yangzhou did, of course, have a regional economic base which emerged clearly to view after the decline of the Grand Canal and the abrogation of the salt monopoly. Although even in this later period the city still seems to have served as Jiangbei's gateway, it is worth noting with respect to the theoretical framework that most larger cities, according to Hohenberg and Lees, will be found to have a place in both the network and the central place hierarchy.[52] Network system theory, however, helps to explain why, as the center of the interregional salt trade, Yangzhou does not seem to be well embedded in Jiangbei. If the key systemic property of a network city is considered to be nodality within the network rather than centrality within the region, then the city's failure to fulfill roles at lower levels of the marketing hierarchy, as seems to be the case in Yangzhou as well as Hankou does not need to be explained in terms of departure from a central place norm.[53] In fact, Yangzhou's economic role in Jiangbei in the eighteenth century is probably best conceptualized as that of an extractive "funnel," through which salt flowed out of the hinterland but little flowed back in.

SPATIAL ORGANIZATION IN YANGZHOU

The mixture of administrative, economic, and strategic functions that Yangzhou served were reflected in the city's physical features. These features changed over time, although a certain "stability of urban form" was apparent in Yangzhou at least from the Southern Song.[54] The changes were partly due to the number of times the city was destroyed and rebuilt through the centuries but may also be explained in terms of the changing nature of the city itself. During the eighteenth century, the significance of the salt trade was especially evident in the city's morphology. The particular features of the city at this time can best be appreciated through a comparison of Qing Yangzhou with the city's earlier forms.

In the transition from the Tang to the Song, the physical transformation of the city was marked. The Tang city walls, unfortunately unrecorded in any extant map, have been partially uncovered by archaeological work and appear to have enclosed a much larger area than any subsequent construction. They included both the earlier city space of Guangling, on the Shugang plateau, and the later space covered by the Qing city.[55] The size of the Tang city is consistent both with the significance of Yangzhou as an international emporium and with the concentration of urban functions within the walls of administrative cities during this time.

Great physical destruction must have accompanied the late Tang disturbances for in the year 958 the short-lived Later Zhou regime (951–960) found it necessary to construct walls to enclose the southeastern section of the Tang city. This may have set the pattern for later construction.[56] In the course of the Southern Song, a complex "triple walled" (*sancheng*) city was constructed, the southern segment of which was known as the "*dacheng*" (Great Wall or alternatively Great City). Here were situated the important civil administrative offices, military offices and barracks, temples, granaries, and schools. The second wall, known as the "Baoyou Wall" after the Baoyou period

(1253–1258) of the reign of Emperor Lizong (reign 1225–1264), was constructed well to the north of the first. Communication between the two areas thus enclosed was provided by a third, much smaller enclosure known as the "*jiacheng*," a term which could be roughly translated as the "wall in between."[57]

The late date of construction of the Baoyou wall, and hence also of the connecting enclosure, points to the primacy of military considerations in the creation of the Southern Song complex.[58] In fact the constant threat posed by the Jin empire to Song territories in the twelfth and thirteenth centuries meant that throughout the Southern Song period Yangzhou's significance was strictly of a strategic nature. The Great Wall nonetheless had all the formal features of a capital and its careful, even ornamental, symmetry did full justice to the ancient cosmological tradition within which space was delineated and rendered manageable and comprehensible. Much of its detail was reproduced in the Yangzhou of Ming-Qing times.

The suggestion that cities in late Imperial China had a binuclear character is supported by the case of Yangzhou.[59] From the Southern Song through to the Qing the western end of the city held steady importance as the domain of officialdom. The Great Wall was rectangular in form and was divided along its north-south axis by a canal which ran parallel to the avenue linking the north and south city gates. All of the offices of the civil administration and related institutions such as the Temple of the City God, the school and academy, and the Public Relief Treasury (*bianmin ku*) were situated to the west of the canal while the ordinary residential area (such as it was) appears to have been on the eastern side.[60] Military offices were dispersed but, undoubtedly for reasons of space, were more heavily concentrated on the eastern side. The functional division of the city was clear, without being rigid.

No record of wall construction exists for the Yuan period[61] but the early Ming reconstruction echoed the plan of the Southern Song Great Wall, though covering only part of its area.[62] Again the city was divided by an internal canal parallel to the north-south avenue and again the offices of the field administration were clustered on the western side. The salt inspectorate (*chayuan*), which was, of course, a bureaucratic office, was situated on the eastern side[63] but this appears to be in accordance with the Song arrangement. Spatial differentiation between the field and the salt administrations continued to be made as the city grew, reflecting the ambivalent position of the salt administration in the overall structure of the imperial administration.

The east-west division of the city was duplicated on larger scale when the enclosed area was extended in the sixteenth century. The original Ming wall, constructed in haste to enable Ming forces to beat off a rival aspirant to the throne, measured only nine *li* all around and could not easily accommodate a growing urban population.[64] To its east sprang up a large commercial suburb which, by the middle of the sixteenth century, was pressing hard on the banks of the Grand Canal to its east, leaving virtually no room for the construction of a new wall necessary for defense against the sixteenth-century pirate raids. After pirates had sacked this suburb in 1556, the new wall was eventually built, joining with the original city's eastern wall and more than doubling the enclosed area.[65] The eastern stretch of the city moat now constituted a second internal canal which could be crossed by bridge but passage between the two sections of the city was restricted to the two gates in the wall which divided them. The two sections were distinguished from each other by the self-explanatory terms "Old City" (*jiucheng*) and "New City" (*xincheng*) and presented to the eye the contrast to be expected between a planned and an unplanned settlement. Judging by the map of the city in Qing times, the streets in the Old City were laid out in a regular, almost geometrical pattern while those of the New City were arranged rather haphazardly.

In the course of the Manchu conquest of China Yangzhou was virtually destroyed. Rights to the city were fiercely contested by the Southern Ming generals appointed to defend Huainan, and in the summer of 1644 it was subjected to a month long siege by one of their number, the notorious Gao Jie (d. 1645). The occupation of the city by the Manchus in May of the following year was accompanied by brutal slaughter and the wanton destruction of property.[66] During the early years of the Qing, however, the city was quite rapidly restored with apparently few changes being initiated. In these politically difficult years, it may even have seemed to the new rulers especially important that this shattered symbol of Ming resistance should be reconstructed in its old image and likeness.

Early efforts towards restoring the physical fabric of the city signaled to the city's surviving inhabitants that the new order was clearly to be in some respects continuance of the old. One of the few recorded activities of the first Qing prefect, Hu Qizhong, was to undertake restoration of the prefectural school or "school temple" (*xuegong*), one of the most important emblems of the city's administrative status. Repairs to the city walls soon afterwards confirmed that the city was to be reshaped with some precision in accordance with the Ming model. The physical and the functional distinctions between the Old and New

Cities were retained and even the original east-west division internal to the Old City was preserved. The only office of the field administration to be located east of the Old City's central canal was the Ganquan county yamen, newly constructed after the creation of this county in 1732. The offices of the salt censor continued to be situated on the east side of the Old City but the rambling establishment of the salt controller with its twenty bureaus and countless employees, was located in the New City.[67]

The curious physical structure of the city meant that the notion of a city "center" made no geographical sense in the context of the city as a whole. The location of centers of activity, whether commercial, bureaucratic, or cultural, tended anyway to be determined by the interaction of intra-and extra-mural forces. The New City, for example, did exhibit a certain tropism towards the Old, which reflected its origins as a suburb, but other influences served to create hubs of activity, which were independent of the New-Old nexus. In particular, commercial activities tended to cluster at points convenient to external trade routes.[68]

Yangzhou's main trading district was in the southwestern corner of the New City, near to the customs station and to the most convenient exit from the city to the Grand Canal. Access to the Old City, through Little East Gate (*Xiao dong men*), was also convenient from here and commercial activity in fact extended through the gate to the southeastern corner of the Old City. Business interests in this area appear to have been mixed. The names of streets such as Unhulled Rice Lane (*Caomi hang*), in the Old City, and Mutton Lane (*Yangrou hang*), in the New City, suggest that wholesale trade in basic commodities was pursued in the near vicinity of the retail outlets for silks and satins, bridal hairpieces, jewelry and cosmetics, which were concentrated in this part of this city.[69] Daily markets were also held in this neighborhood. In the nineteenth century, if not before, the Jingjiang and Hubei *huiguan*, or native-place associations, were located here, while not far to the east were the premises of other native-place associations.[70]

Commercial activities were not restricted to the southwest corner. Markets were held at a number of other New City gates as well as at the Kaiming Bridge in the Old City. The orientation of the New City to the Old, reflected in the commercial activity around the Little East Gate, is visible again at the Greater East Gate, where the city's main book market was held and storytellers practiced their craft. The canal running south to north along the western perimeter of the New City, outside the Old City wall, was a commercial zone in itself, lined with

Ctr for Cartographic Research and Spatial Analysis, Michigan State University

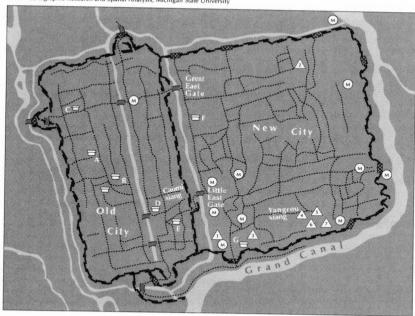

based on map in *Jiangdu xianzhi 1884.*

Official Sites

A Jiangdu County yamen
B Prefectural yamen
C Zheng Family mansion
D Anding Academy
E Ganquan County yamen
F Salt Controller's yamen
G Customs Office

Ⓜ Identified Market Sites

△ Merchant Guilds
1 Jingjiang huiguan
2 Shan-Shaan huiguan
3 Hubei huiguan
4 Lingnan huiguan
5 Anhui huiguan
6 Hunan huiguan
7 Jiangxi huiguan

Fig. 10. Qing dynasty Yangzhou

restaurants, taverns, and brothels.[71] On the whole, however, commercial activities seem to have taken place more at the city's edge than its heart: it was at its perimeters that Yangzhou made exchanges with the world beyond.

In the course of the eighteenth century, however, commercial functions began to spill out of the city. To the north of the New City, covered markets were created along the north bank of the city moat, dealing in luxury goods. Some minor native-place associations were also quartered here, though no details concerning them are known.[72]

Subsequently commercial interests were extended to the south bank as well, the two areas being distinguished by the names of, respectively, "Upper Trade Street" and "Lower Trade Street" (*Shang, Xia maimai jie*).[73] The extension of local commercial interests was evident also in the mushrooming of teahouses, taverns, and even restaurants along the waterway leading to Shugang, which was a popular tourist route.[74] Further afield again, to the northeast of the city, were extensive fish markets, supplied by fishermen carrying their catch from up to seventy *li* away.[75]

The crowded conditions of the city meant that not everyone could find room to live within it. A visiting Frenchman noted:

> Over against the East Side [of the city] there stands a Bridge and a large Suburb; the crowd is always so great at this Place, that the Bridge prov'd too narrow for the Passengers, so that it was found absolutely necessary to keep a large Ferry-Boat about thirty Paces distance, which is scarcely sufficient to carry all that come. . .[76]

The expansion of the city beyond its walls in the mid-Qing period was in some respects simply a repetition of what had taken place under the Ming. If the enlarged Ming city was not able to contain the city population of the eighteenth century, this could perhaps be explained simply by reference to the enormous population growth between the sixteenth and eighteenth centuries. An important difference between these periods, however, lies in the stimulus given to Yangzhou's growth by the reforms in the salt monopoly in the early seventeenth century. These reforms, initiated by the Ming and retained under the Qing, signified that much greater numbers of salt merchants than previously now actually lived in Yangzhou and, more importantly, that larger private fortunes were amassed. Given the general prosperity of the eighteenth century and the importance of the inland waterway system as a trade route, Yangzhou would surely have thrived during this period even in the absence of the salt merchants. It was their presence, however, that ensured the city's exceptional vitality.

The influence of salt merchant wealth in the city was, of course, pervasive, and affected the organization and use of city space in a number of ways. Its most visible effect, however, was in the splendid gardens and villas which they created. This development was mainly an extra-mural phenomenon but did reflect a real spatial extension of the urban area of Yangzhou, an extension forced by the decreasing amount of land available within or directly outside of the city's walls. Only the very wealthiest families could afford to own gardens within the city, and gardens identified as located near the city walls prove on the whole to be earlier in date of construction than those located further away.[77]

The development of the gardens took place mainly northwest of the city, towards Shugang, where the ancient city of Guangling had stood. Here, along the shores of a little lake connecting with the moat, one site after another was developed in magnificent style. Featuring pavilions on hillocks, strange rock formations carefully crafted from specially imported stones, and ornate villas surrounded by blossoming trees, the gardens together made an impressive spectacle. By the middle of the eighteenth century, they formed a continuous stretch between the northwest corner of the city and Shugang, reaching down around the western and southern walls as well. A contemporary description conveys a sense of the progressive development of the area:

> Fifty years ago I climbed up to Pingshantang [on Shugang]. The gardens north of the city were like a tapestry. Only beyond the Guanzhuangmu Shrine was there a stretch of wilderness. . . . Last year in spring I went there again to find that what had been neglected was now beautiful, what had been in pieces was prospering. . . and sight-seers were everywhere.[78]

Until the decline of the salt merchants' fortunes in the early nineteenth century, the gardens were an important part of city space. They allowed the illusion of escape from the bustle of the city proper, were the site of literary gatherings, and attracted innumerable visitors to Yangzhou, particularly during festivals. In a very particular way they distinguished the Qing city from its predecessors, marking it as the product of actions and interactions taking place within the society of that time. The contrast between the Qing and Southern Song cities in respect of their spatial formation is especially telling. During the Southern Song, the extension of city space beyond the limits of the Great Wall was entirely for purposes of defense. During the Qing, a similar extension was wholly for the purposes of leisure and display.

Ultimately, of course, the salt merchants' influence on the city was limited by the strength of the preexisting order. The basic spatial organization of the city had been set by a precedent which it served Qing diplomacy to observe and by a tradition which supported the social distinctiveness of the gentry-official stratum. This allowed the Old City, with its yamens and schools, to remain rather aloof. It had its share of restaurants and teahouses but these were located on its fringe: some within the *enceinte* at the south gate, one at the west gate and a few in the commercial county abutting the Little East Gate, which led into the New City.[79] On the whole, however, the Old City must have presented a relatively staid appearance. Li Dou, Yangzhou's eighteenth-century Baedeker, found little within its precincts worth mentioning.

One significant addition the Old City enjoyed through the beneficence of the salt merchants was the Anding Academy, constructed in 1735. This would have been an interesting case of merchant penetration of the gentry-official-side of the city if, as Ping-ti Ho has stated, this was purely for the education of sons of salt merchants.[80] According to Li Dou, however, the academy was founded as a "place for training scholars of the prefecture" and although in the list of graduates he appends to his account many of those included were not in fact from Yangzhou prefecture, there is little to suggest a systematic connection between merchants and students.[81] As an institution serving the prefecture and supporting its talented scholars with stipends of three *taels* a month,[82] the Anding Academy properly belonged in the vicinity of state institutions. It added to, rather than took from, the Old City's air of attention to affairs of government.

At the beginning of this article it was stated that the influence of the state on the formation of space in China was particularly marked in the case of Yangzhou. Such influence is evident in the resilience of the Old City, but in this respect Yangzhou was not an exceptional case. While bureaucratic structures remained in place, it was only to be expected that bureaucratic space would be retained. In Yangzhou, however, bureaucratic structures also served in quite specific ways to stimulate the city's commercial vitality. Insofar as this vitality was due to the advantages of Yangzhou's location, it was ensured by the river administration, which implemented policies designed to maintain the inland waterway system. The salt monopoly even more directly encouraged the flow of wealth into the city.

The fact remains that merchants, not officials, created Yangzhou's gardens, which constituted the most significant development of city space during the eighteenth century. Yet the special status of salt merchants, and especially of the head merchants, brought them virtually into the category of official merchants. Their privileged position was manifest early in the eighteenth century when, in 1705, they usurped the place of the local officials to greet the Kangxi emperor on his arrival in Yangzhou.[83] Later in the century, the intimacy of their relationship with the throne became increasingly apparent as their efforts to "return imperial grace" (baoxiao), which took the form of substantial contributions to government coffers, were acknowledged by a grateful monarch.[84] They fêted the Qianlong emperor during each of his six southern tours and were honored by his visits to the gardens of some of the most powerful merchants. When honorary ranks were bestowed upon them, the distinction between official and merchant, shen and shang, was not exactly abrogated but was certainly compromised.

A short and perhaps apocryphal tale makes an appropriate conclusion here. Supposedly referring to the construction of Yangzhou's famous white stupa (bai ta), it touches on a small but significant aspect of the creation of Yangzhou's gardens, which is that the imperial visits themselves inspired the merchants to ever greater efforts in this domain. On one occasion, so the story goes, the emperor was visiting the Great Rainbow Garden (Dahongyuan). Struck by its similarity to a garden islet in Beijing, the site of a Lamaist stupa, he expressed his regret that there was no stupa to complete the picture. According to Xu Ke's rendering of the tale,

[The merchant] Jiang heard this and hastily bribed some attendants to draw him the shape of the stupa. Having obtained the drawing, he assembled workmen and prepared materials and in one night the stupa was completed. The following day, Emperor Gaozong visited the garden again, saw the stupa in its majesty and marvelled at it. Thinking it false, he went up to it, but it was composed of brick and stone. He enquired of its origins and sighed, saying: "The wealth of the salt merchants is extraordinary!"[85]

YANGZHOU SOCIETY

In the eighteenth century, gardens were the hallmark of Yangzhou. "Hangzhou abounds in mountains and lakes," ran the saying, "Suzhou abounds in markets; Yangzhou abounds in gardens."[86] In the same way, the salt merchants of Yangzhou came to epitomize Yangzhou society, a perception so strongly reinforced by modern scholarship that it is now sometimes forgotten that the salt merchants were not actually from Yangzhou at all.[87] As Ping-ti Ho has observed, they mostly hailed rather from Huizhou prefecture in Anhui, and the northern provinces of Shanxi and Shaanxi.[88] Merchants of local ancestry, whether of Yangzhou or elsewhere in Jiangbei, were conspicuous by their absence.

This should not occasion great surprise. "The *foreigner* is of course ubiquitous," notes Polanyi of premodern trading groups.[89] The Huizhou and Shanxi merchants of late Imperial China had their equivalents in the Hanseatic and Venetian merchants of medieval and early modern Europe. From Ping-ti Ho's seminal study of Chinese native place associations, it is clear that merchant mobility was so well-established a fact of life in late Imperial China that it had become institutionalized.[90] More recent research has provided detailed accounts of the activities of immigrant merchants in a number of important commercial cities.[91]

That immigrant merchants were a general phenomenon in late Imperial China does not mean that they always and everywhere played the same role with the same effects. The position of these merchant groups in the "host" localities will be found to differ from case to case in accordance with the strength of their total resources (economic, political, social) relative to those of the society they are penetrating or in which they are seeking to participate. To take two ends of the spectrum, the *keshang* (guest merchants) in recently colonized eighteenth-century Guizhou were obviously in a very strong position vis-à-vis the local society while the Ningbo clique was by contrast in a relatively weak position in the complex, cosmopolitan society of nineteenth-century Shanghai, much as they may have profited from their activities there.[92]

In most, if not all cases, the activities of the nonnative merchants in the host society will prove to have substantially altered the society in question, or rather to have created a different sort of society. The transformation of Yangzhou society under the influence of the salt merchants has been depicted as follows by Richard Strassberg:

> The effect which the rise of the merchants had on Yangchow society was less a case of a nouveau riche achieving dominance over former elites than a blending of the traditional stratifications. Aristocrats, officials, gentry, scholars, soldiers, merchants, artisans, and performers crossed economic, political, philosophical, and class lines to a greater extent than ever before. . . . The old elite, anxious to preserve its privileges, entered into symbiotic relationships with those who had come to the forefront under the new dynasty. It was no longer

unusual for official families to develop ancillary commercial operations, nor was it outlandish for merchants to adopt literati tastes and purchase degrees. This process of expansion and overlapping of legitimate social rôles was more pronounced in Yangchow than anywhere else.[93]

There can be no doubt that, as this passage suggests, the great wealth of the salt merchants helped break down old social barriers in Yangzhou in this period. In evidence, Ping-ti Ho has demonstrated the enormous success of salt merchant families in the civil examination system. No doubt for this reason the once paradoxical term *shenshang* (gentry-merchants), which has elsewhere been recognized as current in the late Qing, was in use in Yangzhou at least by 1733, and then in reference to individuals active in Yangzhou in the middle of the preceding century.[94]

Whether this phenomenon was indicative of long-term changes general within Chinese society is a moot point. In itself, it did not have notable consequences particular to Yangzhou much beyond the beginning of the nineteenth century, when the power of the salt merchants was on the wane. There were, however, other consequences for Yangzhou society, which become clear when we examine the composition of Yangzhou society from the perspective of native place origin.

Establishing the local or subethnic identity of individuals or groups in the heterogeneous population of a large city such as Yangzhou poses considerable methodological problems. As William T. Rowe indicates in his study of Hankou, it is often difficult to distinguish between native and nonnative of the city or locality. A family might be resident in a city for a number of generations and still retain its original registration or have indeed changed registration and still be described as hailing from the original place or have changed registration to a third place and yet be a long-term resident of the city.[95] This last phenomenon was marked in Yangzhou, where many salt merchant families had altered their registration to that of the neighboring county of Yizheng rather than to Jiangdu or Ganquan,[96] possibly because land was easier to obtain in Yizheng. The fact remains, however, that Yangzhou was full of people who were described as being in some way or other not of Yangzhou. In the following discussion, which focuses on the correlation between place of origin and position in the urban occupational structure, it is assumed that this was significant rather than otherwise.

Skinner estimates Yangzhou's population ca. 1843 at somewhere around 175,000, ranking it twentieth in size among cities of China proper.[97] In the eighteenth century, its population may have been proportionally greater and had long included very large numbers of immigrants. In the late Ming nonnatives were held to outnumber natives by ten to one,[98] which may not be literally true but suggests a phenomenon of some scale. From very soon after the infamous siege of 1645, Yangzhou was again attracting immigrants to its precincts. Some came to engage in the salt trade while others, including a number of prominent scholars and artists, were drawn to the city by a mixture of economic and social motives.[99] Through the later seventeenth and eighteenth centuries, officials, merchants, and scholars together composed the dominant group of extra-local residents in a city which had a high proportion of immigrants over all.

The most significant group of extra-local origin in Yangzhou comprised the salt merchants, who, as noted above, were overwhelmingly from Shexian county in Huizhou, Anhui. Of the prominent merchant families in the eighteenth century, many seem to have arrived in the second half of the seventeenth century so that by the middle of the eighteenth century they were well established in the city, with fathers, brothers, sons, nephews, and grandsons being represented variously in the salt trade, the examination lists, the bureaucracy, and even scholarly circles. Ping-ti Ho provides some salient examples.[100] These immensely wealthy and powerful merchants were responsible for those aspects of eighteenth-century Yangzhou which made it known as a beautiful, prosperous, cultured, and commercially vital city. In addition to creating gardens, they initiated and financed Yangzhou's prestigious educational institutions, founded welfare centers, built bridges and roads, financed and managed famine relief granaries, and supported its firefighting services.[101]

There were also numerous lesser groups of merchants of extra-local origin in Yangzhou. The geographical origins of these merchants and their corporate strengths are difficult to gauge because of lack of information on the guild organizations in the city, a conventional index to merchant presence. According to a late Qing county gazetteer, there were in Yangzhou six provincial native-place associations, representing merchants from Shan-Shaan (Shanxi and Shaanxi), Hunan, Jiangxi, Hubei, Anhui, and Guangdong (*Lingnan huiguan*), along with the three prefectural guilds of Zhenjiang, Shaoxing, and Jiaxing. These were apparently in existence before the Taiping disturbances[102] and it is possible that they dated back to the late eighteenth century. Judging by the examples of Suzhou and Hankou, the seventeenth and eighteenth centuries were a period when native-place associations proliferated[103] and there is evidence of at least nascent development of native-place associations in eighteenth-century Yangzhou.[104] It seems unlikely, however, that the number of associations in Yangzhou was at all comparable to that in Suzhou or Hankou. Except in respect of the salt trade, Yangzhou was simply not as important a port for either regional or interregional trade as the great commercial cities of the south.

Given the buying capacity of the salt merchants and their reputation for profligacy, it might reasonably be suggested that the consumer market was a major attraction for other merchants coming to Yangzhou. A direct connection between a highly specialized consumer market and the "various departmental and county native-place associations" is suggested by the fact that the latter were located just opposite the covered markets lining the north bank of the city moat, where merchants from all parts of the empire conducted a busy trade in a variety of rare and precious goods.[105] Li Dou supplies much incidental information about individual immigrant merchants but apart from Shexian, almost no place of extra-local origin is mentioned sufficiently frequently to appear as significant. Zhenjiang, however, is described as a major place of origin for those involved in the retail trade in silks[106] and we may speculate about the economic activities of some of the other merchant groups. Merchants from Shan-Shaan were also participants in the salt trade and were undoubtedly involved in the money market as well. The Hunanese were probably engaged primarily in the rice trade and would have benefited in this respect from being in close contact with the Lianghuai salt merchants, who were themselves active in the rice trade and had responsibility for the management and financing of famine relief granaries both in Yangzhou and on the coast.[107] Shaoxing merchants supplied the city with wine for its many taverns, which were much frequented by visiting scholars from Zhejiang.[108] Merchants from Anhui, other than the salt merchants, were probably engaged in the tea and timber trades, common domains of commercial activity for natives of this province.

Literati constituted another significant group of nonnatives in the city. Salt merchants served as patrons to eminent scholars whose presence in Yangzhou in turn attracted men "from hundreds and thousands of *li* away. . . . There were great discussions and enormous gatherings, each [participant] wrangling with the visitor for the sake of esteem and glory."[109] The Anding and Meihua academies, both financed by salt merchant subscriptions, were also a significant attraction for visiting scholars, whether teachers or students.[110] A strong cultural community was, of course, characteristic of the administrative city, where the higher educational institutions tended to be concentrated.[111] In Yangzhou this community was strengthened and enriched through the resources made available from the profits of the salt trade. The same resources created a sizeable market for cultural products, most notably books and paintings, which created economic opportunities for sojourning scholars and artists. Some did very well from the exploitation of this market. Shi Panzi, a native of Shanxi, specialized in the production of half-inch miniature paintings of beautiful women. The demand for these enabled him to charge thirty pieces of gold for each piece of work, which must have provided him with a very comfortable standard of living.[112]

The nonnative origins of incumbents of office in Yangzhou need no special explanation since regulations prohibited an official from serving in his native province. It is worth noting, however, that officials, like the salt merchants, attracted many literati to Yangzhou. The powerful salt controller Lu Jianzeng (1690–1768) was a noted patron of visiting scholars and gathered around him some very talented men, some of whom resided with him for years on end. A list of thirty-two of Lu's associates provided by Li Dou includes four natives of Jiangbei with the remainder coming mainly from Anhui, Southern Jiangsu, and Zhejiang.[113] Many of these, of course, were only briefly in Yangzhou, but they were part of a large transient population which had a significant role to play in Yangzhou's cultural and economic life. Li Dou was hardly exaggerating when he wrote that "of the great scholars and high officials in the empire, there are none who do not come here."[114] The "great scholars" included Hui Dong (1697–1758) and Dai Zhen (1724–1777), who were among Lu Jianzeng's guests in Yangzhou and were employed by him on literary projects.[115]

Yangzhou's population of transients was seasonally boosted by an influx of tourists who did much to stimulate the city's consumer economy by their patronage of its many restaurants, taverns, and teahouses. There were thirteen important festivals in Yangzhou each year and on these occasions people from nearby cities, towns, and rural areas flocked into the city to see the sights and participate in the festivities. The canals in and around the city were crowded with boats as the visitors were ferried to and from temples and gardens, returning to the city to "drink and talk their fill" at popular resorts. At these times, prices for services in the city increased dramatically.[116]

Mingling with the officials, merchants, scholars, petty entrepreneurs and tourists of nonlocal origin were those we may loosely describe as the local people. Among these were local literati, who made their own special contribution to cultural life in Yangzhou. Yangzhou's *baguai* (eight eccentric) painters, for instance, included five natives of Jiangbei, of whom two were from Yangzhou's home counties.[117] Li Dou records the names and achievements of a large number of less prominent artists and calligraphers in Yangzhou, of whom a substantial minority were natives of Yangzhou's home counties or are described as *Yangzhou ren* (person of Yangzhou), a lesser number coming from other parts of Jiangbei. These native sons must have occupied a fairly marginal position in society since they were all but excluded from entry in the local gazetteers, an oversight noted by Li Dou.[118] Lu Jianzeng's exclusive and brilliant literary circle, which is said to have admitted no salt merchants,[119] included very few local scholars or artists. This is perhaps not surprising when we consider that the real achievements of Yangzhou natives in the field of scholarship actually came fairly late in the city's history. Most of the representatives of the *"Yangzhou xuepai"* (Yangzhou school), a group which included scholars from other parts of Jiangbei, were in fact not born till later in the eighteenth century.[120]

Yet even Yangzhou's prominent artists, who were active through the middle of the century, found it difficult to establish a footing in the city. Zheng Banqiao (1703–1765), the most famous of the "eight eccentrics" and one of Lu Jianzeng's circle, came to Yangzhou to sell his paintings whenever times were bad on the land but found it necessary in turn to seek employment as an official when the market for his paintings failed to make ends meet.[121] Gao Fenghan (1683–1749), who also enjoyed Lu's patronage and is sometimes numbered among the "eight eccentrics," is said to have ended his life in poverty and hunger.[122]

For educated men without degrees or special talent there were opportunities of employment in local government offices, where the endless paperwork created a steady demand for clerical skills. The importance of local talent in supplying this need is well recognized.[123] The presence of the salt administration meant that in Yangzhou there was an unusually large number of openings in this domain. Under the salt controller alone, the number of subordinate clerks must have reached into the hundreds.

There were many other avenues of employment for local people. Jade, lacquerware, lanterns, cosmetics, and hair ornaments were all typical Yangzhou products developed from local expertise and labor.[124] The distinctiveness of Yangzhou hairstyles and Yangzhou cuisine suggests two other domains of local expertise,[125] later to be reflected in the expression "*Yangzhou san dao*" (the three knives of Yangzhou), a reference to the tools of trade of the chef, the barber, and the pedicurist. The importance of the service industries as domains of employment for Yangzhou people was probably as marked in their native city in this period as later in Shanghai.[126] Local people otherwise served in all sorts of menial professions: the men as laborers, porters, boatmen, and peddlers, the women as concubines, in whom Yangzhou did a thriving trade; domestic servants, wet-nurses in the orphanage, and common prostitutes.[127] The demand for theater and entertainment of various sorts provided an outlet for local talent, particularly with the development of Yangzhou opera in the last quarter of the eighteenth century.[128] Above all, there were the markets, where anything and everything was bought and sold and where storytellers, acrobats, and even salt smugglers could try by day or night to wrest a living from the city. In many of these areas of employment, Yangzhou natives were joined by immigrants both from elsewhere in Jiangbei and from outside the region.[129]

Assessing the position of Yangzhou's local gentry in the city is complicated by the emergence of gentry of nonnative, salt merchant ancestry, numbers of whom had declared new local loyalties by altering their registration to Jiangdu, Ganquan, or Yizheng. Within a generation or two of making its fortune, many a merchant family had altered its registration and was providing the leaders of Yangzhou society. This was true, for example, of the Zheng family, whose forbears came to Yangzhou from Shexian around the turn of the seventeenth century and changed registration at some time before the end of the dynasty. The four brothers of the third generation of this family appear to have been born and raised in Yangzhou and in the late Ming all of them owned gardens just outside the city.[130] Zheng Yuanxun together with his nephew Zheng Weihong were both graduates of the last Ming metropolitan exam, held in 1643, and both men were highly active members of local society. These men died in the course of the Ming-Qing transition but Weihong's brother, Weixu, and his cousin, Weiguang, went on to gain degrees and hold office under the Qing.[131] The Zheng Family Mansion in Yangzhou was a noted enough landmark to be recorded on the city map in the late Qing county gazetteer.[132] It was situated where gentry families typically lived, near to the schools and academies of the Old City.

Another stratum of gentry, emerging to prominence rather late in the annals of Yangzhou, can be distinguished from the merchant-gentry or gentry with merchant origins although there were marriage ties between the groups.[133] Members of this stratum were officials and scholars who generally owned greater or lesser amounts of land in the rural areas of Yangzhou and Yizheng, but were on the whole insignificant as owners of urban property and initiators of urban development. They did, however, participate in the economic and cultural life of Yangzhou and their number included some very wealthy men. The noted bibliophiles Qin Enfu (1760–1843) and Jiang Fan (1761–1831) must have possessed considerable wealth to amass and house their impressive libraries. The source of Jiang's wealth is clear from the fact that he was impoverished by a drought in 1785 and had to sell off his thousands of books "in order to eat."[134] The well-known scholar-official Ruan Yuan (1764–1849), who served as patron to Jiang Fan after the latter fell on hard times, owned property in both Ganquan and Jiangdu counties and also had business interests in Yangzhou, doing a profitable trade in the reeds grown for fuel on the sandbars at the riverine town of Guazhou, to the city's south.[135] Ruan's cousin, Jiao Xun (1763–1820), was another prominent representative of the local, landowning gentry, although the fact that he spent some time employed as a tutor in Yangzhou suggests that his resources were relatively limited. No doubt he, like Jiang Fan, was affected by the drought of 1785 and perhaps by the floods of the following year.[136]

Jiang Fan and Jian Xun were both involved in the compilation of the 1810 edition of the Yangzhou gazetteer, a gargantuan work of seventy-two volumes, which is notable for its dearth of references to the salt merchants and their activities over the preceding century. Since local scholars were in a minority among the compilers, this cannot be used as evidence of local chauvinism on their part. It does, however, suggest that the distinction between gentry and merchants continued to be felt as significant in Yangzhou. This distinction had a spatial expression, for while members of the local elite were periodically resident in the city, they also maintained a certain distance from it. In the vicinity of Yangzhou, they had alternative centers of activity where they did not have to compete with the salt merchants.[137] These included nearby market towns, of which Guazhou was the most significant, and also rural enclaves such as the Beihu (north lakes) area, where the Yangzhou Ming loyalist, Wang Yuzao (a metropolitan graduate of 1643), retired from the world.[138] Beihu lay in the northwestern part of Ganquan county and both the Jiao and Ruan families owned land there.[139] In the later eighteenth century, Ruan Yuan had a villa on his land, a rural equivalent of the villas which the salt merchants established outside of the walls of Yangzhou.[140] Noteworthy residences, villas, and gardens of other prominent county families likewise tended to be situated at some distance from Yangzhou.[141]

The importance of Beihu as a focus for local identity is reflected in the existence of a little gazetteer, *Beihu xiaozhi* (Little Gazetteer of North Lakes) written by Jiao Xun, and its sequel, *Beihu xuzhi* (Gazetteer of North Lakes, Continued), compiled by a younger scion of the Ruan family, Ruan Xian.[142] But the local literati, including Jiao, also identified strongly with Yangzhou. This is quite evident from the outpouring of works on local history, topography, and literature in the later eighteenth and early nineteenth centuries. The authors of these various works include natives of other parts of Jiangbei, most notably Liu Baonan (1791–1855), from Baoying.[143] The merchant families had by contrast little to contribute in this domain. In fact, the literary celebration of Yangzhou took place mainly after the city's period of greatest prosperity, at a time when the salt merchants were increasingly deserting the city. It could be said that while the immigrant merchant families had created the eighteenth-century city, their departure allowed local gentry to reappropriate it.

Viewed from the perspective of native-place origins, Yangzhou society does not appear quite as Richard E. Strassberg's portrayal suggests. First, the *"nouveau riche"* do indeed appear to have gained dominance over "traditional" elites, although this may have been the more easily achieved by virtue of the relative weakness of the local elite after the devastation of Yangzhou in the mid-seventeenth century. Second, the implication of indiscriminate mingling and the disappearance of social divisions conveyed in Strassberg's description is contradicted by the evidence of a correlation between occupation and native-place origin within the city. Social and economic power in Yangzhou rested largely in the hands of a wealthy immigrant group, which dominated control of the major trading resource of the city's hinterland. Natives of the locality either occupied a subordinate position in the urban social structure or maintained a certain distance from the city. The occupational profile of the eighteenth-century city rather resembles that of a colonial city in which "power (economic, social, political) is principally in the hands of a non-indigenous minority."[144]

CONCLUSION

In recent years, Yangzhou's long-neglected gardens have been restored and local authorities have begun to publish tourist handbooks and popular histories, featuring tales of the eighteenth-century salt merchants. These developments will help fix the image of Qing Yangzhou as a city of merchants and gardens, an image which differentiates it from other cities in the wealthy Lower Yangzi area. And merchants and gardens are, of course, precisely what make Yangzhou an interesting place: they provide the characters and the setting for a colorful eighteenth-century drama.

This image should not be allowed to obscure the fact that Yangzhou had features in common with other Chinese cities in the late Imperial period. I have tried here to show that the bureaucratic city, with its characteristic spaces and institutions, held its own in Yangzhou throughout the period of the rise of the merchants. Visitors to eighteenth-century Yangzhou were dazzled by the city, but they also found it familiar.

But Yangzhou society could not have been duplicated elsewhere in the Lower Yangzi region. Strategically positioned as it was between North and South China, Yangzhou lay in the overlapping margins of two worlds and it bore the marks of both. South of the Yangzi lay not only its markets but also the sources of its entrepreneurial talent and much of its cultural inspiration. These are the things of which the strongest traces remain, both in written records of the times and in the restored remnants of Yangzhou's eighteenth-century gardens. From the north, however, came a different order of things: salt from the coast, fish from the lakes, and a steady stream of people seeking a share in the city's prosperity. From this perspective, a history of eighteenth-century Yangzhou as a city of salt merchants and gardens seems incomplete. As we have seen, there were other people in Yangzhou, and other spaces.

In very general terms, of course, the composition of society in Yangzhou did not differ much from that of the other large commercial cities in late Imperial China, all of which appear to have had significant numbers of sojourners or long-term residents of extra-local origin. In Hankou, as in Yangzhou, immigrant merchants dominated society while natives of the local area occupied the lowest and most marginal places in the city's occupational structure.[145] It seems unsatisfactory, however, to describe this heterogeneity only in general terms, as something common to the populations of all of these cities. It is a characteristic which lends itself rather to an analysis of the structures of dominance within Chinese society, which should in turn allow insights into how these structures were variously experienced and responded to by the members of this society. There certainly seems something more than a Confucian conservatism in the attitude of Zheng Banqiao who, as magistrate of Weixian, was wont to "order his retainers to kick [the salt merchants in audience with him], or have them seized by the head, branded like criminals, and thrown out."[146]

How to conceptualize, describe, and account for these structures is another matter. In the case of Yangzhou, as indicated earlier, I have found the model of the colonial city helpful. The dominance of this city in its region, the exercise of power over urban functions by a nonlocal group, the wealth of the city combined with the lack of real economic diversity in its hinterland, are all factors which bring to mind the example of primate cities in colonial and postcolonial countries. The operation of the salt monopoly in Jiangbei could well be described in terms used to analyze the structure of trade in a place such as Haiti where "licences to trade, means of transport, and processing facilities are in the hands of nonlocal merchants" with the result that "vertical trade" (the export of a few specialized lines of primary production) flourishes with no real returns being made to the producers.[147] Needless to say, the protection and patronage offered by the state to the salt merchants also has a parallel in the creation of the power structures in colonial societies, where the flag has usually followed and sometimes preceded the penetration of the original societies by foreign traders.

The similarity with the experience of certain colonial societies extends to the long-term effects of the salt monopoly and imperial water control policies on Jiangbei. Although the causes of the once constant floods have been largely removed and the Lianghuai salt monopoly has long since disappeared, Jiangbei continues even now to show all the hallmarks of underdevelopment relative to Jiangnan. Despite the backwardness of the northern part of the province, a recent demographic survey found that it was in Xiahe and the coastal region of Jiangbei that the lowest levels of economic development and urbanization were to be found.[148] Undoubtedly related to Jiangbei's long experience of disadvantage relative to Jiangnan is the continuing social and economic marginalization of Jiangbei migrants in Shanghai, apparent at least from the second half of the nineteenth century.[149] This phenomenon is reminiscent of the "internal colonialism" syndrome as described of certain postcolonial societies where, despite formal political and even superficial cultural integration between the dominant and subordinate groups, the structural inequalities of the old colonial society are seen to have been perpetuated in a cultural division of labor.[150]

To extend this analogy would take us beyond the scope of this article. I have employed it here merely to indicate the dimensions of the particular structure of dominance which pertained in Yangzhou under the Qing. It is of course more common among Western sinologists to describe Chinese cities by the extent to which they systematically vary from the cities of preindustrial Europe.[151] A comparison of the cities discussed in this book, however, suggests the need for a greater diversity of models to explain the diversity of urban experiences in late Imperial China. Perhaps it is to an alternative range of urban centers and economic models that we should now be looking for further insights into the functioning of individual cities.

Chapter 5

Shanghai: An Emerging Jiangnan Port, 1683–1840

Linda Cooke Johnson

Conventional interpretations of the development of the city of Shanghai usually begin with its creation as a European treaty port in 1843; the prevailing impression has been that prior to that time Shanghai was a fishing village, the county seat for a marginal region on the edges of the Empire, or at best, in the words of a contemporary European observer in the 1860s, an "insignificant third-class Chinese city."[1] But its later selection as a western treaty port belies such an interpretation, for, with the exception of Hong Kong and Singapore, most of the cities that later became important colonial outposts did not spring into being at the moment of European occupation, but had initially attracted Western attention precisely because they were already commercial centers in their own rights. That this was also true in the case of Shanghai has not been generally recognized.

Even scholarly examinations of the development of Shanghai have tended to concentrate largely on the city's history after 1843; the only two full length books in English on Shanghai, Rhoads Murphey's *Shanghai, Key to Modern China* (1953), and Betty Peh-T'i Wei's *Shanghai, Crucible of Modern China* (1987), each devote only a single introductory chapter to the city's history before 1843.[2] Recent interest in social and economic history has generated several serious articles on specific aspects of nineteenth century Shanghai,[3] but the earlier history of the city and its emergence as a major coastal port prior to the Treaty of Nanking has been neglected.[4] The story of Shanghai as an emerging port in the Qing period is testimony to increasing commercialization of the internal economy of the Jiangnan region in the middle to late Qing period, and indirectly, to the effects of international markets.

JIANGNAN PORTS

South central China as defined by the watershed of the Yangzi River has been one of the richest regions of China for over two thousand years. As early as the Zhou dynasty, the states of Shu, Chu, and Wu, located in the upper, middle, and lower Yangzi respectively, were renowned for their distinctive cultures and phenomenal productivity. In modern terminology, G. W. Skinner has identified the Yangzi valley as made up of several linked "macro-regions," comprising the upper-Yangzi region, modern Sichuan province (ancient Shu), the middle-Yangzi, which includes parts of Hubei, Henan, and Anhui provinces (much of ancient Chu), and the lower Yangzi area, comprising the delta of the river, most of Jiangsu province and parts of Jiangxi, Anhui, and Zhejiang (ancient Wu).[5]

The great cities of the Jiangnan region were Suzhou, Hangzhou, and Nanjing. Two had been imperial capitals: Hangzhou in the Southern Song and Nanjing in the early Ming, while the third, Suzhou, had been the capital of the sometime state of Wu. In the prosperous setting of the lower Yangzi, no single city dominated the region over the long duration, no one had eclipsed the others even at its height. By the Qing period all three were major administrative centers. Hangzhou was the capital for Zhejiang province, Suzhou was the capital for Jiangsu, and Nanjing served as the seat of the governor-general for the *Liangjiang* provinces: Jiangsu, Zhejiang, and Jiangxi.

These three major cities were also ports—Hangzhou was a coastal port for Zhejiang, Nanjing a Yangzi River port and Suzhou, discussed in two papers by Michael Marmé and Paolo Santangelo in this volume, was a principal port on the Grand Canal. Yangzhou, on the north side of the river, was a Grand Canal port which occupied a special niche in the economic and cultural life of Jiangnan, as demonstrated in Antonia Finnane's paper in this volume. The region also supported subsidiary ports such as Zhenjiang, Ningbo, Fuzhou, and Shanghai. Such ports, commercial in nature, and as centers for commerce, were also subject to government levies and tariffs.

Tariffs had been levied on imports and exports to and from coastal ports since at least the Song dynasty.[6] According to the system of Customs stations established under the Kangxi emperor in 1688, the four southern coastal provinces, Jiangsu, Zhejiang, Fujian, and Guangdong each had a principal customs' collection station, located at Guangzhou in Guangdong province, at Quanzhou in Fujian, at Ningbo in Zhejiang, and at Songjiang in Jiangsu province.[7] These stations were in turn each served by a network of smaller tariff stations along the coast, and in the case of Jiangsu province, along the Grand Canal and Yangzi River as well. Since the Song dynasty a station had been located at Shanghai.

Shanghai first attracted notice as a county seat in the Song and flourished as a coastal port in the Song and Yuan periods, but underwent a period of decline and contraction in the Ming. It revived in the Qing; in the mid-eighteenth century the main Customs' station was transferred from Songjiang to Shanghai and Shanghai was made the exclusive station for tariff collections on "outside" commerce for Jiangsu Province. By the Qianlong era (1736–1796) Shanghai had again become a major coastal port; the city continued to thrive in the opening decades of the nineteenth century and, according to at least one scholarly assessment, Shanghai by 1840 could be numbered among the twenty or so largest cities in China.[8] The history of that development in terms of the indigenous Jiangnan economy and the coastal trade of China will be the subject of this paper.[9]

HISTORICAL DEVELOPMENT OF SHANGHAI

The modern city of Shanghai is favorably situated in geographic terms, located on a short but deep tributary to the Yangzi in the delta region close to the mouth of the river. The delta is a natural site for a coastal port, offering a gateway to the Jiangnan region where much of the Empire's grain, tea, cotton, and silk were produced. Shanghai's anchorage, which today is a half-mile wide basin at the confluence of Suzhou Creek (formerly the Wusong River) and the Huangpu River, is protected from storms and attack from the sea, but offers easy access to the Yangzi and the coast. The Huangpu joins the Yangzi at Wusong, about twelve miles north of the city and less than twenty miles from the open sea. Inland access is provided by the Wusong River, which leads to Suzhou, some seventy miles west of Shanghai, the capital of Jiangsu province during the Qing period (the capital was moved to Nanjing in the twentieth century). Suzhou was one of the great preindustrial manufacturing centers of China, and was a major inland port for the Grand Canal. Thus, Shanghai functions as a gateway to China's interior; in the Qing dynasty the port served as the connecting point between the circulation of internal commerce via the Grand Canal and that of coastal and ocean shipping routes.[10]

Although local histories claim a genealogy for Shanghai dating back as far as the Qin dynasty, geological evidence shows that the site of the present city was created by the extension of the Yangzi delta seaward during the first millennium A.D. Prior to the seventh or eighth century the region was still submerged or at best a marshy extension of coastal sands. Even in the Tang dynasty the site of Shanghai was quite literally "on the sea."[11] Popular tradition has it that Shanghai began as a small fishing village called "Hu" or "Hudu," near a fishing spot on the south bank of the Songjiang River.[12] This village grew to become a market town in the Song dynasty. The area was part of Huating county, which in turn was part of Suzhou prefecture. The prefecture was included in the East Jiangnan (Jiangnan dong) circuit.[13]

Historically, Shanghai was only one of a succession of ports located in the vicinity. The alluvial soil and shifting waterways of the delta region formed an unstable terrain where streams and rivers frequently changed course, creating new land where water or marsh had formerly been, and cutting new waterways where none had existed before.[14] A port city in the same general area appears to have been an integral part of the natural and commercial ecology of the region for well over a thousand years. In the Tang dynasty, a naval garrison was located in what today would be the western suburbs of Shanghai. A temple near the site, constructed in the Sui or early Tang was still in existence in the Song.[15] By the Song, however, this port had been superseded by a much larger market town, Qinglong zhen, which was situated on what was, at that time, a broad and protected harbor.[16]

The Wusong River, which today is no more than a creek, was a major waterway in the Tang dynasty, then called the "Songjiang," flowing due east from Lake Tai to the seacoast in modern Chuansha, just south of the mouth of the Yangzi itself.[17] Tributary to the Wusong was the Qinglong River, which flowed north from the fens of Huating county. A wide estuary was created at the confluence of these two streams, not far from the site of the modern airport near Hongqiao in today's Shanghai suburbs.[18]

Meanwhile the future Huangpu River, on whose banks Shanghai city would later stand, had begun as a small stream, or by some accounts a man-made drainage sluice,[19] and was successively widened and deepened through a combination of drainage and diking efforts and the natural scouring actions of the water itself until, by the Song period, it had developed into a substantial tributary to the Songjiang River.[20]

Qinglong market town was at the height of its prosperity from the late Tang through early Song periods. It served as the seaport for

Suzhou and the whole Lake Tai region, and as the collection point for the produce from five counties. Its position was enhanced when Hangzhou became the Southern Song capital; Qinglong served then as a military and naval base as well as a commercial port. Evidence of Qinglong's commercial significance can be seen in the establishment of an office of the Deputy magistrate for Land and Water control in the early Song.[21] By 1077 receipts for commercial taxes outstripped all other sources of government income from Huating county. In the early twelfth century, Qinglong was selected as the location for an office of the Superintendency of Foreign Trade, a branch of the Liang Zhe system of the Hubu (ministry of finance), in charge of the trade and tax collections for five counties.[22] So active and prosperous was the city that it was popularly known as "little Hangzhou."[23]

The shifting sands of the delta that had created the estuary could also obliterate it; silting of its harbor signaled doom for Qinglong. As early as the eleventh century the port was already experiencing serious problems which made it too shallow for larger ships; oceangoing junks and warships had to anchor out in the Wusong River. Although efforts were made to dredge the harbor, the river had begun to shift its channel and scour a new bed away from the Qinglong estuary, eventually leaving no trace of harbor or river on present topography.[24]

As Qinglong lost commerce, the adjacent town of Shanghai profited. Its river, the Huangpu, captured the drainage of the southern fens from the Qinglong. A twelfth century map shows both streams approximately the same size, but as the one diminished, the other increased.[25] Shanghai was officially designated as a market town in 1074. The countryside was prosperous and its population was expanding. In 1292, the five northern *xiang* of Huating county were subdivided to form a new county, Shanghai county, part of Songjiang *fu* (prefecture) in the Liang Zhe circuit; Shanghai market town was designated as its seat.[26] Meanwhile a second Office of Overseas Trade was opened in Shanghai in the late thirteenth century, and only a few years later the bureau in Qinglong was permanently closed, making Shanghai the exclusive office for the lower Jiangnan region.[27] A county college was established in 1294 and a new taxation office was set up in the 1298–1308 period. Contrary to conventional views of Mongol devastation, the Yuan dynasty was a period of flourishing trade, commercial growth, and expanded ocean shipping in Shanghai.[28]

A Yuan map shows a sprawling town, without walls, but having important county offices, a Yuan naval garrison and the headquarters for the grain tribute. The city had twenty-seven stone bridges, a city

temple—though not the same city temple that existed in the Qing—
and a temple dedicated to Tian Hou, the traditional deity of sea-
farers.[29] As Yuan power waned in the latter part of the fourteenth
century, Shanghai was included in the territory claimed by the rebel
salt merchant Zhang Shicheng, who made his headquarters at Suzhou
between 1357 and 1369, an offense that saddled the Suzhou region with
a punitively high grain tax from the early Ming period on, as Michael
Marmé has described in his paper on Suzhou in this volume.[30]

Shanghai's prosperity, based primarily on coastal shipping, continued only as long as the Ming capital was located at Nanjing. When
the capital was transferred to Beijing in 1421, Shanghai was reduced to
a peripheral site. When imperial prohibitions were issued banning sea
traffic, it suffered from loss of trade and cutbacks in naval protection
that initiated a three hundred year decline. The town shrank in size
and population. One index of relative prosperity has traditionally been
the numbers of successful *jinshi* candidates produced by a given locality. Shanghai *jinshi* degree holders had reached an all-time high with
thirteen successful candidates during the Yongle period, before the
move of the Ming capital and the effects of naval cutbacks. These numbers declined dramatically in the latter part of the Ming.[31]

Another indication of the city's decline was its assumption of a
defensive attitude, signaled by construction of the city wall, creating
a barrier between Shanghai and the sea. Loss of naval defenses had
opened the city to pirate depredations in the latter part of the Ming
period.[32] After repeated attacks in the first half of the fifteenth century
the local magistrate authorized construction of a protective seawall.[33]
Though the reason for the building of the city wall and a protective
embankment is specifically related in the county history to defense
against pirate attacks, the latter part of the Ming and early Qing saw
extensive construction of city walls throughout China. In the lower
Yangzi region, walls like the one at Shanghai were usually built of
earth and faced with masonry, fired brick, or tile.[34]

By the late Ming, Shanghai was a fully walled town surrounded by
a protective moat, smaller than it had been in the Song and Yuan
periods, a little over a mile in diameter.[35] The temple of the Shanghai
city god was dedicated in 1602,[36] though the selection of this Song
official as the city's "patron saint" may well have taken place earlier.[37]

By the Qing period the topography had changed still more. The
Qinglong River had disappeared, and the Songjiang, now known as
the "Wusong *jiang*," which had always followed a channel from Lake
Tai to the coast, was joined by the Huangpu. As a result of dredging in

the Ming dynasty, the channel of the Wusong had been shifted, to make a turn to the north just above Shanghai city. It then flowed north to join the Yangzi at Wusongkou rather than emptying into the sea east of Shanghai.[38] Between the mid-fifteenth century and the reign of Kangxi, Shanghai lost many of its former port functions and reverted to the status of a county seat, whose principal distinction lay in the development of a local cotton handicraft industry.

COTTON AND COMMERCE

The sandy alluvial soil of the coastal Jiangnan region where Shanghai was situated, while only marginally suited for rice cultivation, was ideal for cotton. The humid climate around Shanghai provided the right conditions for spinning long fiber cotton yarn with a high tensile strength. With the introduction of more efficient technology in the thirteenth century, cotton gradually became the leading cash crop of the entire region, and its cultivation, processing, spinning and weaving became principal handicraft occupations for peasant families.[39] Songjiang prefecture, including Shanghai county, became the center of much of Jiangsu's cotton production. The eastern sections of the prefecture, where the soil was alluvial and sandy, produced primarily cotton and the western counties where heavier soils and more abundant fresh water were suitable for paddy fields produced mainly rice. Exchange between the two regions increased commercialization as eastern farmers bought rice and the people of the western sections purchased cotton for handicraft industries of spinning and weaving. So large a percentage of arable land in Shanghai county was planted in cotton that it was obliged to import rice from external sources both for food and to meet grain tax quotas.[40]

Commercialization brought about by cotton cultivation, sales of yarn and cloth, and the purchase of grain and other commodities was reflected in a continuing rise in the numbers of market towns in Shanghai county from the fifteenth through the nineteenth centuries.[41] Outstripping population growth, this increase in market towns reflected the pace of continuing commercialization in the countryside.[42]

The development of rural cotton production was supplemented by handicraft manufacturing in Songjiang and Suzhou, where silk weaving and cotton processing were two of the most important of a number of handicraft industries.[43] Cultivation, processing raw cotton, hand spinning, and weaving rough cloth could be done in peasant homes, and while cloth produced in this manner was satisfactory for local domestic use, it was not so much a cash crop as a subsistence necessity. By contrast, to produce cotton cloth that would be in demand in markets throughout China required specialized weaving looms and techniques, and dyeing and finishing processes that used large scale equipment and heavy labor, which were well beyond the capacity of peasant households or individual shops.[44] This type of heavier handicraft industry flourished in the western region, especially in cities such as Songjiang and Suzhou, while in the eastern areas where the cotton was grown, small-scale peasant family handicraft predominated. The massive cotton production of Shanghai and adjacent areas also required large scale merchandising.[45]

Raising the level of production from a peasant sideline to a handicraft industry developed through the combined efforts of brokers, manufacturers, and merchants. The brokers purchased cotton in all states, raw, yarn or homespun from peasant households and local markets, and transported it to the larger towns for finishing where big industrial workshops wove, dyed, rolled, polished, and finished various types of cotton textiles. As many as 20,000 workers were employed in Suzhou in this industry in the mid-Qing.[46] The range of textiles varied from the heavy blue cotton cloth, which resisted wind and cold, popular with northern farmers, to cotton damasks and lawns so fine that they were suitable for imperial underwear. Once the cloth was finished, merchants took over merchandising and shipping to meet the demands of the empire for Jiangnan cotton. The traditional transport route to the north was via the Grand Canal and inland waterways, but after the lifting of the prohibitions on sea traffic, an increasing volume of cotton was shipped from Shanghai by sea to coastal destinations.

Shanghai's fortunes in the Qing period were built on cultivation of cotton as a cash crop, on importing soy-cake fertilizer for the cotton fields, on cotton products as a local handicraft industry, and on transportation for both cotton fertilizer at one end of the production process and for finished cotton textiles at the other end. Fertilizer was a necessity because cotton cultivation exhausted the soil easily and required additional nutrients for sustained yields. The main source of fertilizer was soybean cake, which was not available locally and had to be imported from Shandong and Guandong (Liaodong). A lucrative two-way trade developed between Shanghai and ports in Shandong and Guandong. Beans, bean products, and especially fermented soy-cake fertilizer were imported from the north and in return, cotton yarn, cloth, and tea were shipped out of Shanghai to northern ports.

Cotton brokers and transport merchants dealt in bean products and fertilizer on the routes south to Shanghai and in cotton cloth, tea, and mud from the banks of local waterways, sold in the north as fertilizer to fill the ships on the return trips north.[47] Bean products and fertilizer were high bulk, low value cargoes, but cotton cloth and yarn were high value and lighter in bulk; consequently trips north carrying cotton also required the addition of ballast, usually in the form of mud and sand from the banks of the Huangpu. Labor gangs filled the ballast bags with mud and sand; ships' masters and cotton brokers became involved with the labor disputes that frequently arose among the low paid mud-workers and their bosses.[48] Regular removal of mud and sand from the banks of the Huangpu almost certainly helped widen the river, alleviate silting problems, and enhance the anchorage for deep water shipping.[49]

CUSTOMS AND TARIFFS

Cotton and commerce together were responsible for the first stage of Shanghai's economic revival in the Qing when the city again became a major coastal port. However, one more additional factor that was critical to the emergence of Shanghai must be considered: the impact of government policies that regulated commerce and determined the laws governing coastal and ocean shipping. Just as the Ming prohibitions had precipitated the decline of Shanghai, the lifting of those prohibitions by the Kangxi emperor in 1684 boosted coastal ports by permitting ocean shipping and expanded opportunities in coastal trade, leading to the city's revival in the Qing. Kangxi's proclamations were designed to reopen but also to control ocean shipping, and a salient feature of the new regulations was rigorous enforcement of new and existing provisions in order to tax trade and eliminate corruption.

A new system of external trade tariffs was established, and in 1688 four principal Customs offices were opened in the four southern coastal provinces: at Guangzhou (Canton) in Guangdong, Quanzhou in Fujian, Ningbo in Zhejiang, and Songjiang in Jiangsu. The Customs' division for Jiangsu was known as the "Jianghai Guan," "River and Sea Customs," in contrast to the coastal collection centers in Guangdong, Fujian, and Zhejiang, which were "Hai Guan," or "Sea Customs" only. Each main station also had a number of branches, which in the case of the Jianghai Guan included principal offices at Nanjing, Yangzhou, and Songjiang, and branches at Zhenjiang, Liuhekou, Shanghai, Changzhou, and other towns, altogether some twenty-two river and coastal ports.[50] Tariffs were of two kinds, charged on cargo by weight or value, and by vessel based on size as determined by length. A fully laden ship paid both fees, while an empty one paid only the vessel charges. Cargo fees in the mid-eighteenth century ranged from a low of 2 percent to a high of about 6 percent.[51]

The new regulations were still subject to local variations. One of these involved Shanghai and a rival port, Liuhekou, in Zhenyang county, Taicang *zhou*. Customs regulations in the Ming had divided collection of tariffs in such a way that northern commerce transported by the Grand Canal or by coastal routes was directed through Liuhekou, while trade from southern regions was processed at Shanghai.[52] Such regulations probably reflected conditions in the early Ming when the Songjiang River still ran due east to the sea, and for this reason ships from Shanghai found it extremely difficult if not impossible to navigate north across the massive outflow of the Yangzi with its tides and cross currents. But, after the shift of the river's channel to the north where it joined the Yangzi, Shanghai ships could make northern voyages as easily as could those from Taicang. Although by the early Qing the port at Liuhekou was fast silting up and going the way of Qinglong, these regulations were still on the books, but they may well have been honored more in the breach than in the observance.

Guild records show that groups or cliques (*bang*) of northern shipping merchants from Shandong and Guandong were active in Shanghai as early as the Shunzhi period even before the lifting of the prohibitions.[53] Junk masters and shipping merchants from Shanghai and nearby localities competing with the northerners in the same cotton and fertilizer transport formed the "Sand-junk Merchants' *huiguan*" in 1685.[54] The early success of these merchants and their continuing activities testify to a lively trade in spite of nominal restrictions and competition from Liuhekou.

The main Jianghai Guan station in Jiangsu had originally been located at the prefectural capital, Songjiang, but important subsidiary stations were also active at Longjiang near Nanjing and at Yangzhou, the celebrated salt monopoly port on the north bank of the Yangzi. These three stations and their branch offices effectively divided up the responsibilities of collecting the tariffs on local, river and coastal traffic, and imports and exports to regions of the Southern Ocean (Nanyang) and other foreign ports. The Shanghai gazetteer reported that the resulting situation permitted confusion in trade, duplication of collections efforts, and opportunities for evasion and corruption.[55]

Shanghai's future was assured when a second imperial edict, issued by the Yongzheng emperor in 1730, moved the main Jianghai Guan office from Songjiang to Shanghai and gave it precedence over rival stations at Nanjing and Yangzhou by making it the exclusive customs station for "outside" or external commerce. The local Shanghai gazetteer gives the credit for this change in policy to Jiangsu governor Zhang Kai, who memorialized to the emperor in 1725, asking that a permanent Circuit Inspector be appointed at Shanghai to oversee the Su-Song-Tai Circuit, comprised of Suzhou, Songjiang, and Taicang, in order to collect tariffs and "control unlawful elements." Only in this way could the integrity of officials be guaranteed and proper duties collected. "Moreover," the governor said, "Shanghai is a remote place where there are many coves by the sea where evildoers can appear and disappear at will, and where robberies proliferate." With the appointment of a Circuit Intendant to inspect such practices, "villainous rebels will be suppressed, and Shanghai will be transformed into a safe place."[56]

These suggestions were implemented as a part of the reforms undertaken in the Yongzheng reign; the Office of the Circuit Intendant (colloquially known as the "*daotai*") at Shanghai was provided with increased authority and personnel. The Intendant, who was responsible for military defense as well as tariffs, received a direct Imperial appointment, thus ranking his office above that of the county magistrate and making the Intendant the highest official at Shanghai.[57] By 1735, Shanghai had become the major port of entry and exit for the produce and coastal traffic of the whole lower Yangzi region. The relocation of the Circuit and Customs authorities had far-reaching effects on foreign trade as well, for in spite of Canton's monopoly on western trade after 1760, other ports including Ningbo, Quanzhou, and Shanghai were still open to foreign commerce other than European, and a lively trade with Japan and "Nanyang" continued to flourish.[58]

Shanghai performed two functions, one official and the other commercial. In its official role, as a county seat for Shanghai *xian*, it was on the lowest level in the governing hierarchy of county, prefecture, and province. Its location as the seat for the Su-Song-Tai Circuit, however, placed it in effect two rungs higher because the circuit encompassed not only Shanghai's home prefecture of Songjiang but also a second prefecture, Suzhou, and Taicang (an autonomous semi-prefecture). The circuit *daotai* had a direct imperial appointment as compared with the standard bureaucratic appointments of county and prefect magistrates.[59] As the site of the main customs station for external trade, the city assumed a special role in official and commercial matters. Above all, it was the city's burgeoning commercial activities that elevated it to prominence in the internal circulation of Chinese trade, and by extension, international trade.

The expansion of commerce in the Qianlong, Jiaqing, and early Daoguang periods that lay behind Shanghai's economic development in the Qing also affected the city's physical growth. By the mid-eighteenth century, Shanghai had already outgrown its city walls and was creating a busy commercial suburb with bustling wharves and boat yards between the city's East Gate and the banks of the Huangpu.[60]

The city's two diverse roles, one official, the other commercial were reflected separately in the city's physical morphology. Official aspects, such as the county magistrate's offices, the City Temple, and the new Circuit Intendant's office were inside the walls of the city. The activities associated with commercial functions such as wharves, go-downs, the Jianghai Customs' station and the native-place associations, or *huiguan*, from other parts of China, were located outside the walls in the suburbs that were rapidly expanding. Nearly all of the growth of Shanghai, both inside and outside the walls of the city, can be attributed to mercantile and commercial interests—merchants who reconstructed the City Temple and Yu Gardens and built enormous guild complexes in the suburbs. By the latter part of the Qing dynasty, Shanghai was in effect a city constructed very largely by its guilds and trade organizations.

SHANGHAI'S GUILDS

In the absence of more comprehensive urban statistics, we turn to records of the activities of Shanghai's guilds, *huiguan* or native-place associations and *gongsuo* or common-trade organizations,[61] for an indirect but vivid index of Shanghai's growing prosperity and engagement in Jiangnan produce and coastal trade. The Qing revival began with groups of transport merchants organized in informal cliques or *bang*, dating back to the beginning of the dynasty. As early as the Shenzhi reign, one such *bang* of merchants from Guandong and Shandong, who dealt in beans and soy-cake fertilizer, established a trade association, which was later incorporated as the "Guan-Shandong *gongsuo*".[62]

The quickening pace of commercial activity following the lifting of the prohibitions stimulated the second such organization, again made up of transport merchants and ships' masters, who were engaged in the cotton and soybean trade; they established the Sea Merchants *huiguan*, commonly known as the "Sandjunk" *huiguan*. The activities of this group or clique of ships' masters and associated merchants had begun early in the Kangxi reign although the guild was not formally recognized until 1715.[63] The name was derived from the boats known as "sand-junks" that were employed for coastal shipping on routes between Shanghai and Shandong, Tianjin, Liaodong, and points north. In contrast to the Guan-Shandong *bang*, the "Sandjunk" merchants were local men from Shanghai and adjacent towns such as Baoshan, and Chongming Island, all within the Su-Song-Tai circuit.[64] The guild combined functions of a common-trade organization for ships' masters and owners with those of a native-place association. Its premises were located on "South Huiguan Street" by the wharves in the east suburbs of the walled city. There its members constructed an elaborate guild-hall, temples to Tian Hou and other deities, and a large array of go-downs, docks, shipbuilding facilities, and wharves.[65] It was one of the largest and most influential of the Shanghai guilds for nearly two hundred years.

A dichotomy between locals and outsiders can be seen emerging at Shanghai in the Kangxi period. The first trade association was made up of outsiders, merchants from Guandong and Shandong. The second, the local "Sand-junk *huiguan*" was followed by at least two more outsiders' guilds that combined native-place services with common-trade interests. The Zheshao *gongsuo* of merchants from Shaoxing in Zhejiang was established in 1736, with offices on Quanxin Street inside the city. They were active in a variety of trades including finance, charcoal, butchering, wholesaling, and retail shops.[66] The Huining *huiguan* of tea merchants from Anhui opened in 1755, although its merchants had been active in the city much earlier.[67] The activities of both of these new guilds supplemented the trade conducted by the "Sandjunk" merchants rather than competing directly with them.

Shanghai was not party to the European tea trade at this time, but did trade in teas with northern coastal ports. The teas shipped by the Anhui merchants were collected at Shanghai for transport north, via the Grand Canal, or by sea to northern ports such as Tianjin. From here teas were carried inland to Beijing and to the cities and towns of the north, and probably to border regions as well where a lively exchange in tea and horses had long been in evidence.

When British merchants first arrived in Shanghai they found a "Northern Tea Warehouse" in operation, but shipment of tea to southern ports such as Canton was prohibited.[68] Some of the Anhui tea shipped from Shanghai probably found its ultimate destination in Moscow and St. Petersburg, but not at this date in London. Southern tea, including that destined for Europe, went directly from the tea producing regions by inland routes to Canton. However, the early date of the Anhui merchants' association and the size and strength of their guild testify to a substantial trade in northern tea dating from the early Qianlong period.

The thriving commercial climate of the city quickly attracted growing numbers of merchants and their guilds; numbers of guilds and diversity of trades both increased, though it was always difficult to distinguish between *huiguan* and *gongsuo* by name, since even native-place associations often used the term *gongsuo* in their titles and vice-versa.[69] Merchants and ships' masters from Fujian established the Quanzhang *huiguan* in 1757, and began construction of its guildhall in 1769.[70] The presence of large numbers of ships' masters and merchants, who specialized in sugar, lumber, and other products from the southern coastal regions of Fujian and Taiwan, indicates expansion of trade on the southern routes in the Qianlong period. The Fujian guild was quickly followed by another group of southern coastal transport merchants from more distant ports; the Chaozhou *huiguan* was founded in 1783 by Guangdong merchants from three counties. Their activities brought additional "Nanyang" trade in sugar, lumber, and other southern goods to Shanghai.[71]

One of the most powerful of all of the "outsider" guilds, the "Siming *gongsuo*," which in spite of its name was actually a native-place association, was established by merchants from Ningbo and Shaoxing in Zhejiang in 1796, early in the Jiaqing reign. In part its members came from an internal split in the earlier Zheshao guild, but in part they also represented a new group led by the Fang family of Ningbo.[72] This association established a very large compound west of the North Gate of the city, on land that would later be claimed by the French Concession. It became known as the "Ningbo Guild," and its members were involved in the money trade, tobacco, opium, shipping, and construction.[73] (Locations of the guilds are shown on the map of Shanghai, Fig. 11.)

More Fujian merchants were attracted to Shanghai in the Jiaqing and early Daoguang years. A second Fujian guild, the "Jianting *huiguan*," was probably established in 1796 (though it was not registered by the magistrate until 1822); it was made up of merchants from Jianning and Tingzhou who specialized in paper, rope, and palm fiber products.[74] A third Zhejiang guild, the "Zhening *huiguan*," of Ningbo merchants was first set up in 1819, formally registered in 1829. The Fang lineage from Ningbo was prominent in this guild also.[75] Sojourners from Fujian and Zhejiang constituted the majority of "outsiders" in Shanghai in the period prior to the Opium War, but they were joined by equally large numbers of Cantonese after 1843.

A second Guandong guild was established in 1830 by merchants from two counties on the coast; originally called the "Chaohui *gong-suo*," it was actually a native-place association.[76] It was this guild that later became infamous as the "Swatow Opium Guild." While most of the *huiguan* represented groups from outside Jiangsu province, at least one Jiangsu group of merchants also established a native-place association. This was the "Juzi" *gongsuo*, representing merchants from Qing-kou market town in the area of Jiangsu north of the river, Jiangbei.[77]

Associations raised funds by levying fees and collecting donations from their membership, whose names and contributions were occasionally made public—probably not in full, for reasons that will become evident below. Charitable activities conducted by native-place associations benefited fellow countrymen, widows, orphans, the destitute, and those who died far from home. The initial establishment and subsequent maintenance of each association, with its enclosed compound, temples, halls, gardens, dormitories, mortuaries, and cemeteries represented a very substantial financial investment in Shanghai business.

The size of these guilds and the scale of the expenditures required to construct a typical "outsider" native-place association can be gauged from a description of the "Quanzhang *huiguan*." The compound was located in the eastern suburbs, just north of the "Little East Gate" of the city, and consisted of:

> . . . two main halls, one dedicated to Guandi, and the other to Tian Hou, a large stage for theatrical performances, two *kan-lou* buildings, corridors, courtyards, etc., and, in the center of the main courtyard, a precious bronze *ding* weighing over 1,000 catties, inscribed with the names of the contributors.

In addition, the guild owned more than thirty *mu* of land for a graveyard and an additional forty *mu* of fields. On surplus land the guild constructed houses to lease out, proceeds from which were used for charities.[78] The establishment of such a guild and the construction of its halls and gardens was no small undertaking; the profits that paid the dues that supported these associations were clearly substantial.

Meanwhile a second type of guild, which was made up of merchants engaged in a common trade, handicraft, or service, was also established at Shanghai. These organizations also used the term *gong-suo*, now applied in a more specific manner than had been the case

with principally native-place associations such as the Siming or
Chaohui *gongsuo*. Membership in these groups, while frequently drawing on cliques from various regions such as Suzhou, Ningbo, and
Shaoxing, always included and usually was dominated by Shanghaiese.
The earliest such organization was probably the "Finance *gongsuo*,"
whose activities were said to have dated back to the Kangxi period,
although the organization was not formally registered until 1776. Its
offices were located in the "Nei Yuan," an inner garden in the West
Garden complex of the City Temple.[79] The "Construction Workers'
gongsuo" is also said to have originated at a very early date, but was
not formally registered until much later.[80] Among the common-trade
associations of the Qianlong period were a "Cotton Trades *gongsuo*,"
the "Bean Association," the "Fresh meat (butchers') *gongsuo*," a
Medicinal guild and even one that dealt in hats from Peking for
officials.[81]

Most of the common-trade organizations were made up of merchants in wholesale or retail operations or in banking, but several also
were engaged in transport. At least two were also engaged in international trade. The "Northern and Southern Wholesale Commodities
Association" was established in 1808, and, as the name suggests, managed transport of merchandise from northern and southern ports.
Among the commodities it traded were foreign textiles.[82] Indeed, foreign cotton, *xiyang bu* appeared in Customs' lists as early as 1785.[83]
The "Sugar, Candy and Imported Goods Association" was established
in c. 1822 by Fujian merchants dealing in sugar and foreign goods.[84]

Common-trade organizations typically did not have large compounds nor did they provide religious or charitable services to members. Their offices were located in or near the gardens of the City Temple or the adjacent Yu Gardens. They basically provided trade and
handicraft services for the growing city and its mercantile community;
contributions to a general fund provided a rudimentary form of insurance against bankruptcy for the merchants enrolled in certain of these
common-trade organizations. Instead of providing benevolent services
for members as the native-place associations normally did, common-
trade organizations contributed to local Shanghai charities such as the
Tongrentang which provided soup kitchens and other benevolent services to the poor, the Heyitang which dispensed medicine to the poor,
and the Yuyingtang which cared for foundlings, to cite only a few.

Native-place associations typically had large compounds which
served as a home-away-from-home for members while common-trade
organizations had more modest premises, a courtyard or a pavilion in

the Yu or City Temple gardens. But the most visible distinction between native-place associations and common-trade organizations lay in
their respective locations inside and outside the city walls. At Shanghai
as at other cities, the territory inside the walls was largely reserved for
official, religious and educational functions, residences, and retail
shops. In the center of the walled city were county offices, the *xian* college, and the City Temple with its adjacent gardens. Here also were
located the offices and courtyards of the common-trade organizations,
symbolically situated in the heart of the city. Street names such as
"Avenue of Great Peace," "Lung Men Academy Street," "County
Office South Street," and "Street in Front of the Circuit Office"
reflected the dignity of prevailing official attitudes.

Native-place associations, by contrast, were usually located outside
the city wall and were distinguished by their large compounds which
included halls and temples for local deities, theatrical stages, enclosed
gardens and courtyards, business offices, hostels for sojourning merchants, mortuaries, cemeteries, and even tracts of land devoted to rental housing. A single exception was the "Zheshao" *gongsuo* guild,
whose offices were located on Quanxin Street inside the north gate of
the city, but their temple, halls, and dormitories were located outside
the city, in the *Laocha* or "Old Water-gate" section of what would
later become the international sector of Shanghai after its opening as
a European treaty port in 1843. Typically native-place associations
bought or rented land, constructed the guild premises and also built
workshops, retail shops, warehouses, hongs, wharves, and constructed
rental housing and purchased large tracts of land in the outlying suburbs for cemeteries. Several even owned country villas.

Street names in the suburbs were stridently commercial in nature.
"South Hui Guan Street," "Pickled Melon Lane," "Foreign Hong
Street," and "Salt Wharf," were all names of the streets in the suburbs
east of the city walls.[85] The activities of these guilds and construction
of their various properties had major formative effects on the development of the suburbs and distribution of urban space in Shanghai. Their
location outside the walls also had symbolic overtones, designating
these associations as "outsiders."

The pattern of guild construction expanded outward in succeeding
years. The earliest guilds were usually built closest to the city and later
guilds were farther away. Cemeteries, which were initially outside the
ring of suburbs, were moved outward as the suburbs grew ever more
congested during the course of the nineteenth century. By 1840, nearly
every important building, hall, temple, and garden in Shanghai and its

sprawling suburbs, except for government structures, owed its existence to one or another of the native-place or common-trade associations. The east suburbs of Shanghai were thick with "outsider" native-place compounds and offices, while inside the city similar numbers of "insider" trade organizations were clustered in the City Temple and Yu Gardens. In all, twelve guilds existed in the Qianlong period and by 1830 there were twenty-one native-place and common-trade guilds at Shanghai. The location of Shanghai's guilds in the early nineteenth century is shown on the map below.

The guilds did more than affect the physical layout of Shanghai; they also reflected its economic health. The gardens and pavilions of the "insiders" within the walls and the extensive compounds of the native-place associations in the suburbs represented proud statements of conspicuous consumption. Construction of guilds amounted to a visible form of capital investment. But while the nature of that investment in land, construction, and services can be detailed, its fiscal contribution is more difficult to estimate. Individual lists of contributors to native-place associations and charitable organizations are preserved, but only in part. While such lists, often inscribed on commemorative vessels or plaques, served public relations functions, the actual size of an individual's contribution was generally expressed in symbolic rather than real numbers. These records are fragmentary and partial at best. The currencies cited offer a bewildering combination of copper cash *wen*, silver *taels* and Carolus or Mexican dollars *yuan*, such that a composite figure would in any case be difficult to construct.

An effort to compile figures from the fragmentary existing records of capital investment would still be inadequate, for wealth was customarily concealed. As one source reported in the case of banking, the capitalization of small banks and medium-sized banks might be generally known, ranging between 500 *taels* for the smallest shops to 1,000 *taels* for middle-sized operations, but "big money shops," whose backers were all said to have been very wealthy men, showed only 3,000 to 5,000 *taels* on the books, although the actual investments were certainly far larger.[86] Wealth was often hidden to forestall taxation or the many "voluntary" contributions to which merchants were subjected. Therefore it is unlikely that the real totals expended on the construction and maintenance of guild premises, much less the actual size of the contributions by their members to Shanghai's economy, will ever be known.

In spite of the lack of hard fiscal data, an effort can be made to estimate the contribution of the guilds to Shanghai's economy on the

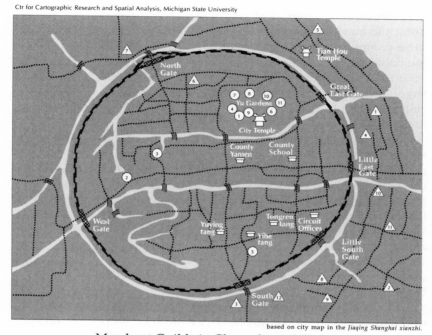

Ctr for Cartographic Research and Spatial Analysis, Michigan State University

based on city map in the *Jiaqing Shanghai xianzhi.*

Merchant Guilds in Chronological Order

○ Common-trade Associations
  1 Cotton gongsuo
  2 Silk Merchants gongsuo
  3 Tea Merchants gongsuo
  4 Fresh Meat gongsuo
  5 Medicinal Herbs gongsuo
  6 "Nei Yuan" Financial gongsuo
  7 Beijing Hat gaongsuo
  8 Southern and Northern Commodities gongsuo
  9 Ready-made Clothing gongsuo
  10 Sugar, Candy and Imported Goods gongsuo
  11 Bean-oil and Bean-cake Fertilizer gongsuo

△ Native-place Associations
  1 Guanshandong bang
  2 Sand-junk Merchants' huiguan
  3 Huining huiguan
  4 Quanzhang huiguan
  5 Chaozhou huiguan
  6 Zheshao gongsuo
  7 "Siming" gongsuo (Ningbo, Zhejiang)
  8 Zhening huiguan
  9 Juchi gongsuo
  10 Jianting huiguan
  11 Chaohui
  12 Jiangxi huiguan

Fig. 11. Qing dynasty Shanghai

basis of the type and number of guilds established in the period prior to the Opium War based on their respective construction projects and investments.[87] These projects are detailed in the guild records in the local gazetteers.[88]

For the native-place associations capital expenditures involved buying or renting land, constructing temples, stages, halls, gardens, dormitories, mortuaries, and cemeteries. For common-trade associations, the material expenses of construction were less significant since these groups usually had smaller quarters in a courtyard or structure in the public gardens, but their investments often included a fund for insurance for members, so that their capital investments were actually larger than their real estate holdings would suggest. Both types of guilds frequently raised funds for repair and refurbishment of their premises.

One inscription from Zheshao *gongsuo* in early Daoguang period shows contributions over one hundred and sixty thousand cash, no doubt a very partial listing of actual contributions.[89] Other records suggest that very large sums were raised to found a major *huiguan*, with lesser amounts required for repair and maintenance.[90] Though much of the endowment for any guild was obviously concealed, the sums involved may have been very large indeed. Capital investments for *qianzhuang* banks ranged from 5,000 to 10,000 *taels* for a small or medium-sized establishment up to estimates of well over twenty thousand for some of the major banks at Shanghai—and there were over a hundred banks in the "Finance Guild."[91]

The capital required to establish a guild can conservatively be estimated on the basis of such fragmentary figures, as perhaps 20,000 *taels*, about the amount of capitalization suggested for a large bank at this time. For a native-place association expenses included the purchase of land and construction of buildings. Some very large native-place guilds such as the "Sandjunk" Merchants, Siming, and Chaozhou associations invested far more than did smaller guilds and must have far exceeded this figure. For a common-trade organization capital investments might be estimated at 10,000 *taels*, or half the investment of a typical native-place association, close to the capital requirements of a mid-sized native bank.[92] Repairs or refurbishments could then be estimated at one-half the cost of establishing a common-trade organization, or 5,000 *taels*, about the amount required for a small bank,[93] although here again the costs of rebuilding one of the larger native-place compounds would have far exceeded this average figure. In this manner some idea of the contribution of the guilds to Shanghai's economy can be statistically demonstrated, bearing in mind that the figures represent estimates only and are designed to show the approximate rate of investment, not actual totals.

Presented in this manner, the data can be interpreted in several different ways. One method is to construct an index of Shanghai's prosperity over time, another is to estimate the cumulative totals of

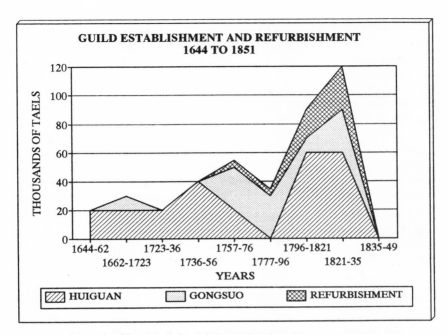

Fig. 12. Shanghai Guild Establishment and Refurbishment 1644–1851 [based on *SHXXZ* (1918) 3:1a–15b; and Du Li, pp. 5–7]

capital investments in Shanghai's economic growth. A chronological chart of guild investments shows periods of activity alternating with slower growth. A peak of activity can be seen in the mid-Qianlong period, 1757–1776, followed by a slowdown in late Qianlong, 1777–1796. Business flourished in the Jiaqing reign, 1796–1821, and reached a peak in the early Daoguang period, 1821–1835, with an estimated investment of 120,000 *taels*. After 1835 virtually all guild activity came to a halt.

While the rest of China was experiencing what is now recognized as a nationwide "Daoguang depression," linked to the silver drain and opium imports plus the cumulative effects of population expansion, Shanghai's economy was still strong through 1830 or even 1835. The population in this region, already large by the Ming dynasty, had grown only relatively slowly; the region was heavily commercialized, enabling it to support a much denser population than predominantly agricultural areas; and opium was as much an economic asset, due to its effects on the banking industry, as it was a social deficit at Shanghai. The net result was that the 1820s and early 1830s were an era of "Daoguang prosperity" in Jiangnan. Beginning in the early 1830s a marked contraction occurred in Shanghai's economic activity, heralded by the collapse of the market in "Nankeen" cotton exports and followed by the Opium War; this depression affected commerce and guild activity, and appeared to linger through much of the 1840s.

In a very real sense the guilds were responsible for the physical growth of the city. Common-trade associations renovated the courtyards and gardens and built the halls and pavilions of the Yu Gardens, the Gardens of the City Temple and the West Garden. Native-place associations constructed the suburbs with magnificent compounds, wharves, jetties, boatyards, warehouses, and go-downs. They built rental housing on speculation, bought land and laid out cemeteries. Each new investment extended the geographical and physical area of the city. After 1835, investments remained static, with no new guilds constructed after that date and repairs made to only one.

GRAIN

Since the Yuan dynasty, the Su-Song-Tai circuit had been subject to an unusually high tax in the form of grain tribute to the capital. Early in the Ming dynasty, in 1395, the quota for Suzhou alone stood at 1.8 million *piculs*, almost a tenth of the total tax for the entire empire.[94] In spite of later reductions the grain quota remained punitively high well into the Qing period. Meanwhile, commercialization of cash crops expanded and cotton replaced rice as a major crop; as a result grain also had to be imported for local consumption. Transport of rice from the upper and middle Yangzi regions became a major industry at Suzhou in the mid-Qing period.[95] The collection point for the Grain Tribute had customarily been at Suzhou; grain tribute barges made their way north to the capital via the slow but safe route of the Grand Canal. As long as the tribute grain was shipped by canal, it had little direct economic effect at Shanghai, apart from purchases needed to meet local quotas.

Occasionally in the past, problems with the Canal had made it necessary to ship the tribute by sea, but these instances were exceptions. However, in the 1820s flooding on the Yellow River caused serious disruptions in the Canal, and for several years the sea route was the only recourse. These floods were only a prelude to the mighty change in the course of the River from the former southern route to a new northern route, which was not ultimately completed until 1853.

The change of course began in the early 1820s with intermittent flooding, and by 1840 the Grand Canal was unnavigable north of Jinan. When the Canal was inoperable and transport by sea was necessary, Shanghai became the principal port for embarkation. Shipment of the grain tribute was first transferred temporarily to Shanghai in 1824 when the government hired—or more likely commandeered 1,560 sea-going junks to carry 1,600,000 *shi* of grain to Tianjin. For several years shipment alternated between the Canal when operable and by sea when necessary. But, as conditions on the Yellow River worsened, shipment by sea became the normal course, though the headquarters of the Grain Tribute fleet was not formally moved from Suzhou to Shanghai until much later in the early 1850s.[96]

Since the flat-bottomed barges that had transported the grain tribute by canal were unsuited for sea transport, the *hai-fang* prefect at Shanghai, in charge of coastal defense, and by extension, the grain tribute, commissioned the construction of seaworthy junks, and hired large numbers of privately owned "sand-junks." In spite of low government transport rates, masters of the commandeered ships actually profited from the government's new demands, since transport of grain to the north could be combined with shipments of beans and fertilizer south on the return trip. Cotton was allowed duty free as "private commerce" on the northern voyages and junks no longer sailed from Shanghai with mud and sand for ballast. The local economy at Shanghai profited from construction and ship building and new jobs that resulted from the transfer of the grain fleets. On the negative side, however, gangs of unemployed Canal boatmen sought work in Shanghai and caused local disturbances.

FINANCE

Finance was yet another activity that made a major contribution to Shanghai's growth. The first native banks or *qianzhuang* shops in Shanghai were established by Suzhou and Ningbo bankers and merchants, using profits from the import and sale of charcoal. Additional capitalization came from wealthy Suzhou merchants with profits from pawn shops, or from Suzhou gentry landlords. Suzhou, with its long history as the center of commerce, had pioneered in the development of banking in the Jiangnan region, closely followed by Ningbo bankers, who were also engaged in finance at Shanghai from the Qianlong period on. Shanghai merchants invested profits made from the soy-cake and cotton trade.[97] The "Finance *gongsuo*," colloquially known as the "Nei Yuan," had members from the Suzhou, Ningbo, and Shanghai *bangs*, but was conducted in sufficient part by local men to rate a location in the inner precincts of the City Temple.[98]

These small banks were all members of the "Nei Yuan" *gongsuo* which operated much like other trade associations; it performed an essential service for the *qianzhuang* banks of Shanghai by operating a daily clearing house, where proprietors of money shops and banks met each afternoon to compare and rectify their books. Due to this system, notes could easily be drawn on one establishment and paid at another, and bank notes issued by member banks and shops circulated freely in Shanghai, providing ready credit and a convenient alternative to cumbersome exchanges in various different currencies. The rapid increase in numbers of *qianzhuang* banks in the later Qianlong reign reflects an increase in commercial services, goods and prices, and expansion of the money supply.[99] According to the history of banking at Shanghai, the number of finance shops and *qianzhuang* banks grew from eighteen in 1776 to eighty-eight in 1796 to a total of one hundred-and-twenty by 1858.[100] An actual count of the establishments listed in an inscription of 1798, however, shows one hundred and twenty-five money shops or "sources" (*yuan*).[101]

Expanding trade and commerce played a major role in the development of financial services, but so also did foreign silver. Shanghai was located at a critical juncture where Chinese and foreign currencies, including silver, were exchanged well before the actual arrival of westerners at the port. Bank notes had first been issued at Suzhou in lieu of silver in the seventeenth century.[102] But silver was preferred. As early as the 1780s, accounts at Suzhou were customarily expressed in silver dollars rather than in *taels*. Increasing use of actual silver and substitute bank notes in transactions at Suzhou and in Shanghai in the 1820s on is documented by Wang Yeh-chien. The shortage of silver that developed in China after 1830 exacerbated the tendency to substitute paper for silver and also encouraged the development of the "Suzhou system" of using opium or notes issued on opium in lieu of silver.[103] Bank notes compensated for the silver drain in the local setting, and opium, which underwrote lucrative loans at high rates of interest, can be seen as an economic asset. Local banking played an important part in all these developments.

Financial figures from the 1850s reveal the general composition of the banking business at Shanghai in more detail, and shed some light on the earlier state of financial development in the city. Of the one hundred-and-twenty banks operating at Shanghai in 1858, fifty were classified as very small shops, with a capitalization of between 500 and

1,000 *taels*; their business was purely local in character. Eight to ten *qianzhuang* were classified as "big money shops," whose backers were all said to have been very wealthy men, although the books showed only a capitalization of between 3,000 and 5,000 *taels*. These shops dealt primarily with the "sand-junk" transport business, shipping, cotton brokers, and the bean-cake fertilizer trade—all of which constituted "big business" at Shanghai.[104]

The remaining shops, perhaps sixty in number at this date, were middle-sized operations. They dealt in two distinct types of business: the financing of local manufacturing, including commercial loans, and opium. Such banks financed imports of opium, bought illegally off Western ships or imported by the various merchants. The opium was sold locally and up river at places such as Yangzhou, Nanjing, and Suzhou. Notes issued by Shanghai banks on opium commanded a relatively longer term and higher rate than other types of business, resulting in profits of between 8 percent and 10 percent per month. The business was both illegal and highly speculative; it could at best produce profits of up to 120 percent per year, or at worst result in quick bankruptcy.[105] From the documented increase in Western opium sales and the demonstrated rate of expansion in Chinese banking, there appears to be good reason to believe that Shanghai banks were deeply involved in the opium business long before 1842.

INTERNAL TRADE

The principal motive force behind Shanghai's growth was commerce, of which by far the greater proportion was internal. A recent article on the development of Shanghai commerce in the early Qing states that as early as 1740 the total trade passing through the Jianghai Customs is estimated at nearly fourteen million *taels*, while customs receipts came to almost 80,000 *taels*. These figures are said to represent a little over half of the volume of traffic that passed through Canton at a comparable period.[106] Tariff quotas were steadily raised from 23,000 *taels* in 1690 to 38,000 in 1722 to 62,000 in 1735, and finally to 77,000 in 1764, and finally stabilized at 73,000 between 1815 and 1838.[107] By the 1820s, the annual trade through the port of Shanghai is estimated to have reached approximately 30 million *taels*.[108]

This evidence of commercial prosperity is reinforced by descriptions of early western visitors, indicating that a massive volume of trade flowed through Shanghai's port. A visitor to the port of Shanghai in 1834 described it as ". . . a forest of innumerable masts" where native shipping was double that at Canton.[109]

Rhoads Murphey has estimated that trade at Shanghai as reported in the 1832–1834 period made the city already one of the leading ports of the world, with a volume of shipping equal to or greater than that of London in the same period.[110] John King Fairbank noted that immediately after the opening of the treaty port in 1844, Shanghai's annual imports from North China alone were said to have been worth $10 million a year, while those from the south were valued at perhaps twice as much.[111]

A Jianghai Customs' Handbook from Qianlong 50 (1785) lists the various products on which duties were charged. Prominent among these items are all kinds of silk and cotton textiles, damask, lace, yarn, thread, and bulk cotton, which together comprise the largest category of the inventory, paper, paper products and books, other manufactured items, foodstuffs and comestibles including tea, items of clothing, hides and leather products, wood and bamboo manufactured items and bulk lumber, metal tools, straw and grass bulk and woven items, dyes, drugs, and medicines.[112]

Shanghai county and Songjiang prefecture were prime cotton producing areas; cotton raised and spun by peasant families in the countryside was woven, dyed, and polished in towns and cities such as Shanghai, Songjiang, and Suzhou. By contrast, silks came from Suzhou, Nanjing, and areas to the west of Shanghai. Paper, wood, and bamboo products were major manufactures at Suzhou. Shanghai's function as Suzhou's seaport is clearly evident in the lists of this customs' manual. Other products known to have been important in Shanghai's economy such as bean, bean-cake fertilizer and bulk tea are not included in the handbook; quite probably the duties on these products were collected independently by the licensed brokers and transport merchants of the "Northern Tea Warehouse," "Sand-junk Merchants'" guild and the bean brokers guild.[113] At the date of the handbook, in 1785, these products that made their way in and out of the port of Shanghai were virtually all destined for the internal Chinese market; the strength of that market and degree to which Shanghai was deeply embedded in its Jiangnan hinterland is reflected in the prosperity of the port.

EFFECTS OF FOREIGN TRADE

Shanghai may be seen as a "broker city," a critical point of transshipment between the river junks and barges of inland waterways of Jiangnan and the deep draft shipping of the coastal commerce. Jiangnan silk figured in the export market at Canton and "Nankeen" cotton also enjoyed a strong demand before 1830. Imports of foreign silver and exports of products such as silk and cotton that were ultimately destined for foreign markets played an increasing role in stimulating commercial prosperity. Tea, however, was a special case because prior to 1844 tea exports from Shanghai were restricted to northern destinations; Anhui and Fujian teas made their way to Canton by circuitous overland routes, not through the port of Shanghai.

Silk, grown throughout the Jiangnan region, with major manufacturing centers in Suzhou and Nanjing, was a standard export item. Silk products figured prominently in the tariff list of 1785.[114] A probable idea of the value of pre-opium war silk at Shanghai can be gained by examining the figures for the years immediately after the opening of the port. In 1845, Shanghai shipped 5,146 *piculs* of raw silk, which amounted to 48.7 percent of the total for Canton and Shanghai combined; the percentage rose steadily between 1845 and the 1850s until Shanghai shipped fully 92 percent of all raw silk exports.[115] In spite of the increased trade through Shanghai, the values remained limited, no more than L 40,000 in 1846 and in 1847.[116]

Cotton provides the most dramatic example of both positive and negative impacts of foreign demand on the local economy of Shanghai. The greatest part of the market for Jiangnan cotton was indigenous but there was also a substantial foreign demand. In the late eighteenth and early nineteenth century European markets sold large quantities of a heavy cotton fabric, usually dyed with indigo, known as "Nankeen," which was much in demand for gentlemen's breeches in Britain and America in the eighteenth and early nineteenth centuries. Most "Nankeen" cotton was grown and spun in peasant households in Songjiang prefecture, and sent for dyeing and finishing to Songjiang, Shanghai, or Suzhou.

In spite of its name, "Nankeen" cotton had no direct connection with the city of Nanjing, but rather referred to the southern half of Jiangsu province which was popularly known as "Nanjing *sheng*," or "Nanjing province." So the name for the distinctive blue cotton cloth from Songjiang prefecture in Nanjing *sheng* came to be "Nankeen."[117] Finished bolts were shipped out of Shanghai to Canton for international sale.[118] Canton statistics therefore reflected Jiangnan production.[119] The graph in Fig. 13 shows recorded exports of "Nankeens" from Canton between 1786 and 1835.

Recorded sales at Canton began in 1786 with a modest 372,000 bolts, but soon rose to an average of over one million bolts per year, sold to foreign merchants in the years between 1795 and 1810. Trade

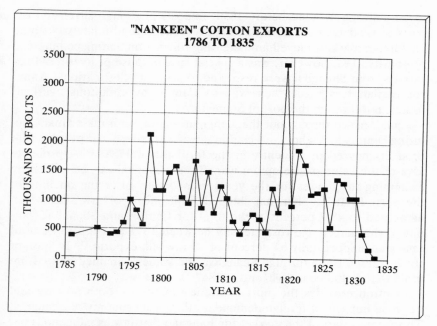

Fig. 13. "Nankeen" Cotton Exports 1786–1835 [based
on Quan, "Mien fang zhiyeh," p. 40]

fell off somewhat between 1810 and 1815, with average shipments of
600,000 bolts annually. But from 1817 to 1820 cotton exports increased
dramatically. One million, two hundred twenty-nine thousand bolts
were exported in 1817, and this total rose to over *three million* bolts in
1819. Thereafter until 1830 the average annual export was well over
one million bolts.[120] But after 1830 the trade totally collapsed, and
with it the entire Shanghai economy appears to have suffered a severe
contraction.

Chinese records do not indicate the immediate cause of the dramatic fall in cotton textile exports. Chinese scholars have attributed some
of the problem to imports of foreign yarn from Bengal, which undercut
production from local producers and spinners.[121] But, internal factors
alone do not seem to be sufficient to account for the very dramatic
fall of cotton exports in the early 1830s. External causes may well
have played a major role in the collapse of the Chinese market in
"Nankeens."

In looking for market factors to explain the collapse of cotton exports, two possibilities may be suggested: first, competition from machine manufactures and second, disruption of trade relations. In what appears to be a classic case of indirect economic imperialism, the bottom dropped out of Chinese cotton textile exports at exactly the same period that British power-loom production of cotton textiles quadrupled in quantity and halved in price.[122] Prices of raw cotton on world markets also were reduced owing to the invention and by the 1830s widespread use of the cotton gin in America. Thus, international competition can be seen as a powerful factor.

Trade relations were also significant, since the collapse of the cotton textile export market at Canton coincided with the cessation of the British East India Company's monopoly on the China trade in 1834.[123] Cottons shipped out of Canton prior to 1834 had been handled by the East India Company, as was virtually all legitimate British trade. The company imported Indian raw cotton and cotton textiles into Canton and brought Chinese "Nankeens" and fine Indian cottons to Britain, but in order to protect its own imports, had historically refused to carry exports of British manufactured cottons to Asia. As British manufactures grew, textile merchants began to search for foreign markets.

In his classic study of the China trade, Michael Greenberg notes that the decisive pressure against the East India Company's monopoly came from Manchester, whose textile manufacturers opposed the import of foreign textiles. The Company's monopoly was regarded as an obstacle to development of export markets.[124] Opposition increased to the point where, by 1829, the textile manufacturers mounted a major campaign against the Company, and by 1834 were successful in persuading Parliament to revoke the Company's monopoly on the China trade.[125]

The American market was also critical. Americans were buyers of Chinese cotton prior to the mid-1800s. American merchants bought "nankin" at Canton in quantities such that, in the words of Horace Greeley, "In my early boyhood Chinese cotton fabrics, known as Nankins . . . , were extensively worn, even by the poor, in New England."[126] But the trade began to be reversed with imports of American made cotton textiles in small quantities in 1820; by 1828 cotton sales were beginning to make a significant reduction in the outflow of American silver.[127] When the East India Company's monopoly was revoked, the market was thrown wide open—to the manifest advantage of the Americans, who increased their sales of cotton textiles at Canton from $15,000 in 1826 to $192,000 in 1833; by 1838 the value of American cotton textiles reached half-a-million dollars. In 1841, some

500,000 pieces of American cotton textile goods were imported into Canton.[128]

East India Company's loss of control of the Canton market was the initial blow, but the *coup-de-grace* in the cotton trade was delivered by the Americans. The market for "Nankeens" was hit simultaneously with resistance to foreign yarn, competition in price and quality from British and American machine manufactures, and disruption of accustomed channels of trade at Canton. Imports of foreign cotton textiles replaced exports of Chinese cottons, reversing the marketing pattern in a very short period of time. The international market economy was outside the control and probably even the comprehension of Chinese merchants. All that was apparent at Shanghai was that orders for "Nankeens" suddenly diminished and then evaporated altogether.

At Shanghai the effects of the drop in cotton "Nankeen" exports were devastating. Whether caused by the cotton decline or coincidental with it, a sudden economic chill hit Shanghai. Immediately virtually all guild construction and repair ceased. Collapse of the cotton textile market was followed in short order by the curtailment of trade due to the Opium War, effects of famines in the Subei and Shandong regions, and insolvency among local banks. Prosperity, as reflected in guild activities, did not resume until the mid-1850s.

CONCLUSION

The boom at Shanghai, which began with the lifting of the prohibitions on sea traffic in 1684, was initially based on cotton and transport. It expanded through dramatically increasing commercialization during the course of the eighteenth and early nineteenth centuries. Internal services such as banking, construction and comestibles grew to match the expansion of commerce and the city's increasing population. Between 1685 and 1840 Shanghai grew from a typical county seat and local marketing center to a major coastal port city. In the mid-eighteenth century the city's population was around 120,000.[129] One hundred years later, in the mid-nineteenth century, European visitors estimated the population at around 230,000.[130] Shanghai was clearly a city of substance and importance by anyone's measure.

The city's growth involved internal immigration, principally from Zhejiang and Fujian, even Guandong, and in some cases may have represented a displacement of resources from those regions to the newly flourishing city. In general, however, Shanghai's economic effect on the Jiangnan region appears to have been beneficial. During the period under discussion in this paper, there is no evidence to support

Fei Xiaotong's image of Shanghai as a parasite-city, sucking the life-blood from the countryside.[131]

Shanghai's engagement in foreign trade was also a factor in its growth during this period. The boom in "Nankeen" exports between 1790 and 1830 and the effects of its subsequent collapse illustrate the fragile nature of foreign demand. Other foreign products, especially opium, remain more problematical during this period, though it appears that opium had close connections with the growth of banking.

This picture of Shanghai's prosperity was not, however, without shadows. The effects of international competition were devastatingly illustrated when "Nankeen" collapsed. Resources displaced from other locations to Shanghai might be more vulnerable there. The transfer of the Grain Tribute from Suzhou to Shanghai is an early indication of an erosion of important economic functions from the prefectural and pro-vincial capital to the periphery. And men and commerce from places as distant as Huizhou, Quanzhou, Ningbo, Shaoxing, the Fujian coast, and Canton followed the wealth to Shanghai.

Appendices

Appendix One

> *Note: The work of G. William Skinner in analyzing geographical regions of China and marketing networks is central to three of the five papers in the volume. The following summary of Skinner's concepts is provided by Professor Marmé. (ed.)*

Skinner's work remains the most ambitious and sophisticated attempt to provide a regional framework for the study of premodern China. Arguing that, given premodern transport and communications, geography imposes significant costs on the exchange of goods and messages, Skinner posits a relatively stable division of China into nine essentially autonomous macroregions. The exchange of goods and services within each of these macroregions was more significant than exchanges with neighboring regions. Such exchange was organized through a nested hierarchy of markets. At the low end of the scale, one found sparsely populated areas with relatively backward technology and a low level of commercialization. Insofar as such areas engaged in trade with the outside, they bartered raw materials, foodstuffs, and crude handicrafts for luxuries. At the opposite extreme was the central metropolis, the most densely populated and highly commercialized portion of the macroregion. The most skilled workers and the most advanced available technology were concentrated there; such areas specialized in the production of luxuries. They traded these (comparatively expensive) goods for raw materials, foodstuffs, and simple handicrafts.

In time, higher centers converted their comparative advantage—in skills, in technology and in resources—into structural ones. The central metropolis integrated the region, systematizing exchanges within the macroregion in ways which served its interests and perpetuated its dominance. The result of this patterning of transactions was a shift of resources (hence of wealth, population, cultural amenities, *and* power) from lower to higher levels of the marketing hierarchy, from the border regions toward the central metropolis.

Skinner's model is not static. Regions have their ups and downs, each region following its own rhythms. In the medium to long term, at least, each macroregion (and regional metropolitan, regional city, greater city, local city, central market town, intermediate market town, and standard market town system) will have a dominant center. The location of that center at any given moment depends, however, on a host of factors—political context, climactic change, technological level, the skill and cohesion of elites at point A versus the skill and cohesion of elites at point B. Thus, the Lower Yangzi macroregion had to have a central metropolis, but nothing preordained that that central metropolis be Suzhou, or Hangzhou, or Nanjing.

Finally, it is often useful to speak of the core and periphery of these regions. The precise geographical referent will vary with context and level under discussion. In the first place, the core can be defined narrowly or broadly. Thus on the map depicting China's macroregions (Skinner, "Regional Urbanization in Nineteenth-Century China," in Skinner (ed.) *City in Late Imperial China*, p. 214), the Lower Yangzi macroregion's core includes Hangzhou, Suzhou, Nanjing, Yangzhou and Shanghai even though, at any given moment, four of those cities were dominated by (hence peripheral to) the fifth. The central metropolis was the core of the macroregion's core; one can thus speak of other areas in the core as peripheral in relation to it. Each region (in the case of the Lower Yangzi macroregion, Skinner describes three, centered on Hangzhou, Suzhou, and Nanjing) had its own core, a principle which can be extended all the way down the marketing hierarchy. Whatever the level and scope, references to the core and periphery should be understood to describe dynamic relationships, not static locations.

See Skinner (ed.), *The City in Late Imperial China*, 3–31, 211–351, 521–553 and G. William Skinner, "Presidential Address: the Structure of Chinese History," *Journal of Asian Studies* 44 (1985), pp. 271–292.

Appendix Two

Table One: Population, Product and Tax Burden in Early Ming Wu and Changzhou Districts, Suzhou Prefecture

Assume 4.8 *shi* of husked rice per person per annum, 5.48 mouths per household, and an average yield of 2.25 *shi* of husked rice per *mu*.

Wu

Households × Mouths per Household × Rice per Person per
    Annum = Estimated Product
$$61,857 \times 5.48 \times 4.8 = 1,627,086.50 \; shi$$
Minimum (Maximum) Acreage × Yield per *mu* = Total Agricultural
    Output
$$381,655 \; (469,796) \times 2.25 = \quad 858,723.75 \; shi$$
$$(1,057,041.00 \; shi)$$
Total Agricultural Output − Tax Exported = Total Agricultural Output
    Available for Consumption
$$858,723.75 \; -130,549 = \; 728,174.75 \; shi$$
$$(1,057,041.00) - 130,549 = (926,492.00 \; shi)$$
Agricultural Output Available for Consumption ÷ No. of
    Households = Agricultural Output per Household
$$728,174.75 \div 61,857 = 11.72 \; shi/\text{Household}$$
$$(926,492.00) \div 61,857 = 14.98 \; shi/\text{Household}$$

Changzhou

Households × Mouths per Household × Rice per Person per
    Annum = Estimated Product
$$86,178 \times 5.48 \times 4.8 = 2,266,826.10 \; shi$$
Minimum (Maximum) Acreage × Yield per *mu* = Total Agricultural
    Output
$$969,840 \; (1,237,818) \times 2.25 = \; 2,182,140.00 \; shi$$
$$(2,785,090.50 \; shi)$$
Total Agricultural Output − Tax Exported = Total Agricultural Output
    Available for Consumption
$$2,182,140.00 \; -418,177 = \; 1,763,963.00 \; shi$$
$$(2,785,090.50) - 418,177 = (2,366,913.50 \; shi)$$
Agricultural Output Available for Consumption ÷ No. of
    Households = Agricultural Output per Household
$$1,763,963.00 \div 86,178 = 20.47 \; shi/\text{Household}$$
$$(2,366,913.50) \div 86,178 = 27.46 \; shi/\text{Household}$$

Household numbers are based on *Suzhou fuzhi* 1884, 13:3b, 9a–b. Household size is drawn from *Juqu zhi* 1689, 6. Consumption of rice per person per annum is calculated in Marmé, "From Rout to Hegemony," 210–212; this assumes 2,200 *kcal* per day and seventy percent of income spent on food. Acreage from *Wu xian zhi* 1933, 45:1a–2b, 46:1a–3b, 47:1a–3a, was converted to twentieth century standard *mu* (using Perkins, *Agricultural Development in China*, p. 314). Hills and marsh were then excluded, and average yields calculated: Marmé, "From Rout to Hegemony," 213–216. Tax exported was based on quotas cited in *Gu Su zhi* 1506, 15 as analyzed in Marmé, pp. 216–219.

Table Two: Population Versus Local Food Supplies in Late Imperial Wu and Changzhou

	Wu	Changzhou
Maximum Agricultural Output Available (Less Taxes Exported)	926,492.00 *shi*	2,366,913.50 *shi*
Households (1376)	61,857 HH	86,178 HH
X 5.48 Mouths/HH	338,976 Mouths	472,255 Mouths
X 4.8 *shi*/annum = Minimum Agricultural Output Required (1376)	1,627,086.50 *shi*	2,266,826.10 *shi*

	Wu	Changzhou and Yuanhe
Indigenous Population (1820)	1,734,238 Mouths	757,491 Mouths
X 4.8 *shi* per annum	8,324,342.40 *shi*	3,635,956.80 *shi*
DEFICIT (1820)	7,397,850.40 *shi*	1,269,043.30 *shi*
Sojourners (1820)	375,418 Mouths	107,663 Mouths
X 4.8 *shi* per annum	1,802,006.40 *shi*	516,782.40 *shi*
TOTAL DEFICIT (1820)	9,199,856.80 *shi*	2,302,608.10 *shi*

Sources: 1376 figures are drawn from Table one, above. 1820 population figures are from GXSZFZ 1883, 13: 9a–b. Sojourners are calculated as the number of males in excess of the sex ratio assumed for the indigenous population (109.8:100).

Note: In 1725 Changzhou *xian* was divided into Changzhou and Yuanhe, two *xian*.

Appendix Three

Name Changes of Suzhou, Tang through Qing

618	Wu jun 吳郡
621	Su zhou 蘇州
742	Wu jun 吳郡
757	Su zhou 蘇州
897	Wu Yue guo 吳越國
901	Wu guo 吳國
907	Su zhou 蘇州
917	Zhong Wu fu 中吳府
924	Zhong Wu jun 中吳軍
975	Su zhou 蘇州
1115	Pingjiang fu 平江府
1277	Pingjiang lu 平江路
1356	Longping fu 隆平府
1357	Pingjiang lu 平江路
1368	Suzhou fu 蘇州府
GSZ	1:7a–19a

NOTES

Preface

1. Readers unfamiliar with the G. William Skinner's concept of macro-regions might wish to consult "Appendix one" where this concept is summarized.

2. In its earliest form, the vast territory called "Jiangnan" included modern Zhejiang, Fujian, Jiangxi, Jiangsu, and Hubei provinces, but the later and more specific Tang circuit was confined to only those portions of Jiangsu, Anhui, and Zhejiang lying south of the Yangzi river. In the latter Tang, the region was divided into the Jiangnan East and Jiangnan West circuits. Zhejiang and a portion of Fujian were included in the East Jiangnan circuit with its capital at Hangzhou while Jiangsu and Anhui and some portion of Hubei were in the West Jiangnan circuit with its capital at Suzhou. *Zhongguo gujin diming dazidian*, new edition (Taibei: n.d. [1980]) p. 326.

3. G. William Skinner, "Regional Urbanization in Nineteenth Century China." In *The City in Late Imperial China* (Stanford: Stanford University Press, 1977), pp. 211–249, especially p. 238.

Introduction

1. G. William Skinner, ed. *The City in Late Imperial China*; Mark Elvin and Skinner. eds. *The Chinese City Between Worlds* (Stanford: Stanford University Press, 1974).

2. A brief list of monographic titles would include David Buck, *Urban Change in China* (Madison: University of Wisconsin Press, 1977); Kenneth Lieberthal, *Revolution and Tradition in Tientsin, 1949–52* (Stanford: Stanford University Press, 1980); William T. Rowe, *Hankow: Commerce and Society in a Chinese City, 1796–1889* and *Hankow: Conflict and Community in a Chinese City, 1796–1895* (Stanford: Stanford University Press, 1984 and 1989); Gail Hershatter, *The Workers of Tianjin, 1900–1949* (Stanford: Stanford University Press, 1986); Emily Honig, *Sisters and Strangers: Women in the Shanghai Cotton Mills, 1919–1949* (Stanford: Stanford University Press, 1986); David

Strand, *Rickshaw Beijing* (Berkeley: University of California Press, 1989); and Marie-Claire Bergère, *The Golden Age of the Chinese Bourgeoisie* (Cambridge: Cambridge University Press, 1990).

3. F. W. Mote, "A Millennium of Chinese Urban History: Form, Time and Space concepts in Soochow," *Rice University Studies* 59 (1973), pp. 35–65; Mote, "The Transformation of Nanking, 1350–1400," in Skinner, *City in Late Imperial China*, pp. 101–154.

4. Skinner, *City in Late Imperial China*, p. 219.

5. Robert Hartwell, "A Cycle of Economic Change in Imperial China: Coal and Iron in Northeast China, 750–1350," *Journal of the Economic and Social History of the Orient* 10 (1967), pp. 102–159.

6. The classic study is of course Ping-ti Ho, "The Salt Merchants of Yangchou: A Study of Commercial Capitalism in Eighteenth-Century China," *Harvard Journal of Asiatic Studies* 17 (1954), pp. 130–168.

7. See Carol A. Smith, "Regional Economic Systems," in Smith, ed., *Regional Analysis*, Vol. 1 (New York: Academic Press, 1976), pp. 3–63. For a classic exposition of the model, see August Losch, "The Nature of Economic Regions," *Southern Economic Journal* 5 (1938), pp. 71–78.

8. Ch'ao-ting Chi, *Key Economic Areas in Chinese History* (London: Allen and Unwin, 1936); Shiba Yoshinobu, *Sōdai Kōnan keizaishi no kenkyū* [A study of the economic history of Song-dynasty Jiangnan] (Tokyo: Tōyō bunka kenkyūjo, 1988); Fu Yiling, *Mingdai Jiangnan shimin jingji shitan* [A preliminary study or urbanites in Ming-dynasty Jiangnan] (Shanghai: Renmin chubanshe, 1957); and *Ming-Qing nongcum shehui jingji* [Rural society and economy in the Ming and Qing] (Hong Kong: Sanlian shudian, 1961).

9. Among his various works on this subject, see especially Douglass North, "Location Theory and Regional Economic Growth," *Journal of Political Economy* 6:3 (1955), pp. 243–258. For a neatly contrasting negative model, see Michael Hechter, *Internal Colonialism: the Celtic Fringe in British National Development, 1536–1966* (Berkeley: University of California Press, 1975), chapter 5.

10. See Emily Honig, "Pride and Prejudice: Subei People in Contemporary Shanghai," in Perry Link, Richard Madsen, and Paul G. Pickowicz, eds. *Unofficial China: Popular Culture and Thought in the People's Republic* (Boulder: Westview Press, 1989), pp. 138–155.

11. E. A. Wrigley, "A Simple Model of London's Importance in Changing English Society and Economy, 1650–1750," *Past and Present* 37 (1967), pp. 44–70; David R. Ringrose, "Madrid and the Castilian Economy," *Journal of European Economic History* 10:1 (1981), pp. 481–490. The initial theoretical

work on this subject was Bert Hoselitz, "Generative and Parasitic Cities," *Economic Development and Cultural Change* 3:3 (1955), pp. 78–94.

12. See Ye Xian'en, *Ming-Qing Huizhou nongcun shehui yu dianpu zhi* [Rural society and the tenancy system in Ming and Qing Huizhou] (Hefei: Anhui renmin chubanshe, 1983).

13. James Vance, *The Merchant's World: The Geography of Wholesaling* (Englewood Cliffs: Prentice-Hall, 1970).

14. For but a few examples, see Wang Jiafan, "Ming-Qing Jiangnan *shizhen jiegou ji lishi jiazhi chutan*" [a preliminary investigation of the structure and historical importance of market towns in Ming and Qing Jiangnan], *Huadong shifan daxue xuebao* 1984:1, pp. 74–83; Shih-chi Liu, "Some Reflections on Urbanization and the Historical Development of Market Towns in the Lower Yangtze Region, ca. 1500–1900," *American Asian Review* :1 (1984), pp. 1–27; and Liu Shiji, *Ming-Qing shidai Jiangnan shizhen yanjiu* [A study of market towns in Ming and Qing Jiangnan] (Beijing: Zhongguo shehui kexue chubanshe, 1987).

15. See Jan de Vries, *European Urbanization, 1500–1800* (Cambridge: Harvard University Press, 1984).

16. Fei Hsiao-tung, "Small Towns in Northern Jiangsu," in Fei, *Rural Development in China: Prospect and Retrospect* (Chicago: University of Chicago Press, 1989), p. 159.

17. Antonia Finnane, "Prosperity and Decline under the Qing," Ph.D. diss., Australian National University, 1987, chapter 4.

18. A representative selection of this literature appears in *Ming-Qing mengya yanjiu lunwen ji* [Collected essays on the sprouts of capitalism in the Ming and Qing periods] (Shanghai: Shanghai renmin chubanshe. 1981).

CHAPTER 1: SUZHOU 1150–1550

List of abbreviations:

GSZ 1506: *Gu Su zhi*, 1506; (reprinted Taipei: 1965).
GXSZFZ 1883: *Guangxu Suzhou fuzhi*, 1883; (reprinted Taibei: 1970).
MGWXZ 1933: *Minguo Wu xianzhi*, 1933; (reprinted Taibei: 1970).

1. In Northern Song Kaifeng, the saying went, "Su Hang baishi fandu, dishang Tian gong (at Suzhou and Hangzhou the hundred things multiply many times; it is Heaven's palace on earth)." Fan Chengda (1126–1193) cited the proverb, "Tianshang Tian gong, dishang Su Hang" (In heaven above, there is the heavenly palace; on earth, there is Suzhou and Hangzhou), in his *Wu jun*

zhi. The adage does not appear to have attained its modern form until the thirteenth century. See: Liao Zhihao et alia, *Suzhou Shihua* [Historical talks on Suzhou], (Nanjing: Jiangsu renmin chubanshe, 1980), pp. 47–52.

2. Edmund H. Worthy, Jr., "Diplomacy for Survival: Domestic and Foreign Relations of Wu Yueh, 907–978," in Rossabi, ed. *China Among Equals: The Middle Kingdom and its Neighbors, 10th–14th Centuries* (Berkeley: University of California Press, 1983), pp. 17–44.

3. Charles O. Hucker, *A Dictionary of Official Titles in Imperial China* (Stanford: Stanford University Press, 1975), p. 45.

4. *GSZ* 1506, 1:7b–19a.

5. Ibid., 7:3a–4a. In 1217 a portion of Kunshan was designated Jiading county; in, 1375 Chongming county was added to Suzhou prefecture; and in 1497, the independent sub-prefecture (*zhou*) of Taicang was created from parts of Kunshan, Changshu, and Jiading counties. Only the addition of Chongming modified the borders of Suzhou prefecture.

6. Etienne Balasz, "Une carte des centres commerciaux de la Chine à la fin du XIe siècle" [A map of the commercial centers in China at the end of the eleventh century], *Annales: économies, sociétés, civilisations* 12.4 (1957), p. 591.

7. Ordinary prefectures in Song were designated *zhou* (the same character later used to designate sub-prefectures); places of extraordinary importance were called "*fu*"—Superior Prefectures in Hucker's rendering. See Hucker, *Dictionary of Official Titles*, p. 45. On the Northern Song capital at Kaifeng, see Robert M. Hartwell, "A Cycle of Economic Change in Imperial China: Coal and Iron in Northeast China 750–1350," *Journal of the Economic and Social History of the Orient* 10 (1967), pp. 107–159 and Edward A. Kracke, "Sung K'ai-feng: Pragmatic Metropolis and Formalistic Capital," in John W. Haeger, ed. *Crisis and Prosperity in Sung China* (Tucson: University of Arizona Press, 1975), pp. 49–77.

8. John W. Haeger, "1126–1127: Political Crisis and the Integrity of Culture," in *Crisis and Prosperity in Sung China*, pp. 143–161; Jacques Gernet, *Daily Life in China on the Eve of the Mongol Invasion 1250–1276* (Stanford: Stanford University Press, 1962), pp. 22–23.

9. *MGWXZ* 1933, 53:23a–24b.

10. Marco Polo, *Travels of Marco Polo* (New York: Dell Press, 1961), pp. 277, 278–279. On Song Hangzhou, see Etienne Balasz, "Marco Polo in the Capital of China," in Balasz, ed., *Chinese Civilization and Bureaucracy* (New Haven: Yale University Press, 1964), pp. 79–100 and Gernet, *Daily Life in China*.

11. G. William Skinner, "Introduction: Urban Development in Imperial China," in G. William Skinner, ed., *The City in Late Imperial China* (Stanford: Stanford University Press, 1977), p. 17.

12. See Miyazaki Ichisada, "Mindai So-Shō chiho no shidaifu to min shū—Mindai shi sobyo no kokoromi" [The literati and the masses in the Suzhou-Songjiang region during the Ming—a preliminary study of Ming history], *Shirin* 37.3 (1954), pp. 1–33.

13. Marie-Claire Bergère, "Shanghai ou l'autre Chine, 1919–1949" [Shanghai or "the Other China," 1919–1949], *Annales* 34 (1979), pp. 1040–1064.

14. William T. Rowe, *Hankow: Commerce and Society in a Chinese City, 1796–1889* (Stanford: Stanford University Press, 1984) and *Hankow: Conflict and Community in a Chinese City, 1796–1895* (Stanford: Stanford University Press, 1989).

15. Liao, *Suzhou shihua*, p. 70.

16. Liang Gengyao, "Song Yuan shidai de Suzhou" [Suzhou in the Song and Yuan period], *Wenshi zhexue bao* 31 (1982), pp. 235–243.

17. GXSZFZ 1883, 13:2a–b; Robert M. Hartwell, "Demographic, Political and Social Transformations of China, 750–1550," *Harvard Journal of Asiatic Studies* 47 (1988), p. 391, citing the work of J. Steurmer.

18. See John R. Shepherd, "Rethinking Tenancy: Explaining Spatial and Temporal Variation in Late Imperial and Republican China," *Comparative Studies in History and Society* 30.3 (1988), pp. 403–431.

19. Evelyn S. Rawski, *Agricultural Change and the Peasant Economy of South China* (Cambridge: Harvard University Press, 1972), pp. 41, 52–53 emphasizes that concentration on low yield, high quality strains was characteristic of this area throughout the late imperial period.

20. Shiba Yoshinobu, *Commerce and Society in Sung China* (Ann Arbor: Center for Chinese Studies, University of Michigan, 1970), pp. 55–56. See also the evidence drawn from nearby Xiuzhou (now Songjiang and Jiaxing), cited by Liang, "Song Yuan shidai de Suzhou," p. 269.

21. On the cosmological significance of the Chinese city, see Paul Wheatley, *The Pivot of the Four Quarters* (Chicago: Aldine Press, 1971).

22. Liang, "Song Yuan shidai de Suzhou," p. 306 notes sixty-three bridges circa 1010, 222 in 1190 and 288 circa 1380. On Huang Xie, compare Liao, *Suzhou shihua*, p. 72 with the discussion in David Johnson, "The City-God Cults of T'ang and Sung China," *Harvard Journal of Asiatic Studies* 45 (1985), pp. 366–368.

23. Liao, *Suzhou shihua*, p. 21.

24. Data from *GSZ* 1506, juan 29, marshaled in Liang, "Song Yuan shidai de Suzhou," p. 316. The figures omit temples which vanished from the record as well as from the landscape. They also ignore regular rebuilding (necessary for survival down the ages) and periodic enlargements (often as significant as the original foundation).

25. Liang, "Song Yuan shidai de Suzhou," p. 316–317; as the discussion in David Johnson, "City-God Cults," pp. 413–414 suggests, Suzhou's maintenance of this organization in Song is a sign of backwardness.

26. Liang, "Song Yuan shidai de Suzhou," p. 318.

27. Ibid., pp. 318–319.

28. Ibid., p. 316. Note that the guild chose a geographical designation which had not been used for official purposes for over five hundred years.

29. Thus the decline in temple building in the Ming may not only reflect changes in the nature of activity rather than decline in level but it may also reflect changes in the ways in which, and the degree to which, commerce and manufacture were privately organized in the early Ming.

30. G. William Skinner, "Regional Urbanization in Nineteenth-Century China," in *The City in Late Imperial China*, pp. 230–231.

31. Liang, "Song Yuan shidai de Suzhou," pp. 309–312.

32. Date on elite residence is drawn from *MGWXZ* 1933, 39 *shang*: 4b–30a; 39 *zhong*: 1b–10a; and 39 *xia*: 2a–10b. It is marshaled in Marmé, "Population and Possiblility in Ming (1368–1644) Suzhou: A Quantified Model," *Ming Studies* 12 (Spring 1981), p. 47 (Table XI). Given the importance of the *yin* privilege—permitting sons of successful officials to enter the elite without sitting for examinations—in Song times, examination lists provide a misleading picture of its composition. The generosity of R. M. Hartwell, who made his painstaking reconstruction of the Suzhou elite in Song available to me, alone enables me to make categorical statements regarding its composition.

33. Herbert W. Franke, "Chia Ssu-tao (1213–1275): A 'Bad Last Minister'?" in Arthur F. Wright and Denis Twitchett, eds., *Confucian Personalities* (Stanford: Stanford University Press, 1962), pp. 229–231; Lo Jung-pang, "Maritime Commerce and the Sung Navy," *Journal of the Social and Economic History of the Orient* 12 (1969) pp. 57–101.

34. *MGWXZ* 1933, 53: 25a.

35. Hangzhou's prefectural population fell from 391,259 households in 1225 to 360,850 in 1290 and 216,165 in 1393. As Shiba Yoshinobu, "Ningbo

and Its Hinterland," in *The City in Late Imperial China* p. 399 makes clear, this stagnation affected economic activity throughout the region.

36. *GXSZFZ* 1883, 13: 2b–3a.

37. Liang, "Song Yuan shidai de Suzhou," pp. 274–276 discusses the growing importance of Liujiagang—later Taicang—in the Yuan. The population estimate is from Liang, p. 323.

38. Liang, "Song Yuan shidai de Suzhou," pp. 307–308, 319.

39. Ibid., p. 308.

40. Skinner, "Introduction: Urban Development in Imperial China," p. 17.

41. Edward L. Dreyer, *Early Ming China: A Political History 1355–1435* (Stanford: Stanford University Press, 1982), pp. 12–64 (especially pp. 58–59); Frederick W. Mote, *The Poet Kao Ch'i, 1336–1374* (Princeton: Princeton University Press, 1962).

42. Zhu Yunming, *Jiuchao yeji* [Unofficial history of nine reigns], 1511, 1:14b.

43. The best known of the casualties was Gao Qi—See Mote, *The Poet Kao Ch'i*, pp. 234-243—but there were many others. The land tax was, however, the most lasting of the early Ming policies. It is discussed (among many other places) in Lu Shiyi (1611–1672), "Su-Song fuliang kao" [Examination of the excessive taxes in kind in Suzhou and Songjiang] in *Lu, Futing xiansheng yishu* [Posthumous works of Lu Futing (Shiyi)] (Beijing: 1889) *juan* 19; Gu Yanwu, "Su Song erfu tianfu zhi zhong" [On the heaviness of the land tax in the two prefectures of Suzhou and Songjiang], *Rizhilu Jishi* [Collected explanations of the Record of things learned daily] 1670, *juan* 4; Wu Jihua, *Mingdai shehui jingji shilun cong* [Collected discussions of Ming social and economic history] (Taibei: Taiwan xuesheng shuju, 1970) volume 1, pp. 19–24, 52–63; Mori Masao, "Minsho Kōnan no kanden ni tsuite" [On official fields in early Ming Jiangnan], *Toyōshi kenkyū*, 19 (1960–1961), pp. 315–336, 433–450; and Lin Jinshu, "Shilun Mingdai Su Song erfu de zhongfu wenti" [Concerning the question of heavy taxes in the two prefectures of Suzhou and Songjiang during the Ming], *Mingshi yanjiu luncong* 1 (1982), pp. 91–123.

44. Military households may well be omitted from these totals. This would modify the picture (a disproportionate number of soldiers being stationed in the capital region); it would not transform it.

45. Yuan population figures are drawn from Liang Fangzhong, *Zhongguo lidai hukou, tiandi, tianfu tongji* [Statistics on population, culivated area and the land tax throughout Chinese history] (Shanghai: Shanghai renmin chubanshe, 1980), pp. 181–182 (Table 49); Ming figures from *Da Ming huidian* [Sta-

tutes of the Ming dynasty] (1587), 19:3b–6a and *Zhejiang tongzhi* [Complete gazetteer of Zhejiang province] (1934), pp. 72–74. I am indebted to G. William Skinner for boundaries of the Hangzhou, Suzhou and Nanjing regions. In several instances, regional boundaries run through prefectures. In all these cases, half the total population was allocated to one region, half to the other. On balance, this procedure should understate the population of the Suzhou region and overstate that of the others.

46. See Mori Masao's seminal article, "Minsho Kōnan no kanden ni tsuite" [On official fields in early Ming Jiangnan] *Tōyōshi kenkyū*, 19 (1960–1961) pp. 315–336, 433–450.

47. Zhu Yunming, *Jiuchao yeji*, 1:14b–15a.

48. The average rate was derived by dividing the total quota for official land—2,625,930+ *shi*: Zhou Liangxiao, "Mingdai Su Song diqu de guantian yu zhongfu wenti" [The question of official fields and heavy taxes in Ming Suzhou and Songjiang] in *Mingdai shehui jingji shilun ji* [Collection of historical discussions of society and economy in the Ming dynasty] (Hong Kong: Chongwen shudian, 1975), p. 130 which cites Gu Yanwu, who was quoting Kuang Zhong (Suzhou prefect 1430–1443)—by the amount of official land given in GSZ 1506, 15: 3a–3b (2,990,000 *mu* of *guantian* plus 1,633,800 *mu* of *chaomo* or [newly] confiscated land).

49. *MGWXZ* 1933, 54:1a–2a; 55:6b–9b, 19a–19b; *GXSZFZ* 1883, 18:29b–32b. The data is summarized in Marmé, "From Rout to Hegemony: Suzhou 1368–1550," Ph.D. diss. (Berkeley: University of California, 1986), Table 3.4. Note that the tax reductions preceded—and were probably connected to—the Hu Weiyong purge of 1381.

50. Official tax quotas from *Hongwu Suzhou fuzhi* [Hongwu gazetteer of Suzhou Prefecture] (1379), *juan* 10; tax rates—in paper notes, from *Ming huiyao* [Important documents of the Ming] (1887) (1972 reprint, Taibei), 57:1. This was converted to *shi* using the 1385 value of notes as recorded in Ray Huang, *Taxation and Governmental Finance in Sixteenth-Century Ming China* (Cambridge: Cambridge University Press, 1974), p.70: "2.5 *guan* per picul of grain." Given early Ming inflation, use of 1385 grain prices probably results in significant underestimate of trade volume.

51. See Chuan Han-sheng and Richard A. Kraus, *Mid-Ch'ing Rice Markets and Trade: An Essay in Price History* (Cambridge: Harvard University Press, 1975).

52. *MGWXZ* 1933, 44:3a–b.

53. Mud dredged from the canals was in demand as fertilizer: see Atsutoshi Hamashima, "The Organization of Water Control in the Kiangnan Delta in the Ming Period," *Acta Asiatica* 38 (Mar 1980), pp. 71, 74.

54. On water control, see Mark Elvin, "Market Towns and Waterways: The County of Shang-hai from 1480 to 1910," in *The City in Late Imperial China*, pp. 441–473; Peter C. Perdue, "Official Goals and Local Interests: Water Control in the Dongting Lake Region during the Ming and Qing Periods," *Journal of Asian Studies* 41.4 (1982), pp. 747–765; and R. Keith Schoppa, *Xiang Lake—Nine Centuries of Chinese Life* (New Haven: Yale University Press, 1989).

55. *MGWXZ* 1933, 42: 16b–17a; 43:2a, 8a, 12b; 63:9a–b (Xia Yuanji).

56. Mori, "Minsho Kōnan no kanden no tsuite," p. 443 (citing *Ming shi*, juan 153); Terada Takunobu, "Mindai Soshū heiya no nōka keizai ni tsuite" [On the peasant economy of the Suzhou plain in the Ming] *Toÿoshi kenkyū*, 16.1 (1957), p. 4.

57. We must remember that there were three levels of taxation: the tax quota, the wastage allowance (in Ming Suzhou wastage averaged one *shi* for every two assessed) and customary fees ("squeeze"). The customary fees were deducted first; the ratio between tax proper and wastage seems to have been relatively constant. Thus, a shortfall of four million *shi* in seven years meant that taxpayers had evaded one *shi* in seven of the 4,000,000 demanded annually as tax and wastage, not one *shi* in five of the 2,810,000 owed as tax quota. The amount collected as customary fees is unknown. *GXSZFZ* 1883, 12:10a provides the figure for officially audited tax "including waste" in 1498; deficits are those for the early fifteenth century.

58. Data (summarized in Marmé, "From Rout to Hegemony," Table 3.1) in *MGWXZ* 1933, 9:1b–2a, 3b, 6a, 8b–12a, 12b–13b; 10:6b–29a; *juan* 12; 13:23b–24a; 15:23a–23b; *juan* 16. Yongle rates of success were only surpassed—and then just barely—by the men of Changzhou in the first half of the sixteenth century.

59. Wu Kuan (1436–1504), *Paoweng jiacang ji* [Collection from the family storehouse of (Wu) Paoweng (Kuan)] (1508) (Sibu congkan ed. Shanghai: Shanghai Commercial Press, 1935–1936), 63:6b–7b.

60. The entries in *MGWXZ* 1933, 63:6b–26b for prefect and district magistrate were compared with the tables indicating year of appointment. Comparison with other editions of the local gazetteers indicates that this was a stable list, reflecting conventional definitions of good government.

61. See Mi Chu Wiens, "Changes in the Fiscal and Rural Control Systems in the Fourteenth and Fifteenth Centuries," *Ming Studies* 3 (Fall 1976), p. 53; Edward L. Farmer, *Early Ming Government: the Evolution of Dual Capitals* (Cambridge: Harvard University Press, 1976), p. 47; Frederick W. Mote, "The Transformation of Nanking, 1350–1400," in *The City in Late Imperial China*, p. 145; *Da Ming huidian* (1587 edition) 19:21a–b.

198   CITIES OF JIANGNAN IN LATE IMPERIAL CHINA

62. Bao Yanbang, "Mingdai caoyun de xingcheng ji qi fuyi xingzhi" [On the form of grrain transport and the nature of corvée labor during the Ming dynasty], *Zhongguo shehui jingji shi luncong* 1 (1981), p. 297.

63. The reforms are analyzed by Huang, *Taxation and Governmental Finance*, pp. 101–102; for rice prices, see *ibid.*, p. 52.

64. In his recent work on the seventeenth century crisis, Jack A. Goldstone argues that population played a much more important role in stimulating economic activity than did the import of New World silver. Jack A. Goldstone, "East and West in the Seventeenth Century: Political Crises in Stuart England, Ottoman Turkey and Ming China," *Comparative Studies in Society and History* 30.1 (1988), pp. 107–110, 115–116. Velocity of circulation only increases if additional people are brought into the market; the effect should be the same if a fixed number of people become involved in market transaction on a more regular basis. Thus, even if the supply of silver and copper did not change and the population did not grow, monetizing tax payments should have stimulated economic activity.

65. Shiba Yoshinobu, *Commerce and Society in Sung China*, p. 112.

66. *MGWXZ* 1933, 52 *shang*:9b. On silk production in this area during the Ming, consult Song Yingxing's *Tiangong kaiwu* (1637), chapter two; English translation by E-tu Zen Sun and Shiou-chuan Sun, *T'ien-kung K'ai-wu, Chinese Technology in the Seventeenth Century* (University Park: University of Pennsylvania Press, 1966). For a slightly later period, see E-tu Zen Sun, "Sericulture and Silk Textile Production in Ch'ing China," in W. E. Willmott, ed., *Economic Organization in Chinese Society* (Stanford: Stanford University Press, 1972), pp. 84–99.

67. Citations from the *GSZ* 1506 and *Wu yi zhi* (1529) are conveniently marshaled in *MGWXZ* 1933, 51:15a.

68. *Linqing zhou zhi*, cited in Fu Yiling, *Mingdai Jiangnan shimin jingji shican* [A preliminary study of urban dwellers in Ming dynasty Jiangnan] (Shanghai: Shanghai renmin chubanshe, 1957), p. 84.

69. The ready entry of peasants into cotton textile production was not true for the best grades of cloth, as Linda Cooke Johnson notes in her paper. Evidence concerning how much of what grade was produced and by whom in Ming times is extremely sparse. On cotton, see Craig Dietrich, "Cotton Culture and Manufacture in Early Ch'ing China," in *Economic Organization in Chinese Society*, pp. 109–135.

70. *Qianlong Wujiang xianzhi*, cited in Liu Shiji, "Ming Qing shidai Jiangnan diqu de zhuanye shizhen (*zhong*)" [Specialized market-towns in Jiangnan in the Ming and Qing periods (middle)], *Shihuo* 8 (1978), p. 331; on the late

Chenghua boom, see Peng Zeyi, "Cong Mingdai guanying zhizao de jingying fangshi kan Jiangnan sizhiye shengchan de xingzhi" [The managerial pattern of the state-owned textile industry and the character of silk textile production in Ming dynasty Jiangnan] in *Ming Qing zibenzhuyi mengya yanjiu lunwen ji* [Essays investigating the shoots of capitalism in the Ming and Qing] (Shanghai: Shanghai renmin chubanshe, 1981), p. 322.

71. See Shih Chin, "Peasant Economy and Rural Society in the Lake Tai Area, 1368–1840," (Berkeley: Ph.D. diss, 1981), p. 167. Shih argues that elite control was only broken in the Qing.

72. George B. Cressey, *Land of the 500 Million* (New York: McGraw Hill, 1934), p. 192.

73. Hsiao-tung Fei, *Chinese Village Close-up* (Beijing: New World Press, 1983), pp. 108–109.

74. The classic work on standard marketing areas is G. William Skinner, "Marketing and Social Structure in Rural China," *Journal of Asian Studies*, 24 (1964–1965), pp. 3–43; 195–228. Note that Skinner himself argues that, in conditions like the Yangzi delta, standard markets will disappear: see Skinner, "Rural Marketing in China: Revival and Reappraisal," in Stuart Plattner, ed., *Markets and Marketing* (Lanham, Maryland: University Press of America, 1985), pp. 21–22.

75. Xie Guozhen, *Mingdai shehui jingji shiliao xuanbian zhong* [Anthology of historical materials on Ming society and economy] (Fuzhou: Fujian renmin chubanshe, 1980), pp. 114–116, citing the Qianlong period (1736–1796) *Zhenze xianzhi* [Gazetteer of Zhenze county] and *Wujiang xianzhi* [Gazetteer of Wujiang county]. In Ming times, these two counties were the single county of Wujiang.

76. *Chongzhen Wu xianzhi* [Chongzhen gazetteer of Wu county] (1643), 10:3a; *GSZ* 1506, 14:28b, 26a.

77. Skinner, "Cities and the Hierarchy of Local Systems," in *The City in Late Imperial China*, pp. 285–287, 347–351 and *passim*. This was the third of eight ranks.

78. Zhu Yunming, *Zhu shi jilue* [Collected Works of Zhu [Yuanming] (1588) (Taibei, Guoli zhongyang tushuguan, 1971), 19:10b.

79. Pu Ch'oe, *Ch'oe Pu's Diary: A Record of Drifting Across the Sea*, trans. John Meskill. (Tucson: University of Arizona Press, 1965) pp. 92–94; Wang Qi (1432–1499), *Yupu zaji* [Miscellanea of the Orchard Dweller], 1500, *juan* 5, reprinted in Xie, *Mingdai shehui jingji shiliao xuanbian zhong*.

80. See map in Skinner, *City in Late Imperial China*, Fig. 2, p. 15.

81. Mote, *The Poet Kao Ch'i*, pp. 234–243.

82. Shifting residence patterns were calculated from data in *MGWXZ* 1933, 39 *shang*: 4b–3a; 39 *zhong*: 1b–10a; 39 *xia*: 2a–10a. See also the comment in *Chongzhen Wu xianzhi* (1643), 10:1b.

83. Gong Dingxiang (1524–1596), cited in Angela Ning-jy Hsi, "Social and Economic Status of the Merchant Class of the Ming Dynasty, 1368–1644" (Ph.D. diss. University of Illinois, 1972), p. 31.

84. *GSZ* 1506, juan 29; Liu Yung-ch'eng, "The Handicraft Guilds in Soochow during the Ch'ing Dynasty," *Chinese Studies in History* 15 (1981–1982), p. 126.

85. Fu Yiling, *Mingdai Jiangnan shimin jingji shican*, p. 87. This passage is cited repeatedly in PRC scholarship on the "shoots of capitalism." For an English translation, see Mi Chu Wiens, "Cotton Textile Production and Rural Social Transformation in Early Modern China," *Journal of the Institute of Chinese Studies of the Chinese University of Hong Kong* 7.2 (1974), p. 527.

86. Peng Zeyi, "Cong Mingdai guanying zhizao de jingying fangshi kan Jiangnan sizhiye shengchan de xingzhi," p. 334–344.

87. Liang, "Song Yuan shidai de Suzhou," p. 308.

88. The quotation is from *GSZ* 1506, 17:11b; compare *Hongwu Suzhou fuzhi* (1379), 5:7a–10a and *GSZ* 1506, 17:5b–12a.

89. *GSZ* 1506, 18:2b.

90. Cao Zishou, "Wu xian cheng tu shuo," in Gu Yanwu, *Tianxia junguo libing shu* [On the strengths and weaknesses of various prefectures and districts in the Empire] (1662), *ce* 5: 12a.

91. Cited in *MGWXZ* 1933, 53:1a.

92. Liu Shiji, "Ming Qing shidai Jiangnan diqu de zhuanye shizhen (*xia*)" [Specialized market-towns in Jiangnan in the Ming and Qing periods (last part)] *Shihuo* 8 (1978), p. 371. Given the reference to fourteen provinces, this passage presumably dates from the period 1413–1428.

93. *GSZ* 1506, 18:8a.

94. On the rice market at Hushu in Qing times, see Chuan and Kraus, *Mid-Ch'ing Rice Markets and Trade*, pp. 59–65.

95. *GSZ* 1506, 17:11b–12a.

96. *Wanli Changzhou xianzhi* [Wanli gazetteer of Changzhou county] (1598), 12:3b–7a; *Chongzhen Wu xianzhi* 1643, 15:9a–13b.

97. See the passages from the *Silkworm Classic* (*Can jing*) of Huang Xingzeng (1490–1540), cited in *MGWXZ* 1933, 51:16b.

98. The stress should apparently fall on "relatively," not "deserted." See Ch'oe, *Ch'oe Pu's Diary*, p. 92.

99. *GSZ* 1506, 14:26a, 28b.

100. *Chongzhen Wu xianzhi* 1643, 10:1b.

101. This conclusion is based on a comparison of the distribution of *li/tu* (giving a rough map of early Ming population in Wu and Changzhou) with distribution of villages and market towns in the 1506, 1598, and 1643 editions of the local gazetteers. For data, see *MGWXZ* 1933, *juan* 21–23. For the procedures used, see Marmé, "From Rout to Hegemony," chapter 4, footnote 67.

102. Data from *GXSZFZ* 1883, 13:3b, 9a–b. For a detailed explanation of the assumptions made and techniques employed, see Marmé, "From Rout to Hegemony," Statistical Appendix to Chapter Four: Population.

103. Xie Guozhen, *Mingdai shehui jingji shiliao xuanbian, zhong,* pp. 144–145, citing *Haicheng xian zhi.* In spite of Fu Chonglan's corrective "Lun Ming Qing shiqi Hangzhou chengshi de fazhan," *Zhongguo shi yankiu* 4 (1983), pp. 69–79, the emphasis in Ming times must have been on Suzhou just as a comparable boast in Song would have implicitly stressed Hangzhou.

104. The brittle nature of Ming fiscal arrangements is a central theme of Huang's *Taxation and Governmental Finance.*

105. Based on data in the gazetteers, taxes were remitted—in whole or in part—once every seven years between 1368 and 1572; water control projects were undertaken on average once every seven years; and the crucial posts of prefect and district magistrate were occupied by "illustrious officials" 45 percent of the time. Although one would have to analyze similar materials for other areas to prove Suzhou was better treated than other parts of the empire, it is highly likely that it was. Evidence for Suzhou is marshaled in Marmé, "From Rout to Hegemony," chapter three.

106. Ping-ti Ho, *Studies on the Population of China, 1368–1953* (Cambridge: Harvard University Press, 1959), p. 22 corrected the Ming figures. Others (most recently Robert M. Hartwell, who summarized his results in, "[Review of] *Man and Land in Chinese History: An Economic Analysis* by Kang Chao," *Journal of Asian Studies* 47 (1988), p. 336) have argued for a substantially higher figure for the empire as a whole. However, few would argue for a substantial undercount in late fourteenth-century Suzhou. The government's ability to accumulate and use information on populations of this size in earlier periods is most striking in the case of Tang dynasty Dunhuang: see Arthur F.

Wright and Denis C. Twitchett (eds), *Perspectives on the T'ang* (New Haven: Yale University Press, 1973), pp. 47–85 and 121–150.

107. The fact that this population was concentrated in a relatively small area, an area with the best in premodern transport networks, must have facilitated such regimentation. See Dwight Perkins, *Agricultural Development in China (1368–1968)* (Chicago: Aldine Press, 1969), p. 179.

108. Wang Ao's suggestions on tax administration are cited in Mori Masao, "Jūroku seiki Taiko shūhen chitai ni okeru kanden seido no kaikaku," [Reform of the official field system in the Lake Tai region during the sixteenth century], *Toyōshi kenkyū*, 22:1 (1963), pp. 71, 74.

109. The weakness of extended kinship organization is documented in the Appendices to Chapter Five, Marmé, "From Rout to Hegemony," pp. 308–430. On guilds, see Liu Yung-ch'eng, "Handicraft Guilds in Soochow," p. 126.

110. On guilds, see Liu Yung-ch'eng, "Handicraft Guilds in Soochow," pp. 116–123 (Table One) and *Ming Qing Suzhou gongshangye beike ji* [Collected inscriptions on handicraft industries in Suzhou in the Ming and Qing periods] (Nanjing: Jiangsu renmin chubanshe, 1981). For "charitable estates," see *MGWXZ* 1933, 31:11a–26a. The archetype of this family corporation (the Fan) was the only one founded in the Song; three were established in the Ming, fifty–seven in the Qing.

111. Yuan Zhi, *Xutai xiansheng ji* [Collected works of Mr. Xutai (Yuan Zhi)], n.d., 16:19b–21a.

112. *MGWXZ* 1933, 16:9b.

113. In addition to tax remission and famine relief, there were officially sponsored cemeteries for paupers; see *MGWXZ* 1933, 41:27b–30a. Accounts of illustrious officials and local notables also refer to acts of charity with some regularity.

114. Cao Zishou, "Wu xian cheng tu shuo," in Gu, *Tianxia junguo libing shu, ce* 5:11b–12a.

115. The most detailed treatment of Zhou Chen in English is Mette Siggstedt, "Zhou Chen: The Life and Paintings of a Ming Professional Artist," *Bulletion of the Museum of Far Eastern Antiquities* 54 (1982), pp. 1–239, which reproduces the entire series. More readily accessible is Color Plate 12 in James Cahill, *Parting at the Shore: Chinese Painting of the Early and Middle Ming Dynasty, 1368–1580* (New York: Weatherhill, 1978).

116. Marmé, "From Rout to Hegemony," Statistical Appendix to chapter four, pp. 203–207.

117. Fu Yiling, *Mingdai Jiangnan shimin jingji shican*, p. 87, citing Cao Shipin from *Ming Wanli shilu* [Veritable Records of the Wanli reign, Ming dynasty], juan 361.

118. *MGWXZ* 1933, 54:1b–2a.

119. For a clear summary of these incidents, see Tsing Yuan, "Urban Riots and Disturbances," in Jonathan D. Spence and John E. Wills, Jr., eds, *From Ming to Ch'ing* (New Haven: Yale University Press, 1979), pp. 287–290, 292–296, 302–308.

120. Some may have been seasonal workers, or underemployed members of households seeking the highest return for their labor. In either of these cases, they would not have depended on finding employment that day in order to survive.

121. E. P. Thompson, *The Making of the English Working Class* (New York: Vintage Press, 1963), p. 9.

122. For detailed evidence for this assertion, see the examination of the elite in Marmé, "From Rout to Hegemony," chapter five and appendices.

123. The last point is made by Gail Hershatter, *The Workers of Tianjin, 1900–1949* (Stanford: Stanford University Press, 1986), pp. 113–114. The rise of guilds in late Ming and early Qing Suzhou may thus have facilitated the militancy of craftsmen in the early Qing (on which, see Tsing Yuan, "Urban Riots and Disturbances," pp. 302–308).

124. See Fu Yiling, *Ming Qing shidai shangren ji shangye ziben, passim.* On the most important of these groups, see the classic study of Fujii Hiroshi, "Shinan shōnin no kenkyū" [A study of the Xin'an merchants], *Tōyō gakuhō*, 36 (1953–1954), pp. 1–44, 180–208, 335–388, 533–563 and Harriet T. Zurndorfer, *Change and Continuity in Chinese Local History: the Development of Hui-chou prefecture, 800–1800* (Leiden: E. H. Brill, 1989).

125. This statement is based on estimates of per capita income developed by Paul Bairoch, estimates cited by Fernand Braudel, *The Perspective of the World* (New York: Harper and Row, 1984), p. 534. Living standards at the end of the eighteenth century were, to be sure, higher in North America—but there were very few people in North America. Since Bairoch's estimate refers to China as a whole, and living standards at the core of its most prosperous macroregion must have been somewhat higher than average, his figure for China must be too low for Suzhou in particular and the Lower Yangzi macroregion in general.

126. Very few premodern cities exceeded a hundred thousand residents; those that did were almost always capital cities. See Fernand Braudel, *The*

204   CITIES OF JIANGNAN IN LATE IMPERIAL CHINA

Structures of Everyday Life (New York: Harper and Row, 1981), pp. 525–531, and Jan De Vries, *European Urbanization, 1500–1800* (Cambridge: Harvard University Press, 1984), pp. 242–243, and passim.

CHAPTER 2: LATE MING URBAN REFORM AND THE POPULAR UPRISING IN HANGZHOU

[*Author's note:* The present paper in its English translation is a revision of an earlier version: Fuma Susumu, "Minmatsu no toshi kaikaku to Kōshū minpen" [Late Ming urban reform and the popular uprising in Hangzhou] published in *Tōhō gakuhō*, no. 49. 1977 pp. 215–262. Although new findings from research undertaken since the article's original appearance have been incorporated in preparing this translation and the accompanying notes, the main argument is unchanged. Endnotes in the present translation have been shortened and made more explicit by insertion of page number references to Chinese texts. Interested readers will find citations from Chinese texts quoted more extensively in the original Chinese in the notes of the earlier Japanese version of the paper.

Certain issues, such as the appropriateness of the term "gentry rule" or the interpretation of the prominent role played by "idlers" or "vagabonds" in the protest—interpretations common to the original sources—demand additional consideration and will be taken up in future research.

Although the original article appeared some fifteen years ago, it is still quoted with some frequency. For a recent discussion of some of the issues taken up in this paper, see: Richard Von Glahn, "Municipal Reform and Urban Social Conflict in Late Ming Jiangnan," *Journal of Asian Studies*, Vol. 50, no. 2 (May 1991), 280–307.]

1. On reforms of rural village taxation and labor service systems, see any of these major research studies: Hamashima Atsutoshi, *Mindai Kōnan nōson shakai no kenkyū* [Rural society in Jiangnan during the Ming dynasty] (Tokyo: Tokyo Daigaku Shuppankai, 1982); Iwami Hiroshi, *Mindai yōeki seido no kenkyū* [Studies on the statute labor system in the Ming dynasty] (Kyoto: Dōhōsha, 1986), and Mori Masao, *Mindai Kōnan tochi seido no kenkyū* [A study of the land system in Jiangnan during the Ming dynasty], (Kyoto: Dōhōsha, 1988).

2. *Chongzhen Songjiang fuzhi* [Chongzhen gazetteer of Songjiang prefecture] 1631, 11:22a; Gu Yanwu, *Tianxia junguo libing shu* [Strengths and weaknesses of various prefectures and districts in the Empire] 1662, 6:78b.

3. Lu Kun, *Quwei zhai quanji* [Complete works from the Quwei studio] 1889, jikutiaochen, 3a; Lu Kun, *Shizheng lu* [A record of practical statecraft] 1889, 2:84a.

4. *Huang Ming tiaofashi liezuan* [Imperial Ming Legal Code], (1966 Tokyo reprint: Koten Kenyukai), p. 692.

5. See reference materials included in Fuma Susumu, "Minmatsu Shinsho no toshi bōdō" [Urban riots in the late Ming and early Qing], *Chūgoku minshū*

Notes

hanran shi [History of Chinese popular uprisings], ed. Tanigawa Michio and Mori Masao. Vol. 4, (Tokyo: Heibonsha, 1983), pp. 99–103, 403–409. Also Tanaka Masatoshi, "Minpen kōso nuhen" [Popular uprisings, rent resistance and servant uprisings], *Sekai no rekishi* [History of the World]; vol. XI (Tokyo: Chikuma shobō, 1961); Liu Yan, "Mingmo chengshi jingji fazhan xia de chuqi shimin yundong" [The early city residents' movements under the development of the urban economy in the late Ming] in *Zhongguo ziben zhuyi mengya wenti taolun ji* [Collected essays discussing the 'Sprouts of Capitalism' issue] vol. 1. (Beijing: Sanlian shudian, 1957); Liu Zhiqin, "Shilun Wanli minbian" [A Discussion of Popular Uprisings in the Wanli reign-period], in *Ming Qingshi guoji xueshu taolunhui lunwen ji* [Collected essays from an International symposium on Ming and Qing historical issues], (Tianjin: Tianjin Renmin chubanshe, 1982).

6. *Wanli Jiaxing fuzhi* [Wanli Gazetteer of Jiaxing Prefecture] 1600, 8:8b "Kecheng, fu mentan."

7. *Kangxi Jiaxing fuzhi* [Kangxi Gazetteer of Jiaxing prefecture] 1681, 18: 53b–56a.

8. Ibid.

9. *Tianqi Haiyan xian tujing*, [Tianqi gazetteer of Haiyan county] 1624, 6: 31b–32a: Feng Gaomo, "Cai yihou shimin qusi bei" [text from the stele erected by citizenry to commemorate the occasion of Magistrate Cai's departure from office].

10. Ibid., 6:31b–33a.

11. *Wanli Changzhou fuzhi*, [Wanli Gazetteer of Changzhou prefecture] 1618, 12:33a–34a.

12. Ibid., 12:35b.

13. Ibid., 12:34a–b.

14. Gu Yanwu, *Tianxia junguo libing shu*, 8:39a–42b, on "huojia." *Ding Bin, Ding Qinghui gong yiji* [Surviving Works of Ding Qinghui (Ding Bin)], 1638, 2:3a–11a; 5:10a–12b. For additional details, see Fuma Susumu, "Minmatsu han chihōkan shihen" [Student movements against local bureaucrats in the late Ming period], *Tōhō gakukō*, 52 (Kyoto, Kyoto Daigaku Jinbun Kagaku Kenkyūjo, 1980), pp. 601–602, and "Mindai Nankin no toshi gyōsei" [Urban administration in Ming Nanjing] in *Zen kindai ni okeru toshi to shakai sō*, ed. by Nakamura Kenjirō (Kyoto: Kyoto Daigaku Jinbun Kagaku Kenkyūjo, 1980), pp. 245–297.

15. *Wanli Jiading xianzhi* [Wanli Gazetteer of Jiading county] 1605, 6:10a; Gu, *Tianxia junguo libing shu*, 6:22b–23a.

16. Jiang Liangdong, *Zhen Wu lu*, [Record of Pacification in Wu district (Suzhou)], (original date of composition unclear, but probably in the Wanli period).

17. Ibid., siwen: 10b–11a. A *bao* usually consisted of one hundred households, a *jia* of ten households; together the nested system based on tens of households was known as *baojia*.

18. On the students' uprising, see Fuma, "Minmatsu han chihōkan shihen," pp. 595–622.

19. *Zhen Wu lu*, tiaoyi, 1a–b.

20. Ibid., 1b–3a.

21. On Xu Yikui, *Zhigong dui* [The Weavers' Response], refer to the following works: Fujii Hiroshi, "Chūgoku ni okeru shin to kyū—shokkō tai no bunseki o meguru shomondai" [Old and new in China—several problems involved in the analysis of shokko tai], *Tōyō Bunka*, 9 (1952); Peng Zeyi, "'Zhigong dui' shiliao nengshuo Ming zhongguo shougongye zibenzhuyi mengya de wenti ma?" ["*Zhigong dui*, on the problem of whether this material can explain the rise of handicraft industry leading to the development of the 'sprouts of capitalism" in China], in *Zhongguo ziben zhuyi mengya taolun ji* [Collected Essays on the "Sprouts of Capitalism" Issue], vol. 2 (sequel), (Beijing: Sanlian shudian, 1960), pp. 430–456.

22. *Ming Lu*, [Statutes of the Ming dynasty], juan 14, "Military laws." According to "the curfew," travel on city streets was largely prohibited after dark. According to Yabuuchi Kiyoshu, "Chūgoku no tokei" [Clocks of China], *Kagaku shi kenkyū*, 19 (1951) and Hashimoto Manpei, *Nihon no jikoku seido*, [The Japanese System of Time], (Tokyo: Hanawa Shobo 1966); the Chinese used a variable method for determining the evening and nighttime hours. Consequently, we can estimate that the hours of the night curfew varied according to the season. According to the *Ming Shi* and *Da Ming ershi nian suici xinchou (1541) Datongli* [The Official Calender of the Ming Dynasty for the year 1541], it is estimated that the night curfew extened from around 7:25 in the evening to 4:00 in the morning in the spring or autumn seasons.

23. *Zhen Wu lu*, tiaochen, 2a–b.

24. Kitamura Hironao, "Minmatsu Shinsho ni okeru jinushi ni tsuite" [On landlords in the late Ming and early Qing], *Rekishigaku kenkyū* 140 (1949). This was later included in Kitamura's *Shindai shakai keizaishi kenkyū* [Studies in Qing socio-economic history], (Kyoto: Ōsaka Shiritsu Daigaku Keizai Gakkai, 1972), pp. 18–49.

25. *Zhen Wu lu*, tiaochen, 2a.

26. Ibid., tiaochen, 8a–9a.

27. *Wanli Hangzhou fuzhi*, [Wanli Gazetteer of Hangzhou prefecture] 1579, "Biographies of Virtuous Conduct," 89:21a–b.

28. Ibid., 31:2b.

29. Shen Shixing, *Shen Wending gongji*, [Collected words of Shen Wending (Shen Shixing)], containing: *"Lunfei jiandu"* [Correspondence from the Grand Secretariat] 1:70b, 1:74b.

30. Lu Kun, *Shizheng lu*, 2:88a.

31. *Wanli Hangzhou fuzhi* [Wanli gazetteer of Hangzhou prefecture], 7:34a–35a.

32. Ibid., 7:34a–35a.

33. Ibid.

34. Ibid.

35. The table is based upon a comparison of the number of *ding* tax units arrived at by converting the number of *mu* area units into the number of *jian*. Chen Shan, the editor of the *Wanli Hangzhou fuzhi*, later put forth a radical critique of the reform in suggesting the complete abolition of the city tax burden which had been instituted to achieve fiscal relief for the countryside. Chen noted that, "When discussing these issues we must find the basis of the problem, but today we are only discussing the differences between seven *jian* and twenty *jian*, instead of addressing [the real problem of] of the 50,000 *jian*, which is unjustly demanded, so our people can't be released from this tax burden." *Wanli Hangzhou fuzhi*, 7:34a–35a.

36. Fang Yang, *Fang Chu'an Xiansheng ji*, [Collected writings of Fang Chu'an (Fang Yang)], 1615, 16:37b–38a.

37. *Wanli Hangzhou fuzhi*, 7:34a–35a.

38. On the relationship of the *jianjia* levy, *zhongjia* and *huofu*, see *Wanli Hangzhou fuzhi*, 7:30b–31b, 89:21a.

39. Ibid; 7:32a–33a.

40. Ibid., "Biographies of Virtuous Conduct," 89:21a–b.

41. Cui Jiaxiang, "Mingwu jishi," [Miscellaneous Notes from the Mingwu Studio], included in *Yanyi zhilin*, [Literary Miscelany of Haiyan County] 1623, 48:25a.

42. *Wanli Hangzhou fuzhi*, 89:21a–b. Further biographical information on Ding Shiqing is cited in note 52.

43. Ibid., 89:21a–b

44. Chen Shan's critical remarks are from the *Wanli Hangzhou fuzhi*, 7:32a–33a.

45. Chen Shan's father studied with Wang Shouren as did Chen himself during his youth. Chen was said to have raised high expectations for his future success on the part of Wang Shouren. Lu Shusheng, *Lu Wending gongji*, [Collected works of Lu Wending (Lu Shusheng)] 1616, 6:33a–39b, provides details on Chen's life and career. He is said to have been a model of all that a member of the gentry should be. He was especially active in water control works and in benevolent relief for the poor. It is also reported that Chen "was willing to speak out on any matter concerning his home region and that his concern led to the correction of an exceedingly large number of problems.

46. The following are research materials valuable for the study of the Hangzhou military uprising:

(a) Wang Shizhen, "Zhang (da)sima ding Zhe erluan zhi" [History of General Zhang's Supression of the Two Rebellions in Zhejiang], in Zhang Jiayin, *Julai Xiansheng ji*, [Collected Writings of (Zhang) Julai (Zhang Jiayin)], (1594), "appendix."

(b) Zhu Guozhen, "Hangzhou bingbian" [Military rebellion in Hangzhou] in *Huang Ming dashi ji*, [Chronicle of the August Ming Dynasty], (n.d.), juan 41.

(c) Cui Jiaxiang, 'Mingwu jishi," in *Yanyi zhilin*, juan 48.

(d) Zheng Shunchen, "Da sima Zhang Gong jinglue Zhe zhen bingbian shimo" [Complete history of General Zhang's successful suppression of the military rebellion in Zhejiang], in *Julai Xiansheng ji*, "Appendix."

(e) Wang Zudi, "Da sima Zhang Gong kanding Zhe zhen bingbian ji," [History of General Zhang's sucessful suppression of the military rebellion in Zhejiang, city (Hangzhou)], in *Julai Xiansheng ji*, "appendix."

(f) Yao Shilin, "Jian zhi bian" [Miscelany of Things Seen and Heard], in *Yanyi zhilin*, juan 53. In addition to these there are numerous materials on the military uprising, but as far as the author knows, these do not go beyond having value as secondary sources.

47. See: Wang Shizhen, "Zhang (da) sima ding Zhe erluan zhi." Zheng shunchen, "Da sima Zhang Gong jinglue Zhe zhen bingbian shimo", states that "the cash did not circulate in the market. Its value was not more than the equivalent of copper." The "new cash" suggests the Wanli *tongbao*. On the difference in value of "northern cash" and "southern cash" see *Ming Shi*, juan 81:5, "shihuo" "currency."

48. See: Cui Jiaxiang, "Mingwu jishi."

49. Wang Shizhen, "Zhang (da) sima ding zhe erluan zhi."

50. Wang Zudi, "Da sima Zhang gong kanding Wulin minbian ji," [A Record of General Zhang's successful supression of the popular uprising at Wulin (in Hangzhou)], in *Julai Xiansheng ji*, 1594, 46b.

51. Wang Shizhen, "Guanglu dafu taizi taibao binbu shangshu zeng shaobao Julai Zhang gong muzhi ming," [Epitaph of the Minister of War, Zhang Jiayin], in Zhang Jiayin, *Julai Xiansheng ji*, 1594, 65:30a.

52. The following materials, which are briefly introduced here, are important sources for the study of the Hangzhou popular uprising:

(a) Wang shizhen, "Zhang (da) sima ding Zhe erluan zhi." [Record of General Zhang's supression of two uprisings in Zhejiang] in *Erluan zhi* [Record of the two rebellions] (see the same title in *Jilai Xiangsheng ji* 1594, "Appendix.") This is a narrative of Zhang's meritorious service in putting down the military and civilian uprisings. Wang, the author, was a friend with close personal ties to Zhang. The epitaph on Zhang's tomb was in fact written by Wang. (see note 51.) As that epitaph attests, when Zhang came to supress the Hangzhou uprising, he conferred with two people on remedial measures: Lu Guangzu and Wang Shizhen. This suggests that Wang's account has some historical value. Nevertheless, since Wang's version is told from the standpoint of praising Zhang, it denigrates and devalues the popular uprising and Ding Shiqing. That the negative historical evaluation of the Hangzhou uprising became the permanent interpretation of the incident can be largely attributed to the great influence of Wang's account. (The description of the Hangzhou popular uprising in the following works is based largely on the *Erluan zhi*: Zhang Xuan, *Xiyuan wenjian lu* [Record of Zhang "Xiyuan's" [Xuan] Observations], 1940 juan 83, "Suppressions," Zhang Jiayin. Shen Guoyuan, *Huang Ming congxin lu* [Reliable Record of the Ming dynasty], juan 35. Wen Bing, *Dingling zhulue* [Notes on Mixcellaneous Matters of the Wanli Reign], juan 7, "Hangzhou Military Revolt," Fang Kongzhao, *Quan bian lue ji* [Record of Protecting the boundaries], juan 11. Feng Menglong, *Zhengguang zhinang bu* [Compliment of Expanding Wisdom], juan 8. "Pacifying the Rebellion of the military and the people."

(b) Zhu Guozhen, "Hangzhou bingbian," [Hangzhou Military Rebellion] in *Huang Ming dashi ji*, Zhu was a native of Huzhou prefecture in Zhejiang. As Zhu was enroute to sit for the provincial examinations, he saw General Zhang from his carriage. he was responsible for editing the *Huang Ming dashi ji*. Although he made use of Wang Shizhen's *Er luan zhi*, he provides a narrative record not found in other sources.

(c) Cui Jiaxiang, "Mingwu jishi," juan 48. Cui was a native of Jiaxing prefecture in Zhejiang province. Subjectivity, a concern in Wang Shizhen's account, is not a difficulty in this source; again, Cui provides insights not seen in other sources and his work is exceedingly important.

(d) Qian Youwei, "Da sima Zhang Gong jinglue Zhe zhen minbian zhuan" [Chronicle of General Zhang's successful supression of the popular uprising in Zhejiang city (Hangzhou)], in *Julai Xiansheng ji*, 1594, "appendix."

(e) Wang Zudi, "Da sima Zhang Gong kanding Wulin minbian ji," [Record of General Zhang's successful supression of the popular rebellion at Wulin (in Hangzhou)] and by the same author, "Da sima Zhang gong kanding zhezhen bingbian ji" in Zhang Jiayin, *Julai Xiansheng ji* 1594, "appendix."

(f) Yao Shilin, *Jian zhi bian*, juan 1. Yao happened to be in Hangzhou at the time of the military and civilian uprisings. He was an eye witness to both events and his account is therefore highly valued as a historical source.

(g) Qu Jiusi, *Wanli wugong lu* [Record of military engagements in the Wanli period] 1612, juan 2, "Zhejiang."

53. Wang Zudi, "Da sima Zhang Gong kanding Wulin minbian ji," 45a.

54. Qu Jiusi, *Wanli wugong lu*, 2:6a.

55. Wang Zudi, "Da sima Zhang Gong kanding Wulin minbian ji," 45a.

56. Qu Jiusi, *Wanli wugong lu*, 2:6a.

57. Details on Shen Jin and Shen Pian are provided in Huang Ruheng, *Yulin ji* [Notes from the (Master) of the "Yulin" (Studio) [e.g. Huang Ruheng], 1624, 17:24a–25b, "Sichuan anchasi qianshi Shen Gong xingzhuan" [Biography of Shen (Pian)'s activities as an official in Sichuan]. This source vigorously defends Shen Pian, who at the time of the Hangzhou uprising was most hated by the local citizenry.

58. *Wanli Hangzhou fuzhi*, 56:35b.

59. Ibid., 59:10a.

60. Zhu Guozheng, "Hangzhou bingbian;" Qu Jiusi, *Wanli wugong lu*, 2:6a.

61. Cui Jiaxiang, "Mingwu jishi," 48:25a.

62. *Hangzhou Wanli fuzhi*, 56:35b.

63. *Ming shilu* [Veritable Records of the Ming [dynasty]], (1966 reprint: Taibei: Zhongyang yanjiuyuan lishi yuyan yanjiusuo), "Wanli", p. 1916.

64. Qian Youwei, "Da sima Zhang Gong jinglue Zhe zhen minbian chuan," 32b; Wang Zudi, "Da sima Zhang Gong kanding Wulin minbian ji," 46b.

65. Zhu Guozhen, "Hangzhou bingbian," 41:13a; Qu Jiusi, *Wanli wugong lu*, 2:6a.

66. Zhu Guozhen, "Hangzhou bingbian," 41:13a. On Ding's arrest, see Wang Shizhen, "Zhang (da) sima ding Zhe erluan zhi;" Qian Youwei, "Da sima Zhang Gong jinglue Zhe zhen minbian zhuan;" and Wang Zudi, "Da sima Zhang Gong kanding Wulin minbian ji." These accounts suggest that he was arrested for a different, unrelated matter. The accounts by Wang Shizhen, Qian Youwei, and Wang Cidi are also written from a perspective that views Ding as a villain and General Zhang as having performed a great service in

putting down the rebellion. Zhu's and Cui's observations are written from a fairer standpoint, one that records Ding's arrest as having stemmed from his involvement in efforts to reform the labor service system. They are probably more reliable.

67. Qian Youwei, "Da sima Zhang Gong jinglue Zhe zhen minbian zhuan."

68. Wang Zudi, "Da sima Zhang Gong kanding Wulin minbian ji."

69. Cui Jiaxiang, *Ming Wu jishi*. 48:25a.

70. The description of Ding Shiqing in sources cited in notes 40 and 42 is dated to the years before Wanli 10. Therefore the evaluation is 180 degrees different from that in other sources, such as, for example, Wang Shezhen's account.

71. Zhu Guozhen, "Hangzhou bingbian," 41:13a; and Yao Shilin, *Jian zhi bian*, 53:4a. juan 1.

72. Zhu Guozhen, "Hangzhou bingbian," 41:13b.

73. Wang Zudi, "Da sima Zhang Gong kanding Wulin minbian ji;" Qu Jiusi, *Wanli wugong lu*, 2:7b.

74. Yao Shilin, *Jian zhi bian*, 53:4a.

75. Qian Youwei, "Da sima Zhang Gong jinglue Zhe zhen minbian zhuan," 33a.

76. Zhu Guozhen, "Hangzhou bingbian," 41:13b. Wang Zudi, "Da sima Zhang Gong kanding Wulin minbian ji."

77. Wang Shizhen, "Guanglu dafu taizi taibao binbu shangshu zeng shaobao jiali Zhang gong Muzhi ming," in Zhang Jiayin, *Julai Xiansheng ji*, 1594, 65:30b; and Wang Shizhen, "Zhang (da) sima ding Zhe erluan zhi," 26a.

78. Ibid.

79. Dong Fen, "Yushi Dafu zuosima Zhang Gong ding Zhe bian ji," [Censorate Officials' Supression of the Rebellion in Zhejiang] in Zhang Jiayin, *Julai Xiansheng ji*, "Appendix," 59a.

80. Wang Shizhen, "Zhang (da) sima ding Zhe erluan zhi," 26b; Wang Zudi, "Da sima Zhang Gong kanding Wulin minbian ji," 48b.

81. Wang Zudi, 48b.

82. Wang Shizhen, "Zhang (da) sima ding Zhe erluan zhi," 26b.

83. Ibid., 27a.

84. Ibid., 28b.

85. Ibid., 27b. and Yao Shilin, *Jian zhi bian*, 53:4b.

86. Qian Youwei, "Da sima Zhang Gong jinglue Zhe zhen minbian zhuan."

87. Dong Fen, "Yushi Dafu zuosima Zhang Gong ding Zhe bian ji," in *Julai Xiansheng ji*, "appendix." Zhang Jiayin, who proved successful in pitting the soldiers against the civilians, also included punishment for the military alongside other remedial measures. The military itself succeeded in distancing itself from the two ringleaders of the military uprising, Ma and Yang, who were punished by beheading.

88. Yao Shilin, *Jian zhi bian*, 53:4a.

89. A biography of Chai Xiang is included in *Kangxi Renhe xianzhi* [Kangxi Gaxetteer of Renhe county], 1687, juan 16, "Biographies."

90. Qu Jiusi, *Wanli wugong lu*, 2:7b.

91. On Mo Rui, see *Wanli Hangzhou fuzhi*, 57:24a. He was a *juren* of the first year of Wanli, from Qiantang (county); for his biography, see *Minguo Hangzhou fuzhi* [Republican Gazetteer of Hangzhou Prefecture] 1912, juan 134.

92. On Ma Sancai, see Mao Kun, *Mao Lumen Xiansheng wenji* [Collected writings of Mao Lumen (Kun)], 25:15a–17b.

93. Qu Jiusi, *Wanli wugong lu*, 2:7b.

94. Cui Jiaxiang, "Ming Wu jishi," 48:25b.

95. The locations of the homes of Shen and Mo are discussed in Ke Rulin, "Wulin dizhai kao" [Notes on homes in Wulin], in *Wulin Zhanggu cong-bian* [Collected anecdotes on Wulin (Hangzhou)], XII, 1889, 7b–8a. On the home of Ma Sancai, see: Sun Zhilu, *Er Shen Ye Lu* [Unofficial records of events of the Ming period], n.d. 5:21a.

96. *Kangxi Qiantang xianzhi*, [Kangxi Gaxetteer of Qiantang county], 1718, 21:4a. Chen Shan's home was located in the Taiping (district) of Qiantang county; see, *Guochao xian zhenglu* [Biographies of the present dynasty (Ming)], "Epitaph of Chen Shan," 102:12a.

97. Wang Zudi, "Da sima Zhang Gong kanding Wulin minbian ji," 46a.

98. Fang Yang, *Fang Chu'an Xiangsheng ji*, 16:46a–47b.

99. *Wanli Hangzhou fuzhi*, 19:4b.

100. As used here, the concept of "gentry rule" is based largely on Shigeta, "Kyōshin shihai no seiritsu to kōzō," [The establishment and structure of gentry rule] in vol. XII of *Iwanami sekai rekishi* (Tokyo: Iwanami, 1971); this essay was later published in Shigeta, *Shindai shakai keizai shi kenkyū* [Qing Economic and Social History], (Tokyo, Iwanami, 1975). However, Mr. Shigeta emphasizes "gentry rule" in rural society. His theory of "gentry rule" will be discussed in a future essay.

101. Zhu Guozhen, "Hangzhou bingbian," 41:13a.

102. *Ming shilu*, (Wanli ten, yiyou), p. 2321; "Popular rebellion in Hangzhou:" Ding Shiqing, who was a homeless person from Shangyu county in Zhejiang, planned [this event]; by fanning resentment against the gentry, he made use of the opportunity to provoke people to revolt. He led protests, destroyed the towers and gates, burned down the houses of gentry and officials, and [encouraged] looting."

103. Lu Ben, *Dufu Liangzhe dingbian yusong lu*, [Preface to the Record of Supressing Rebellion in Zhejiang by Zhang Jiayin], in Zhang Jiayin, *Julai Xiansheng ji*, "appendix," 1a–3a.

104. Zhang Siwei, *Tiaolu tang ji* [Collected writings from the Tiaolu Studio] (1596), 19:28b–29b, "Response to Zhang Julai."

105. For example, Liu Yan, "Mingmo chengshi jingji fazhan xia de chuqi shimin yundong," cited in note 5 above. "On top of lacking a clear plan for their struggle, they also lacked clear political aims. The major goal of civilian struggles went no further than attempts to lighten the violent pillaging of commerce and handicraft industries and thereby strive for the development of greater freedom of commercial production." This view, one exclusively from the perspective of the anti-eunuch popular uprising, should be revised.

106. Wan Zudi, "Da sima Zhang Gong kanding Wulin mingbian ji," 45b.

107. Li E, *Dongcheng zaji* [Miscellaneous notes on the Eastern Capital (Hangzhou)], "Zhicheng shi jing tu" [Views/maps of the city] (1728) 2:11a. Yao Zhen, "Chujiatang Qionghuayuan Tongshengmiao ji" [Notes on the Tongsheng temple in the Qionghua garden] (1423) in Zhou Jing, *Zhao Zhonglu fulu* [Records of Zhao Zhong] in *Wulin Zhanggu Congbian*, XXI, 1933, pp. 11b–13a.

108. Although a Qing period work, Yao Siqin's, "Donghe Zhao Ge" [Songs of the East River] in *Wulin Zhanggu Congbian*, XVII, 1892, 22b indicates a concentration of weavers living near the river. (See map.) A song from Yao's work tells of how nearby dyeworks turned the foam on the river to the colors of the rainbow.

109. *Wanli Hangzhou fuzhi*, 34:15b–16a.

110. Additional historical materials indicating that those people who joined the uprising were renters include Lu Guangzhu, "Zeng Zhang Julai Huanchao Xu," [Recollections of Zhang Julai] in *Lu Zhuangjian Gong Yi Gao*, [Posthumous writings of Lu Zhuangjian (Guangzhu)], 1629 unpaginated.

111. Qu Jiusi, *Wanli wugong lu*, 2:6b.

112. Cui Jiaxiang, "Ming Wu jishi," 48:24b–25a.

113. Qian Youwei, "Da sima Zhang Gong jinglue Zhe zhen minbian chuan," 31b.

114. He Canran, *Liuyu xuan chugao* [Preliminary drafts from the Liuyu Studio] 1608, yijia, 13a.

CHAPTER 3: URBAN SOCIETY IN LATE IMPERIAL SUZHOU

[*Author's note:* This essay was completed as part of the project on Ming-Qing social and economic development, financed by the Consiglio Nazionale delle Richerche.]

List of abbreviations:

HCJSWB 1826: *Huangchao jingshi wenbian* [Dynastic Memorials on Statecraft] (reprinted: Taipei: 1964).
JSMQBK 1956: *Jiangsu sheng Ming Qing yilai beike ziliao xianji* [Selected Inscriptions from stele in Jiangsu in the Ming and Qing periods] (Nanjing: Sanlian shudian, 1956).
MQSZBKJ 1981: *Ming Qing Suzhou gongshangye beike ji*, [Collection of stele on industry and commerce in Suzhou during the Ming and Qing] (Nanjing 1981).

1. The area is one of many lakes and canals, at an altitude of between three and five metres. The mildness of the climate is due in part to Lake Taihu (surface area 2,250 square kilometers); temperatures range from 0 degrees in winter to 28 degrees Celsius in summer. Average annual percipitation exceeds one meter, concentrated during the summer monsoon.

2. Gu Yanwu, *Tianxia junguo libing shu* [Strengths and weaknesses of various prefectures and districts in the Empire]. 1662; [original draft ed., n.d.] (1935 Shanghai reprint; 1964 Tokyo), 5:194.

3. *Huangchao yudi tongkao* [Dynastic Memorials on Statecraft] 1826; (1964 Taipei reprint), 31:11.

4. Ibid., 31:11.

5. The "four talents" were the friends Gao Qi (1336–1374), Xu Ben (1335–1380), Zhang Yu (1333–1385) and Yang Ji (1333–1383).

6. Cited in Hong Huanchun, "Lun Ming Qing Suzhou diqu huiguan de xingzhi ji qi zuoyang" [On the nature and functions of guilds in Suzhou during the Ming and Qing], *Zhongguo shi yanjiu* [Research in Chinese history] (1980) vol. 2, p. 3.

7. Wang Yi (1432–1499), *Yupu zaji* [Miscellaneous notes from a residential garden], 5, cit, in Xie Guozhen, ed., *Mingdai shehui jingji shiliao xuanbian* [An anthology of historical materials on Ming society and economy] (Fuzhou: Fujian renmin chubanshe, 1980), p. 111. See: also *Qianlong Suzhou fuzhi* [Qianlong gazetteer of Suzhou prefecture] 1748, 3:17–18.

8. Ch'oe Pu, "P'yohaenok" [Notes on a long voyage (1488–1490)] 2:21, in *Yŏnhaeng nok sŏnjip* [Collection of Accounts of Missions to Beijing] (Seoul: Minjok munhwa mungo kanhaeghoe, 1984) vol I, pp. 40, 129. Three-and-a-half centuries later, a French traveler, Isidore Hedde, exalted with analogous terms the beauty and richness of Suzhou that he described as "the greatest town of the world" in Isidore Hedde, *Description methodique des produits divers* [Organized description of various products] (Paris: Saint-Etienne, 1848) and L.B.O (liphant) "Excursion to the City of Suchau," *Chinese Repository* 1845, pp. 584–87.

9. Oliphant, *Narrative of the Earl of Elgin's Mission to China and Japan in the years 1857, 1858, 1859*, (Edinburgh: Blackwood, 1859), p. 130.

10. *Yongzheng zhupi yuzhi* [Imperial endorsements and edicts of the Yongzhong reign], 1887 (1965 reprint Taibei), 4/10/9 9:5365–66.

11. Gilbert Rozman, *Urban Networks in Ch'ing China and Tokugawa Japan* (Princeton: Princeton University Press, 1973), p. 6.

12. See: G. William Skinner, "Cities in the Hierarchy of local systems," in Arthur Wolf, ed., *Studies in Chinese Society* (Stanford: Stanford University Press, 1978), pp. 1–77.

13. Suzhou's survival as a concentrated urban zone depended on a complex and efficient logistical organization. An example: in 1640 there was a revolt when, in spite of a good harvest, there were delays in the delivery of rice, delays which entailed price increases. Eight years later, many citizens starved to death after ships carrying food were a month late in arriving (this incident is described in Pierre-Etienne Will, *Burocratie et famine en Chine au XVIII siècle* [Bureaucracy and Famine in 18th c. China]. (Paris-the Hague: Mouton, 1980), p. 162, citing Ye Shaoyuan, *Qi Zhen Jimenlu* [Records of the Tianqi and Chongzhen reigns], n.d., 2:6b, 7:12b. Li Xu's memorials in the Kangxi period show variations in the price of rice with respect to quantity imported from these regions. *Wen xian congbian* [Collection of documents of the Imperial Palace] n.d. (Taibei: Tailian guofeng chubanshe, 1964), pp. 871, 876. In 1734 a significant proportion of Hubei and Hunan rice (ten million dan), loaded at

Hankou and transported on the Yangzi River, was bound for Suzhou. (See: Chuan Hanshen and Richard Kraus, *Mid-Ch'ing Rice Markets and Trade: An Essay in Price History* (Cambridge: Harvard University Press, 1975).

14. *Jinpingmei cihua* [Notes and commentaries on the *Jin Ping Mei*] n.d. (1986 reprint Hong Kong), p. 737.

Luxury and waste in Suzhou were commonly criticized in sections in the local gazetteer on customs and ethics: *Qianlong Suzhou fuzhi* 1748, 3:29–31. Also see the description of luxuries in *Jinpingmei cihua* cited above.

15. See: Mark Elvin, "Market Towns and Waterways in the County of Shanghai from 1480 to 1910," in G. William Skinner, ed., *The City in Late Imperial China* (Stanford: Stanford University Press, 1978), pp. 459–61.

Concerning the phenomenon of the peasants leaving their fields in the same period and the same area, cf. also He Liangjun, *Siyou zhai congshuo*, [Collected dissertations from the Four Friends Studio], 1573 (Beijing, 1959), 13:111–12.

16. Examples of poverty and want are depicted in Feng Menglong's short stories; see the seventh, the twentieth and the thirty-fifth stories in Feng, *Xingshi hengyan* [Constant Words to Awaken the World], 1672 (1986 reprint: Beijing: Renmin chubanshe).

17. Gu Yanwu, *Tianxia junguo libing shu*, 4:55.

18. Nakayama Mio, "Shindai senki Kōnan no bukka dōkō" [Price trends in Jiangnan in the early Qing], *Tōyōshi kenkyū*, vol. 37, 4 (1979), pp. 77–106.

19. Quoted in [Nagel's] *China* (Geneva: Nagel Publishers, 1973), p. 1006.

20. Zhang Haishan's proposal to use public and private capital for the drainage of Wusong river, after the famine of 1804 is one example of this decline; *HCJSWB* 1826, 43: 3a–4a.

21. In *Qianlong Wujiang xianzhi* [Qianlong gazetteer of Wujiang county], 1749, 12:8; Zhao Zhenye complained that the wealthiest families, not content with a monopoly of land, took control of water resources to exploit peasants and fishermen, and on the whim of growing aquatic plants, they undid years of work of dredging the waterways.

22. *HCJSWB* 41:3a. The price differences between local and external markets stimulated rice smuggling and export. See: Will, *Burocratie et famine en Chine* . . . , pp. 188–89.

23. Robert Fortune, *Two Visits to the Tea Countries of China and the British Plantations in the Himalaya* (London: Murray, 1853) Vol. I, p. 186.

24. Gu Yanwu, *Zhaoyuzhi, Jiangnan 8, Suzhoufu* [Compendium of His-

torical Geography: Suzhou Prefecture in Jiangnan # 8], cited in Xie Guozhen, *Mingdai shehui jingji shiliao xuanbian* vol. II, p. 113.

25. The Wu school, whose main representatives were Jiang Sheng (1721–1799) and Yu Xiaoke (1729–1777), accepted the influence of the so called "Han school" as opposed to that of the "Song school."

26. *Qianlong Suzhou fuzhi* 1748, 3:26–27.

27. One such garden was at Zhouzhengyuan, built by the censor Wang Xiancheng in the sixteenth century; after his death it passed into the hands of other persons of note, including Wu Sangui's son-in-law.

28. Spence writes: "As presented in the poems written by Cao Yin's circle, this social life was an ideal round of drinking and poetry parties, interspersed with well chosen bucolic outings, Thus, we find Cao Yin watching the harvesting in the autumn, enjoying the snow in winter, going on the lake in summer to enjoy the lotus and the cool breezes, yearning for the simple life of fisher-folk in their little village, or traveling in spring to see the blossoms . . . " Jonathan Spence, *Ts'ao Yin and the K'ang-hsi Emperor: Bondservant and Master* (New Haven: Yale University Press, 1966), p. 65.

29. For a description, see: M. Martini, *Novus Atlas Sinensis* (Amsterdam: Blaeu, 1655), p. 101; perhaps the most lively description of the free and amorous life in Suzhou is in Zhang Dai, *Tao'an Mengyi* [Dreams and memories of Tao'an], c. 1644 (1978 reprint, Taipei). Note especially: pp. 1:9, 4:52–54, 5:69–70, 6:84.

30. See: Elvin, "Market-towns and Waterways," pp. 241–42; Will, *Burocratie et famine en Chine. . . .*

31. See: Lawrence Kessler, *K'ang-hsi and the consolidation of Ch'ing Rule, 1661–1684* (Chicago: University of Chicago Press, 1976) pp. 33–39; Charles O. Hucker, "Su-chou and the agents of Wei Chung-hsien," *Silver Jubilee Volume of the Zinbun-kagaku-kenkyuśyo. Kyoto University* (Kyoto, 1954) pp. 224–256 and Hucker, *Two Studies on the Ming* (Ann Arbor: University of Michigan Press, 1971).

32. On the fates of Gu Yanwu and Gu Bingguan, see: Willard Peterson, "The Life of Ku Yen-wu (1613–1682)," *Harvard Journal of Asiatic Studies*, 28 (1968), pp. 124, 133–56.

33. Lin Zexu, *Lin wenzhong gong zhengshu, Jiaji: Jiangsu zougao* [Memorials of Lin Zexu, first collection, Jiangsu] (1966 reprint, Taibei) p. 150. According to the witness of a Qing official, Yin Huiyi (1691–1748), at seven years of age a girl could already spin cotton, and by twelve or thirteen, she was able to weave, earning in one day more than an adult's living. *HCJSWB*, 36:5–6.

Concerning textile work productivity, cf. the episodes of the two widows who were able not only to earn their living and to pay all their debts, but also to accumulate large savings. Peng Zeyi, ed., *Zhongguo jindai shougongye shi ziliao* [Source materials on the history of handicraft industry in modern China] (Beijing: Zhonghua shuju, 1962), pp. 235–36.)

34. *Guanyu Jiangning zhizao Caojia dangan shiliao*, [Archival materials concerning the Cao family supervisors of the Nanking Imperial Factories] (Beijing: Renmin chubanshe, 1975; 1977 reprint, Taibei), p. 101.

35. Ye Shaoyuan, *Qi Zhen jiwenlu*, 7:11, cit. in Peng Zeyi, "Qingdai qianqi Jiangnan zhizao de yanjiu" [Study of Textile manufacture in Jiangnan in the Early Qing] *Lishi Yanjiu* 1983: 3 p. 93. See: also Sun Pei, *Suzhou zhizaoju zhi* [Treatise on the manufactories of Suzhou] 1686 (reprint, Nanjing: Jiangsu renmin chubanshe, 1954), 9:88.

36. Peng Zeyi, "Qingdai qianqi Jiangnan zhizao de yanjiu" [Study of textile manufacture in Jiangnan in the early Qing] *Lishi Yanjiu* 1963, 4, p. 93, citing *Gushan bichen* [Pencil dust on mountains and valleys] n.d., 4:10.

37. On the fame of Suzhou silk, see Tang Zhen, *HCJSWB* 1826, 37:1; *Kangxi Wujiang xianzhi* [Kangxi gazetteer of Wujiang county] 1684, 17:23; *Qianlong Wujiang xianzhi* 1749, 5:14.

38. Qianlong Wu xianzhi [Qianlong gazetteer of Wu county] 18th century, 52a:5, quoting *Qianlong Zhangzhou xianzhi* [Qianlong gazetteer of Zhangzhou county] 1766.

39. Xu Daling, ed., *Zhongguo zibenzhuyi mengya wenti taolunji* [Collected discussions on the "sprouts of capitalism" issue in China] (Beijing: Sanlian shudian, 1957–1960), p. 900, citing *Chongzhen Wu xianzhi* [Chongzhen gazetteer of Wu county] 1642, 29:41. The fabrics in greatest demand were satin and taffeta.

40. Between 1770 and 1780 300/400 dye-houses worked in Suzhou, and looms surpassed the number of 10,000. See: Shang Yue, "Qingdai qianqi Zhongguo shehui de tingzhi, bianhua, he fazhan" [Stagnation, change and development in Chinese society in the early Qing], *Zhongguo zibenzhuyi mengya wenti taolunji*, vol. I, p. 200. Furthermore, historical sources of Wanli period describe the industrial area of the city, on the east side, as an uninterrupted succession of shops and factories, with thousands of artisans. *Ming Shilu: Shenzong* [Veritable Records of the Ming: Shenzong reign], 361:5–6. Each area had its own specialized profession; copper shops, for instance, were concentrated in the western side of the city. *Qianlong Suzhou fuzhi* 1748, 12.

41. Mulberry cultivation, breeding of silkworms and spinning of silk were performed within family units. Silk production was a complicated process, requiring a steady supply of mulberry leaves and a light, airy and warm room,

for breeding, where humidity needed to be kept to a minimum. According to Gu Lu, the peasants from the hills near lake Taihu considered the third and fourth lunar months as "silk worm months". During this period red leaves were pinned to doors, and a series of taboos came into effect, prohibiting social practices such as visits, talking loudly in the room where the silk worms were, collecting taxes, celebrating marriages or funerals. The object of these prohibitions was to concentrate all energies on the silk harvest, to protect the crop, and, to some degree, to keep breeding methods secret. Gu Lu, *Qingjia lu* 4:3–5, cited in Shi Minxiong, *Qingdai sizhigongye de fazhan* [Development of the silk industry in the Ming period] (Taibei: Taixian commercial Press, 1968), pp. 31, 33. These families also took care of silk reeling, using simple machinery that, rather than requiring a large initial capital outlay, necessitated a considerable pool of labour. This process needed to be undertaken swiftly in order to avoid a deterioration of the silkworm cocoons. On occasion, the cocoons were purchased directly by merchants and spinning mills, though in general silk breeders preferred to sell finished raw silk, for which they could charge far more. The great works finished with the selling of the product on the place or at the temporary markets.

For a description of silk production in Huzhou prefecture, see: Ting Yueh-hung, "Sericulture in Hu-chou as seen in the *Hu-chou fu-chih*," *Papers on China* 23 (1970), p. 36. Also see: Zhang Luxiang, *Nongshu* [Book of Agriculture], *HCJSWB* 1826, 36:8–10.

42. See: inscriptions *JSMQBK* 1956, p. 71; see also Liu Yongcheng, "Lun Qingdai guyong laodong" [Wage labor in the Qing period], *Lishi Yanjiu* 4 (1962), pp. 109, 114.

43. *JSMQBK* 1956, p. 217, 233; Liu Yongcheng, "Lun Qingdai guyong laodong," p. 109 and 111. He Bingdi also mentions a guild of leather artisans who immigrated from Nanjing, Yuanning (He, *Zhongguo huiguan shilun* [An historical survey of landsmannnschaten in China] (Taibei: Xuesheng shuju, 1966), pp. 50–51.

44. Kangxi visited a shipyard in order to examine the project of a new vessel called a *huangchuan* (Spence, *Ts'ao Yin and the K'ang Hsi Emperor*, pp. 71–72); There was a guild of local artisans, and another of Muslim immigrants. See: He, *Zhongguo huiguan shilun*, p. 51.

45. Gu Yanwu, *Zhaoyuzhi, Jiangnan 8, Suzhoufu*, cited in Xie Guozhen, ed., *Mingdai shehui jingji shiliao xuanbian*, II, p. 113.

46. Zhang Dai, *Tao'an Mengyi*, 5:63.

47. On the origin of the two systems at the beginning of Ming dynasty, see Saeki Yuichi, "Minzen hanki no kiko—ō chōkenryoku ni yoru shō aku o megutte" [Textile families in the first half of the Ming dynasty] *Tōyō bunka kenkyūjo kiyō* 8 (1956), pp. 167–210, especially 170–183.

48. Sun Pei, *Suzhou zhizaoju zhi* 1686, 4:18, 10:92–100; *Ming Shilu*, Xuanzong 85:9–10; Xizong 73:1.

49. Sun Pei, *Suzhou zhizaoju zhi*, 3:5.

50. See: Paolo Santangelo, "The Imperial Factories of Suzhou: Limits and Characteristics of State Intervention during the Ming and Qing dynasties," in Stuart Schram, ed. *The Scope of State Power in China* (Hong Kong: St. Martin's Press, 1989), p. 275.

51. See: *Daoguang Suzhou fuzhi* [Daoguang gazetteer of Suzhou prefecture] 1824, 21:30–31.

52. See: Peng Zeyi *Zhongguo jindai shougongye shi ziliao*, I, pp. 391–93.

53. Throughout this period there was friction between private owners and the authority of Suzhou's Imperial Factories, demonstrating that the government's actions were of little concrete value and could easily be disregarded. Thus, in 1653 a number of jihu were called up as "foremen." Peng Zeyi, "Qingdai qianqi Jiangnan zhizao de yanjiu," p. 95. Two years later the Minister for Finance responded favorably to complaints made by the auditor Yang Maogong, prohibiting the drafting of *jihu*. Ibid., pp. 92–93, citing *Qingdai chaodang*, Shunzhi 12/5/16.; also see, Sun Pei, *Suzhou zhizaoju zhi* 1686, 1:3.

54. *Da Qing huidian* [Collected Statutes of the Qing] Guangxu ed., 1899, (1963 reprint, Taibei), 201:8; and *MQSZBKJ*, 1981, p. 1–3. In 1708, two Superintendents of Imperial Factories, Cao Yin and Li Xu wrote to Kangxi: "Wages are very low. . . . All these craftsmen, though properly enrolled on pay ledgers, are in realty common folk employed to work. . . . If we decided to rescind this practice, these poor craftsmen would leave in search of work. They cannot afford not to work . . . " *Guanyu Jiangning zhizao Caojia . . .* , p. 54.

55. See: Nakayama Hachirō, "Mindai no shokusenkyoku" [Imperial Textile Manufactures in the Ming] *Hitotsubashi ronsō* 9:5 (1948), pp. 479–502.

56. See: Xu Daling, ed., *Zhongguo zibenzhuyi mengya wenti taolunji* v. I, p. 79.

57. Indeed, the decline of the Imperial Factories, in part due to the flight of workers, can be attributed to the poor treatment and exploitation of craftsmen at the hands of administrators, intermediaries, supervisors. (See: Saeki Yuichi, "Minzen hanki nokiko—ō chōkenryoku ni yoru shō aku o megutte," pp. 186–93) Another factor in this decline lay in an opening up of the market, leading to more opportunities for private businesses.

In another example which illustrates both the decline of the imperial factories and the emiseration of the textile workers, Suzhou Prefect Kou was praised by Gu Yanwu for his efforts to help thousands of unemployed textile artisans (*jihu*) in 1623, when Kou commissioned them to produce textiles for the state. *Guangxu Suzhou fuzhi* [Guangxu gazetteer of Suzhou prefecture] 1883, "Kougong muzhi" [Epitaph for Prefect Kou], 17:21.

58. *Ming Shilu: Shenzong*, 361:5, Wanli 29/7/dingwei, 380:3 Wanli 31/1/ yihai.

59. Yokoyama Suguru, *Chūgoku kindaika no keizai kōzō* [The economic structure of Chinese modernization] (Tokyo: 1972), p. 3, citing *Jiajing Songjiang fuzhi* 1522–1567, juan 4.

60. Yin Huiyi (1691–1748) wrote: "Although there is much money to be earned in silk, the demand for cotton cloth is such that it is a far more profitable sector. If we examine the prefectures of Suzhou and Songjiang in Jiangnan we see that they are the wealthiest. In these places, even poor people become rich, with cotton, not silk. . . ." *HCJSWB* 1826, 36:6. But, in spite of evidence that large silk spinning and weaving businesses were present in seventeenth century Suzhou, the majority of cotton production in traditional China—apart from the final processes of dyeing and calendaring—was carried out on a family basis and not by the large businesses the market would seem to have been able to support. See the discussion by Chao Kang, *The Development of Cotton Textile Production in China* (Cambridge: Harvard University Press, 1977), pp. 31–47.

61. Lin Cong's 1454 memorial denounces the impoverishment of poorer workers and the growing wealth of merchants and pawnbrokers during the passage from dependence on the state to dependence on the private sector. Other sources show that craftsmen having fled to one of the two capitals set up their own workshops. *Ming Shilu, Yizong Shilu*, 239:8. Also see Saeki, "Minzen hanki no kiko—ō chōkenryoku ni yoru shō aku o megutte," p. 192, citing *Huang Ming jingshi wenbian*.

62. Such rich families could easily find a way to be replaced by people from orphanages or hospices, and their inscription in the registers of textiles was a device in order to avoid heavier duties. Saeki, "Minzen hanki no kiko—ō chōkenryoku ni yoru shō aku o megutte," pp. 209, n. 100, 210 n.102, citing *Huang Ming jingshi wenbian*.

63. See: Sun Pei, *Suzhou zhizaoju zhi* 1686, 12:107.

64. Peng Zeyi, "Qingdai qianqi Jiangnan zhizao de yanjiu," p. 93 n.1

65. Qin Shan, *Songwen, HCJSWB* 1956, 28:8.

66. It is not a coincidence that so many of these merchants predisposed towards trade and smuggling with Japan came from Huizhou. See: Miyazaki Ichisada, "Minshinjidai no Soshū to keikōkyō to hattatsu," pp. 306–319, especially p. 309.

Gu Yanwu, describes Huizhou merchants as industrious and parsimonious, "A few months after marrying, [they] leave, often for as long as ten years at a time, so that if father and son met they would not recognize one another. The richest merchants travel with an assistant and many agents, all of whom are scrupulously honest, in whom the merchant places full trust, in whose care he leaves huge fortunes [. . .]," Gu Yanwu, *Zhaoyuzhi, Jiangnan 11, Huizhoufu*, cited in *Mingdai shehui jingji shiliao xuanbian*, II, pp. 91–92.

67. Hong Huanchun, "Lun Ming Qing Suzhou diqu huiguan de xingzhi ji qi zuoyong," p. 4.

68. Zhang Kui (zi Xiuwo) was well known in Suzhou for his refined tastes, his homosexual love affairs, and his disorderly life. He is mentioned in Yu Huai's *Banqiao zaji* a collection of notes on life in leisure areas of Nanjing at the end of Ming Dynasty. See: Yu Huai, *Banqiao zaji* [Diverse Records of the Wooden Bridge] c. 1696, (1928 reprint Shanghai), p. 14; Also see: Howard Levy, *A Feast of Mist and Flowers: the Gay Quarters at Nanking at the end of the Ming* (Yokohama: n.p., 1967), p. 85–86

69. In Qian Yong, *Lüyuan conghua* [Collected talks on roaming through gardens] 1838 (Suzhou: Zhenxin shushe, 1870), "Sun Chunyang," 24:640–41.

70. Gu Lu, *Wuqu fengtu lu* [On popular customs of Suzhou] *Xiaofang Kunshai yudi conglu*, 6:35. On Gu Lu, see He Liangjun, *Siyou zhai congshuo* [Collected dissertations from the Studio of the Four Friends] 1569–1579 (1959 reprint, Beijing), 6:134.

71. *Minguo Wu xianzhi* 1933, 52a:5.

72. *MQSZBKJ* 1981, the various shops are described in inscriptions, respectively pp. 115–17, 392, 267–68.

73. Gu Gongxie, *Xiaoxiaxianji zhaichao*, cited in Xie Guozhen, ed., *Mingdai shehui jingji shiliao xuanbian*, II, p. 85.

74. Hong Huanchun, "Lun Ming Qing Suzhou diqu huiquan de xingzhi ji qi zuoyang," p. 6. The city's evident prosperity and the shops of many stories are depicted in Xu Yang's painting of Suzhou in the Qianlong period, "Gusu fanhua tu." See: Liaoning Provincial Museum, *Qing: Xu Yang, "Gusu fanhua tu"* ["Old Suzhou Picture of Prosperity" by Xu Yang, Qing dynasty] (Hong Kong: Commercial Press, 1988).

75. On the contradiction between "authorized middle-men" (*guanya*) and "illegal middle-men" (*siya*), see the text of the 1844 stone inscription, MQSZBKJ 1981, pp. 258–59.

76. This point is supported by the stone inscription of the seventh year of Tianqi (1627), in *MQSZBKJ* 1981, pp. 240–41.

77. An inscription dated 1772 of the guild "Qianjiang huiguan," *MQSZBKJ* 1981, p. 19; He Bingdi, *Zhongguo huiguan shilun*, p. 102

78. On the Jiangxi guild, see the carved inscription, *MQSZBKJ* 1981, pp. 345–49. This problem is also discussed by He, *Zhongguo huiguan shilun*, p. 38, Hong Huanchun, "Lun Ming Qing Suzhou diqu huiguan de xingzhi ji qi zuoyong," p. 12.

79. See: Yang Lien-sheng, "Government Control of Urban Merchants in Traditional China," *Qinghua xuebao* 8, (1970), pp. 186–209.

80. Hong Huanchun, "Lun Ming Qing Suzhou diqu huiguan de xingzhi ji qi zuoyong," pp. 12–13.

81. On the numbers of guilds at Suzhou: Liu Yongcheng lists 122 *gongsuo* and 40 *huiguan*, in total 162 guilds, a figure Liu considers approximate. Liu "Lun Qingdai guyong laodong," p. 22. Hong Huanchun lists 90 guilds in, "Lun Ming Qing Suzhou diqu huiguan de xingzhi ji qi zuoyong," pp. 7–11. He counts approximately 60 guilds created between the seventeenth and nineteenth centuries, on the basis of the members' job and geographical origin; He, *Zhongguo huiguan shilun*, pp. 39, 50–51.

82. Liu Yongcheng, "Lun Qingdai guyong laodong," pp. 44–45.

83. *MQSZBKJ* 1981, pp. 19–21, 22.

84. See: the 1850 stone inscription, *MQSZBKJ* 1981, p. 122; also: Hong Huanchun, "Lun Ming Qing Suzhou diqu huiguan de xingzhi ji qi zuoyong," p. 15.

85. Peng Zeyi, *Zhongguo jindai shougongye shi ziliao*, p. 30–31.

86. Inscriptions support this point, *JSMQBK* 1956, pp. 120–21.

87. Bradstock Timothy, "Ch'ing Dynasty Craft Guilds and Their Monopolies," *Qinghua xuebao*, 15 (1983), p. 152.

88. Hong Huanchun, "Lun Ming Qing Suzhou diqu huiguan de xingzhi ji qi zuoyong," p. 14.

89. See: inscriptions in *MQSZBKJ* 1981, pp. 138–140.

90. For instance, the regulations of jewellers' guild of Suzhou in 1902 prohibited acceptance of stolen goods. See: inscriptions in *MQSZBKJ* 1981, pp. 173–74; and *JSMQBK* 1956, p. 148.

91. *Da Ming huidian*: *Wanli*, 20:1–4.

92. See: Sun Pei, *Suzhou zhizao zhi* 1686, 1:3. The gazetteer of the Yuanhe district composed during the Qianlong reign demonstrates that still in

the eighteenth century the term *jihu* could be used with its original financial implications: "The population of eastern Suzhou to a large degree works in textiles, and the names of these textile firms are registered in government ledgers". *Qianlong Yuanhe xianzhi* [Qianlong gazetteer of Yuanhe county], 18th century, 10:7; see also *Minguo Wuxian zhi* 1933, 51:5.

93. Liu Yongcheng distinguishes between three types of *jihu*: the richest category had nothing to do with production, and therefore considered themselves as *zhangfang*; the middle group took part in the manufacturing process, hiring their own workers, while the poorest *jihu*, although independent were short of capital and therefore worked exclusively for the *zhangfang*, Liu, "Lun Qingdai guyong laodong," p. 40.

94. See for instance the memorial sent by the Superintendent of Suzhou Imperial Factories, Li Xu, where the *jihu* are treated as independent producers. *Wenxian congbian* [Collection of documents of the Imperial Palace] n.d. (Taibei: Tailian guofeng chubanshe, 1964), p. 886.

95. *Qianlong Yuanhe xianzhi*, 10:7.

96. *Zhenze xianzhi*, juan 25, cited in Saeki, "Minzen hanki no kiko—ō chōkenryoku ni yoru shō aku o megutte,," "p. 199 n. 32. See: also "Xitai manji" juan 4, cited in Peng Zeyi, "Qingdai qianqi Jiangnan zhizao de yanjiu," p. 64.

97. *Kangxi Zhangzhou xianzhi* [Kangxi gazetteer of Zhangzhou county] 1684, 3:11–12; *Kangxi Suzhou fuzhi* [Kangxi gazetteer of Suzhou prefecture] 1693, 21:7; this subject is also mentioned in *Gujin tushu jicheng* [Synthesis of books and illustrations] 1725, "Kaogong dian," 10:95385, cited in Peng Zeyi, *Zhongguo shougongye shi ziliao*, I, p. 101.

98. According to the quoted sources, the economic activity in this area was prosperous during the Ming and Qing dynasties, with the exception of the transitional period. (For example see *JSMQBK* 1956, p. 1).

99. See: *Tongzhi Huzhou fuzhi* [Tongzhi gazetteer of Huzhou prefecture], juan 33, cited in Xu Daling, ed., *Zhongguo zibenzhuyi mengya wenti taolunji*, I, p. 368.

100. See: Mark Elvin, *The Pattern of the Chinese Past*, (Stanford: Stanford Univesity Press, 1973) pp. 283–84; Peng Zeyi, "Qingdai qianqi Jiangnan zhizao de yanjiu," pp. 91–116.

101. See: *Minguo Wuxian zhi* 1933, 51:22, cit. in Peng Zeyi, ed., *Zhongguo jindai shougongye shi ziliao*, II, p. 428. In the Ming era, in the 1601 *Veritable Records*, there were already reports confirming the existence of wage

labour in textile and dyeing workshops. For an example, see *Ming shilu: Shenzong*, 361:5–6. In one 1822 stone inscription the term is used also for a big textile factory which is at the same time a commercial firm. *MQSZBKJ* 1981, p. 25.

102. At the beginning of Qing dynasty, the Superintendent of Suzhou Imperial Textile Factories, Chen Youming, confirms that artisans—including those working for the Imperial Factories—worked scattered at home. *Ming Qing shiliao*, [Documents of the Ming and Qing] (Shanghai: Commercial Press, 1930–1936), 3:286b.

103. The main function of the Imperial Factories was political; they supplied the Imperial family and the Court with clothes and dresses, the army with uniforms and standards, or the Emperor with presents for dignitaries of the tributary states and rewards for civil and military officials.

104. *Guangxu Jiading xianzhi*, juan 29, cited in Nishijima Sadeo, *Chūgoku keizai shi kenkyū* [Studies in the History of the Chinese Economy], (Tokyo: Tokyo Daigaku shuppankai, 1966), p. 885.

105. See: *Shenghu zhuzhi ci* [Collection of the Bamboo Branch from Shengze and Huzhou] cited in Xie Guozhen, ed., *Mingdai shehui jingji shiliao xuanbian*, II, p.69. On Shengzezhen, see: He Bing, *Guoji muyi daobao*, 4,5, p. 36, cit. in Peng Zeyi, *Zhongguo shougongye shi ziliao*, I, p. 220, where it is reported that commissions ranged from 50 to 100 and more *wen* per *pi* of cloth sold.

106. See: Kojima Yoshio, "Shinmatsu Minkokushoki Soshūfu no kinuorigyō to kiko no dōkō" [Silk industry and weaver's movement in Suzhoufu in late Ming and early Qing], *Shakai keizai shigaku*, 34:5 (1969), pp. 37–38.

107. See: Yokoyama Sugeru, "Shindai no toshi kinuorimonogyō no seisan deitai" [The mode of production in the urban silk industry in the Qing], *Shigaku kenkyū*, (1968) 105:53–54; Peng Zeyi, ed., *Ming Qing zibenshuyi mengya yanjiu lunwen*, pp. 350–60.

108. See: *HCJSWB* 1826, 36:6, where Yin Huiyi (1691–1748), on the subject of the flourishing economies in Suzhou and Songjiang, recounts that cotton, thanks to its low price and wide diffusion, had become the populace's major source of income. At seven or eight years of age a girl could already spin cotton, and by twelve or thirteen, she was able to weave. This was undoubtedly one of the reasons why big cotton manufacturers did not develop. By contrast, the *jihu* which succeeded in expanding the most, turning into proper factories, were those which devoted to silk processing. At the beginning of the Qing dynasty these firms were subject to restrictions on the number of looms allowed per company. This restriction remained in force until the end of the

226   CITIES OF JIANGNAN IN LATE IMPERIAL CHINA

seventeenth century. Kang, *The Development of Cotton Textile Production in China*, p. 30.

109. In the histories of Wuxian it is noted that in spite of the fact that little cotton was grown in the area, people in the countryside and the city worked at spinning and weaving cotton, "despite the scarcity of cotton production, those families dedicated to spinning and weaving cotton do so full time, not only in the villages but also in the city". *Minguo Wuxian zhi* [1933], 51:15.

110. *Qianlong Wujiang xianzhi* 1748, 5:14; 38:7–8, cited in Fu Yiling, *Ming Qing shidai shangren yi shangye ziben* [Merchants and commercial capital in the Ming and Qing], (Beijing: Renmin chubanshe, 1956), p. 16.

From that period onwards Shengze textiles were particularly prized, and the town became a destination for thousands of interprovincial merchants. This economic growth explains how Shengze, from a small village of fifty to sixty families at the beginning of the Ming dynasty, swelled into a major city numbering fifty thousand inhabitants by the Qing. The whole Wujiang district benefitted from such sustained economic growth: at the end of the fifteenth century there were three market-villages (*shi*) and four market-towns (*zhen*); towards the middle of the sixteenth century the total stood at ten and four respectively, and in the seventeenth century ten and seven. *Qianlong Wujiang xianzhi* 1749, 1:2a, 4:1b, cited in Fu, op. cit. p. 19.

See also the case of Zhenze, *Qianlong Zhenze xianzhi* [Qianlong gazetteer of Zhenze county] 1:2a, 4:1b, cit. in Fu Yiling, Beijing, 1980, p. 19: village with few dozens of families during Mongol domination, doubled between the fifteenth and the sixteenth century, and in the eighteenth century reached a population of two or three thousand families.

111. Feng Menglong, *Xingshi hengyan*, 18:370–93. As we may see from notes and memoirs of other contemporary authors, this story was a common one. Zhang Han tells the tale of a wine seller who, around 1480, following problems caused by a flood that ruined his cellars, turned his hand to weaving. He began with one loom, and then, after selling the finished silk, bought himself another, and then another, until he owned more than twenty. Zhang Han, *Songchuang mengyu* [Dream from a window [looking out on] pine trees] 1593, 6:119. A similiar case is that of Pan Bicheng, recorded by Shen Defu, *Wanli yehuo bian* [Collection of informal notes of the Wanli era] 1619, (1959 reprint Beijing) 28:713.

112. See: *HCJSWB* 1826, 37:1.

113. *Fenglu xiaozhi*, 3:7, cited in Xu Daling, ed., *Zhongguo zibenzhuyi mengya wenti taolunji*, I, pp. 79, 204. And Ibid., I, p. 200. Furthermore, according to *Yongzheng zhupi yuzhi* 1887, 42:76–77, 48:101–102, during Yongzheng's reign, there were at least 100,000 calenderers in the city. From

gazetteers and commercial yearbooks we may calculate an average of between twelve and thirteen thousand looms in Suzhou in the eighteenth century.

114. By 1900, according to the *Suzhou shi qing* cited by Peng Zeyi, there had been a big reduction in the number of these big companies, while the *Minguo Wuxian zhi* 1933, put the number of these companies at fifty-seven by 1911. Peng, *Zhongguo jindai shougongye shi ziliao*, II, pp. 428–30, 452. A 1913 prospectus on Suzhou accounting companies show that one company controlled 600 looms, six companies between 300 and 400 looms, twenty-seven between 100 and 260, and the remaining twenty-three companies between 25 and 90.

115. *Xitai manji*, 4, cit. in Hong Huanchun, "Lun Ming Qing Suzhou diqu zibenzhuyi mengya chubu kaocha" [An investigation of the discussion of the sprouts of capitalism question in the Suzhou area in the Ming and Qing dynasties], *Ming Qing zibenzhuyi mengya yanjiu lunwenji* [Collection of discussions of the research on the sprouts of capitalism in the Ming and Qing] (Shanghai: Renmin chushuban, 1981), p. 428.

116. *JSMQBK* 1956, p. 16 gives the text of a 1734 stone inscription in Changzhou.

117. *Wujiang xian zhi*, 13:6, cited in Peng, *Zhongguo jindai shougongye shi ziliao*, p. 945. Only when these conditions were met do we find a clean break with the land and a complete dependence on the "sale of labor" as defined by Lenin.

118. See: *Gujin tushu jicheng* "Fangyu huibian, Zhifang dian," 687:13960, cited in Peng Zeyi, *Zhongguo shougongye shi ziliao*, I. Also: *Qianlong Changzhou xianzhi* 1766, 16:8; *Qianlong Yuanhe xianzhi*, eighteenth century, 10:7; *Gujin tushu jicheng*, "Jingji huibian, Kaogong," 10:95385; Saeki Yuichi, "Senroppyakuichi nen shokuyō no hen o meguru shomondai" [Problems concerning the 1601 textile workers' rebellion], *Tōyō bunka kenkyūjo kiyō*, vol 45 (1968); Fan Lian (1540–?), *Yunjian jumu chao* [Notes on [my] personal experiences among clouds] n.d., cited in Fu, *Ming Qing shidai shangren yi shangye ziben*, p. 12. Such sources indirectly confirm the existence of a flourishing labor market and support the contention that the lives of many artisans depended already on their employment in the *jihu*.

119. In the sixteenth century, registers defined two categories, upper (*shang*) and middle (*zhong*): "On the basis of income and wealth, textile workers are divided into the categories of upper and middle." See: *Ming shilu*, Shizong, 172:4, Jiajing 14/2/yisi.

120. See: Ibid. 172:4–5, Jiajing 14/2/yisi.

121. There is a wealth of material to be found in the *Veritable Records* of the Ming period detailing protests against a rise in the amount of goods requested by the state above and beyond agreed quotas. See: for instance *Ming shilu*, Yingzong, 317:9, 339:4; Xianzong, 101:2; Xiaozong, 54:1, 61:1–2, 158:2, 170:5; Wuzong, 13:8–9; Shizong 34:4–6, 172:4, 285:1; Muzong, 48:6, 66:13; Shenzong, 42:5, 93:2, 121:7, 285:11 Also on this subject: *Da Ming huidian*, 37:31. There are also references to this practice, particularly among shops in the capital in the *Ming shilu* (cf. for instance Xuanzong, 8:10; Shizong, 25:9–10; Muzong, 44:6–7; Shenzong, 417:2).

122. Peng Zeyi, "Qingdai qianqi Jiangnan zhizao de yanjiu," p. 63.

123. Sun Pei, *Suzhou zhizaoju zhi* 1686, 4:18, 10:99–100.

124. On wages, see: Sun Pei, *Suzhou zhizaoju zhi* 1686, 5–6:23–37; MQSZBKJ 1981, pp. 15–17; *Qianlong Zhangzhou xianzhi*, 1766, 16:8, *Kangxi Zhangzhou xianshi* 1684, 3:11–12; *Qianlong Yuanhe xianzhi* 18th century, 10:7; *Kangxi Suzhou fuzhi* 1693, 21:7; see also the inscription of the beginning of 1735, in MQSZBKJ (1981), pp. 15–17.

125. As well as various types of picketing and retaliatory action against workers unwilling to take industrial action or abstain from work, we also find an example of a singular punishment meted out to one "blackleg." During a strike of calenderers, organized by a certain Dou Guibi in 1670. "Since Wang Minghou did not dare to take part in the protest, his punishment was to pay some singers from a theatre company to perform so that all the other craftsmen downed tools and followed the entertainment". *MQSZBKJ* 1981, p. 54.

126. See: inscriptions in *MQSZBKJ* 1981, pp. 15–17, 24–25; and *JSMQBK* 1956, pp. 5–6, 13–14. Several strikes and remostrances happened also in other economic fields, as in paper production (note: the 1756 stone inscription, *MQSBKJ* 1981, pp. 89–92).

127. For revision of earlier views, see: Fu Yiling, "Wo duiyu Mingdai zhongye yihou guyong laodong de zairenshi" [My reevaluation of wage labor after the middle Ming], *Lishi Yanjiu*, (1961) 3, pp. 62–63. A model of struggle and conflict between the owners of the means of production and men who freely offer their labor seems simplistic, not only because the differentiation between the two categories is unclear, but also because the situation is complicated by the presence of other categories, such as the *baohang*. See: Luo Yaojiu's observation, "Mingdai zhongye de guyong laodong shi zhibenshuyi xingzhi de ma?" [Does the wage labor of the mid-Ming period have a capitalistic nature?] *Lishi Yanjiu*, (1961) 1, pp. 55–73.

128. Stone inscription, 1734, *JSMQBK* 1956, p. 16.

129. There are cases of protest against extortion and acts of corruption

perpetrated by supervisors and foremen of the Imperial Factories authorities. For example, a memorial stone was erected by textile workers in 1741 as a warning against officials who abused their position to extort money from the children of deceased or retired craftsmen in exchange for the authorization that would allow them to take the place of their parent: *JSMQBK* 1956, pp. 17–18.

130. See: Sun Pei, *Suzhou zhizaoju zhi* 1686, 1:2, 12:106; *Mingshi*, 82:1664; *Ming shilu*: Shenzong, 380:3–4; Wanli 3/2/yichou, 360:2 Wanli 30/5 mouchen.

131. See, for instance: *Ming shilu*: *Shenzong*, 89:5–6 Wanli 7/7/yichou; 93:2 Wanli 7/11/dingsi; 116:3 Wanli 9/9/mouyin; 121:7 Wanli 10/2/jiayin; 139:7 Wanli 11/7/guimao; 380:3 Wanli 31/1/yihai.

132. The following incident was reported in Ming records: where, among other things, it is reported that two new tax inspectors "took it upon themselves to increase the levy per loom to three *qian*. This measure gave rise to much discontent amongst the people, and rumors sprang up everywhere. Weaving businesses closed shop, and workers found themselves plunged into poverty, famished and ready to follow anybody. Thus Huang was stoned to death, and the house belonging to Tang was burnt down, as was that of the noble Ding. The rebels were unarmed, they did not steal anything. Indeed, they warned people living near the houses that were to be burned down so that they could keep the flames from spreading and from damaging innocent people." *Ming shilu*: *Shenzong*, 361:5.

133. Ge Cheng, nicknamed Xian, "the wise," was a textile worker who became legendary for his part in the 1601 revolt, and for the act of self-accusation, which saved many of his fellow workers from arrest and punishment. In the *Veritable Records* the incident is described in the following manner:
Ge Cheng presented himself at the Prefecture of his own will, where he gave himself up and asked to be punished in lieu of the demonstrators who, because of their strong indignation, could not be held responsible for their actions. The citizens of Suzhou—he said—are quick-tempered, impulsive and ready to heed hear-say. They are so poor that they wake up in the morning without knowing if they will eat during the day; if they don't find work, they will not survive. He had noted that many thousands of dyers had been left penniless when their companies had closed down, and that many thousands of craftsmen found themselves in the same condition after the weaving businesses had locked them out." See: *Ming shilu*: *Shenzong*, 361:5.

134. Wen Bing, *Dingling zhulue, Liuyue Suzhou minbian* [The Suzhou June revolt] c. 1669 (1976 reprint Taibei), pp. 364–66.
Sun Long's accusations are also recorded in the *Shilu* as follows:

"The rebel Ge Xian (Cheng) and others incited the crowd to burn, plunder and murder; together they surrounded the Imperial Manufacturers offices to extort the abolition of taxes." (*Shenzong*, 361:5).

According to the local Suzhou gazetteer, however, Ge Cheng only joined the fray after the revolt was already under way. His biography in the *Suzhou fuzhi* (94:4–5) begins: "Ge Xian, formerly Cheng, was by trade a weaver. In 1601 the eunuch Sun Long was tax superintendent at Suzhou. [. . .] All textile workers wishing to sell their goods at the market had to pay a tax of 3 *fen* for every *pi* of material. The people of Suzhou reacted to this by closing down their shops and their workshops. The crowd first went to Yang [Tang] and Xu's houses, attacking and killing; next they set alight Assistant Ding's dwelling. [. . .] In the exact moment when the revolt broke out, Ge Cheng was in Kunshan. Hearing news of the revolt, he and his brother came to Suzhou". *Kangxi Suzhou fuzhi* 1693, 94:4.

A memorial tombstone erected in 1673 for Ge Cheng bears a different, somewhat idyllic account of his role in the revolt:

In 1601 the eunuch Sun Long set up tolls in every port in Jiangnan. Nothing escaped taxation, not rice nor salt, not fruit nor wood, not fowl nor pork. [. . .] In response the people of Suzhou closed up their workshops and demonstrated in the streets. It was then that the valiant Ge Cheng appeared, taking charge of the situation as he brandished a palm leaf fan. Around a thousand people answered his call [. . .] Ge swore before them that: "What has taken place today happened in the name of the sovereign to liberate the people from evil. Therefore, it having been an act of goodness, who can be against us? Whoever wishes to follow me, do so, whoever wants to go home, do so." Everybody followed him. They all went to Tang Shen's house, destroying it, heaping up his possessions and burning them. But when somebody tried to make off with one of Tang Shen's possessions, such as one of his antique vases, Ge had him killed as an example. This made him more popular still, and yet more followers joined his ranks. The tax officials were terrified by the uprising, and thought of calling in the army. Only the Prefect Zhu Bianyuan objected: the army should be used solely against foreign enemies; it was not possible to send in the troops against a revolt just to eliminate the ring leaders; the damage caused by army intervention would far exceed any possible advantages. It was not wise to fly in the face of the people's anger; calling in the army would be like putting more wood onto the fire. . .*JSMQBK* 1956, p. 383.

135. See: Hucker, "Su-chou and the agents of Wei Chung-hsien," 224–56. Among others, Yan Peiwei, son of a rich merchant, and the textile merchant Yang Nianru took part in the uprising.

136. *Qianlong zhupi yuzhi* [Imperial endorsements of the Qianlong era] Qianlong, 13/4/26; 13/6/29. The above translation is based on this source, but is supplemented with further information supplied by the following texts. *Guang-*

xu Suzhou fu zhi [Guangxu gazetteer of Suzhou prefecture] 1883, 149:6; *Da Qing Gaozong Qianlong shilu* [Veritable records of the Qianlong reign] in the *Da Qing shilu*, 315:4–5.

137. *Da Qing Gaozong Qianlong shilu*, 502:33.

138. *Wenxian congbian*, pp. 92–93; *JSMQBK* 1956, pp. 62–67.

139. Examples from different parts of the empire, with a focus on the situation in the capital, are documented in the following sections of the *Ming shilu*: Xuanzong, 40:9, 63:5; Yingzong 47:6, 49:8; Xianzong, 112:1; Xiaozong, 49:8, 61:1; Wuzong, 114:1–2.

140. *Minguo Wuxian zhi*, 1933, 52a:5, quoting *Qianlong Changzhou xianzhi*.

141. *Guangxu Suzhou fuzhi*, 1883, 3:31–32, reports examples of hooligans who took advantage of festivals in order to illicitly make money and enjoy at the expense of honest people.

142. Ibid., 3:36.

143. Ueda Makoto, "Minmatsu Shincho Kōnan no tōshi no burai o meguru shakai handei" [Urban "bully groups" in Jiangnan during the late Ming and early Qing], *Shigaku zasshi*, vol. 90, no. 11 1981, pp. 1648–49 quotes passages from *Jiangnan tongzhi*, juan 65; *Jiangwanli zhi*, juan 3.

144. *Taicang zhouzhi* [Gazetteer of Taicang (independent) zhou] juan 5; *Baoshan xianzhi* [Gazetteer of Baoshan county] juan 1; *Nanxiangzhen zhi* [Gazetteer of Nanxiang village], juan 12, cit. in Ueda, "Kōnan no tōshi no burai o meguru shakai handei," pp. 1623–24.

145. Ibid., pp. 1636–40.

146. *JSMQBK* 1956, pp. 231–36.

147. *Guangxu Suzhou fuzhi*, 1883, 3:27.

148. See: *Qingchao wenxian tongkao* [General history of the institutions and critical examination of the documents and studies of the Ming and Qing] 1747, 23:29 [*kao* 5056] (1958 reprint, Taibei). Also *JSMQBK* 1956, p. 67–69, where the collective responsibility of each group of five calenderers is described in detail, as well as the control duty of people in charge for surveillance at various levels, from *baotou* to factory-supervisors. On calenders, also see Yokoyama Suguru, "Shindai ni okeru tanpugyuō no keiei deitai" [The form of management of calendering in Qing times], *Tōyō shi kenkyū* vol. 19, no 3. (1960) pp. 337–349; vol. 4, 1961, pp. 451–467.

149. *Ming shilu*: Taizu, 135:4; *Mingshi*, 77:1878.

150. *Yongzheng zhupi yuzhi* 1887, 48:101 Yongzheng 1/4/5. The italics are mine. In another passage it is observed that amongst thousands of calenderers there are indeed some good men who work honestly for their living. Nevertheless, most of them are ruffians who goad their workmates, gather gangs together to escape police checks, and then cause disturbance upon disturbance. The passage goes on to suggest that as it is impossible to stop these people from working, it is a good idea to seek out and punish the troublemakers. Ibid., 42:76–77.

151. *JSMQBK* 1956, pp. 55–57.

152. See: Song Yingxing, *Tiangong kaiwu* [Exploitation of the work of nature] 1637 (1983 reprint, Hong Kong), 2:96; Chu Hua, *Mumian* [Cotton], n.d. [late 18th century] reprint in *Shanghai zhanggu cishu* [Collection of Shanghai Historical Miscellany], (Shanghai: Shanghai tongsheshi, 1936) p. 11. For an illustration of the stone, see Rudolf Hommel, *China at Work: an Illustrated Record of the Primitive Industries of China's Masses, whose life is toil, and thus an account of Chinese civilization*, (New York, 1937; 1969 reprint Cambridge Mass: M.I.T. Press), p. 193. This volume is also useful for its descriptions of Chinese textile techniques.

153. JSMQBK 1956, pp. 55–56; Also, Terada Takanobu, "Soshu tanpogyo no keiei deitai" [Management of calendering in Suzhou] *Tōhoku daigaku bundakubu kenkyū nenpō*, 18 (1968), pp. 130–38.

154. *Yongzheng zhupi yuzhi* 1187, 42:76–77. To be exact, one *fen*, one *li* and three *hao* per *pi* of cloth. Later, this sum was increased. See also the inscription dated 1670 and 1693: JSMQBK 1956, pp. 53–56, 66, 68, 70, 74–75, 77–79, 85 See also: Terada Takanobu, "Soshō chihō ni oleru toshi mengyōshōnin ni tsuite" [Urban cotton merchants in Suzhou and Songjiang], *Shirin* 416 (1958), p. 65.

155. Yokoyama, "Shindai ni okeru tanpugyō," vol. 3 (1960), pp. 337–49; vol. 4, (1961), pp. 451–67.

156. See inscriptions, JSMQBK 1956, p. 43; *Yongzheng zhupi yuzhi* 1887, 42:76; Yokoyama, "Tanpugyō no seizan kozo," pp. 63–143.

157. *Fengjing xiaozhi* [Short gazetteer of Fengjing (county)] n.d., n.p., 10:5.

158. The following, based on date compiled by Quan Hansheng, "Qingdai Suzhou de chuaibuye" [Calendaring in Suzhou during the Qing dynasty], *Xin Ya xuebao* 13 (1975), pp. 424–426; this source has been supplemented with data from Terada's statement, ("Soshu tanpogyō no keiei deitai," p. 150), Its figures concern values and rates of calenderers' wages, of rice prices, and the ratio between the silver tael and the copper coin, from 1665 to 1872 in Suzhou. Also see: the 1715 stone inscription, in JSMQBK 1956, pp. 65–67.

159. See: the 1779 stone inscription, in *MQSZBKJ* 1981, pp. 77–78.

160. See: stone inscriptions of Qianlong 44 and 60, *JSMQBK* 1956, pp. 77–79.

161. See: Quan, "Qingdai Suzhou de chuaibuye," p. 428; Terada, "Soshu tanpogyō no keiei deitai," pp. 147–49. Price fluctuations may have been related to the increasing use of foreign currency (*yangqian*); cf. Quan, "Qingdai Suzhou de chuaibuye," pp. 409–36 on the price trend in Suzhou in the seventeenth and eighteenth centuries, compare respectively Ye Mengzhu, *Yueshibian* [A survey of the age] c. 1690 (1982 reprint Taibei, 7:157–66, and *Minguo Wu xianzhi* 1933, 52:4a.

In *MQSZBKJ* 1981, note the following inscriptions:
a. Kangxi 9, p. 54
b. Kangxi 32, pp. 55–57
c. Kangxi 40, pp. 62–65
d. Kangxi 54, pp. 65–67
e. Kangxi 59, pp. 68–71
f. Qianlong 4, pp. 74–76
g. Qianlong 60, pp. 78–79
On Calenderers strikes see: Ibid., pp. 53–57, 62–65, 74–76.

162. See: *Yongzheng zhupi yuzhi* 1887, 48:101–2 Yongzheng 1/4/5; 42:76–77.

Calendering (polishing) was an indispensable process, rendering cotton cloth more durable, giving it greater sheen. These processes were especially important for the green and blue cotton cloth ordered by merchants from Northern provinces. See *Qing tongkao*, juan 23, which reports 400 calendring workshops and no less than 10,000 calenderers. According to the *Qianlong Yuanhe xianzhi* [Qianlong gaxetteer of Yuanhe county], 10:7, cit. in Chen Zhaonan, *Caizheng jingji yuekan*, 11,7,1961, p.29., there were around 20,000 calenderers in Suzhou.

163. *JSMQBK* 1956, inscription of Kangxi 59, pp. 68–71.

164. See for instance the 1715 stone inscription *JSMQBK* 1956, pp. 65–67), where authorities clearly take side for cloth merchants. Other attempts of creating associations were repressed in 1723, in 1729 and in 1730. See: *Yongzheng zhupi yuzhi* 1887, 7:4457–58, 4470, 8:4415; Quan, "Qingdai Suzhou de chuaibuye," pp. 430–431; 434.

165. *Yongzheng zhupi yuzhi* 1887, *ce* 8, Yongzheng 1/5/24.

166. Ibid., *ce* 8 Yongzheng 1/4/5.

167. The 1701 inscription is recorded in *JSMQBK* 1956, pp. 63–64.

168. According to the names featuring on the stele, we can deduce that at least 276 *baotou* took part in this organization, in as much as the document is

underwritten by twenty-two *jiazhang*, "overseers" representing 264 ordinary members, plus twelve "foremen" (*fangzong*). See: Terada, "Sōshu tanpogyō," p. 132.

169. The 1720 inscription is recorded in *JSMQBK* 1956, pp. 68–71.

170. Ibid., pp. 68–71.
Editor's Note: The following scheme has been used to translate the sometimes confusing Chinese terms:

fangzhang = foreman, a worker selected from among his peers to be responsible for their performance.

   baotao = contractor, manager or proprietor (distinctions between these are not always clear), a person who managed and made contracts for one or more workshops or factories.

jiazhang = *jia*-overseer, a rotating post of foreman selected from among the *baotou* who made up a *jia* to be responsible for their performance.

fangzong = "general supervisor" of the calendaring trade, selected from among the *baotou* who made up several *jia*, thus this person supervised the *jia*, and through them, the workshops or factories.

171. *JSMQBK* 1956, p. 25; see also Peng Zeyi, *Ming Qing zibenshuyi mengya yanjiu lunwen*, p. 353.

172. *Yongzheng zhupi yuzhi* 1887, 42:24 Yongzheng 7/12/2, 7:4458.

173. *Yongzheng zhupi yuzhi* 1887, 42:23–24 (7: 4457), and 76–77 (8:4514–4515).

174. Ibid., 70:27 Yongzheng 7/12/4. This record relates that a gang of bandits, calling themselves "the heroes of justice," who practiced martial arts, dealt in magic and sorcery and committed numerous crimes, operated on the coast. During investigations taoist books containing charms and spells were discovered in the house of a certain Fan Longyou, subsequently arrested. Also arrested were twenty or so calenderers bound by a secret pact, whose names were discovered on a list of sect members.

175. *Yongzheng zhupi yuzhi*, 1887, 42:23; 42:76–77.

176. On May 5, 1768 several monks from Zhejiang were lynched. That same year three beggars were arrested by local police. See: Kuhn, "Political Crime and Bureaucratic Monarchy: a Chinese Case of 1768," *Late Imperial China* (1987) 8:1, pp. 86–87. This essay examines in detail the contradictions between bureaucratic and imperial authorities in their strategies against these mass psychoses.

CHAPTER 4: YANGZHOU: A CENTRAL PLACE
IN THE QING EMPIRE

List of abbreviations:

BHXZ 1808: *Yangzhou Beihu xiaozhi* [Gazetteer of Beihu, Yangzhou]; reprinted Taibei, 1983.

JQGQXZ 1810: [*Jiaqing*] *Ganquan xianzhi* [Jiaqing Gazetteer of Ganquan county].

GXGQXZ 1881: [*Guangxu*] *Zengxiu Ganquan xianzhi* [Guangxu reedition of Ganquan county gazetteer]; reprinted Taibei, 1983.

GXJDXZ 1883: [*Guangxu*] *Jiangdu xian xuzhi* [Guangxu Gazetteer of Jiangdu county, continued]; reprinted Taibei, 1970.

QLJNTZ 1737: [*Qianlong*] *Jiangnan tongzhi* [Qianlong Complete gazetteer of Jiangnan]; reprinted Taibei, 1967.

JQLHYFZ 1806: [*Jiaqing*] *Lianghuai yanfa zhi* [Jiaqing gazetteer of the Lianghuai salt monopoly].

XZLHYFZ 1905: [*Xuanzong*] *Lianghuai yanfa zhi* [Xuanzong gazetteer of the Lianghuai salt monopoly].

WLYZFZ 1603: [*Wanli*] *Yangzhou fuzhi* [Wanli gazetteer of Yangzhou prefecture].

YZYZFZ 1733: [*Yongzheng*] *Yangzhou fuzhi* [Wanli gazetteer of Yangzhou prefecture]; reprinted Taibei, 1975.

JQYZFZ 1810: [*Jiaqing*] *Yangzhou fuzhi* [Jiaqing gazetteer of Yangzhou prefecture]; reprinted Taibei, 1974.

QLZLTZZ 1755: [*Qianlong*] *Zhili Tongzhou zhi* [Qianlong gazetteer of Tongzhou independent sub-prefecture]; reprinted Taibei, 1968.

1. See, Marcel Granet, *The Religion of the Chinese People, trans.* Maurice Freedman (Oxford: Blackwell, 1975), p. 36; John K. Fairbank, *The United States and China,* 3rd ed. (Cambridge, Mass.: Harvard University Press, 1971), p. 16.

2. G. William Skinner, "Regional Urbanization In Nineteenth-Century China," in Skinner ed., *The City in Late Imperial China* (Stanford: Stanford University Press, 1977), pp. 211–249. See especially maps 1 and 2, pp. 214–215. Skinner by no means ignores administrative and strategic influences in China's spatial organization, but he does concede that his "approach gives some analytical precedence to commercial as against other central functions." Skinner, "Cities and the Hierarchy of Local Systems," in Skinner ed., *The City in Late Imperial China*, p. 276.

3. Skinner, "Cities and the Hierarchy of Local Systems," p. 346.

4. Jean-Christophe Agnew, *Worlds Apart*: *The Market and the Theater in*

Anglo-American Thought, 1550–1750 (Cambridge: Cambridge University Press, 1986), p. 18.

5. Zhao Ye (fl.40–80 a.d.), cited in Zheng Zhaojing, *Zhongguo shuili shi* [A history of water control in China] (Changsha: Shangwu yinshuguan, 1939), p. 190.

6. In James Legge, *The Chinese Classics, 5: The Ch'un Ts'ew with the Tso Chuen* (Oxford: The Clarendon Press, 1865–95; Hong Kong: Hong Kong University Press, 1960), pp. 818–819.

7. Sima Qian, *Shiji* [The Record of History], vol. 2 (Beijing: Zhonghua shuju, 1959), p. 731.

8. *Hou Han Shu* [History of the Later Han] vol. 6 (Beijing: Zhonghua shuju, 1971), p. 3561. On the archaeological record of wall building on this site, see Ji Zhongqing, "Yangzhou gucheng zhi bianqian chutan" [Preliminary investigation of changes in the foundations of the ancient city of Yangzhou], *Wenwu*, no. 9, 1979, pp. 43–56.

9. Nanjing bowuyuan, "Yangzhou gucheng 1978 nian diaocha fazhuo jianbao" [Brief report on the 1978 investigation and excavation of the ancient city of Yangzhou], *Wenwu*, no. 9, 1979, p. 35.

10. *Hou Han Shu*, vol. 6, p. 3561.

11. *Shiji*, vol. 2, p. 840; vol. 6, pp. 2822–2823.

12. Fernand Braudel, *Capitalism and Material Life, 1400–1800*, trans. Miriam Kochan (London: Weidenfeld and Nicolson Ltd., 1973), p. 389.

13. Bao Zhao (405–466), *Bao Canjun jizhu* [Bao Canjun's collected works with commentary] (Shanghai: Shanghai guji chubanshe) 1980, p. 13.

14. Lao Gan, "Duiyu Nanjing chengshi de jidian renshi" [Several issues concerning the city of Nanjing], cited in Frederick Mote, "The Transformation of Nanking," in Skinner, *The City in Late Imperial China*, pp. 121–122.

15. Chi Ch'ao-ting, *Key Economic Areas in Chinese History* (London: G. Allen and Unwin, 1936), p. 105.

16. *Song shu* [History of the Liu Song], vol. 2 (Beijing: Zhonghua shuju, 1974), pp. 1033, 1054–55.

17. Arthur E. Wright, *The Sui Dynasty* (New York: Alfred A. Knopf, 1978), pp. 158–161.

18. On Yangzhou in the Tang-Song period, see Quan Hansheng, "Tang Song shidai Yangzhou jingji jingkuang de fanrong yu shuailuo" [Economic

prosperity and decline in Yangzhou during the Tang-Song period], in *Guoli Zhongyang yanjiuyuan lishi yuyan yanjiusuo jikan*, 1974: 11, p. 149–176. On Yangzhou under the Southern Ming, see Frederic Wakeman, Jr., *The Great Enterprise: The Manchu Reconstruction of Imperial Order in Seventeenth-Century China* (Berkeley: University of California Press, 1985), chapters 5 and 7, passim. On the importance of the Yangzi and Huai garrison systems in the military organization of the Yuan dynasty, see Ch'i-ch'ing Hsiao, *The Military Establishment of the Yuan Dynasty* (Cambridge, Mass.: Harvard East Asian Monographs, 1978). The size of the military establishment in late thirteenth-century Yangzhou was noted by Marco Polo: H. Yule, *The Book of Ser Marco Polo* rev. (H. Cordier, vol. II) (London: John Murray, 1903), p. 154.

19. Yao Wentian, *Guangling shilue* [Brief Account of Guangling] (Kaifeng, 1812), preface, n.p.

20. On the Grand Canal, see inter al. Quan Hansheng, *Tang Song diguo yu yunhe* [The Tang and Song Empires and the Grand Canal] (Shanghai: Academia Sinica, 1946); Jung-Pang Lo, "The Controversy over Grain Conveyance during the Reign of Qubilai Qaqan, 1260–94," *Far Eastern Quarterly*, vol. 13, no. 3 (May 1954), pp. 263–285; Ray Huang, *The Grand Canal During the Ming Dynasty, 1368–1644*, Ph.D. diss., University of Michigan, 1964; Harold C. Hinton, *The Grain Tribute System of China (1845–1911)* (Cambridge: Harvard University Press, 1956). My conclusions concerning the Salt Transport canal are based on Finnane, *Prosperity and Decline under the Qing: Yangzhou and its Hinterland, 1644–1810*, Ph.D. diss. Australian National University, 1985, passim, but see especially p. 229 ff.

21. *Qingchao wenxian tongkao* [Encyclopedia of historical records of the Qing Dynasty], Shitong ed. (Taipei: 1963), 55:5367. *Jinshen quanshu* [Complete guide to officials], 1855 ed., 2:46a.

22. Skinner, "Cites and the Hierarchy of Local Systems," p. 314 ff.

23. *QLJNTZ* 1737. 20:23b. Haimen was, however, resurrected as an independent sub-prefecture (*ting*) in 1775. *Qingchao tongdian* [Collected Statutes of the Qing Dynasty], 92:2715.

24. *Yangzhou fuzhi* 1810, (hereafter *YZFZ*), 5:15a–16b.

25. I.e. in its mid to late Qing form. See Bureau of Foreign Trade, Ministry of Industry, *China Industrial Handbooks: Kiangsu* (Shanghai: 1933; Taipei: Ch'eng Wen Publishing Company, 1973), pp. 6–8.

26. *QLJNTZ* 1737, 4:4b, 106:2a–b.

27. See Finnane, "Bureaucracy and Responsibility: A Reassessment of the River Administration under the Qing," *Papers on Far Eastern History*, 30 (September 1984), pp. 165–166.

28. Thus, in Tong Jun, *Jiangnan yuanlin zhi* [Gazetteer of Jiangnan Gardens, 1937 (Beijing: Zhongguo gongye chubanshe, 1963). The gardens of Yangzhou are the only example provided from the area north of the Yangzi.

29. Huang Junzai, *Jinhu langmo* [Desultory writings from the golden inkpot], 1.7b, in *Jinhu qimo* [Seven writings from the golden inkpot] (Shanghai: Saoye shanfang, 1929).

30. This area is also referred to as Subei. For a discussion of the meaning of Subei, see Emily Honig, "The Politics of Prejudice: Subei People in Republican Era Shanghai," *Modern China*, vol.15 No. 3 (July, 1989), p. 270, n.1. Honig notes the equivalence of the terms Jiangbei and Subei (ibid., p. 243) but the word Subei, while now more commonly used to denote this area, appears to be of relatively recent origin. In the context of Qing China, it seems more appropriate to speak of Jiangbei.

31. This region posed the greatest difficulties in water control during the Ming-Qing period and much was written on it by officials and their advisers. See inter al. Bao Shichen, "Xiahe shuili shuo" [On water control in Xiahe], in *Anwu sizhong: zhongqu yishao* [Four Works from Mr Anwu: Suggesting the Middle Way], 1872 ed. (Taipei: Wenhai chubanshe, 1969), 1:28a–30b; Zhang Pengge, "Zhi Xiahe shui lun" [On hydraulic management of water in Xiahe], in Chen Henghe ed., *Yangzhou congke* [Collected writings from yangahou] (Jiangdu: 1936); Zhu Xie, *Zhongguo yunhe shiliao xuanji* [Collected Historical Materials on the Grand Canal of China] (Beijing: Zhonghua shuju, 1962). See also Richard E. Strassberg, *The World of K'ung Shang-jen: A Man of Letters in Early Ch'ing China* (New York: Columbia University Press, 1983), pp. 117–122, 208–212. Kong Shangren served briefly as a river official in this area in the late seventeenth century, so he was well acquainted with its problems.

32. Li Dou, *Yangzhou huafang lu* [An account of Yangzhou's pleasure craft], ca. 1795, (Taipei: Shijie shuju, 1963), 13:2.

33. Hu Huanyong, *Lianghuai shuili* [Water control in the Lianghuai region] (Nanjing: Zhengzhong shuju, 1947), p. 2. See also John Lossing Buck, *Land Utilization in China* (New York: Paragon Reprint Corporation, 1968), Map. 4, p. 27; G. B. Cressey, *China's Geographic Foundations: A Survey of the Land and its People* (New York: McGraw-Hill Book Co., 1934), pp. 86–87.

34. Zhu, *Zhongguo yunhe*, p. 148.

35. This summary is derived from too many scattered items of information to document fully here. On the general range of products within Yangzhou prefecture (with scant attention given to quantities, place or importance) see *JQYZFZ* 1810, *juan* 61. On economic activity in the rural area surrounding

Yangzhou, see Zhu Zongzhou, "Qingdai qianqi Yangzhou chengshi jingji" [The urban economy of Yangzhou in the first half of the Qing period) *Yangzhou shiyuan xuebao: shehui kexue ban*, 1984:2, p. 115; On rice agriculture and fishing in the lakes area to the north of Yangzhou, see Jiao Xun, *BHXZ* 1808, 1:8b–12a; for a general description, again with scant attention to quantities and general economic significance, see British Legation and Embassy Archives, China, FO 228/747, Report from Frederick Oxenham (Consul at Zhenjiang), June 28, 1884, p. 117.

36. *QLZLTZZ* 1755, 17:18b. Chen Zugui (ed.), *Mian* (Cotton), pt. 1 (Beijing: Zhonghua shuju, 1957), p. 111.

37. Wang Shuhuai, "Qingmo minqu Jiangsusheng chengshi de fazhan" [Urban development in Jiangsu in the late Qing early republican period], *Zhongyang yanjiuyuan jindaishi yanjiusuo jikan*, vol. VIII (October, 1979), pp. 65–97; note especially pp. 68–71. Further on the economy of the region, see Finnane, "The Origins of Prejudice: The Malintegration of Subei in Late Imperial China," in *Comparative Studies in Society and History*, forthcoming.

38. Yang Dequan, "Qingdai qianqi Lianghuai yanshang ziliao chuji" [Preliminary collection of materials on the Lianghuai salt merchants of the earlier Qing period], *Jianghai xuekan*, 45 (November 1962), p. 45.

39. This is clear from prohibitory edicts. See *JQLHYFZ* 1806, 27:1a–b.

40. Li Cheng, *Huaicuo beiyao* [Essentials of the Huainan salt trade], 1823, 5:2b. Hsiao Kung-chuan, *Rural China: Imperial Control in the Nineteenth Century* (Seattle: University of Washington Press, 1972), pp. 47–49.

41. See *JQLHYFZ*, 1806, 29:1a–b.

42. For a list of crimes needing to be dealt with by local magistrates in this area, see the memorial of Jiangsu governor Chen Dashou (1702–1751) in *XZLHYFZ*, 1905, 13:11a–12a.

43. For merchant contributions to hydraulic maintenance in the eighteenth century, see *XZLHYFZ*, 1905, *juan* 65. The major contributions are tabulated in Suzuki Tadashi, "Shinsho ryogai ensho ni kan-suru ikkosatsu" [An enquiry into the Lianghuai salt merchants in the first part of the Qing], *Shien*, 36 (March 1946), pp. 1, 23–124, but this list is far from exhaustive.

44. *Da Qing lichao shilu* [Veritable Records of the Qing Dynasty], Qianlong 1419, 9a–10b.

45. See Ping-ti Ho, "The Salt merchants of Yang-chou: A Study of Commercial Capitalism in Eighteenth-Century China," *Harvard Journal of Asiatic Studies*, 17 (June 1954), pp. 130–168.

46. De facto responsibilities in this regard were formalized after 1753. Li Shixu ed., *Xuxingshui jinjian* [The Golden Mirror of Waterway Inspection Continued], 1832 Shanghai: (Shangwu yinshuguan, 1936), 88:1977.

47. *XZLHYFZ*, 1905, 4:1b–2a.

48. On the smuggling of Lianghuai salt, see Xu Hong, *Qingdai Lianghai yanchang de yanjiu* [A study of the Lianghuai salt yards in the Qing period] (Taibei: Jiaxin shuini gongsi, 1972), pp. 127–181.

49. Paul M. Hohenberg, and Lynn Hollen Lees, *The Making of Urban Europe, 1000–1950* (Cambridge: Harvard University Press, 1985), pp. 66–70.

50. See Skinner, "Regional Urbanization," p. 217. But Rowe differs from Skinner on the issue of the integrity of regional trade systems: William T. Rowe, *Hankow: Commerce and Society in a Chinese City, 1796–1889.* (Stanford: Stanford University Press, 1984).

51. Quan, "Tang Song shidai Yangzhou," pp. 170–174.

52. Hohenberg and Lees, *Making of Urban Europe*, p. 71.

53. Hohenberg and Lees, *Making of Urban Europe*, p. 240. See Rowe, *Hankow*, p. 62.

54. See F. W. Mote, "A Millennium of Chinese Urban History: Form, Time and Space Concepts in Soochow," in *Rice University Studies*, vol. 59, no. 4 (Fall 1973), p. 39.

55. Ji, "Yangzhou gucheng," p. 44, Fig. 1.

56. Ibid., p. 53.

57. Diagrams of both the Song city complex and, in greater detail, the *dacheng* by itself are to be found in *YZYZFZ*, 1733, *JQYZFZ* 1810. They are reprinted in Yule, *The Book of Ser Marco Polo*, pp. 155–156.

58. Ji, "Yangzhou gucheng," pp. 53–54.

59. Skinner, "Introduction; Urban Social Structure in Ch'ing China," in Skinner, *City in Late Imperial China*, p. 533. This feature is not, however, peculiar to Chinese cities. See Hohenberg and Lees, *Making of Urban Europe*, p. 33.

60. According to Quan Hansheng, such civilians as remained in Yangzhou under the Southern Song lived in easily combustible thatched huts: "Tang Song shidai Yangzhou," p. 170.

61. This is consistent with the general antagonism of the Mongols towards the construction of city walls. See Sen-dou Chang, "The Morphology of Walled Capitals," in Skinner ed., *The City in Late Imperial China*, p. 75.

62. *JQYZFZ*, 1810, 13:1b–2a.

63. *Weiyang zhi* [Gazetteer of Weiyang (Yangzhou)] 1542, 1:16a–b. The faded condition of the original print does not lend itself easily to reproduction nor is it even entirely legible. Normally one would expect to find a map of this sort reproduced in later editions of the gazetteer (as with the map of the Southern Song). Why this was not so in the case of the Ming map is probably answered by the fact that the Old City (*jiu cheng*) of Qing times basically preserved the Ming form.

64. This was the salt-worker rebel, Zhang Shicheng (1321–1367), who was in control of most of the districts neighboring Yangzhou when Ming forces took the city in 1357. See L. Carrington Goodrich and Chaoying Fang, *Dictionary of Ming Biography, 1368–1644* (New York: Columbia University Press, 1976), p. 99. *Yuan shi* [Yuan History], vol. 2 (Beijing: Zhonghua shuju, 1976), 46:971.

65. *JQLHYFZ*, 1806, 44:16b. On the pirate troubles, see Kwan-wai So, *Japanese Piracy in Ming China During the 16th Century* (East Lansing: Michigan State University Press, 1975). The author does not, however, refer to the attack on Yangzhou, nor is the city marked as one of the places besieged in Jiangnan.

66. The classic account of the sacking is Wang Xiuchu, "Yangzhou shi ri ji" [Record of ten days in Yangzhou], *Zhongguo jindai neiluan waihuo lishi gushi congshu* [Stories of internal strife and external calamities in modern Chinese history] (Taipei: Guangwen shuju), pp. 229–243. For an English translation, see Lucien Mao, "A Memoir of Ten Days' Massacre in Yangchow," *Tienhsia Monthly*, vol. 4, No. 5 (May, 1937), pp. 515–537.

67. *JQYZFZ*, 1810, 19:1a 13:3b, 5:20b. On the significance of the school temple, see Stephen Feuchtwang, "School-Temple and City God," in Skinner, *City in Late Imperial China*, pp. 581–608.

68. The case of Yangzhou thus supports the hypothesis advanced by Skinner in "Urban Social Structure," pp. 527–528.

69. Li Dou, *Yangzhou*, 9:6–24.

70. Zhu Zongzhou, drawing largely on Li Dou, discusses the businesses in this general area although without reference to the significance of their location: Zhu, "Qingdai qianqi Yangzhou," pp. 113–114.

71. Li Dou, *Yangzhou*, 9:57, 1:41, 9:11, 9:58, 9:68.

72. Ibid., 3:8. This reference is cited in He Bingdi, *Zhongguo huiguan shilun* [*An Historical Survey of Landsmannschaften in China*], (Taipei: Xuesheng shuju, 1966), p. 60.

73. Li Dou, *Yangzhou*, 6:1.

74. Ibid., passim.

75. Ibid., 1:20–21.

76. J. B Du Halde, *The General History of China*, vol. 1, (London: J. Watts: 1741), p.141.

77. Six of the eight famous gardens of the Kangxi period (*ba jia hua yuan*) [one of which actually dated from the Ming dynasty] were situated close to the city walls. The gardens are plotted in a picturesque representation in Zhao Zhibi, *Pingshantang tuzhi* [Illustrated gazetteer of Pingshantang] (Yangzhou: ca. 1765), frontpiece, entitled: "Figure 1: Complete vista of Shugang and the Baozhang Canal." The wealthiest garden owners in the eighteenth century included Jiang Chun, the Ma brothers, and the Huang brothers, all salt merchants or of salt merchant families. Their gardens were all located within the crowded confines of the New City. On Jiang, see Ho, "Salt Merchants," pp. 159–160. His city garden (he also owned extra-mural gardens) was named "Kangshan": Qian Yong, *Lüyuan conghua* [collected talks on roaming through gardens) (Suzhou: Zhenxin shushe, 1870), 20.7b. On the Ma brothers, see Ho, "Salt Merchants," p. 157. On the four Huang brothers, two of whom owned gardens in the city, see Li Dou, *Yangzhou*, 12.85.

78. Qu Fu (fl.1736), "Yangzhou Dongyuan ji" [Account of Yangzhou's "Eastern Garden"], in Zhao, *Pingshantang tuzhi*, 9:21b–22a.

79. Li, *Yangzhou*, 7:14, 1:41, 9:26.

80. Ping-ti Ho, *The Ladder of Success in Imperial China* (New York: Science Editions, 1964), p. 202.

81. Li, *Yangzhou*, 3:9 ff.

82. *XZLHYFZ*, 1905, 151:3a.

83. Jonathan Spence, *Ts'ao Yin and the K'ang-hsi Emperor Bondservant and Master* (New Haven: Yale University Press, 1966), p. 144.

84. Suzuki, "Shinsho ryogai ensho," pp. 123–124. Sadeki's documentation is summarized in Thomas A. Metzger, "T'ao Chu's Reform of the Huaipei Salt Monopoly (1831–1833)," *Papers on China (Harvard)*, 16, pp. 3–4.

85. Xu Ke, *Qingbai leichao* (Taibei: Shangwu yinshuguan, 1966), 7:14–15. The salt merchant referred to is probably Jiang Chun (see above, n. 82). The stupa was actually built in the grounds of the Lianxing Temple, some distance from the Dahongyuan but visible from it. According to Xu Ke's version, the comparable site in Beijing was in Nanhai garden, but it is in fact in Beihai.

86. Li, *Yangzhou*, 6:39.

87. E.g. Honig, "Politics of Prejudice," p. 260.

88. Ho, "Salt Merchants," pp. 143–144. Ho's description suggests an equal weighting of these groups within the salt merchant community but even in the Ming, when Shan-Shaan merchants were relatively prominent, the overwhelming number of successful merchant families were from Shexian district in Huizhou. Of 285 second-degree (*juren*) graduates from Ming salt merchant families, 162 were from Shexian. Other districts prominently represented were Jingyang and Sanyuan in Shanxi, with a total of thirty-six graduates, and Datong in Shanxi, with five graduates. *JQLHYFZ*, 1806, *juan* 48.

89. Karl Polanyi, "The Economy as Instituted Process," in Polanyi, Conrad M. Arensberg, and Harry W. Pearson, eds., *Trade and Market in the Early Empires: Economies in History and Theory* (Glencoe, Illinois: The Free Press, 1957), p. 260.

90. He, *Zhongguo huiguan shilun*.

91. See Rowe, *Hankow*, especially pp. 213–251; Fan Jinmin, "Ming Qing shiqi huoyue yu Suzhou de waidi shangren" [Outsider merchants sojourning in Suzhou in the Ming Qing period], in *Zhongguo shehui jingjishi yanjiu*, 1989:4, pp. 39–46.

92. Claudine Lombard-Salmon, *Un exemple d'acculturation chinoise: la province du Gui zhou au XVIIIe siècle* [A case of Chinese acculturation: Guizhou province in the eighteenth century] (Paris: École francaise d'Extrême-Orient, 1972), pp. 249–286; Susan Mann Jones, "The Ningpo Pang and Financial Power at Shanghai," in Mark Elvin and G. William Skinner eds., *The Chinese City Between Two Worlds* (California: Stanford University Press, 1974), pp. 73–96.

93. Strassberg, *The World of K'ung Shang-jen*, pp. 127.

94. *YZYZFZ*, 1733, 13.5b. For a recent discussion of the term, see Susan Mann, *Local Merchants and the Chinese Bureaucracy, 1750–1950* (Stanford: Stanford University Press, 1987), pp. 21–23, 231–232.

95. Rowe, *Hankow*, p. 237.

96. A prominent example is that of the family of Jiang Chun, discussed by Ho, "Salt Merchants," pp. 159–160. One of the largest property owners in Yangzhou, Jiang Chun, of Shexian extract, bore Yizheng registration: Li, *Yangzhou*, 12:1. Ping-ti Ho elsewhere correctly describes Yizheng as a "virtual appendage" of Jiangdu. Ho, *The Ladder of Success*, p. 254.

97. Skinner, "Regional Urbanization," pp. 238, 248, figs. 1 and 2.

98. *WLYZFZ*. 1603, preface, p. 3a.

99. See Strassberg, *World of K'ung Shang-jen*, p. 117 ff. Winston Ding Yee Wu, *Kung Hsien (ca. 1619–1689)*, Ph.D diss., Princeton University, p. 5ff.

100. Ho, "Salt Merchants," pp. 158–166.

101. Some of these activities were undertaken through the private initiatives of individual merchants but they were also institutionalized through a system of levies paid into the Salt Transport Treasury (*yunku*). See Saeki, *Shindai ensei*, pp. 276–277.

102. Negative evidence of this is that special note is made of the more recent founding of the *Hubei huiguan* in the nearby market town of Xiannuzhen. *GXJDXZ* 1883, 12b:8b–9a. The Zhenjiang (Jingkou) *huiguan* is not listed in the text but it is marked on the map provided in this edition.

103. Lu Zuoxie, "Shilun Ming Qing shiqi huiguan de xingzhi he zuoyong" [Appraisal of the nature and functions of native-place associations in the Ming and Qing periods], in Nanjing daxue lishixi Ming-Qingshi yanjiu shibian, *Zhongguo ziben zhuyi mengya wenti lunwenji* [Collected essays on the sprouts of capitalism in China] (Nanjing: Jiangsu renmin chubanshe, 1983), pp. 172–211.

104. He Bingdi makes reference to Li Dou's tantalizingly vague statement concerning "all the departmental and district *huiguan*" located in the built-up area north of the city wall and concludes that Yangzhou probably had one of the greatest concentrations of huiguan in the empire. He infers much, however, from his impression of the city's great wealth, which did not necessarily involve a great diversity of economic activity. He, *Zhongguo huiguan shilun*, p. 60.

105. Li, *Yangzhou*, 3:8.

106. Ibid., 9:18.

107. *JQLHYFZ*, 1806, 152:1b, 3a ff; *QLZLTZZ*, 1755 4:21a–b.

108. Li, *Yangzhou*, 13:2. *Ganquan xianzhi*, 1810 (hereafter *GQXZ*), 6:22a.

109. Cited in Zhang Shunhui, *Qingdai Yangzhouxue ji* [Account of the Yangzhou Learning in the Qing Dynasty] (Shanghai: Renmin chubanshe, 1962), p. 9. The greater number of visiting literati recorded by Li Dou came either from within Jiangsu or from the neighboring provinces of Anhui and Zhejiang. Li, *Yangzhou*, 4.14–42; 10.70–80; 12.19–67; 15.28–47. See also, Ho, "Salt Merchants," pp. 156–157.

110. Li, *Yangzhou*, 3:9 ff. The Meihua Academy initially developed as an official entreprise, was later incorporated with the Anding Academy, but was eventually restored to an independent footing with the same close organizational and financial relationship to the salt monopoly as that held from the beginning by the Anding Academy. Li, *Yangzhou*, 3:8, 3:19; *XZLHYFZ*, 1905, 151:4b.

111. See Tilemann Grimm, "Academies and Urban Systems in Kwangtung," in Skinner, *City in Late Imperial China*, pp. 485–487.

112. Li, *Yangzhou*, 2:92.

113. Ibid., 10:39–68.

114. Ibid., 10:92.

115. Ibid., 10:39, 10:41. For biographies of these two scholars, see Arthur W. Hummel, *Eminent Chinese of the Ch'ing Period (1644–1912)* (Washington: United States Government Printing Office, 1943), pp. 357–358, 695–699.

116. Li, op. cit., 4:4, 11:3.

117. See Wang Huan, *Yangzhou bajia huazhuan* [Lives and works of Yangzhou's eight painters] (Taibei: Da Zhonghua chuban gongsi, 1970).

118. Li, *Yangzhou*, 2:61 ff. Ten of the names listed carry a Huizhou designation, these men making up the only other numerically significant group.

119. Ibid., 10:46.

120. Zhang, *Qingdai Yangzhouxue ji*, passim. The exceptions were Wang Zhong (1745–1794) and Wang Niansun (1744–1832).

121. Wang Jiansheng, "Zheng Banqiao Shengping kaoshi" [A study of the life of Zheng Banqiao], in *Donghai xuebao*, 7 (June, 1976), p. 79.

122. Wang, *Yangzhou bajia huazhuan*, p. 155.

123. T'ung-Tsu Ch'ü, *Local government in China Under the Ch'ing* (Cambridge: Harvard University Press, 1962), pp. 36–37.

124. Zhu, "Qingdai qianqi Yangzhou," p. 113–114. See also Li, *Yangzhou*, 3:6, 4:3, 6:1.

125. Li, op. cit., 9:24, 11:49.

126. Honig, "Politics of Prejudice," p. 248.

127. Li, *Yangzhou*, passim. On wet-nurses, see *XZLHYFZ*, 1905, 152:13b–14a; on concubines, see Du Halde, *General History of China*, p. 142.

A more detailed account of the concubine business is to be found in Dorothy Yin-Yee Ko, *Toward a Social History of Women in Seventeenth Century China*, (Ph.D. diss., Stanford University, 1989), pp. 87–90.

128. See Colin Mackerras, "The Theatre in Yang-chou in the Eighteenth Century," *Papers on Far Eastern History*, 1 (March, 1970), pp. 1–30.

129. Li, *Yangzhou*, 9:29, 11:43, 45.

130. Ibid., 8:3–5.

131. *YZYZFZ* 1733, 29:56a; *JQYZFZ* 1810, 49:41a, 48:8a, 48:11b–12a. Yuanxun was a *fushe* (restoration society) member; see *Fushe xingshi*, (anon., n.d.), rare books collection, National Library, Taipei. On the *fushe*, see William S. Atwell, "From Education to Politics," in William Theodore de Bary ed., *The Unfolding of Neo-Confucianism* (New York: Columbia University Press, 1975), pp. 333–367. Both Yuanxun and Weihong were also members of the local literary society, the *Zhuxi xushe*: *JQYZFZ* 1810, 31.27a.

132. I can only speculate that this was originally the property of this family. No other family of this surname appears as prominently in Yangzhou's records and Zleng is, moreover, a typical Shexian surname (though one shared, of course, by the Xinghua painter, Zheng Banqiao). See *Shexian zhi*, 1937 ed., 1:6a.

133. Ruan Yuan offers a case in point. His grandmother was sister to the merchant, Jiang Chun. Li, *Yangzhou*, 12:30.

134. *GXJDXZ* 1883, 25:3a; *GXGQXZ* 1881, 24.23a. See Hummel, *Eminent Chinese*, pp. 137–138.

135. Zhu, "Qingdai qianqi Yangzhou," p. 115. For Ruan Yuan's biography, see Hummel, *Eminent Chinese*, pp. 399–402. He spent much of his official leave in Yangzhou and took a great interest in the city. See his forward to Li Dou, *Yangzhou*, and his two postscripts, written in 1834 and 1839, in Ruan Yuan, *Yanjingshi zaixuji* [Collected writings from the Yanjing Studio, continued], ca.1844, (bound with *Yanjingshi ji*), 3:6a–b.

136. For Jiao's biography, see Hummel, *Eminent Chinese*, pp. 144–145. Jiang Fan's biography in Hummel states that the drought took place over the two years of 1785–86, but 1786 was in fact a year of heavy rains and serious floods. *JQNYZFZ*, 1810, 13:4a–b.

137. *JQYZFZ*, 1810, 16:9b–10a.

138. Zhao Erxun comp., *Qing shi gao* [Draft history of the Qing], vol. 45 (Beijing: Zhonghua shuju, 1977), 287.13826–7.

139. On the Jiao family, see *BHXZ* 1808, *juan* 6. Also in this work, Jiao

Xun includes a biographical note on his wife's grandfather, Ruan Chengchun, through whom he must have been related to Ruan Yuan. According to this note, the family had actually lived at Gongdeqiao in the Beihu area for generations, despite an Yizheng registration: 4:29a.

140. Ruan Yuan, *Yanjingshi zai xuji*, 5:17a.

141. *GXJDXZ*, 1883, 19:6b–7a.

142. In Chen Henghe, *Yangzhou congke*.

143. Ruan Yuan, Jiao Xun, Jiang Fan, Liu Wenqi (1789–1856), and Wang Zhong (1745–1794), in addition to Li Dou and Liu Baonan, all produced works of local interest. See individual biographies in Hummel, *Eminent Chinese*.

144. Anthony D. King, "Colonial Cities: Global Pivots of Change," in Robert J. Ross and Gerard J. Telkamp, eds., *Colonial Cities* (Dordrecht: Martinus Nijhoff Publishers, 1985), p. 10.

145. Rowe, *Hankow*, passim, but on the natives of the locality see especially pp. 217–219.

146. Cited in William Henry Scott, "Yangzhou and its Eight Eccentrics," in Scott, *Hollow Ships on a Wine-dark Sea and Other Essays* (Quezon City: New Day Publishers, 1976), p. 62. I am grateful to Mr. Scott for sending me this article.

147. E. A. J. Johnson, *The Organization of Space in Developing Countries* (Cambridge, Mass.: Harvard University Press, 1970), p. 96.

148. Du Wenzhen, *Jiangsusheng renkou* [The population of Jiangsu] (Nanjing: "Jiangsusheng renkou" bianji weiyuanhui, 1984), p. 242.

149. Honig, "The Politics of Prejudice."

150. The seminal article on internal colonialism is Pablo González-Casanova, "Internal Colonialism and National Development," *Studies in Comparative International Development*, 1, 4, (1965), pp. 27–37. The theory is developed more fully in Michael Hechter, *Internal Colonialism: The Celtic Fringe in British National Development*, 1536–1966 (Berkeley and Los Angeles: University of California Press, 1977). I am grateful to William T. Rowe for drawing my attention to Hechter's work. See further Finnane, "The Origins of Prejudice: the Malintegration of Subei in Late Imperial China."

151. See for example Mote, "Tranformation of Nanking," and Elvin, "Chinese Cities Since the Sung Dynasty," in Philip Abrams and E. A. Wrigley eds., *Towns in Societies: Essays in Economic History and Historical Sociology* (Cambridge: Cambridge University Press, 1978), pp. 79–89.

CHAPTER 5: SHANGHAI: AN EMERGING JIANGNAN PORT,
1683–1840

[*Author's note:* I would like to thank Professors Dilip K. Basu, Edmund Burke, III, and Susan Mann, Frederic Wakeman, Jr., Evelyn S. Rawski, William T. Rowe, Edward T. Graham, Bryna Goodman and Harris I. Martin for their help and comments on earlier versions of this paper.]

List of abbreviations:

> *HCBK:* Chu Hua, *Hucheng beikao* [Draft history of "Hu" city (Shanghai)] (late 18th century); reprinted in *Shanghai zhanggu cishu* [Collection of Shanghai historical miscellany] (Shanghai: Shanghai tungsheshi, 1936) *juan* one.
> *JQSHXZ: Jiaqing Shanghai xianzhi* [Jiaqing gazetteer of Shanghai county], 1814; reprinted Taibei, 1970.
> *MGSHXZ: Minguo Shanghai xianzhi* [Republican gazetteer of Shanghai county], 1935; reprinted Taibei, 1975.
> *SHDGZL: Shanghai daguan zeli* [Handbook of the main Shanghai Custom House], 1785; (Shanghai: Jianghai Guan, Hubu, 1785).
> *SHXXZ: Shanghai xianxuzhi* [Continued gazetteer of Shanghai county], 1918.
> *TZSHXZ: Tongzhi Shanghai xian zhi*, Tongzhi gazetteer of Shanghai county] 1871.

1. William F. Mayers, N. B. Dennys and Charles King, *The Treaty Ports of China and Japan* (London: Trubner and Co, 1867; 1977 reprint, San Francisco), p. 350.

2. Rhoads Murphey, *Shanghai, Key to Modern China* (Cambridge: Harvard University Press, 1953); Betty Peh T'i Wei, *Shanghai, Crucible of Modern China* (Oxford: Oxford University Press, 1987). On a closely comparable city see: William T. Rowe, *Hankow, Commerce and Society in a Chinese City, 1796–1889* (Stanford: Stanford University Press, 1984) and *Hankow, Conflict and Community in A Chinese City, 1796–1895* (Stanford: Stanford University Press, 1989).

3. Several outstanding examples of such studies include: Mark Elvin, "Market Towns and waterways: the county of Shanghai from 1480 to 1910," in G. William Skinner, ed., *The City in Late Imperial China* (Stanford: Stanford University Press, 1977), pp. 441–473; Susan Mann Jones, "The Ningpo Pang and financial power in Shanghai," in Mark Elvin and Skinner, eds., *The Chinese City Between Two Worlds* (Stanford: Stanford University Press, 1974), pp. 73–96; and Elvin, "The administration of Shanghai: 1905–1914" in *The Chinese City Between Two Worlds*, pp. 239–262.

4. Although details of the pre-treaty port history of the city have not been prominent in English language discussions, certain aspects have been addressed by contemporary Chinese scholars: Quan Hansheng, "Yapien zhanzhang yiqian Jiangsu de mienfang zhiyeh" [The cotton spinning and weaving industry in Jiangsu prior to the Opium War], *Tsing Hua Journal of Chinese Studies*, New Series, 1.3 (1958), pp. 1–45; Zou Yilin, "Shanghai dichu zuicao de dui waimao yanggang Qinglong zhen" [Qinglong Market-town, the earliest commercial port in the Shanghai region], *Zhonghua wenshi bientcong* 1 (1980), pp. 119–129. Specifically devoted to the history of Shanghai prior to the Opium war are two important works: Zhang Zhongmin, *Shanghai: cong kaifa zouxiang kaifang, 1368–1842* [Shanghai, from inception to opening, 1268–1842] (Kunming: Yunnan renmin chubanshe, 1990; and Du Li, "Yapien zhanzheng qian Shanghai hanghui xingzhi zhi shanbian" [Changes in the character of the Shanghai guilds prior to the Opium War], paper presented at the conference on the "Sprouts of Capitalism," Nanjing, May 1981; published in *Zhongguo zibenzhuyi mengya wenti lunwenji* [Collected discussions on the question of the "Sprouts of Capitalism" in China], Nanjing, 1983, pp. 141–171. Note that page numbers in entries below refer to the mss. copy, not the Nanjing edition.

5. Skinner, "Introduction, urban development in imperial China," in *City in Late Imperial China*, pp. 11–12; Skinner, "Regional urbanization in 19th century China," Ibid., pp. 211–249.

6. A Superintendency of Foreign Trade (*Shi posi*) was established at Shanghai in either 1277 or 1298, (see the discussion in Note # 27) supervising the merchants and collecting the customary fees and tariffs. Zou, "Qinglong zhen," pp. 27–28. The location of the bureau appears on the Yuan dyansty map of Shanghai, *HCBK*, 18th century, preface: 1b–2a, (reprinted in *SHXXZ* 1918, preface, maps.) Shiba Yoshinobu suggests that such collections were often farmed out to brokers and merchants acting as tax contractors during the Southern Song period. See: *Shiba, Commerce and Society in Sung China* (Ann Arbor: Center for Chinese Studies, University of Michigan, 1970), pp. 178–179.

7. *TZSHXZ*, 1871, 2:14a–b; Huang Huchen, "Qingdai qianji haiwai maoyi de fazhan" [The development of foreign commerce in the early Qing], *Lishi Yanjiu* 4 (1986), pp. 152–155.

8. Skinner, "Regional Urbanization . . . ," p. 248.

9. My work draws principally on Chinese primary sources such as local gazetteers, guild records and inscriptions, customs' handbooks and such materials plus a scattering of pre-1842 European descriptions, supplemented by recent Chinese research.

10. Murphey, *Shanghai*, passim.

11. An authoritative reconstruction of the geography of the Jiangsu coast in the Tang period shows the site of modern Shanghai at the mouth of the Songjiang River, which flowed directly east from Lake Tai. The site of the city was immediately on the coast, the eastern section of today's city would have been underwater. Tan Qixiang, ed., *Zhongguo lishi ditu ji* [Historical Atlas of China], (Beijing: Citu chubanshe, c. 1987), vol. 5, "Sui-Tang," p. 55. Zhang, *Shanghai*, p. 1 suggests that the name, "Shanghai" originated in the names of two creeks, known as "Shanghai" (upper) and "Xiahai" (lower); when the lower creek disappeared, the upper, "Shanghai" remained, located near the village that was known as "Hudu."

12. *HCBK*, 18th century, 1:5a–b. This source provides a generally more colloquial approach to Shanghai's history, apparently designed to fill in omissions in the formal *xian* histories. A more formal chronological account of the history of the city is found in *JQSHXZ*, 1814: juan 1 ff; *SHXXZ*, 1918: 1a–4b; and *MGSHXZ*, 1935, *juan* 1 ff.

13. See: *JQSHXZ*, 1814:1:4b; *SHXXZ*, 1918: 1:4b. and *MGSHXZ*, 1935, *juan* 1 ff.; geographic details are based on *Zhongguo Lishi Ditu Ji*, vol. 5, "Sui-Tang," p. 55.

14. Zou, "Qinglong zhen," pp. 119–120.

15. *TZSHXZ*, 1871, 1:3a; *SHXXZ*, 1918: 1:6a–7b; Zou, "Qinglong zhen," pp. 119–120; Yang Qimin, "Gu Louxian kaolue" [Brief examination of ancient Lou county] in Wang Pengcheng, etc. *Shanghai shi yanjiu* [Research on the history of Shanghai] (Shanghai: Xuelin chubanshe, 1984), p. 34.

16. The routes of the two rivers and the harbor created where they met is shown in the map, whose title indicates a Song date, in *HCBK* 18th century, preface: 1b–2a. Zou, "Qinglong zhen," pp. 121–124.

17. The direct route of the Songjiang river is shown in *Zhongguo lishi ditu ji*, vol. 5, "Sui-Tang," p. 55; vol. 6, "Song-Liao-Jin," p. 22–23.

18. *JQSHXZ*, 1814, 1:4a; Zou, "Qinglong zhen," pp. 124–125.

19. *HCBK*, 18th century, 3: 1a–b.

20. Zou, "Qinglong zhen," pp. 119–120. *Zhongguo lishi ditu ji*, vol. 6, "Song-Liao-Jin," pl.p. 22–23.

21. *HCBK*, 18th century, preface: 2b–3a, and 1:4a–b; Qiao Shuming, "Qinglong zhen de chengshuai yu Shanghai de xingchi" [The height and decline of Qinglong market-town and the rise of Shanghai] in Wang Pengcheng, etc. *Shanghai shi yanjiu*, pp. 37–42.

22. Zou, "Qinglong zhen," pp. 124–125; 128. Also see: Shiba, *Commerce and Society in Sung China*, p. 181; Shiba, "Sung foreign trade," in Morris Ros-

sabi, ed. *China Among Equals* (Berkeley: University of California Press, 1983), p. 105.

23. Qiao, "Qinglongzhen de chengshuai yu Shanghai de xingchi," p. 34; Zou, "Qinglong zhen," p. 125.

24. Zou, "Qinglong zhen," p. 127.

25. The changing courses of the rivers are evident on the maps in *HCBK*, 18th century, preface: 1b–2a, reprinted in Zou, "Qinglong zhen," p. 123.

26. The creation of Songjiang prefecture dates from the early Song, when the short-lived state of Wu-Yueh, whose capital had been at Hangzhou, (see Michael Marmé, "Heaven on earth: the rise of Suzhou, 1127–1550" in this volume, pp. 17–18) was incorporated into the Liang Zhe circuit, within the larger Huainan dong circuit area. *Zhongguo Lishi Ditu Ji*, vol. 6, "Song-Liao-Jin," pp. 22–23.

27. The location of the "Office of Overseas Trade" is shown on the map in *HCBK*, 18th century, preface: 1b–2a; but the exact date of its opening is somewhat obscure, some sources indicating the office was opened in 1277: *TZSHXZ*, 1871:2:4a; *SHXXZ*, 1918:1:9a–b; others 1298; see: Zou, "Qinglong zhen," pp. 127–128.

28. See: Shiba, *Commerce and Society in Sung China*, on the prosperity in Jiangnan during the Yuan period.

29. Tian Hou Temple is shown on the map in *HCBK*, 18th century, preface: 4b–5a.

30. Shanghai was part of the Suzhou region claimed by Zhang Shicheng, rival to Zhu Yuanzhang, who later successfully founded the Ming dynasty, as described in Marmé's "Heaven on earth," pp. 26–27. Also see: Mote and Twichett, eds. *The Cambridge History of China* vol. 7 "The Ming Dynasty," part I, pp. 30–31, 44–47, 64, 190.

31. *MGSHXZ*, 1935:1:24b–25b provides a comprehensive list of earlier *jinshi* degree holders.

32. *HCBK* 18th century, 2:7b; 4:8a; *MGSHXZ* 1935, 1:26a.

33. *HCBK* 18th century, 6:1a–b indicates that the construction of the wall took place in successive stages from 1369 on and records details of the pirate attacks that required this defense. 2:7b; 3:6a, ff.; 6:1a–2b, 11a.; a briefer, more strictly factual account is found in *MGSHXZ* 1935, 1:26b.

34. Sen-do Chang, "The morphology of walled capitals," in *The City in Late Imperial China*, pp. 75–77.

35. Maps in various editions of the county gazetteer show the city as it appeared in the Qing period: *Jiaqing Songjiang fuzhi* [Jiaqing gazetteer of Songjiang prefecture] 1819, maps; *Qianlong Suzhou fuzhi* [Qianlong gazetteer of Suzhou prefecture], 1748; (reprinted Taibei, 1970), maps.

36. According to an inscription in *Shanghai beike ziliao xuanji* [Collection of carved inscriptions from Shanghai] (Shanghai: Shanghai bowuguan, 1980), p. 9, the City Temple of the Qing period was dedicated in Wanli thirty (1602). *HCBK*, 18th century, 6:1a notes that what was probably an earlier city temple was constructed in connection with the building of walls and moats in 1369.

37. *HCBK*, 18th century, 6:33a–b.

38. *Zhongguo lishi ditu ji*, vol. 8, "Qing," pp. 16–17. The main body of the river from Shanghai to Wusong was known as the Wusong River, not the Huangpu, even as late as the first European visits to the site in 1832. See: Lindsay and Gutzlaff, "Amherst Expedition," *Chinese Repository* vol. II (April 1834) p. 549: the *Lord Amherst* visited Shanghai in 1832, sailing up the Wusong River and anchoring in the channel of the river with the city on the right bank; from this description it seems clear that the part of the river now known as the Huangpu was then called the Wusong.

39. Development of the cotton industry in the Shanghai region is described by Quan, "Yapien zhanzhang yiqian . . . ," pp. 1–45; by Elvin in "Market towns and waterways," pp. 441–474. Also see: Yan Zhongping, *Zhongguo mien fangzhi shikao* [A brief history of cotton spinning and weaving in China] (Beijing: keshe chubanshe, 1955) and Craig Dietrich, "Cotton culture and manufacture in Ch'ing China," in W. E. Willmott, ed., *Economic Organization in Chinese Society* (Stanford: Stanford University Press, 1972), pp. 109–135.

40. Zhang describes the exchange between the eastern and western parts of the Shanghai region and resulting development of handicraft industries in the western half: Zhang, *Shanghai*, pp. 27–29 and ff. On the import of rice, see: Chuan Hansheng and Richard Kraus, *Mid-Ch'ing Rice Markets and Trade: An Essay in Price History* (Cambridge: Harvard University Press, 1975).

41. *TZSHXZ*, 1871, 1:9a–10b. Elvin, "Market Towns and Waterways," pp. 441–474.

42. See: Elvin, "Market towns and waterways;" the basic model is explained in G. William Skinner, "Marketing and social structure in rural China, I," *Journal of Asian Studies* 24 (1964) pp. 3–43; 195–228. Zhang also devotes particular attention to the development of market towns: Zhang, *Shanghai*, pp. 335–360.

43. Liu Yongcheng, "Shilun Qingdai Suzhou shou gongyeh hanghui" [A discussion of handicraft guilds in Qing dynasty Suzhou], *Lishi yanjiu* 25 (1959), p. 23.

44. Quan, "Yapien zhanzhang yiqian . . . ," pp. 31–33.

45. On the role of brokers, see: Susan Mann, "Brokers as entrepreneurs in presocialist China," *Comparative Studies in Society and History* 25.4 (1984) pp. 614–636 and *Local Merchants and the Chinese Bureaucracy, 1750–1950* (Stanford: Stanford University Press, 1987), pp. 59–69.

46. Liu, "Suzhou gongyeh hanghui," p. 23; Miyazaki Ichisada, "Min shih-jidai no Soshū to kaikōkyō no hattatsu" [Development of light industry in Suzhou in the Ming and Qing periods], *Tōhōgakuhō* 70 (1951), pp. 64–73, and Quan, "Yapien zhanzhang yiqian . . . ," pp. 1–45.

47. Transport merchants dealing in cotton on trips to the north and carring soy beans and bean products on the return trips to Shanghai formed the Guanshandong *bang* as early as the Shunzhi reign, local merchants responded by forming the so-called "Sandjunk" Merchants Guild in the Kangxi period. The trade was clearly lucrative, and expanded throughout the Qing period.

48. The "Sandjunk Merchants'" Guild employed the "mudworkers," and was accordingly charged by the local authorities with their supervision and control, resulting in a number of ordinances directing the guild to exert greater control over the often unruly workers. Such inscriptions are recorded in *Jiangsu sheng Ming Qing yilai beike ciliao xuanji* [Selected inscriptions (from) stele in Jiangsu province in the Ming and Qing periods] (Nanjing: Sanlian shudian, 1956), pp. 478–479; *Shanghai beike ziliao*, pp. 69, 182, 201; The situation is discussed by Du Li, "Yapien zhanzheng qian Shanghai hanghui . . . ," pp. 24–25.

49. When the British later halted the mud-collectors' activities in front of the consulate site immediate problems with silting ensued and keeping the channel cleared required dredging. British opposition to collection of mud from the banks of the river is recorded in G(eorge) Lanning and S(amuel) Couling, *The History of Shanghai*, Part I (Shanghai: Kelly and Walsh, 1921), p. 282.

50. *TZSHXZ*, 1871, 2:14a–b; and Huang, "Qingdai qianji haiwai maoyi de fazhan," pp. 152–155.

51. *SHDGZL*, 1785; Huang, "Qingdai haiwai maoyi," p. 154

52. Zhang Zhongmin, "Qing qianji Shanghai gang fazhan yanbian xintan" [Discoveries in the evolution of Shanghi's port in the early Qing period] *Zhongguo jingji shi yanjiu*, 1987, no. 3, p. 86. Also, by the same author, Zhang, *Shanghai*, pp. 304–305.

53. *Shanghai beike ciliao xuanji*, the Guanshandong activities are notes in inscriptions on pp. 72, 194.

54. *SHXXZ*, 1918, 3:1a–b. Du Li, "Yapien zhanzheng qian Shanghai hanghui . . . ," p. 20.

55. *TZSHXZ*, 1871, 2:14a–b.

56. Ibid.

57. Skinner, "Cities and the hierarchy of local systems, " in *The City in Late Imperial China*, p. 333.

58. *Shanghai qianzhuang shiliao* [Historical materials on Shanghai *qian-zhuang* (banks)] (Shanghai: Shanghai renmin chubanshe, 1960, 1978), p. 6. A full description of earlier trade along the China coast may be found in Fu Yil-ing, *Mingqing shidai shangren yi shangyeh ziben* [Merchants and merchant capital in the Ming-Qing period] (Beijing: renmin chubanshe, 1956).

59. See: Ch'u Tung-tsu, *Local Government in China Under the Ch'ing* (Stanford: Stanford University Press, 1962), pp. 1–7; chart p. 5.

60. A comparison of maps of the city in sequential Shanghai gazetteers makes the expansion of suburbs evident. See: *JQSHXZ*, 1814, preface: 9b–10a city map, *TZSHZX*, 1871, preface: 13b–14a, 15b–16a city map and map of the suburbs.

61. He Bingdi, *Zhongguo huiguan shilun* [An historical survey of land-smannschaften in China] (Taibei: Xuesheng shuju, 1966). Native place associa-tions in China had begun, according to He, as hostels specializing in housing natives from specific localities, furnishing native cuisine and providing opportu-nities for association with others from the same locality, speaking the same common dialects. These associations were customarily known as *huiguan*, and were distinguished from other merchant and craft organizations known as *gongsuo* or common trade associations. Conventional distinctions between *huiguan* as sojourner hostels and *gongsuo* as trade associations had little significance at Shanghai where the terms appear to be used interchangeably.

62. *Shanghai beike ciliao*, pp. 72, 94–95, the Guanshandong guild was active in the early Daoguang reign (1827); according to an inscription, by 1825 the formal name was the Guanshandong *gongsuo*; but had changed its title to *huiguan* before 1906. For another discussion of this group, see: Du Li, "Ya-pien zhanzheng qian Shanghai hanghui . . . ," p. 21.

63. *SHXXZ*, 1918, 3:1a–b; *Shanghai beike ciliao*, pp. 196, 201.

64. Du Li, "Yapien zhanzheng qian Shanghai hanghui . . . ," p. 22.

65. *SHXXZ*, 1918:3:1a–b.

66. Ibid., 3:4a; Du Li, "Yapien zhanzheng qian Shanghai hanghui . . . ," p. 7; *Shanghai beike ciliao*, pp. 211, 230.

67. *SHXXZ* 1918, 3:1b–2b; *Shanghai beike ciliao*, p. 232.

68. Great Britain, Foreign Office Archive, Public Record Office, London: F.O. 224/43 pp. 158–159.

69. *SHXXZ*, 1918, 3:1; also see Du Li, "Yapien zhanzheng qian Shanghai hanghui . . . .", pp. 7–9 distinguishes among guilds by their functions rather than on the basis of *gongsuo* or *huiguan* terms. He finds three distinct types of organizations at Shanghai product-commodity guilds, commerce-shipping guilds, and handicraft guilds.

70. *SHXXZ*, 1918, 3:3a; *Shanghai beike ciliao*, 233–235.

71. Ibid., 3:2a–b.

72. Jones, "Finance in Ningpo: the *Ch'ien-chuang*, 1750–1880," pp. 58–60; Jones, "Ningpo *pang*," pp. 73–96. The Siming *gongsuo* is also catalogued in *Shanghai beike ciliao*, pp. 259–260.

73. *SHXXZ*, 1918, 3:4a–b.

74. Ibid., 3:5a–6a, Du Li, "Yapien zhanzheng qian Shanghai hanghui . . . ," p. 3–36; *Shanghai beike ciliao*, pp. 275–279; Zhang, *Shanghai*, pp. 260–262.

75. *SHXXZ* 3:6a. On the Fang lineage, see Jones, "Ningpo *pang*," pp. 73–96.

76. Ibid., 3:5a. The name of the Chaohui *gongsuo* was changed to Chaohui *huiguan* in 1865, but in spite of the semantic issue, it had always been a native-place association. I would like to thank Bryna Goodman for her help in identifying the "Opium Guild."

77. Ibid., 3:5b; *Shanghai beike ciliao*, p. 307.

78. *SHXXZ* 1918, 3:2a–b.

79. Ibid., 3:3a–b. *Shanghai beike ciliao*, pp. 252–254. The West Garden, of which the "Nei Yuan" forms a portion, was incorporated into the City Temple grounds in 1781 according to an inscription at the temple, *Shanghai beike ciliao*, p. 22.

80. Du Li, "Yapien zhanzheng qian Shanghai hanghui . . . ," p. 38; *Shanghai beike ciliao*, pp. 309–315, but inscirptions are from the Tongzhi period, 1862–1875.

81. *SHXXZ*, 1918: 3:1b–7b.

82. Ibid., 3:5a.

83. *SHDGZL*, 1785, 9a.

84. *SHXXZ*, 1918, 3:6a.

85. Ibid., maps, and 3:1a–16b.

86. *Shanghai qianzhuang shiliao*, p. 6.

87. For a comparable study of construction as an economic indicator, see David B. Miller, "Monumental building as an indicator of economic trends in northern Rus' in the late Kievian and Mongol periods, 1138–1462," *The American Historical Review* 94.2 (1989), pp. 360–390.

88. Representative contributions are indicated in the description of several guilds in *SHXXZ*, 3:1b–16b, and on inscriptions quoted in *Shanghai beike ciliao*, pp. 208–209.

89. Ibid., pp. 254–255.

90. *SHXXZ*, 3:1b. 2a, 3a, ff.

91. *Shanghai qianzhuang shiliao*, pp. 6–8.

92. Ibid., p. 6.

93. Ibid., p. 7.

94. Chan, "The Chien-wen, Yung-lo, Hung-hsi and Husan-te reigns, 1399–1435," in *Cambridge History*, "Ming" Vol. 7, p. 295. Also see the discussion by Marmé of Suzhou's burdensome grain quota, "Heaven on Earth, the rise of Suzhou 1127–1550," pp. 28–29.

95. Quan and Kraus, "Grain Markets," pp.

96. Harold C. Hinton, *The Grain Tribute System of China: 1845–1911* (Cambridge: Harvard University Press), p. 7; Susan Mann Jones and Philip Kuhn, "Dynastic decline and the roots of rebellion," in *Cambridge History: 10:1 Late Ch'ing*. (Cambridge: Cambridge University Press, 1978), pp. 107–162; Zhang, *Shanghai*, p. 301.

97. *Shanghai qianzhuang shiliao*, p. 6.

98. *SHXXZ* 1917, 3:3a.

99. Ibid., pp. 6–7; Mann, "Finance in Ningbo . . . ," pp. 47–77.

100. *Shanghai qianzhuang shiliao*, p. 7.

101. *Shanghai beike ciliao*, pp. 254–255.

102. Yeh-chien Wang, "Evolution of the Chinese monetary system," in Hou and Yu, eds., *Modern Chinese Economic History* (Taipei: Academia Sinica, 1979), pp. 437–438. Also see: Hamashita, "Foreign trade in China, 1810–1850."

103. Takeshi Hamashita, "Foreign Trade in China, 1810–1850," in Christian Daniels and Grove, eds. *State and Society in China: Japanese Perspectives on Ming-Qing Social History* (Tokyo: University of Tokyo Press, 1984), pp. 408, 425, note 92, p. 431. Edward LeFevor, *Western Enterprise in Late Ch'ing China: A Selected Survey of Jardine, Matheson and Company's Operations* (Cambridge: Harvard University Press, 1968), p. 18.

104. *Shanghai qianzhuang shiliao*, pp. 13–14; 17–18.

105. Ibid., p. 14.

106. Huang, "Qingdai haiwai maoyi . . . ," p. 161.

107. Zhang, *Shanghai*, p. 309.

108. Pan Junxiang and Chen Liyi, "Shijiu shiji houpanji Shanghai shangyeh de yanbien" [Evolution of Shanghai commerce in the late 19th century], *Lishi yanjiu*, 1986.1, p. 154.

109. Lindsay & Gutzlaff, "Voyage of the *Huron*," in *The Chinese Repository*, vol. IV (1834), p. 329.

110. Rhoads Murphey, *The Outsiders* (Ann Arbor: University of Michigan Press, 1970), p. 40.

111. John K. Fairbank, *Trade and Diplomacy on the China Coast* (Cambridge: Harvard University Press, 1953), p. 312.

112. *SHDGZL*, 1785, 3a–43b.

113. Collection of customs' duties by guilds is documented for a later date, in the period of the 1850's when the Lumber Merchants' *huiguan* customarily collected duties, filed the receipts, and issued sailing permits. *SHXXZ*, 1918, 3:8b. Susan Mann shows how government registered brokers often collected taxes of various kinds, including customs' duties, see: Mann, "Brokers as entrepreneurs in presocialist China," pp. 614–636 and *Local Merchants and the Chinese Bureaucracy*, 1750–1950, pp. 59–69.

114. *SHDGZL*, 1785, 7a–10b.

115. Lillian M. Li, *China's Silk Trade: Traditional Industry in the Modern World* (Cambridge: Harvard University Press, 1981), p. 71.

116. F.O. 228/89, "Returns on Trade 1847," p. 125.

117. Quan, "Yapien zhanzhang yiqian . . . ," p. 36. Peng Zili argues that due to the strong foreign demand for "Nankeens" a secondary manufacturing site also developed at Foshan near Canton in Guangdong in the early part of the nineteenth century. Foshan "Nankeens" differed from the original product in that the textile was, to a large extent, manufactured from imported Bengali cotton and yarn, known as "yang sha" or "foreign yarn." Peng Zeyi, "Yapien zhanzhang qian Guangzhou xinxing de qingfang gongyeh" [New prosperity in the light weaving industry in Guangzhou before the Opium War], Lishi yanjiu 1983.3, pp. 109–116. If so, some of the cotton shipped out of Canton might well have come from manufactures at Foshan which did not reflect Jiangnan "Nankeen" production. But this argument has been largely discredited. Philip Huang states that the "oft-cited example of Foshan in Guangdong province (based on the account of an early-nineteenth-century foreign traveller) . . . turns out to be an exaggerated report about silk rather than cotton weaving." Huang, The Peasant Family and Rural Development in the Yangzi Delta, 1350–1988 (Stanford: Stanford University Press, 1990), p. 86.

118. Zhang, Shanghai, pp. 19–193.

119. Quan, "Yapien zhanzhang yiqian . . . ," p. 36.

120. Ibid., p.40.

121. Peng, "Yapien Zhanzhang qian Guangzhou . . . ," p. 114.

122. B. R. Mitchell, European Historical Statistics 1750–1975, 2nd ed. (New York: Facts on File, 1980), p. 449. Also see Phyllis Deane, The First Industrial Revolution 2nd ed. (Cambridge: Cambridge University Press, 1979), pp. 91–92, D. A. Farnie, The English Cotton Industry and the World Market 1815–1896 (Oxford: Clarendon Press, 1979), p. 83, and Joel Mokyr, The Economics of the Industrial Revolution (Great Britain: Rowman and Allanheld, 1988), pp. 59–60.

123. Michael Greenberg, British Trade and the Opening of China, 1800–1842 (Cambridge: Cambridge University Press, 1951), pp. 175–195; Hocheung Mui and Loma H. Mui, The Management of Monopoly: A Study of the English East India Company's Conduct of Its Tea Trade, 1784–1833 (Vancouver: University of British Columbia Press, 1984), pp. 135–136.

124. Greenberg, British Trade, pp. 179–180.

125. Ibid., p. 181.

126. Horace Greeley, Essays Designed to Elucidate the Science of Political Economy, quoted by Edward T. Graham, American Ideas of a Special Relation with China, 1784–1900 (New York: Garland Press, 1988), p. 89.

127. Graham, American Ideas of a Special Relation, pp. 87–88. In 1826 sales amounted to $15,000, by 1832 that figure had risen to $87,000, but in

1833 it jumped to $192,000. By 1838 the value of American cotton textiles reached half a million dollars.

128. Greenberg, *British Trade and the Opening of China*, pp. 185–186.

129. Zhang, *Shanghai*, p. 374. Population figures are given in terms of able-bodied adults registered in the county; if immigrants from other parts of China and children and elderly persons were included, the total would clearly be much higher.

130. Robert Fortune, *Three Years' Wandering Among the Northern Provinces of China* (London: Murray, 1847), p. 104.

131. Fei Xiaotong, *China's Gentry* (Chicago: University of Chicago Press, 1953), pp. 105–107.

GLOSSARY

Anding 安定
Anfeng 安豐
bachi hangshi 把持行市
baita 白塔
bang 幫
bao 保
baojia 保甲
Baoshan 寶山
baotou 包頭
baoxiao 報效
baoyi 包衣
Baoying 寶應
Baoyou 寶佑
Bei hao 北濠
bianmin ku 便民庫
Caishi qiao 菜市橋
Cao Shipin 曹時聘
Cao Yin 曹寅
Caomi xiang 糙米巷
Chai Xiang 柴祥
Changmen 閶門
Changzhou xian 長州縣
Chaohui *huiguan* 潮惠會館
chaomo 抄沒
Chaozhou 潮州
chayuan 察院
Chen (Ms.) 陳氏
Chen Sanmo 陳三謨
Chen Shan 陳善
Chen Yu 陳昱
Chen Yuanmo 陳元謨
Ch'oe Pu 崔溥

Chongchang *he* 沖場河
Chongming *xian* 崇明縣
chuaifang 踹房
chuaijiang 踹匠
Chuansha 川沙
Chujia *tang* 褚家塘
dacheng 大城
Dahong *yuan* 大虹園
Da Qing yitong zhi 大清一統志
daotai 道太
dashu 大叔
ding (tripod) 鼎
ding (person) 丁
Ding Shiqing 丁仕卿
Dong Yue 東越
Dongtai 東臺
dushang 督商
ershu 二叔
Fan Chengda 范成大
fanfu 販夫
fang (district) 坊
fang (enbankment) 防
fangmin 坊民
Fangsheng 放生
Fang Yang 方揚
Feng Gaomo 馮皋謨
Feng Menglong 馮夢龍
Fengmen 葑門
fuhu 富戶
Funing 阜寧
Gao Qi 高啓
Gao Gong 高拱

261

Gaoyou 高郵
Ge Cheng 葛成
Geng Dingxiang 耿定向
gengpu 更舖
gongsuo 公所
Gu Yanwu 顧炎武
Guandi 關帝
Guanghuasi *qiao* 廣化寺橋
Guangling 廣陵
guanjidi jianjia 官基地間架
guantian 官田
Guanxiang (kou) 官巷(口)
Guanzhuangmu 關壯繆
Guazhou 瓜洲
Guiji jun 會稽郡
Gusu 姑蘇
hanghui 行會
hangtou 行頭
haifang 海坊
Haimen 海門
hemai 和買
hengjin 橫金
Hengtang 橫塘
Heyitang 和醫堂
Hongqiao 紅橋
Hongze (Lake) 洪澤
Hu Qizhong 胡蘄忠
Hu Weiyong 胡維庸
Huai (king) 懷
Huai (River) 淮
Huaibei 淮北
Huainan 淮南
Huang Xie 黃歇
Huang Xingzeng 黃省曾
Huangpu 黃浦
Huating 華亭
Hubu 戶部
Hudu 滬瀆
huiguan 會館
Huizhou 徽州
huojia 火甲
huofu 火夫
Hushu 滸墅
jia 甲

Jia Sidao 賈似道
jiacheng 夾城
jian 間
jianjia 間架
jiangjia shui 間架稅
Jiang Fan 江藩
Jiang Liangdong 姜艮棟
Jiangbei 江北
Jiangdu 江都
Jianghai *guan* 江海關
Jianning 建寗
Jianting *huiguan* 建汀會館
jiaofu 腳夫
Jiao Xun 焦循
jiatou 甲頭
jidi jianjia 基地間架
jifang 機房
jigun 積棍
jihu 機戶
Jisheng *miao* 機聖廟
jugong 居工
jun 郡
kanlou 看樓
keshang 客商
Kuang Zhong 況鐘
Laozha 老閘
Lianghuai 兩淮
Liangjiang 兩江
Liang Zhe 兩浙
Lianxi fang 濂溪坊
lijia 里甲
Linqing 臨清
Liu Baonan 劉寶楠
Liuhekou 劉河口
Liujiagang 劉家港
Longjiang 龍江
Loumen 婁門
Lu Jianzeng 盧見曾
Lumu *zhen* 陸墓鎮
lunban 輪班
Ma Sancai 馬三才
Ma Wenying 馬文英
Ma Yinghua 馬應華
maisi zhaojiang 買絲招匠

maixinsi 賣新絲
mentan 門攤
minjidi 民基地
mintian 民田
Mo Rui 莫睿
mu 畝
Mudu zhen 木瀆鎮
Nan hao 南濠
nanhuo 南貨
Nanjing sheng 南京省
Nanyang 南洋
Nei Yuan 內園
paimen fu 排門夫
Panmen 盤門
paping 扒平
Pingan 平安
Pingjiang 平江(府)
Pingshantang 平山堂
Qimen 齊門
Qianjiang huiguan 錢江會館
qianpai 僉派
Qiantang xian 錢塘縣
qianzhuang 錢庄
Qin Enfu 秦恩復
Qin Yunyan 欽允言
Qingkou 清口
Qinglong 青龍
Quanxin jie 穿心街
Quanzhang huiguan 泉漳會館
Renhe xian 仁和縣
Ruan Yuan 阮元
Rugao 如皋
sancheng 三城
sandeng jiuze 三等九則
Shang, Xia maimai jie 上下買賣街
shanghu 上戶
Shang tang 上塘
"Shang you tian tang, xia you Su Hang" 上有天堂, 下有蘇杭
Shaobo 邵伯
Shen Pian 沈梗
Shen Jian 沈鑑
Shen Jin 沈蓳

shenshang 紳商
shengyuan 生員
She xian 歙縣
shi (market/city) 市
shi (measure of grain) 石
Shi Panzi 施胖子
shiyin 市隱
sihang 私行
sihang 絲行
Siming gongsuo 四明公所
Shugang 蜀岡
Songjiang 松江
Subei 蘇北
Sun Chunyang 孫春陽
Sun Long 孫隆
Sun Pei 孫珮
suoguan 所官
Su-Song-Tai dao 蘇松太道
Taihu 太湖
Taicang 太倉
tangzhang 堂長
Tian Hou 天后
Taixing 泰興
taixuesheng 太學生
Taizhou 泰州
Tingzhou 汀州
Tongzhou 通州
Tongrentang 同仁堂
tongxiang 同鄉
tongye 同業
Tu Yunfeng 屠雲鳳
Wang Ao 王鏊
Wang Yuzao 王玉藻
Wangxian qiao 望仙橋
Wei xian 濰縣
Wen Bing 文秉
wokou 倭寇
Wu xian 吳縣
Wu Riqiang 吳日强
Wu Shanyan 吳善言
Wu Yue 吳越
Wucheng fu 蕪城賦
Wujiang xian 吳江縣
Wujun jiye gongsuo 吳君機業公所

wulai 無賴
Wulin 武林
Wusong 吳松
Wusongkou 吳松口
xiangdafu 鄉大夫
Xiannu *zhen* 仙女鎮
Xiaodong *men* 小東門
xiaojia 小甲
Xiaoman 小滿
Xia tang 下塘
Xia Yuanji 夏原吉
Xihe 西河
xincheng 新城
Xinguo 新郭
Xinghua 興化
Xingzai 行在
xinqian 新錢
Xiuzhou 秀州
xiyang bu 西洋布
Xu Yikui 徐一夔
xuegong 學宮
Xumen 胥門
yahang 牙行
yajiang 砑匠
yakuai 牙儈
Yancheng 鹽城
Yang Tingyong 楊廷用
Yangzhou 揚州
Yangzhou *sandao* 揚州三刀
Yangzhou *xuepai* 揚州學派
Yao Wentian 姚文田
yiguan 義官
yin 蔭
yinshi 殷氏
Yixing xian 宜興縣
Yizhe xiang 義澤巷
Yizheng 儀徵
yizhuang 義莊
Yu yuan 豫園
Yuanhe 元和
Yuanmiao guan 元妙觀

Yue 越
Yue qiao 樂橋
Yuecheng shi 月城市
Yunyan *he* 運鹽河
Yuyingtang 育嬰堂
zaoding 灶丁
Zhang Jiayin 張佳胤
Zhang Kai 張開
Zhang Kui 張魁
Zhang Shicheng 張士誠
Zhang Wenxi 張文熙
zhangfang 長房
zhangfang 賬房 (alternative pronoun-
　　ciation zhenfang)
Zhangjia *qiao* 章家橋
Zhebing 浙兵
Zheng Banqiao 鄭板橋
Zheng He 鄭和
Zheng Ruoceng 鄭若曾
Zheng Weiguan 鄭為官
Zheng Weixu 鄭為旭
Zheng Yuanxun 鄭元勳
Zhenhai 鎮海
Zhening *huiguan* 浙甯會館
Zhenjiang 鎮江
Zhenyang *xian* 鎮洋縣
Zhenzhou 真州
Zheshao *gongsuo* 浙紹公所
Zhexi 浙西
zhigong 織工
Zhigong dui 織工對
zhiyong 織傭
Zhou Chen 周臣
Zhou Chen 周忱
Zhu Yunming 祝允明
Zhuchi *gongsuo* 祝其公所
zhuzuo 住坐
zicheng 子城
zongjia 總甲
zongshang 總商
zuiyao 最要

BIBLIOGRAPHY

LOCAL GAZETTEERS

Listed alphabetically by locality

Changzhou

[Kangxi] *Changzhou xianzhi* 康熙長州縣志 [Kangxi Gazetteer of Changzhou county] 1684.

[Qianlong] *Changzhou xianzhi* 乾隆長州縣志 [Qianlong Gazetteer of Changzhou county] 1766.

[Wanli] *Changzhou fuzhi* 萬曆常州府志 [Wanli Gazetteer of Changzhou prefecture] 1618.

[Wanli] *Changzhou xianzhi* 萬曆長州縣志 [Wanli Gazetteer of Changzhou county], 1598.

Fengjing

Fengjing xiaozhi 鳳麓小志 [Short gazetteer of Fengjing] n.d.

Ganquan

[Jiaqing] *Ganquan xianzhi* 嘉慶甘泉縣志 [Jiaqing gazetteer of Ganquan county] 1810.

[Guangxu] *Ganquan xianzhi* 光緒甘泉縣志 [Guangxu gazetteer of Ganquan county] 1881; reprinted Taipei, 1983.

Haiyan

[Tianqi] *Haiyan xian tujing* 天啓海鹽縣圖經 [Tianqi Gazetteer of Haiyan county] 1624.

Hangzhou

[Minguo] *Hangzhou fuzhi* 民國杭州府志 [Republican Gazetteer of Hangzhou prefecture] 1912.

[Wanli] *Hangzhou fuzhi* 萬曆杭州府志 [Wanli Gazetteer of Hangzhou prefecture] 1579; reprinted Taibei, 1965.

Jiading

[Guangxu] *Jiading xianzhi* 光緒嘉定縣志 [Guangxu Gazetteer of Jiading county] 1885.

[Wanli] *Jiading xianzhi* 萬曆嘉定縣志 [Wanli gazetteer of Jiading county] 1605.

Jiangdu

[Guangxu] *Jiangdu xianzhi* 光緒江都縣志 [Guangxu gazetteer of Jiangdu county] 1883; 1970. Reprint Taibei.

Jiangnan

[Qianlong] *Jiangnan tongzhi* 乾隆江南通志 [Complete gazetteer of Jiangnan] 1737; 1967. Reprint: Taibei.

Jiaxing

[Kangxi] *Jiaxing fuzhi* 康熙嘉興府志 [Kangxi Gazetteer of Jiaxing prefecture] 1681.

[Wanli] *Jiaxing fuzhi* 萬曆嘉興府志 [Wanli Gazetteer of Jiaxing prefecture] 1600.

Lianghuai

[Jiaqing] *Lianghuai yanfa zhi* 嘉慶兩淮鹽法志 [Complete gazetteer of the Lianghuai salt monopoly] 1806.

[Guangxu] *Lianghuai yanfa zhi* 光緒兩淮鹽法志 [Gazetteer of the Lianghuai salt monopoly] 1905.

Qiantang

[Kangxi] *Qiantang xianzhi* 康熙錢塘縣志 [Kangxi Gazetteer of Qiantang county] 1718.

Renhe

[Kangxi] *Renhe xianzhi* 康熙仁和縣志 [Kangxi Gazetteer of Renhe county] 1687.

Shanghai

[Jiaqing] *Shanghai xianzhi* 嘉慶上海縣志 [History of Shanghai county in the Jiaqing reign] 1814; 1970. Reprint Taipei.

[Minguo] *Shanghai xianzhi* 民國上海縣志 [Republican Gazetteer of Shanghai County] 1935; 1975. Reprint Taibei.

Shanghai xu xianzhi 上海續縣志 [Continued Gazetteer of Shanghai county] 1918; 1970. Reprint Taibei.

[Tongzhi] *Shanghai xianzhi* 同治上海縣志 [Tongzhi Gazetteer of Shanghai County] 1872; 1975. Reprint Taibei.

Songjiang

[Congzhen] *Songjiang fuzhi* 崇禎松江府志 [Congzhen Gazetteer of Songjiang prefecture] 1631.

[Jiaqing] *Songjiang fuzhi* 嘉慶松江府志 [Jiaqing Gazetteer of Songjiang prefecture] 1819.

Suzhou

[Daoguang] *Suzhou fuzhi* 道光蘇州府志 [Daoguang Gazetteer of Suzhou prefecture] 1824.

[Guangxu] *Suzhou fuzhi*, 光緒蘇州府志 [Guangxu Gazetteer of Suzhou prefecture] 1883; 1960; 1970. Reprint Taibei.

[Hongwu] *Suzhou fuzhi* 洪武蘇州府志 [Hongwu Gazetteer of Suzhou Prefecture] 1379.

[Kangxi] *Suzhou fuzhi* 康熙蘇州府志 [Kangxi period gazetteer of Suzhou prefecture] 1693.

[Qianlong] *Suzhou fuzhi* 乾隆蘇州府志 [Qianlong Gazetteer of Suzhou prefecture] 1748.

[Tongzhi] *Suzhou fuzhi* 同治蘇州府志 [Tongzhi Gazetteer of Suzhou prefecture] 1875.

[Zhengde] *Gu Su zhi* 正德姑蘇志 [Gazetteer of Suzhou] 1506; 1965. Reprint Taipei.

Tongzhou

[Qianlong] *Zhili Tongzhou zhi* 乾隆直隸通州志 [Qianlong Gazetteer of Tongzhou independent sub-prefecture] 1755; 1969. Reprint Taibei.

Wu

[Chongzhen] *Wu xianzhi* 崇禎吳縣志 [Chongzhen Gazetteer of Wu county] 1643.

[Minguo] *Wu xianzhi* 民國吳縣志 [Republican Gazetteer of Wu county] 1933; 1970. Reprint, Taibei.

[Qianlong] *Wu xianzhi* 乾隆吳縣志 [Qianlong Gazetteer of Wu county] n.d. (1736–1796).

Wujiang

[Kangxi] *Wujiang xianzhi* 康熙吳江縣志 [Kangxi Gazetteer of Wujiang county] 1684.

[Qianlong] *Wujiang xianzhi* 乾隆吳江縣志 [Qianlong gazetteer of Wujiang county] 1749.

Yangzhou

[Jiajing] *Weiyang zhi* 嘉靖維揚志 [Jiajing Gazetteer of Weiyang (Yangzhou)] 1542.

[Jiaqing] *Yangzhou fuzhi* 嘉慶揚州府志 [Jiaqing Gazetteer of Yangzhou prefecture]. 1810; 1974. Reprint Taibei.

[Wanli] *Yangzhou fuzhi* 萬曆揚州府志 [Wanli Gazetteer of Yangzhou prefecture] 1603.

[Yongzheng] *Yangzhou fuzhi* 雍正揚州府志 [Yongzheng Gazetteer of Yangzhou prefecture] 1733; 1974. Reprint Taibei.

Yuanhe

[Qianlong] *Yuanhe xianzhi*, 乾隆元和縣志 [Qianlong Gazetteer of Yuanhe county] (1736- 1796).

Zhejiang

Zhejiang tongzhi 浙江通志 [Comprehensive gazetteer of Zhejiang province] 1934.

ALL OTHER WORKS

Agnew, Jean-Christophe. *Worlds Apart: the Market and the Theater in Anglo-American Thought, 1550–1750.* Cambridge: Cambridge University Press, 1986.

Balasz, Étienne. "Marco Polo in the Capital of China." In Balasz, *Chinese Civilization and Bureaucracy.* New Haven: Yale University Press, 1964, pp. 79–100.

————. "Une carte des centrès commerciaux de la Chine à la fin du XIe siècle" [A map of the commercial centers in China at the end of the eleventh century]. *Annales: économies, sociétés, civilisations* (1957) 12:4, pp. 587–593.

Bao Shichen 包世臣. "Xiahe shuili shuo" 下河水利說 [On water control in Xiahe]. In *Anwu sizhong: zhongqu yishao* 安吳四種中衢一勺 [Four works from (Mr.) Anwu: suggesting the Middle Way]. 1872; 1969. Reprint Taibei. 1:28a–30b.

Bao Yanbang 鮑彥邦. "Mingdai caoyun de xingcheng ji qi fuyi xingzhi" 明代漕運的形成及其賦役性質 [On the form of grain transport and the nature of *corvée* labor during the Ming dynasty]. *Zhongguo shehui jingji shi luncong* 中國社會經濟史論叢 1 (1981), pp. 292–351.

Bao Zhao 鮑照. *Bao Canjun jizhu* 鮑參軍集注 [Bao Canjun's collected works and commentary]. (405–466) Shanghai: Shanghai guji chubanshe, 1980.

Bergère, Marie-Claire. *The Golden Age of the Chinese Bourgeoisie.* Cambridge: Cambridge University Press, 1990.

————. "Shanghai ou l'autre Chine 1919–1949" [Shanghai or the other China 1919–1949]. *Annales* 34 (1979), pp. 1040–1064.

Bradstock, Timothy. "Ch'ing Dynasty Craft Guilds and Their Monopolies." *Qinghua xuebao*, 15, (1983), pp. 143–155.

Braudel, Fernand. *Capitalism and Material Life, 1400–1800.* trans. Miriam Kochan London: Weidenfeld and Nicolson Ltd., 1973.

————. *The Perspective of the World.* New York: Harper and Row, 1984.

————. *The Structures of Everyday Life.* New York: Harper and Row, 1981.

Buck, David. *Urban Change in China.* Madison: University of Wisconsin Press, 1977.

Buck, John Lossing. *Land Utilization in China.* New York: Paragon Reprints, 1968.

Bureau of Foreign Trade, Ministry of Industry. *China Industrial Handbooks*: *Kiangsu*. Shanghai 1933; 1973. Reprint Taipei.

Cahill, James. *Parting at the Shore*: *Chinese Painting of the Early and Middle Ming Dynasty, 1368–1580*. New York: Weatherhill, 1978.

Cao Zishou 曹自守. "Wu xian cheng tu shuo" 吳縣城圖說 [Discussion of the map of Wu county city]. In Gu Yanwu, 顧炎武 *Tianxia junguo libing shu* 天下郡國利病書 [Strengths and weaknesses of various regions of the empire] 1662. Sibu congkan ed. 1985. Reprint Shanghai.

Chan, Hok-Lam. "The Chien-wen, Yung-lo, Hung-hsi and Husan-te reigns, 1399–1435." In Mote and Twitchett, eds. *Cambridge History, Ming*. Vol. 7. Cambridge: Cambridge University Press, 1988, pp. 182–304.

Chang Sen-dou. "The Morphology of Walled Capitals." In G. William Skinner, ed., *The City in Late Imperial China*. Stanford: Stanford University Press, 1977. pp. 75–100.

Chen Zugui, ed. 陳祖檠. *Mian* 棉 [Cotton]. Part 1. Beijing: Zhonghua shuju, 1957.

Chi Ch'ao-ting. *Key Economic Areas in Chinese History*. London: Allen and Unwin, 1936.

Ch'oe Pu. *Ch'oe Pu's Diary*: *A Record of Drifting Across the Sea*. trans. John Meskill. Tucson: University of Arizona Press, 1965.

Ch'oe Pu 崔溥. "P'yohaenok" 漂海錄 [Notes on a long voyage (1488–1490)]. In *Yônhaeng nok sônjip*, 燕行錄選集 [Collection of Accounts of Missions to Beijing]. I. Seoul. Minjok munhwa mungo kanhaeghoe, 1984.

Chu Hua 褚華. *Hucheng beikao* 滬城備考 (late eighteenth century) [A Draft History of "Hu-city" (Shanghai)]. Reprint in *Shanghai zhanggu cishu* [Collection of Shanghai Historical Miscellany]. Shanghai: Shanghai tongsheshi, 1936.

———. "Mumian" 木棉 [Cotton].n.d. (late eighteenth century). Reprint in *Shanghai zhanggu cishu*. op. cit.

Ch'ü, Tung-tsu. *Local Government in China Under the Ch'ing*. Stanford: Stanford University Press, 1962.

Chuan, Han-sheng and Richard A. Kraus. *Mid-Ch'ing Rice Markets and Trade*: *An Essay in Price History*. Cambridge: Harvard University Press, 1975.

Cressey, George B. *China's Geographic Foundations*: *A Survey of the Land and its People*. New York: McGraw Hill, 1934.

————. *Land of the 500 Million*. New York: McGraw Hill, 1955.

Cui Jiaxiang 催嘉祥 "Mingwu jishi" 鳴吾紀事 [Miscelaneous Notes from the Mingwu Studio]. In *Yanyi zhilin* 鹽邑志林 [Literary Miscelany of Haiyan County]. 1623.

Da Ming Jiaqing ershi nian suici xinchou datongli 大明嘉靖二十年歲次辛丑大統曆 [Official Calendar of the Ming Dynasty for the year 1541].

Da Ming huidian 大明會典 [Collected Statutes of the Ming], including *Wanli Da Ming huidian* 萬曆大明會典 [Collected statutes of the Wanli reign]. Wanli ed., 1587; 1963. Reprint Taipei.

Da Qing huidian 大清會典 [Collected Statutes of the Qing]. Guangxu ed., 1899; 1963. Reprint Taipei. Yongzheng ed., 1732; Qinglong ed., 1764; Jiaqing ed., 1818.

Da Qing huidian shili 大清會典事例 [Precedents of the Collected Statutes of the Qing]. Guangxu ed., 1899; 1963. Reprint Taipei.

Da Qing huidian shili 大清會典事例 [Sub-statutes of the collected Statutes of the Qing]. Qianlong ed., 1764.

Da Qing Gaozong Qianlong shilu 大清高宗乾隆實錄 [Records of the reign of the Qianlong emperor of the Qing]. In *Da Qing Shilu* 大清實錄 [Records of the Qing dynasty]. Taibei: Hualian chubanshe, 1964.

Da Qing lichao shilu 大清歷朝實錄 [Veritable Records of the Qing Dynasty]. Manchuria: Guowuyuan, 1937; 1965. Reprint Taibei.

Deane, Phyllis. *The First Industrial Revolution*. 2nd ed., Cambridge: Cambridge University Press, 1979.

Dietrich, Craig. "Cotton Culture and Manufacture in Ch'ing China. In W. E. Willmott, ed. *Economic Organization in Chinese Society*. Stanford: Stanford University Press, 1972, pp. 109–135.

Ding Bin 丁賓. *Ding Qinghui gong yiji* 丁清惠公遺集 [Surviving Works of Ding Qinghui (Ding Bin)]. 1638.

Dong Fen 董份. "Yushi Dafu zuosima Zhang Gong ding Zhe bian ji" 御史大夫左司馬張公定浙變記 [Censorate Officials' Supression of the Rebellion in Zhejiang]. In Zhang Jiayin, *Julai Xiansheng ji* 居來先生集, 1594. "Appendix," 59a.

Dreyer, Edward L. *Early Ming China: A Political History 1355–1435*. Stanford: Stanford University Press, 1982.

Du Halde, J. B. *The General History of China*. London: J. Watts, 1741.

Du Li 杜黎. "Yapian zhanzheng qian Shanghai hanghui xingzhi zhi shanbian" 鴉片戰爭前上海行會性質之嬗變 ["Changes in the Character of Shanghai Guilds Prior to the Opium War"]. Paper presented at the Conference on "Sprouts of Capitalism," Nanjing, May 1981; published in *Zhongguo zibenzhuyi mengya wenti lunwenji* 中國資本主義萌芽問題論文集 [Collected discussions on the question of the "sprouts of capitalism" in China]. Nanjing: 1983, pp. 141–171. (Note: page references refer to the mss. copy.)

Du Wenzhen 杜聞貞. *Jiangsusheng renkou* 江蘇省人口 [The population of Jiangsu province]. Nanjing: Jiangsusheng renkou bianji weiyuanhui, 1984.

Elvin, Mark. "The Administration of Shanghai: 1905–1914," in Elvin and Skinner, ed., *Chinese City Between Two Worlds*. Stanford: Stanford University Press, 1974, pp. 239–262.

———. "Chinese Cities Since the Song Dynasty." In Philip Abrams and E. A. Wrigley, eds. *Towns in Societies: Essays in Economic History and Historical Sociology*. Cambridge: Cambridge University Press, 1978, pp. 79–89.

———. and Skinner, eds. *The Chinese City Between Worlds*.

———. "Market Towns and Waterways in the County of Shanghai from 1460 to 1910." In *The City in Late Imperial China*. pp. 441–473.

———. *The Pattern of the Chinese Past*. Stanford: Stanford University Press, 1973.

Fairbank, John King. *Trade and Diplomacy on the China Coast*. Cambridge: Harvard University Press, 1953.

———. *The United States and China*. 3nd ed. Cambridge: Harvard University Press, 1971.

Fan Jinmin 范金民. "Ming Qing shiqu huoyue yu Suzhou de waidi shangren" 明清時期活躍於蘇州的外地商人 [Outsider merchants sojourning in Suzhou in the Ming-Qing period]. *Zhongguo shehui jingjishi yanjiu* 中國社會經濟史研究 1989:4, pp. 39–46.

Fang Kongzhao 方孔炤. *Quan bian lue ji* 全邊略記 [Record of Protecting the boundaries]. n.d.; 1927. Reprint Beiping.

Fang Yang 方揚. *Fang Chu'an Xiansheng ji* 方初菴先生集 [Collected writings of Fang Chu'an (Fang Yang)]. 1615, 16:37b–38a.

Farmer, Edward L. *Early Ming Government: the Evolution of Dual Capitals*. Cambridge: Harvard University Press, 1976.

Farnie, D. A. *The English Cotton Industry and the World Market 1815–1896*. Oxford: Clarendon Press, 1979.

Fei Hsiao-tung (Xiaotong). *Chinese Village Close-up*. Beijing: New World Press, 1983.

———. *China's Gentry*. Chicago: University of Chicago Press, 1953.

———. "Small Towns in Northern Jiangsu." In Fei, *Rural Development in China: Prospect and Retrospect*. Chicago: University of Chicago Press, 1989.

Feng Gaomo 馮皐謨. "Cai yi hou shimin qusi bei" 蔡邑侯市民去思碑 [Text from the stele erected by citizenry to commemorate the occasion of Magistrate Cai's departure from office]. *Tianqi Haiyan xian tujing* 天啓海鹽縣圖經 [Tianqi pictorial gazetteer of Haiyan county], 1624, 6:31b–33a.

Feng Menglong 馮夢龍. *Xingshi hengyan* 醒世恆言 [Constant Words to Awaken to World]. 1627; 1986. Reprint. Beijing: Renmin wenxue chubanshe, 1956.

———. *Zengguang zhinang bu* 增廣智囊補 [Compliment of Expanding Wisdon]. n.d.; 1973. Reprint Taipei.

Feuchtwang, Stephen. "School-temple and City God." In *The City in Late Imperial China*, pp. 581–608.

Finnane, Antonia. "Bureaucracy and Responsibility: A Reassessment of the River Administration under the Qing." *Papers on Far Eastern History* 30 (September 1984).

———. "The Origins of Prejudice: the Malintegration of Subei in Late Imperial China." *Comparative Studies in Society and History*. forthcoming.

———. "Prosperity and Decline under the Qing: Yangzhou and its Hinterland, 1644–1810." Ph.D. diss. Australian National University, 1987.

Fortune, Robert. *Three Years' Wandering Among the Northern Provinces of China*. London: Murray, 1847.

———. *Two Visits to the Tea Countries of China and the British Plantations in the Himalaya*. London: Murray, 1853.

Franke, Herbert. "Chia Ssu-tao (1213–1275): 'A Bad Last Minister'?" In Arthur F. Wright and Denis Twitchett, eds., *Confucian Personalities*. Stanford: Stanford University Press, 1962, pp. 217–234.

Fu Chonglan 傅崇蘭. "Lun Ming Qing shiqi Hangzhou chengshi de fazhan" 論明清時期杭州城市的發展 [On the development of the city of Hangzhou in Ming and Qing]. In *Zhongguo shi yanjiu* 中國史研究 (1982) 4, pp. 69–79.

Fu Yiling 傅衣凌. *Mingdai Jiangnan shimin jingji shitan* 明代江南市民經

濟試探 [A preliminary study of urban dwellers in Ming-dynasty Jiangnan]. Shanghai: Renmin chubanshe, 1957.

————. *Ming-Qing nongcun shehui jingji* 明清農村社會經濟 [Rural society and economy in the Ming and Qing]. Hong Kong: Sanlian shudian, 1961.

————. *Ming Qing shidai shangren ji shangye ziben* 明清時代商人及商業資本 [Merchants and commercial capital in the Ming and Qing]. Beijing: Renmin chubanshe, 1956.

————. "Wo duiyu Mingdai zhongye yihou guyong laodong de zairenshi" 我對於明代中葉以後僱佣勞動的再認識 [My re-evaluation of wage labor after the middle Ming]. *Lishi yanjiu* 歷史研究, (1961) 3, pp. 59–78.

Fujii Hiroshi 藤井宏. "Chūgokushi ni okeru shin to kyū—shokkō tai no bunseki o meguru shomondai" 中國史における新と舊—織工對の分析をめぐる諸問題 [Old and new in Chinese history—several problems involved in the analysis of shokko tai]. *Tōyō Bunka* 東洋文化, no. 9, 1952, pp. 99–103.f

————. "Shinan shōnin no kenkyū" 新安商人の研究 [A study of the Xin'an merchants], *Tōyō gakuhō* 東洋學報 no. 36 (1953–1954), pp. 1–44, 180–208, 335–388, 533–563.

Fuma Susumu 夫馬進. "Mindai Nankin no toshi gyōsei" 明代南京の都市行政 [Urbān administration in Ming Nanjing]. In *Zen kindai ni okeru toshi to shakai sō* 前近代における都市と社會層 ed. by Nakamura Kinjirō. Kyoto: Kyoto Daigaku Jinbun Kagaku Kenkyūjo, 1980.

————. "Minmatsu han chihōkan shihen" 明末反地方官士變 [Student movements against local bureaucrats in the late Ming period]. in *Tōhō gakukō* 東方學報 no. 52. Kyoto: Kyoto Daigaku Jinbun Kagaku Kenkyūjo, 1980, pp. 601–602.f

————. "Minmatsu no toshi kaikaku to Kōshū minpen" [Late Ming urban reform and the popular uprising in Hangzhou]. *Tōhō gakukō* (Kyoto) no 49, 1977, pp. 215–272.

————. "Minmatsu Shinsho no toshi bōdō" 明末清初の都市暴動 [Urban riots in the late Ming and early Qing]. In *Chūgoku minshū hanran shi* 中國民衆叛亂史 [A history of Chinese popular uprisings], ed. Tanigawa Michio and Mori Masao. Vol IV. Tokyo: Heibonsha, 1983.

Fushe xingshi 復社姓氏. (by anonymous author). n.d. [probably seventeenth century]. Taibei: National Library, rare books collection.

Gernet, Jacques. *Daily Life in China on the Eve of the Mongol Invasion 1250–1276*. Stanford: Stanford University Press, 1962.

Goldstone, Jack A. "East and West in the Seventeenth Century: Political Crisis in Stuart England, Ottoman Turkey and Ming China." *Comparative Studies in Society and History* 30.1 (1988), pp. 103–142.

Goodrich, L. Carrington and Chaoying Fang. *Dictionary of Ming Biography, 1368–1644.* New York: Columbia University Press, 1976.

Graham, Edward D. *American Ideas of a Special Relation with China, 1784–1900.* New York: Garland Press, 1988.

Granet, Marcel. *The Religion of the Chinese People.* Trans. Maurice Freedman. Oxford: Blackwell, 1975.

Great Britain, Foreign Office Archives. London: Public Record Office, F.O. 225, F.O. 228, F.O. 747.

Greenberg, Michael. *British Trade and the Opening of China, 1800–1842.* Cambridge: Cambridge University Press, 1951.

Grimm, Tilemann. "Academies and Urban Systems in Kwangtung." in *The City in Late Imperial China*, pp. 475–498.

Guanyu Jiangning Zhizao Caojia dangan shiliao 關與江寧織造曹家檔案史料 [Archivial materials concerning the Cao family supervisors of the Nanking Imperial Factories]. Beijing: Renmin Chubanshe, 1975; 1977. Reprint Taibei.

Gujin tushu jicheng 古今圖書集成 [Synthesis of books and Illustrations Past and Present: the Imperial Encyclopaedia] 1725. 1965. Reprint Taipei.

Gu Lu 顧祿. *Wuqu fengtu lu* 吳趣風土錄 [On popular customs of Suzhou] *Xiaofanghuzhai yudi conglu.* 小方壺齋輿地叢錄. 6:35(4).

Gu Yanwu 顧炎武. "Su Song erfu tianfu zhi zhong" 蘇松二府田賦之重 [On the heaviness of the land tax in the two prefectures of Suzhou and Songjiang]. *Rizhilu Jishi* 日知錄集釋 [Collected explanations of the Record of Things Learned Daily]. Original ed., 1670—(Wanyou wenku ed.), *juan* 4, 1935–1937. Reprint. Shanghai: Shanghai Commercial Press.

———. *Tianxia junguo libing shu* 天下郡國利病書 [Strengths and Weaknesses of Various Prefectures and Districts in the Empire]. 1662. [original draft ed., n.d.] 1935; 1964. Reprint. Shanghai; Tokyo.

———. *Zhaoyuzhi, Jiangnan ba Suzhoufu* 肇域志江南八蘇州府 [Compendium of Historical Geography: Suzhou Prefecture in Jiangnan # 8], unfinished work, seventeen century.

Guochao xian zhenglu 國朝獻徵錄 [Biographies of the present dynasty [Ming]. n.d. 1965. Reprint Taibei.

Haeger, John W. "1126–1127: Political Crisis and the Integrity of Culture." In Haeger ed. *Crisis and Prosperity in Sung China*. Tucson: University of Arizona Press, 1975, pp. 143–161.

Hamashima Atsutoshi. "The Organization of Water Control in the Kiangnan Delta in the Ming Period." *Acta Asiatica* 38 (1980), pp. 69–92.

————. 濱島敦俊. *Mindai Kōnan nōson shakai no kenkyū* 明代江南農村社會の研究 [Rural society in Jiangnan during the Ming dynasty]. Tokyo: Tokyo Daigaku Shuppankai, 1982.

Hamashita, Takeshi. "Foreign Trade in China, 1810–1850." In Christian Daniels and Linda Grove, eds. *State and Society in China: Japanese Perspectives on Ming-Qing Social History*. Tokyo: University of Tokyo Press, 1984, pp. 387–435.

Hartwell, Robert M. "A Cycle of Economic Change in Imperial China: Coal and Iron in Northeast China, 750–1350." *Journal of the Economic and Social History of the Orient* 10 (1967), pp. 102–159.

————. "Demographic, Political and Social Transformations of China, 750–1550." *Harvard Journal of Asiatic Studies* 42 (1982), pp. 365–442.

————. "Review of *Man and Land in Chinese History: An Economic Analysis* by Kang Chao." *Journal of Asian Studies* 47 (1988), p. 335–336.

Hashimoto Manpei. *Nihon no jikokū seido* [The Japanese system of time]. Tokyo: Hanawa Shobō 1966.

He Bingdi 何炳棣. *Zhongguo huiguan shilun* 中國會館史論 [An historical survey of landsmannschaften in China]. Taibei: Xuesheng shuji, 1966.

He Canran 賀燦然. *Liuyu xuan chugao* 六欲軒初藁 [Preliminary drafts from the Liuyu Studio]. 1608.

He Liangjun 何良俊. *Siyou zhai congshuo* 四友齋叢說 [Collected dissertation from the studio of the four friends] 1569–1579; 1959. Reprint Beijing.

Hechter, Michael. *Internal Colonialism: the Celtic Fringe in British National Development, 1536–1966*. Berkeley: University of California Press, 1975.

Hedde, Isidore. *Description methodique des produits divers*, [Organized description of various products]. Paris: Saint-Étienne, 1848.

Hershatter, Gail. *The Workers of Tianjin, 1900–1949*. Stanford: Stanford University Press, 1986.

Hinton, Harold C. *The Grain Tribute System of China: 1845–1911*. Cambridge: Harvard University Press, 1956.

Ho, Ping-ti. *The Ladder of Success in Imperial China*. New York: Science Editions, 1964.

————. "The Salt Merchants of Yang-chou: A Study of Commercial Capitalism in Eighteenth-Century China," *Harvard journal of Asiatic Studies* 17 (1954), pp. 130–168.

————. *Studies on the Population of China, 1368–1953*. Cambridge: Harvard University Press, 1959.

Hohenberg, Paul, and Lynn Hollen Lees. *The Making of Urban Europe, 1000–1950*. Cambridge: Harvard University Press, 1985.

Hommel, Rudolf P. *China at Work: An Illustrated Record of the Primitive Industries of China's Masses, whose life is toil, and thus an account of Chinese civilization*. New York: 1937; 1969. Reprint. Cambridge Mass.: M.I.T. Press.

Honig, Emily. "The Politics of Prejudice: Subei People in Republican Era Shanghai." *Modern China*. Vol. 15, no. 3 (July 1989), pp. 243–274.

————. "Pride and Prejudice: Subei People in Contemporary Shanghai." In Perry Link, Richard Madsen, and Paul G. Pickowicz, eds. *Unofficial China: Popular Culture and Thought in the People's Republic*. Boulder: Westview Press, 1989, pp. 138–155.

————. *Sisters and Strangers: Women in the Shanghai Cotton Mills, 1919–1949*. Stanford: Stanford University Press, 1986.

Hong Huanchun 洪煥春. "Lun Ming Qing Suzhou diqu huiguan de xingzhi jiqi zuoyong" 論明清蘇州地區會館的性質及其作用 [On the nature and functions of guilds in Suzhou during the Ming and Qing (dynasties)]. *Zhongguoshi yanjiu*, 1980, vol. 2, pp. 3–15.

————. "Lun Ming Qing Suzhou diqu zibenzhuyi mengya chubu kaocha 論明清蘇州地區資本主義萌芽初步考慮 [Discussion of the "Sprouts of Capitalism" in the Suzhou region during the Ming and Qing period]. In *Ming Qing zibenzhuyi mengya yangjiu luwenji* 明清資本主義萌芽研究論文集 [Collected Discussions of Research in the "Sprouts of Capitalism" in the Ming and Qing period]. Shanghai: Renmin chubanshe, 1981.

Hoselitz, Bert. "Generative and Parasitic Cities." *Economic Development and Cultural Change* 3:3 (1955), pp. 78–94.

Hou Han Shu 後漢書 [History of the Late Han]. Beijing: Zhonghua shuju, 1971.

Hsi, Angela Ning-jy. "Social and Economic Status of the Merchant Class of the Ming Dynasty, 1368–1644." Ph.D diss. University of Illinois, 1972.

Hsiao, Ch'-ch'ing. *The Military Establishment of the Yuan Dynasty*. Cambridge: Harvard East Asia Monograph, 1978.

Hsiao Kung-chuan. *Rural China: Imperial Control in the Nineteenth Century*. Seattle: University of Washington Press, 1972.

Hu Huanyong 胡煥庸. *Lianghuai shuili* 兩淮水利 [Water control in the Lianghuai region]. Nanjing: Zhongzhong shuju, 1947.

Huangchao jingshi wenbian 皇朝經世文編 [Dynastic Memorials on Statecraft] 1826; 1964. Reprint Taipei.

Huangchao yudi tongkao, 皇朝輿地通考 [General examination of Imperial territory] n.d.

Huang Huchen 黃戶臣. "Qingdai qianqi haiwai maoyi de fazhan" 清代前期海外貿易的發展 [The development of foreign commerce in the early Qing]. *Lishi Yanjiu* no. 4, (1986) pp. 151–170.

Huang Junzai 黃鈞宰. *Jinhu langmo* 金壺浪墨 [Desultory writings from the golden inkpot] in *Jinhu qimo* 金壺七墨 [Seven writings from the golden inkpot]. c. 1873; Shanghai: Saoye shanfang, 1929.

Huang Ming zhishu 皇明制書 [Imperial Ming Laws]; 1967. Reprint. Tokyo: Kotenkenkyukai.

Huang Ming tiaofashi liezuan 皇明條法事類纂 [Imperial Ming Legal Code]. 1966. Reprint. Tokyo: Kotenkenyukai.

Huang, Philip. *The Peasant Family and Rural Development in the Yangzi Delta, 1350–1988*. Stanford: Stanford University Press, 1990.

Huang, Ray. "The Grand Canal during the Ming dynasty." Ph.D. diss. University of Michigan, 1964.

———. *Taxation and Governmental Finance in Sixteenth-Century Ming China*. Cambridge: Cambridge University Press, 1974.

Huang Ruheng 黃汝亨. "Sichuan anchasi jianshi Shen Gong xingzhuan" 四川按察司僉事沈公行狀 [Biography of Shen (Pian)'s activities as an official in Sichuan] in *Yulin ji* 寓林集 [Notes from the (Master) of the "Yulin" (Studio) [e.g. Huang Ruheng]]. 1624, 17:24a–25b.

Hucker, Charles O. *A Dictionary of Official Titles in Imperial China*. Stanford: Stanford University Press, 1985.

———. "Su-chou and the agents of Wei Chung-hsien." In *Silver Jubilee Volume of the Zinbun-kagaku-kenkyusyo. Kyoto*: Kyoto University, 1954, pp. 224–256.

————. *Two Studies on the Ming.* Ann Arbor: University of Michigan Press, 1971.

Hummel, Arthur W. *Eminent Chinese of the Ch'ing Period, 1644–1912.* Washington: United States Government Printing Office, 1943.

Iwami Hiroshi 岩見宏. *Mindai yōeki seido no kenkyū* 明代徭役制度の研究 [Studies on the Statute Labor System in the Ming Dynasty]. Kyoto: Dōhōsha, 1986.

Ji Zhongqing 紀中慶. "Yangzhou gucheng zhi bianqian chutan" 揚州 古城址變遷初探 [Preliminary investigation of changes in the foundations of the ancient city of Yangzhou]. *Wenwu* 文物 no. 9:1979, pp. 43–56.fi

Jiang Liangdong 姜良棟. *Zhen Wu lu* 鎮吳錄 [Record of pacification in Wu (county) (Suzhou)]. n.d. probably Wanli period.

Jiangsu sheng Ming Qing yilai beike ziliao xuanji 江蘇省明清以來碑刻資 料選集 [Selected Inscriptions (from) stele in Jiangsu in the Ming and Qing periods]. Nanjing: Sanlian shudian, 1956.

Jiao Xun 焦循. *Yangzhou Beihu xiaozhi* 揚州北湖小志 [Little gazetteer of Beihu and Yangzhou]. 1808; 1983. Reprint: Taibei.

Jinpingmei cihua 金瓶梅詞話 [Notes and commentaries on the *Jin Ping Mei*]. n.d.; 1986. Reprint. Hong Kong: China Book Press.

Jinshen quanshu 縉紳全書 [Complete guide to officials]. Beijing: 1855.

Johnson, David, "The City-God Cults of T'ang and Sung China." *Harvard Journal of Asiatic Studies*, 45 (1985), pp. 363–457.

Johnson, E. A. J. *The Organization of Space in Developing Countries.* Cambridge: Harvard University Press, 1970.

Johnson, Linda Cooke, *Shanghai: from Market-town to Treaty Port 1274–1858.* Stanford: Stanford University Press, forthcoming.

Jones, Susan Mann, "The Ningpo Pang and Financial Power in Shanghai." In Elvin and Skinner, eds. *The Chinese City Between Two Worlds*, pp. 73–96.

————. "Finance in Ningpo: the *Ch'ien-chuang*, 1750–1880." In W. E. Willmott, ed., *Economic Organization in Chinese Society.* Stanford: Stanford University Press, 1972, pp. 47–77.

Jones, Susan Mann, and Philip Kuhn. "Dynastic decline and the roots of rebellion." In Fairbank and Twichett, eds. *Cambridge History* 10.1 "Late Ch'ing," Cambridge: Cambridge University Press, 1978, pp. 107–162.

Kang, Chao. *The Development of Cotton Textile Production in China.* Cambridge: Harvard University Press, 1977.

Ke Rulin 柯汝霖. "Wulin dizhai kao" 武林第宅攷 [Notes on homes in Wulin (Hangzhou)]. In *Wulin Zhanggu congbian* 武林掌故叢編 [Collected anecdotes on Wulin (Hangzhou)]. XII 1889, 7b–8a.

Kessler, Lawrence. *K'ang-hsi and the consolidation of Ch'ing Rule, 1661–1684.* Chicago and London: University of Chicago, 1976.

King, Anthony D. "Colonial Cities: Global Pivots of Change." In Robert J. Ross and Gerard J. Telkamp, eds. *Colonial Cities.* Dordrecht: Martinus Jijhof Publishers, 1985.

Kitamura Hironao. 北村敬直. "Minmatsu Shinsho ni okeru jinushi ni tsuite" 明末、清初における地主について [On landlords in the late Ming and early Qing]. *Rekishigaku kenkyū* 歷史學研究 140 (1949). This was later included in Kitamura's *Shindai shakai keizaishi kenkyū* 清代社會經濟史研究 [Studies in Qing socio-economic history]. Kyoto: Ōsaka Shiritsu Daigaku Keizai Gakkai, 1972, pp. 18–49.

Ko, Dorothy Yin-yee. *Toward a Social History of Women in Seventeenth Century China.* Ph.D. diss. Stanford University 1989.

Kojima Yoshio 小島淑男. "Shinmatsu Minkokushoki Soshūfu no kinuorigyō to kiko no dōkō" 清末民國初期蘇州府の絹織業と機戶の動向 [Silk industry and Weavers' movement in Suzhoufu in late Ming and early Qing]. *Shakai keizai shigaku,* 社會經濟史學 34:5, (1969), pp. 32–54.

Kracke, Edward A. Jr. "Sung K'ai-feng: Pragmatic Metropolis and Formalistic Capital." In Haeger ed. *Crisis and Prosperity in Sung China,* pp. 49–77.

Kuhn, Philip. "Political Crime and Bureaucratic Monarchy: a Chinese Case of 1768." *Late Imperial China,* (1987) 8:1, pp. 80–104.

Lanning, George, and Samuel Couling. *The History of Shanghai. Part I.* Shanghai: Kelly & Walsh, 1921.

LeFevor, Edward. *Western Enterprise in Late Ch'ing China: A Selected Survey of Jardine, Matheson and Company's Operations.* Cambridge: Harvard University Press, 1968.

Legge, James. *The Chinese Classics. The Ch'un Ts'ew with the Tso Chuen.* Vol. 5. Oxford: the Clarendon Press, 1865–95; 1960. Reprint: Hong Kong.

Levy, Howard. *A Feast of Mist and Flowers: the Gay Quarters at Nanking at the end of the Ming.* Yokohama: n.p., 1967.

Li Cheng 李澄. *Huaizuo beiyao* 淮鹺備要 [Essentials of the Huainan Salt Trade]. 1823.

Li Dou 李斗. *Yangzhou huafang lu* 揚州畫肪錄 [An account of Yangzhou's pleasure craft]. c. 1795. Taibei: Shiji shuju, 1963.

Li E 厲鶚. "Dongcheng zaji" 東城雜記 [Miscellaneous notes on the Eastern Capital (Hangzhou)]. In "Zhicheng shi jing tu" 織成十景圖 [Views/maps of the city]. 1728; *Wulin Zhanggu Congbian*, VI 1881.

Li Shixu. 李世序 ed. *Xuxingshui jinjian* 續行金水鑒 [The golden mirror of waterway inspection, continued]. 1832; 1936. Reprint. Shanghai.

Liang Fangzhong 梁方仲. *Zhongguo lidai hukou tiandi tianfu tongji* 中國歷代戶口田地田賦統計 [Statistics on population, cultivated area and the land tax throughout Chinese history]. Shanghai: Shanghai renmin chubanshe, 1980.

Liang Gengyao 梁庚堯. "Song Yuan shidai de Suzhou" 宋元時代的蘇州 [Suzhou in the Song and Yuan period]. *Wenshizhe xuebao* 文史哲學報 31 (1982), pp. 223–325.

Liao Zhihao 廖志豪. Zhang Hu 張鵠, Ye Wanzhong 葉萬忠 and Pu Boliang 浦伯良. *Suzhou Shihua* 蘇州史話 [Historical talks on Suzhou]. Nanjing: Jiangsu renmin chubanshe, 1980.

Lieberthal, Kenneth. *Revolution and Tradition in Tientsin, 1949–52*. Stanford: Stanford University Press, 1980.

Lin Jinshu 林金樹. "Shilun Mingdai Su Song erfu de zhongfu wenti" 試論明代蘇松二府的重賦問題 [Concerning the question of heavy taxes in the two prefectures of Suzhou and Songjiang during the Ming]. *Mingshi yanjiu luncong* 明史研究論叢 1 (1982), pp. 91–123.

Lin Zexu 林則徐. *Lin Wenzhong gong zhengshu, Jiaji: Jiangsu zougao* 林文忠公政書：甲集江蘇奏稿 [Memorials of Lin Zexu, first collection, Jiangsu]. 1966. Reprint: Taibei.

Lindsay, Hugh H. and Karl Gutzlaff, "Amherst expedition." Vol. II. *Chinese Repository* (1834), pp. 549–552.

Liu Shih-chi. "Some Reflections on Urbanization and the Historical Development of Market Towns in the Lower Yangtze Region, ca. 1500–1900." *American Asian Review*: 1 (1984), pp. 1–27.

Liu Shiji 劉石吉. "Ming Qing shidai Jiangnan diqu de zhuanye shizhen," 明清時代江南地區的專業市鎮 [Specialized market-towns in Jiangnan in the Ming and Qing periods]. *Shihuo* 食貨 8, (1978), pp. 326–337.

————. *Ming-Qing shidai Jiangnan shizhen yanjiu* 明清時代江南市鎮研究 [A study of market towns in Ming and Qing Jiangnan]. Beijing: Zhongguo shehui kexue chubanshe, 1987.

Liu Yan 劉炎. "Mingmo chengshi jingji fazhan xia de chuqi shimin yundong" 明末城市經濟發展下的初期市民運動 [The early city residents' movements under the development of the urban economy in the late Ming]. In *Zhongguo ziben zhuyi mengya wenti taolun ji* 中國資本主義萌芽問題討論集 [Collected Essays Discussing the 'Sprouts of Capitalism' Issue]. Vol. I. Beijing: Sanlian Shudian, 1957.

Liu Yongcheng 劉永成. "Lun Qingdai guyong laodong" 論清代僱佣勞動 [Wage labor in the Qing period]. *Lishi yanjiu*, 1962, 4, pp. 104–128.

————. "Shilun Qingdai Suzhou shou gongye hanghui" 試論清代蘇州手工業行會 ["A Discussion of Handicraft Guilds in Qing dynasty Suzhou"]. *Lishi Yanjiu* 歷史研究. Vol. 25. (1959), pp. 21–46.

Liu Yung-ch'eng (Yongcheng). "The Handicraft Guilds in Soochow during the Ch'ing Dynasty." *Chinese Studies in History* 15 (1981–82), pp. 113–167.

Liu Zhiqin 劉志琴. "Shilun Wanli minbian" 試論萬曆民變 [A Discussion of Popular Uprisings in the Wanli reign-period]. In *Ming Qingshi guoji xueshu taolunhui lunwen ji* 明清史國際學術討論會論文集 [Collected essays from an International symposium on Ming and Qing historical issues]. Tianjin: Tianjin renmin chubanshe, 1982, pp. 678–697.

Lo Jung-pang. "The Controversy over Grain Conveyance during the reign of Qubilai Qaqan, 1260–1294." *Far Eastern Quarterly*. Vol 13, no. 3 (May 1954), pp. 263–285.

————. "Maritime Commerce and the Sung Navy." *Journal of the Economic and Social History of the Orient* 12 (1969), pp. 57–101.

Lombard-Salmon, Claudine. *Une exemple d'acculturation chinoise: la province du Gui zhou au XVIIIe siecle* [A case of Chinese acculturation: Guizhou province in the eighteenth century]. Paris: Ecôle francaise d'Extreme-Orient, 1972.

Lösch, August. "The Nature of Economic Regions." *Southern Economic Journal* 5 (1938), pp. 71–78.

Lu Ben 呂本. *Dufu Liangzhe dingbian yusong lu* 督撫兩浙定變輿頌錄 [Preface to the Record of Supressing Rebellion in Zhejiang]. In Zhang Jiayin, *Julai Xiansheng ji*, 1594, appendix.

Lu Guangzhu 陸光祖. "Zeng Zuosima Zhang Julai Huanchao Xu" 贈左司馬張崌峽還朝序 [Recollections of Zhang Julai]. In *Lu Zhuangjian*

Gong Yi Gao 陸莊簡公遺稿 [Posthumous writings of Lu Zhuangjian (Guangzhu)]. 1629.

Lu Kun 呂坤. *Quwei zhai quanji, jiku tiaochen*, 去偽齋全集, 疾苦條陳 [Complete Works from the Quwei Studio], 1889.

————. *Shizheng lu* 實政錄 [A Record of Practical Statecraft]. 1889.

Lu Shiyi 陸世儀. 'Su-Song fuliang kao" 蘇松浮糧考 [Examination of the excessive taxes in kind in Suzhou and Songjiang]. In *Lu Futing xiansheng yishu* 陸桴亭先生遺書 [Posthumous works of Lu Futing]. Beijing. 1889, *juan*, 19.

Lu Shusheng 陸樹聲, *Lu Wending gong ji* 陸文定公集 [Collected works of Lu Wending (Lu Shusheng)]. 1616.

Luo Yaojiu 羅耀九. "Mingdai zhongye de guyong laodong shi zibenzhuyi xingzhi de ma?" 明代中葉的僱傭勞動是資本主義性質的嗎 [Has the wage labor of the mid-Ming period a capitalistic nature?]. *Lishi yanjiu*, 1961:1, pp. 55–73.

Lü Zuoxie 呂作燮. "Shilun Ming qing shiqu huiguan de xingzhi he zuoyong" 試論明清時期會館的性質和作用 [Appraisal of the nature and functions of native-place associations in the Ming and Qing periods]. *Zhongguo zhiben zhuyi mengya wenti lunwenji*. Nanjing: 1983, pp. 172–211.

Mackerras, Colin. "The Theatre in Yang-chou in the Eighteenth Century." *Papers on Far Eastern History*. 1 (March 1970), pp. 1–30.

Mann, Susan. "Brokers as Entrepreneurs in Presocialist China." *Comparative Studies in Society and History*, Vol. 25, no. 4 (October 1984), pp. 614–636.

————. *Local Merchants and the Chinese Bureaucracy, 1750–1950*. Stanford: Stanford University Press, 1987.

Mao Kun 茅坤. *Mao lumen xiansheng wenji* 茅鹿門先生文集 [Collected Writings of Mao Lumen (Kun)]. n.d.

Marmé, Michael. "From Rout to Hegemony: Suzhou 1368–1550." Ph.D. doctoral diss. U.C. Berkeley, 1986.

————. "Population and Possibility in Ming (1368–1644) Suzhou: a Quantified Model." *Ming Studies* 12 (Spring 1981), pp. 29–64.

Martini, M. *Novus Atlas Sinensis*. Amsterdam: Blaeu, 1655.

Mayers, William Frederick, N.B. Dennys and Charles King. *The Treaty Ports of China and Japan*. N.B. Dennys ed. London: Trubner and Co. Hong Kong: A Shortrede and Co., 1867; 1977. Reprint: San Francisco.

Metzger, Thomas A. "T'ao Chu's Reform of the Huaipei Salt Monopoly (1832–1833)." *(Harvard) Papers on China*. 16 (1962), pp. 1–39.

Miller, David B., "Monumental Building as an Indicator of Economic Trends in Northern Rus'. In the Late Kievian and Mongol Periods, 1138–1462." *The American Historical Review*, Vol. 94, no. 2 (April 1989), pp. 360–390.

Ming huiyao 明會要 [Important documents of the Ming]. 1887. 1972. Reprint: Taibei.

Ming Qing shiliao 明清史料 [Documents of the Ming and Qing]. Shanghai. Commercial Press, 1930–1936.

Ming Qing Suzhou gongshangye beike ji 明清蘇州工商業碑刻集 [Collected inscriptions on handicraft industries in Suzhou in the Ming and Qing periods]. Nanjing: Jiangsu renmin chubanshe, 1981.

Ming Shi 明史 [History of the Ming Dynasty] 1739; 1974. Reprint: Beijing.

Ming Shilu 明實錄 [Veritables Records of the Ming], including: *Shenzong shilu* 神宗實錄 [Veritable records of the Shenzong reign]. *Xuanzong shilu* 宣宗實錄 [Veritable Records of the Xuanzong reign]. *Ming Xizong shilu* 明熹宗實錄 [Veritable Records of the Xizong reign] cited separately. 1940. 1962–1967. Reprint: Taibei.

Mitchell, B. R., *European Historical Statistics 1750–1975*. 2nd ed. New York. Facts on File, 1980.

Miyazaki Ichisada 宮崎市定. "Mindai So-Shō chihō no shi dai fu to min shū—Mindai shi sobyō no kokoromi" 明代蘇松地方の士大夫と民衆—明代史素描の試 [The literati and the masses in the Suzhou-Songjiang region during the Ming—a preliminary study of Ming history]. *Shirin* 史林 37.3 (1954), pp. 1–33.

———. "Minshinjidai no Soshū to keikōkyō no hattatsu" 明清時代の蘇州と輕工業の發達 [Development of light industry in Suzhou in the Ming and Qing periods]. *Ajia shi kenkyū* アジア史研究 no. 4, (1975), pp. 306–319. [Earlier version by same title in *Tōhō gakuhō* 1951:70 pp. 64–73.]

Mokyr, Joel. *The Economics of the Industrial Revolution*. Great Britain: Rowman and Allanheld, 1988.

Mori Masao 森正夫. "Jūroku seiki Taiko shūhen chitai ni okeru kanden seido no kaikaku" 十六世紀太湖周邊地帶における官田度の改革 [Reform of the official field system in the Lake Tai region during the sixteenth century]. *Tōyōshi kenkyū*, 東洋史研究 21.4 (1963) pp. 58–92, 22.1 (1963) pp. 67–87.

————. *Mindai Kōnan tochi seido no kenkyū* 明代江南土地制度の研究 [A Study of the Land System in Jiangnan during the Ming dynasty]. Kyoto: Dōhōsha, 1988.

————. "Minsho Konan no kanden ni tsuite" 明初江南の官田について [On official fields in early Ming Jiangnan]. *Tōyōshi kenkyū* 19 (1960–1961), pp. 315–336, 433–450.

Mote, Frederick W. "A Millennium of Chinese Urban History: Form, Time and Space concepts in Soochow." *Rice University Studies* 59 (1973), pp. 35–65.

————. *The Poet Kao Ch'i, 1336–1374.* Princeton: Princeton University Press, 1962.

————. "The Transformation of Nanking, 1350–1400." In Skinner, ed. *City in Late Imperial China.* pp. 101–154.

Mui, Hoh-cheung and Loma H. Mui. *The Management of Monopoly: A Study of the English East India Company's Conduct of Its Tea Trade, 1784–1833.* Vancouver: University of British Columbia Press, 1984.

Murphey, Rhoads. *The Outsiders.* Ann Arbor: University of Michigan Press, 1970.

————. *Shanghai, Key to Modern China.* Cambridge: Harvard University Press, 1953.

[Nagel's] China. Geneva: Nagel Publishers, 1973.

Nakayama Hachirō 中山八郎. "Mindai no shokusenkyoku" 明代の織染局 [Imperial Textile Manufactures in the Ming]. *Hitotsubashi ronsō* 一橋論叢 9:5, (1948), pp. 479–502.

Nakayama Mio 中山美緒. "Shindai senki Kōnan no bukka dōkō" 清代前期江南の物價動向 [Price trends in Jiangnan in the early Qing]. *Tōyōshi kenkyū*, 東洋史研究 Vol. 37, no. 4, (1979), pp. 77–106.

Nanjing bowuyuan 南京博物院. "Yangzhou gucheng 1978 nian diaocha fajue jianbao" 揚州古城1978年調查發掘簡報 [Brief report on the 1978 investigation and excavation of the ancient city of Yangzhou]. *Wenwu* 9:1979. pp. 33–42.

Nishijima Sadao 西島定生. *Chūgoku keizai shi kenkyū* 中國經濟史研究 [Studies in the History of the Chinese Economy]. Tokyo: Tokyo Daigaku Shuppankai, 1966.

North, Douglass. "Location Theory and Regional Economic Growth," *Journal of Political Economy* 6:3 (1955), pp. 243–258.

(Oliphant, Laurence) L. B. O. "Excursion to the City of Suchau," In *Chinese Repository*, (1845), 14, pp. 584–87.

———. *Narrative of the Earl of Elgin's Mission to China and Japan in the years 1857, 1858, 1859.* Edinburgh: Blackwood, 1859.

Pan Junxiang 潘君祥 and Chen Liyi 陳立儀. "Shijiu shiji houpanqi Shanghai shangye de yanbian," 十九世紀後半期上海商業的演變 [Evolution of Shanghai Commerce in the Late nineteenth century]. *Lishi Yanjiu*, no. 1 1986, pp. 154–165.

Peng Zeyi 彭澤益. "Cong Mingdai guanying zhizao de jingying fangshi kan Jiangnan sizhiye shengchan de xingzhi" 從明代官營織造的經營紡絲看 江南絲織業生產的性質 [The managerial pattern of the state-owned textile industry and the character of silk textile production in Ming dynasty Jiangnan]. In *Ming Qing zibenzhuyi mengya yanjiu lunwenji* 明清資本主 義萌芽研究論文集 [Essays investigating the shoots of capitalism in the Ming and Qing]. Shanghai: Shanghai renmin chubanshe, 1981, pp. 307–344.

———. "Qingdai qianqi Jiangnan zhizao de yanjiu" 清代前期江南織造的研究 [Study of textile manufacture in Jiangnan in the early Qing]. *Lishi Yanjiu*, 1963, 4, pp. 91–116.

———. "Yapien zhanzhang qian Guangzhou xinxing de qingfang gongyeh" 鴉片戰爭前廣州新興的輕紡工業 [New prosperity in the light weaving industry in Guangzhou before the Opium War]. *Lishi Yanjiu*, 1983:3, pp. 109–116.

———. "Zhigong dui shiliao nengshuoming Zhongguo shougongye zibenzhuyi mengya de wenti ma?" "織工對"史料能說明中國手工業資本主義萌芽的 問題嗎? [Zhigong dui, on the problem of whether this material can explain the rise of handicraft industry leading to the development of the "sprouts of capitalism" in China." In *Zhongguo zibenzhuyi mengya wenti taolun ji* 中國資本主義萌芽問題討論集 [Collected essays on the "Sprouts of Capitalism" Issue]. Vol. 2 (sequel). Beijing: Sanlian shudian, 1960, pp. 430–456.

———. ed. *Zhongguo jindai shougongye shi ziliao* 中國近代手工業史資料 [Source Materials on the history of handicraft industry in Modern China]. Beijing: Zhonghua shuju, 1962.

Perdue, Peter C. "Official Goals and Local Interests: Water Control in the Dongting Lake Region during the Ming and Qing Periods." *Journal of Asian Studies* 41.4 (1982), pp. 747–765.

Perkins, Dwight H. *Agricultural Development in China (1368–1968)*. Chicago: Aldine Press, 1969.

Peterson, Willard. "The Life of Ku Yen-wu (1613–1682)." *Harvard Journal of Asiatic Studies*, 28, (1968) pp. 14–56; 29 (1969) pp. 201–247.

Polanyi, Karl "The Economy as Instituted Process." In Polanyi, Canrad M. Arensberg and Harry W. Pearson, eds. *Trade and Market in the Early Empires: Economies in History and Theory.* Glencoe, Illinois: the Free Press, 1957.

Polo, Marco. *Travels of Marco Polo.* [the Marsden translation]. New York: Dell, 1961.

Qian Yong 錢泳. *Lüyuan conghua* 履園叢話 [Collected talks on roaming through gardens] 1838. Suzhou: Zhenxin shushe, 1870.

Qian Youwei 錢有威. "Da sima Zhang Gong jinglue Zhe zhen minbian zhuan" 大司馬張公經略浙鎮民變傳 [Chronicle of General Zhang's successful supression of the popular uprising in Zhejiang city (Hangzhou)]. In *Julai Xiansheng ji*, 1594, "Appendix."

Qianlong zhupi yuzhi 乾隆硃批諭旨 [Imperial endorsements and edicts of the Qianlong reign].

Qiao Shuming 譙樞銘. "Qinglong zhen de chengshuai yu Shanghai de xingqi" 青龍鎮的盛衰與上海的興起 [Height and Decline of Qinglong Market-town and the Rise of Shanghai"]. In Wang Pengcheng et alia. *Shanghai Shi Yanjiu*, pp. 37–42.

Qingchao tongdian 清朝通典 [Collected Statutes of the Qing dynasty]. Shitong ed. Shanghai: Shangwu yinshuguan, 1935: 1963. Reprint: Taipei.fi

Qingchao wenxian tongkao 清朝文獻通考 [General history of the Institutions and critical examination of documents and studies of the Qing dynasty]. 1747: 1958, 1963. Reprint: Taibei.

Qu Fu 屈復. "Yangzhou Dongyuan ji" 揚州東園記 [Account of Yangzhou's "Eastern Garden"]. In *Zhao, Pingshantang tuzhi* eighteenth century; 9: 21b–22a.

Qu Jiusi 瞿九思. *Wanli wugong lu* 萬曆武功錄 [Record of military engagements in the Wanli period]. 1612. 1980. Reprint: Taibei.

Quan Hansheng 全漢昇. "Qingdai Suzhou de chuaibuye" 清代蘇州的踹布業 [Calendaring in Suzhou during the Qing dynasty]. *Xin Ya xuebao* 新亞學報. 13, (1975) pp. 409–436.

———. *Tang Song diguo yu yunhe* 唐宋帝國與運河 [The Tang and Song Empires and the Grand Canal]. Shanghai: Academia Sinica, 1946.

———. "Tang Song shidai Yangzhou jingji jingkuang de fanrong yu shuailuo" 唐宋時代揚州經濟景況的繁榮與衰落 [Economic prosperity and decline in

Yangzhou during the Tang and Song periods]. In *Guoli Zhongyang yanjiuyuan lishi yuyan yanjiusuo jikan* 國立中央研究院歷史語言研究所集刊 1974:11, pp. 149–174.

———. "Yapian zhanzheng yiqian Jiangsu de mianfang zhiye" 鴉片戰爭以前江蘇的棉紡織業 [The Cotton Spinning and Weaving Industry in Kiangsu prior to the Opium War]. *Tsing Hua Journal of Chinese Studies*, New series, I:3 (September 1958) pp. 1–45.

Rawski, Evelyn S. *Agricultural Change and the Peasant Economy of South China*. Cambridge: Harvard University Press, 1972.

Renmin University historical research group, ed. *Zhongguo fengjian jingji guanxi de rogan wenti* 中國封建經濟関係的若干問題 [Some problems concerning feudal economic relations in China]. Beijing: Sanlian shudian, 1958.

Ringrose, David R. "Madrid and the Castilian Economy." *Journal of European Economic History* 10:1 (1981), pp. 481–490.

Rowe, William T. *Hankow: Commerce and Society in a Chinese City, 1796–1889*. Stanford: Stanford University Press, 1984.

———. *Hankow: Conflict and Community in a Chinese City, 1796–1895*. Stanford: Stanford University Press, 1989.

Rozman, Gilbert. *Urban Networks in Ch'ing China and Tokugawa Japan*. Princeton: Princeton University Press, 1973.

Ruan Yuan 阮元. *Yanjingshi zaixuji* 研經室再續集 [Collected writings from the Yanjing Studio, continued] c. 1844. (bound with *Yangjing shi ji* 研經室集.

Saeki Yuichi 佐伯有一. "Senroppyakuichi nen shokuyō no hen o meguru shomondai" 一六〇一年織傭之變をめぐる諸問題 [Problems concerning the 1601 textile workers' rebellion]. *Tōyō bunka kenkyūjo kiyō* 東洋文化研究所集要, 45 (1968), pp. 77–108.

———. "Minzen hanki no kiko—ō chōkenryoku ni yoru shō aku o megutte" 明前半期の機戸王朝權力による学梶をめぐつて [Textile families in the first half of the Ming dynasty]. *Tōyō bunka kenkyūjo kiyō*. Vol. 8, (1956), pp. 167–210.

Santangelo, Paolo. "The Imperial Factories of Suzhou: Limits and Characteristics of State Intervention during the Ming and Qing dynasties." In Stuart Schram, ed. *The Scope of State Power in China*. Hong Kong: St. Martin's Press, 1985, pp. 269–294.

Schoppa, R. Keith. *Xiang Lake—Nine Centuries of Chinese Life*. New Haven: Yale University Press, 1989.

Scott, William Henry. "Yangzhou and its Eight Eccentrics." In Scott. *Hollow Ships on a Wine-dark Sea and other essays*. Quezon City: New Day Publishers, 1976, pp. 53–68.

Shang Yue 尚鉞. "Qingdai qianqi Zhongguo shehui de tingzhi, bianhua, he fazhan" 清代前期中國社會的停止變化和發展 [Stagnation, change and development in Chinese Society in the early Qing]. In *Zhongguo zibenzhuyi mengya wenti taolunji*. Nanjing: 1983, pp. 160–237.

Shanghai beike ciliao xuanji 上海碑刻資料選輯 [Collected carved inscriptions from Shanghai]. Shanghai: Shanghai Bowuguan, 1980.

Shanghai daguan zeli 上海大關則例 [Handbook of the Main Shanghai Customhouse]. Shanghai: Jianghai Guan (Hubu), 1785.

Shanghai qianzhuang shiliao 上海錢庄史料 [Historical Materials on Shanghai *qianzhuang* (banks)]. 2nd ed. 1978. Shanghai: Shanghai renmin chubanshe 1960.

Shen Defu 沈德符. *Wanli yehuo bian* 萬曆野獲編 [Collection of informal notes of the the Wanli era] 1619. 1959. Reprint Beijing.

Shen Guoyuan 沈國元. *Huang Ming congxin lu* 皇明從信錄 [Reliable Record of the Ming dynasty]. 1627, juan 35.

Shen Shixing 申時行. "Lunfei jiandu" 綸扉簡牘 [Correspondence from the Grand Secretarait]. In *Shen Wending gong ji* 申文定公集 [Collected works of Shen Wending (Shen Shixing)]. n.d., 1:70b, 1:74b.

Shepherd, John R. "Rethinking Tenancy: Explaining Spatial and Temporal Variation in Later Imperial and Republican China." *Comparative Studies in History and Society*, 30.3, (1988), pp. 403–431.

Shi Minxiong 施敏雄. *Qingdai sizhigongye de fazhan* 清代絲織工業的發展 [The development of the silk industry in the Qing period]. Taibei: Taixian Commercial Press, 1968.

Shiba Yoshinobu. *Commerce and Society in Sung China*. Ann Arbor: Center for Chinese Studies, 1970.

———. "Ningpo and Its Hinterland." in Skinner, ed. *The City in Late Imperial China*, pp 391–440.

———. 斯波義信 *Sōdai Kōnan keizaishi no kenkyū* 宋代江南経済史の研究 [A study of the economic history of Song-dynasty Jiangnan]. Tōkyō: Tōyō bunka kenkyūjo, 1988.

———. "Sung Foreign Trade." In Rossabi, ed. *China Among Equals*. Berkeley: University of California Press, 1983, pp. 89–115.

Shigeta Atsushi 重田德. "Kyōshin shihai no seiritsu to kōzō" 郷紳支配 の成立と構造 [The establishment and structure of gentry control]. In Vol. XII of *Iwanami sekai rekishi* 岩波世界歴史. Tokyo: Iwanami, 1971; this essay was later published in Shigeta Atsushi 重田德. *Shindai shakai keizai shi kenkyū* 清代社會經濟史研究 [Qing Economic and Social History]. Tokyo: Iwanami, 1975.

Shih Chin. "Peasant Economy and Rural Society in the Lake Tai Area, 1368– 1840." Ph.D. diss. Berkley: University of California, 1981.

Siggstedt, Mette. "Zhou Chen: The Life and Paintings of a Ming Professional Artist." *Bulletin of the Museum of Far Eastern Antiquities* 54 (1982), pp. 1–239.

Sima Qian 司馬遷. *Shiji* 史記 [the Record of History]. Beijing: Zhonghua shu-ji, 1959.

Skinner, G. William. "Cities and the Hierarchy of Local Systems." In Skinner, ed. *The City in Late Imperial China*. pp. 275–351; also see Ibid. in Wolf, ed., *Studies in Chinese Society*. Stanford: Stanford University Press, 1978, pp. 1–77.

――――. ed. *The City in Late Imperial China*. Stanford: Stanford University Press, 1977.

――――. "Introduction: Urban Development in Imperial China." In *The City in Late Imperial China*, pp. 521–553.

――――. "Marketing and Social Structure in Rural China. I–II." *Journal of Asia Studies* Vol. 24, 1964/65, pp. 3–43; 195–228.

――――. "Regional Urbanization in nineteenth century China." In *City in Late Imperial China*, pp. 211–249.

――――. "Rural Marketing in China: Revival and Reappraisal." In Stuart Platt-ner, ed. *Markets and Marketing*. Lanham, Maryland: University Press of America, 1955, pp. 21–22.

Song shu 宋書 [History of the [Liu] Song]. Vol. 2. Shen Yue 沈約 (441–513) comp. Beijing: Zhonghua shuju, 1974, pp. 1033; 1054–55.

Song Yingxing 宋應星. *Tiangong Kaiwu* 天工開物 [Exploitation of the work of nature]. 1637. 1983. Reprint: Hong Kong.

Smith, Carol A. "Regional Economic Systems." In Smith, ed. *Regional Analy-sis*. Vol. 1. New York: Academic Press, 1976, pp. 3–63.

Spence, Jonathan. *Ts'ao Yin and the K'ang-hsi Emperor: Bondservant and Master*. New Haven: Yale University Press, 1966.

Strand, David. *Rickshaw Beijing*. Berkeley: University of California Press, 1989.

Strassberg, Richard E. *The World of K'ung Shang-jen: A Man of Letters in Early Ch'ing China*. New York: Columbia University Press, 1983.

Sun, E-tu Zen. "Sericulture and Silk Textile Production in Ch'ing China." In W. E. Willmott, ed. *Economic Organization in Chinese Society*, Stanford: Stanford University Press, 1972, pp. 79–108.

————. and Shiou-chuan Sun. *T'ien-kung K'ai-wu, Chinese Technology in the Seventeenth Century*. University Park: University of Pennsylvania Press, 1966.

Sun Pei 孫珮. *Suzhou zhizaoju zhi* 蘇州織造局志 [Treatise on the Manufactories of Suzhou]. 1986; Reprint: Nanjing. Jiangsu renmin chubanshe, 1954.

Sun Zhilu 孫之騄. *Er Shen Ye Lu* 二申野錄 [Unofficial records of events of the Ming period]. n.d.

Suzuki Tadashi 鈴木正. "Shinsho ryogai ensho ni kan-suru ikkosatsu" 清代兩淮塩商に關する一考察 [An enquiry into the Lianghuai salt merchants in the first part of the Qing]. *Shien*, 36 (March 1946), pp. 101–134.

Tan Qixiang 潭其驤, ed. *Zhongguo lishi ditu ji* 中國歷史地圖集 [Historical Atlas of China]. Vol. 5. "Sui-Tang." Vol. 6, "Song-Liao-Jin." Vol 7. "Ming." Vol. 8, "Qing." Beijing: Ditu chubanshe, n.d., c. 1987.

Tanaka Masatoshi 田中正俊. "Minpen kōsō nuhen" 民變抗租奴變 [Popular uprisings, rent resistance and servant uprisings]. In *Sekai no rekishi* 世界の歷史 [History of the World]. Vol. XI. Tokyo: Chikuma Shobō, 1961.

Terada Takunobu 寺田隆信. "Mindai Soshū heiya no nōka keizai ni tsuite" 明代蘇州平野の農家經濟について [On the peasant economy of the Suzhou plain in the Ming]. *Tōyō shi kenkyū* 16.1 (1957), 4, pp. 1–25.

————. "Soshō chihō ni okeru toshi mengyōshōnin ni tsuite" 蘇松地方に於ける都市の棉業商人について [Urban Cotton Merchants in Suzhou and Songjiang]. *Shirin* 史林, 41:6, (1958) pp. 52–69.ˢ

————. "Soshū tanpogyō no keiei deitai," 蘇州踹布業の経営形態 [Management of calendaring in Suzhou]. *Tōhoku daigaku bungakubu kenkyū nenpō* 東北大學文學部研究年報 18 (1968) pp. 121–173.

Thompson, E. P. *The Making of the English Working Class*. New York: Vintage, 1963.

Ting Yueh-hung. "Sericulture in Hu-chou as seen in the *Hu-chou fu-chih*." *Papers on China*, 23 (1970) pp. 29–51.

Tong Jun 童儁. *Jiangnan yuanlin zhi* 江南園林志 [Gazetteer of Jiangnan Gardens]. 1937. 1963. Reprint: Beijing.

Ueda Makoto 上田信. "Minmatsu Shincho Kōnan no tōshi no burai o meguru shakai handei" 明末清初江南の都市の無をめる社會關係 [Urban "bully groups" in Jiangnan during the late Ming and early Qing]. *Shigaku zasshi* 史學雜志, Vol. 90 no. 11, (1981), pp. 1619–1653.

Vance, James. *The Merchant's World: The Geography of Wholesaling*. Englewood Cliffs: Prentice-Hall, 1970.

Von Glahn, Richard. "Municipal Reform and Urban Social Conflict in Late Ming Jiangnan." *Journal of Asian Studies* Vol. 50, no. 2 (May 1991), pp. 280–307.

de Vries, Jan. *European Urbanization, 1500–1800*. Cambridge: Harvard University Press, 1984.

Wakeman, Frederic Jr. *The Great Enterprise: the Manchu Reconstruction of Imperial Order in Seventeenth-century China*. Berkeley: University of California Press, 1985.

Wang Jiafan 王家范. "Ming-Qing Jiangnan shizhen jiegou ji lishi jiazhi chutan" 明清江南市鎮結構及歷史價值初探 [A preliminary investigation of the structure and historical importance of market towns in Ming and Qing Jiangnan]. *Huadong shifan daxue xuebao* 華東師範大學學報 1984:1, pp. 74–83.

Wang Huan 王幻. *Yangzhou bajia huazhuan* 揚州八家畫傳 [Lives and works of Yangzhou's eight painters]. Taibei: Da Zhonghua chuban gongsi, 1970.

Wang Jiansheng 王建生. "Zeng Banqiao shenping kaoshi" 鄭板橋生平考釋 [A study of the life of Zheng Banqiao]. *Donghai xuebao* 東海學報, 7 (June 1976), pp. 75–96.⁶⁶

Wang Pengcheng 王鵬程 et alia, *Shanghai shi yanjiu* 上海史研究 [Research on Shanghai history]. Shanghai: Xuelin chubanshe, 1984.

Wang Qi 王錡. *Yupu zaji* 鬱圃雜記 [Miscellanea of the Orchard Dweller]. (1500), 5, reprint in Xie Guozhen. *Mingdai shehui jinji shiliao xuanbian (zhong)* [Anthology of historical materials on Ming society and economy]. Vol. 2, pp. 111–112.

Wang Shizhen 王世貞. "Guanglu dafu taizi taibao binbu shangshu zeng shaobao Julai Zhang gong Muzhi ming" 光祿大夫太子太保兵部尚書贈

少保居來張公墓誌銘 [Epitaph of the Minister of War, Zhang Jiayin]. In Zhang Jiayin, *Julai Xiansheng ji*, 1594, 65:30a.

———. "Zhang (da) sima ding Zhe erluan zhi" 張（大）司馬定浙二亂志 [Record of General Zhang's suppression of two uprisings in Zhejiang]. In *Erluan zhi* 二亂志 [Record of the Two Rebellions]. Also see: same title in Zhang Jiayin, *Julai Xiansheng ji*, 1594, "Appendix."

Wang Shuhuai 王樹槐. "Qingmo minchu Jiangsusheng chengshi de fazhan" 清末民初江蘇省城市的發展 [Urban development in Jiangsu in the late Qing and early Republican periods]. *Zhongyang yanjiuyuan jindaishi yanjiusuo jikan* 中央研究院近代史研究所集刊. Vol. XIII (October 1979), pp. 65–79.ﬁ

Wang, Yeh-chien. "Evolution of the Chinese Monetary System." In Hou and Yu, eds. *Modern Chinese Economic History*. Taipei: Academia Sinica, 1979.

Wang Xiuchu 王秀楚. "Yangzhou shi ri ji" 揚州十日記 [Record of ten days in Yangzhou]. *Zhongguo jindai neiluan waihuo lishi gushi congshu* 中國近代內亂外禍歷史故事叢書 [Stories of internal strife and external calamities in Chinese history]. Vol. 2. Taibei: Guangwen shuji, 1964, pp. 229–243.ﬁ

Wang Zudi 王祖嫡. "Da sima Zhang Gong kanding Wulin minbian ji" 大司馬張公戡定武林民變記 [Record of General Zhang's successful suppression of the popular rebellion at Wulin (in Hangzhou)]; and "Da sima Zhang Gong kanding Zhe zhen bingbian ji" 大司馬張公戡定浙鎮兵變記 [History of General Zhang's successful suppression of the military rebellion in Zhejiang city (Hangzhou)]. In *Julai Xiansheng ji*, 1594, "Appendix."

Wei, Betty Peh-T'i. *Shanghai, Crucible of Modern China*. Oxford: Oxford University Press, 1987.

Wen Bing 文秉. *Dingling zhulue* 定陵註略 [Notes on Miscellaneous Matters of the Wanli Reign], n.d.

———. *Dingling zhulüe, Liuyue Suzhou minbian* 定陵注略六月蘇州民變 [The Suzhou June revolt], c. 1669. 1976. Reprint: Taibei.ˢ

Wenxian congbian 文獻叢編 [Collection of documents of the Imperial Palace] n.d. Taibei: Tailian guofeng chubanshe, 1964.

Wheatley, Paul. *The Pivot of the Four Quarters*. Taibei: Rainbow-Bridge, 1971; originally published Chicago: Aldine Press, 1971.

Wiens, Mi Chu. "Changes in the Fiscal and Rural Control Systems in the Fourteenth and Fifteenth Centuries." *Ming Studies* 3 (Fall 1976), pp. 53–69.

————. "Cotton Textile Production and Rural Social Transformation in Early Modern China." *Journal of the Institute of Chinese Studies of the Chinese University of Hong Kong*, 7.2 (1974), pp. 515–531.

Will, Pierre-Étienne Will. *Burocratie et famine en Chine au XVIII siècle* [Bureaucracy and famine in eighteenth century China] Paris-The Hague: Mouton, 1980.

Worthy, Edmund H. Jr. "Diplomacy for Survival: Domestic and Foreign Relations of Wu Yueh, 907–978". In Morris Rossabi, ed. *China Among Equals: The Middle Kingdom and its Neighbors, 10th–14th Centuries*. Berkeley: University of California Press, 1983, pp. 17–44.

Wright, Arthur F., and Denis C. Twitchett, eds. *Perspectives on the T'ang* New Haven: Yale University Press, 1973.

Wright, Arthur F. *The Sui Dynasty*. New York: Alfred A. Knopf, 1978.

Wrigley, E. A. "A Simple Model of London's Importance in Changing English Society and Economy, 1650–1750," *Past and Present* 37 (1967), pp. 44–70.

Wu Jihua 吳緝華. *Mingdai shehui jingji shi luncong* 明代社會經濟史論叢 [Collected Discussions of Ming Social and Economic History]. Taibei: Taiwan xuesheng shuju, 1970.

Wu Kuan 吳寬. *Paoweng jiacang ji* 匏翁家藏集 [Collection from the family storehouse of (Wu) Paoweng]. 1508, Sibu congkan ed. Shanghai: Shanghai Commercial Press, 1935–1936.

Wu, Winston Ding Yee. *Kung Hsien (c. 1619–1689)*. Ph.D. diss. Princeton University, Princeton, N.J. 1979.

Xie Guozhen 謝國楨. *Mingdai shehui jinji shiliao xuanbian* 明代社會經濟史料選編 [Anthology of historical materials on Ming society and economy]. Fuzhou: Fujian renmin chubanshe, 1980.

Xu Daling 許大齡, ed. *Zhongguo zibenzhuyi mengya wenti taolunji* [Collected discussions on the "sprouts of capitalism" issue in China]. Beijing: Sanlian shudian, 1957–1960.

Xu Hong 徐泓. *Qingdai Lianghuai yanchang de yanjiu* 清代兩淮鹽商的研究 [A study of the Lianghuai salt yards in the Qing period]. Taibei: Jiaxin shuini gongsi, 1972.fi

Xu Ke 徐珂. *Qingbai leichao* 清稗類鈔. Taibei: Shangwu yinshuguan, 1966.

Yabuuchi Kiyoshu 藪內清, "Chūgoku no tokei" 中國の時計 [Clocks of China]. *Kagaku shi kenkyū* 科學史研究, 19 (1951); also in Hashimoto Manpei 橋本萬平, *Nihon no jikoku seido* 日本の時刻制度 [The Japanese System of Time]. Tokyo: Hanawashobō 1966.

Yan Zhongping 嚴中平. *Zhongguo mian fangzhi shigao* 中國棉紡織史稿 [A brief history of cotton spinning and weaving in China]. Beijing: Keshe chubanshe, 1955.

Yang Qimin 楊其民. "Gu Louxian kaolue" 古婁縣考略 ["Brief Examination of Ancient Luo County"]. In Wang Pengcheng, *Shanghai shi yanjiu*. 1984.

Yang Dequan 楊德泉. "Qingdai qianqi Lianghuai yanshang ziliao chuji" 清代前期兩淮鹽商資料初集 [Preliminary collection of materials on the Lianghuai salt-merchants of the earlier Qing period]. Jianghai xuekan 江海學刊, 45 (November 1962), pp. 45–49.fi

Yang Lien-sheng. "Government Control of Urban Merchants in Traditional China." *Qinghua xuebao*, 8, (1970), pp. 186–209.

Yao Shilin 姚士麟. "Jian zhi bian" 見只編, [Miscelany of Things Seen and Heard]. In *Yanyi zhilin*, juan 53.

Yao Siqin 姚思勤. "Donghe Zhao Ge" 東河櫂歌 [Songs of the East River]. In *Wulin Zhanggu Congbian*, XVII, 1892, pp. 22b.

Yao Wentian 姚文田. *Guangling shilue* 廣陵事略 [Brief Account of Guangling]. Kaifeng: n.p., 1912.fi

Yao Zhen 姚震. "Chujiatang Qionghuayuan Tongshengmiao ji" 褚家塘瓊花園通聖廟記 [Notes on the Tongsheng temple in the Qionghua garden]. 1423 in Zhou Jing 周璟, *Zhao Zhonglu fuli* 昭忠錄附錄 [Records of Zhao Zhong]. In *Wulin Zhanggu Congbian*, XXI, 1933, pp. 11b–13a.

Ye Mengzhu 葉夢珠. *Yueshibian* 閱世編 [A survey of the age]. c. 1690; 1982. Reprint: Taibei.

Ye Xianen 葉顯恩. *Ming-Qing Huizhou nongcun shehui yu dianpu zhi* 明清惠州農村社會與佃僕制 [Rural society and the tenancy system in Ming and Qing Huizhou]. Hefei: Anhui renmin chubanshe, 1983.

Yokoyama Suguru 橫山英. *Chūgoku kindaika no keizai kōzō* 中國近代化の經濟構造 [The economic structure of Chinese modernization]. Tokyo: 1972.

———. "Shindai ni okeru tanpugyō no keiei deitai" 清代における踹布業の經營形態 [Form of management of calendaring in Qing times]. *Tōyō shi kenkyū*, Vol. 19, no. 3, (1960) pp. 337–349; 4 (1961) pp. 451–467.

———. "Shindai no toshi kinuorimonogyō no seisan deitai" 清代の都市絹織物業の生產形態 [Mode of production of the urban silk industry in the Qing]. *Shigaku kenkyū*, 史學研究 (1968) 104, pp. 67–78, 105 pp. 52–66.

———. "Tanpugyō no seisan kōzō," 踹布業の生產構造 [Structure of calendaring production] in Yokoyama. *Chūgoku kindaika no keizai kōzō*

中國近代化の經濟構造 [Economic Structure of Chinese Modernization]. Tokyo: Kikeizai Aki shobō, 1972, pp. 63–143.

Yongzheng zhupi yuzhi 雍正硃批諭旨 [Imperial endorsements and edicts of the Yongzhong reign]. 1887; 1965. Reprint Taibei.

Yu Huai (Tanxin) 余懷. *Banqiao zaji* 板橋雜記 [Diverse Records of Wooden Bridge]. c. 1644–1696; 1928. Reprint: Shanghai.

Yuan shi 元史 [History of the Yuan dynasty]. Beijing: Zhonghua shuju, 1976.

Yuan, Tsing. "Urban Riots and Disturbances." In Jonathan D. Spence and John E. Wills, Jr. eds. *From Ming to Ch'ing: Conquest, Region and Continuity in Seventeenth Century China*. New Haven, Yale University Press, 1979, pp. 287–308.

Yuan Zhi 袁裘. *Xutai xiansheng ji* 胥臺先生集 [Collected works of (Yuan) Xutai (Yuan Zhi)]. n.d. 16:19b–21a.

Yule, Sir Henry. *The Book of Ser Marco Polo*. Henri Cordier. Rev. London: John Murray, 1903.

Zhang Dai 張岱. *Taoan mengyi* 陶庵夢憶 [Dreams and Memories of Taoan]. c. 1644; 1978. Reprint: Taibei.

Zhang Han 張瀚. *Songchuang mengyu* 松窗夢語 [Dream from the window (looking out on) pine trees]. 1593; Reprint. Taibei.

Zhang Pengge 張鵬翮. "Zhi Xiahe shui lun" 治下河水論 [On hydraulic management of water in Xiahe]. In Chen Henghe, ed. 陳恒和 *Yangzhou congke* 揚州叢刻 [Collected writings from Yangzhou]. Jiangdu: 1936.

Zhang Siwei 張四維. 復張崌崍 "Fu Zhang Julai" [Response to Zhang Julai] in *Tiaolu tang ji* 條麓堂集 [Collected writings from the Tiaolu Studio]. 1596, 19:28b–29b.

Zhang Shunhui 張舜徽. *Qingdai Yangzhouxue ji* 清代揚州學記 [Account of the Yangzhou learning in the Qing dynasty]. Shanghai: Renmin chubanshe, 1962.

Zhang Xuan 張萱, *Xiyuan wenjian lu* 西園聞見錄 [Record of [Zhang "Xiyuan's" [Xuan] Observations], juan 83, "Suppressions;" 1940. Reprint.

Zhang Zhongmin 張忠民. "Qing qianqi Shanghai gang fazhan yanbian xintan" 清前期上海港發展演變新探 [New Discoveries in the Evolution of Shanghai's Port in the Early Qing Period]. *Zhongguo jingji shi yanjiu* 中國經濟史研究, 1987, no. 3, pp. 85–94.

———. *Shanghai: cong kaifa zouxiang kaifang, 1368–1842* 上海從開發走向開放, 1368–1842 [Shanghai from inception to opening, 1368–1842]. Kunming: Yunnan renmin chushuban, 1990.

Zhao Erxun 趙爾巽 (comp.). *Qing shi gao* 清史稿 [Draft history of the Qing].
Beijing: 1928; 1977. Reprint. Beijing: Zhonghua shuju.[fi]

Zhao Zhibi 趙之璧. *Pingshantang tuzhi* 平山堂圖志 [Illustrated gazetteer of
Pingshantang]. Yangzhou: c. 1765.[fi]

Zheng Shunchen 鄭舜臣. "Da sima Zhang Gong jinglue Zhe zhen bingbian
shimo" 大司馬張公經略浙鎮兵變始末 [Complete history of General
Zhang's successful suppression of the military rebellion in Zhejiang]. In
Julai Xiansheng ji, 1594, "Appendix."

Zheng Zhaojing 鄭肇經. *Zhongguo shuili shi* 中國水利史 [A history of water
control in China]. Changsha: Shangwu yinshuguan, 1939.[fi]

Zhou Liangxiao 周良霄. "Mingdai Su Song diqu de guantian yu zhongfu wenti" 明代蘇松地區的官田與重賦問題 [The question of official fields and
heavy taxes in Ming Suzhou and Songjiang]. In *Mingdai shehui jingji shilun ji* 明代社會經濟史論集 [Collection of historical discussions of society
and economy in the Ming dynasty]. Hong Kong: Chongwen shudian,
1975, pp. 130–142.

Zhu Guozhen 朱國禎. "Hangzhou bingbian" 杭州兵變 [Military rebellion in
Hangzhou]. In *Huang Ming dashi ji* 皇明大事記 [Chronicle of the August
Ming Dynasty]. (n.d.), juan 41.

Zhu Xie 朱偰. *Zhongguo yunhe shiliao xuanji* 中國運河史料選集 [Collected
historical materials on the Grand Canal of China]. Beijing: Zhonghua shuju, 1962.

Zhu Yunming 祝允明. *Jiuchao yeji* 九朝野記. [Unofficial history of nine
reigns]. 1511. n.p. Reprint. Shizong shuju, 1911.

———. *Zhu shi jilue* 祝氏集略 [Collected works of Zhu (Yunming)]. Reprint
of 1558 ed. In *Zhu Shi Shiwen Ji* 祝氏詩文集 [Collected poetry and prose
of Zhu (Yunming)]. Taibei: Guoli Zhongyang Tushuguan, 1971, p. 1832.[m]

Zhu Zongzhou 朱宗宙. "Qingdai qianqi Yangzhou chengshi jingji"
清代前期揚州城市經濟 [The urban economy of Yangzhou in the first half
of the Qing period]. *Yangzhou shiyuan xuebao: shehui kexue ban*
揚州師院學報社會科學版. 1984:2, pp. 114–117.[fi]

Zou Yilin 鄒逸麟. "Shanghai dichu zuicao de duiwai maoyi gang Qinglong
zhen" 上海地區最早的對外貿易港—清龍鎮 ["Qinglong Market-town, the
earliest commercial port in the Shanghai region"]. Vol. 1. *Zhonghua wenshi lun cong* 中華文史論叢 (1980) pp. 119–129.[j]

Zurndorfer, Harriet T., *Change and Continuity in Chinese Local History: the
Development of Hui-chou Prefecture, 800–1800*. Leiden: E. J. Brill, 1989.

INDEX

academy, academies, 1, 85–86, 104, 130, 136, 141, 144, 167
actors, 44, 84
agent boat system, 34
agricultural, agriculture, 12–13, 21–22, 30, 83–84, 107, 125, 126, 171
  commercialization of, 1–13, 21–22, 30, 157
amateur ideal, 44
American(s), 6, 179–180
  American trade, 179 –180
Anding, 136, 141
Anfeng, 125
Anhui, 91, 109, 122, 123, 128, 137, 140, 141, 142, 152, 163, 177
  See: Huizhou; -merchants
Anqing, 122
anti-eunuch uprising, 75
anti-gentry uprising, 62, 75, 76
arsenals, 23
arson, 18, 63, 73
artisan(s), 32, 34, 87–89, 138
artists, 84, 85, 140, 142, 143
avoidance, rule of, 75

Baltimore, 3
bandits, 106, 114
bang(s), 119, 160, 162, 163, 174
bank(s), banking, 31, 117, 125, 131, 133, 134, 141, 154, 159–160, 162, 166, 168, 170–175, 180–181

baojia, 52, 53, 54, 55, 56, 60, 66, 77, 78, 108, 112, 126
Baoshan, 163
baotou, 109, 110, 112, 113, 114, 115
baoxiao, 137
baoyi, 89
Baoying, 122, 123, 146
bean(s), 38, 158, 159, 162, 166, 173, 176
bean-cake fertilizer, 175, 176
Beihu, 145, 146
Beijing, 4, 30, 32, 48, 63, 64, 65, 66, 76, 82, 93, 137, 156, 163
Benevolent association(s), 108, 166
  See: charitable organizations
Bengal, 178
Bergere, Marie-Claire, 15, 19
bianmin ku, 130
Birmingham, 14
boat-building, 23
boatmen, 43, 144, 173
boatyards, 172
bourgeoisie, 43
Braudel, Frenand, 119
Britain, 177, 179
British East India Company, 179–180
brokers, 9, 38, 53, 90, 100, 158, 159, 175, 176
brothels, 133

Caishi qiao, 70, 76

299